AF322844

THE ONSET OF
WORLD WAR

STUDIES IN INTERNATIONAL CONFLICT

Series Editor: Manus I. Midlarsky, *Center for International Relations and Department of Political Science, University of Colorado, Boulder*

THE ONSET OF WORLD WAR
by Manus I. Midlarsky

forthcoming:

THE PRICE OF POWER
by Alan Lamborn

GLOBAL WAR AND STATE-SHAPING PROCESSES
by William Thompson and Karen Rasler

THE PARADOXES OF WAR
by Zeev Maoz

THE ONSET OF WORLD WAR

Manus I. Midlarsky

Studies in International Conflict,
Volume I

Boston
UNWIN HYMAN
London   Sydney   Wellington

Copyright © 1988 By Unwin Hyman, Inc.
All rights reserved

Unwin Hyman
8 Winchester Place, Winchester, MA 01890, USA.

The U.S. Company of
Unwin Hyman, Ltd,
Broadwick House, 15/17 Broadwick Street, London W1V 1FP, UK

Allen & Unwin Australia Pty Ltd,
8 Napier Street, North Sydney, NSW 2060, Australia

Allen & Unwin (New Zealand) Ltd, in association with the Port Nicholson
Press Ltd, 60 Cambridge Terrace, Wellington, New Zealand

Library of Congress Cataloging-in-Publication Data

Midlarsky, Manus I.
  The onset of world war.
  (Studies in international conflict; v. 1)
Bibliography: p. 244
1. International relations—Research.   2. War—Mathematical models.
  I. Title. II. Series.
JX1291.M53   1987   327.1'6   87-3569
ISBN 0-04-497004-8
ISBN 0-04-497005-6 (pbk.)

British Library of Cataloguing in Publication Data

Midlarsky, Manus I.
  The onset of world war.—(Studies in international conflict; v. 1).
1. War
I. Title   II. Series
355'.027'01   U21.2
ISBN 0-04-497004-8
ISBN 0-04-497005-6 Pbk

Set in 10 on 12 point Zapf Book Light by Getset (BTS) Ltd
and printed in Great Britain by Biddles of Guildford

For Liz, Susan, Miriam, and Michael

Contents

List of Tables   xi
List of Figures   xiii
Acknowledgments   xv

1. Introduction   1
2. A Hierarchical Equilibrium   20
3. The Long-Run Instability of Multipolar Systems   44
4. A Distribution of Extreme Inequality   69
5. Conflict Overlap in Systemic Wars   79
6. The Balance of Power, Preponderance, and the Onset of War in
    Polarized Settings   92
7. Structural and Mobilization Wars   131
8. A Comparison between Two Systemic Wars   148
9. Alliance Durability   158
10. Normative Justifications   169
11. Conclusion: International Structure as an Information System   187

Mathematical Appendix A   217
Mathematical Appendix B   221
Tabular Appendix A   231
Tabular Appendix B   237
Tabular Appendix C   240
Bibliography   244
About the Author   255
Index   257

List of Tables

1.1 Hierarchical equilibrium. 11

1.2 Types of war. 14

2.1 Findings of the empirical tests. 38

3.1 The number of countries with r utiles (n_r) with $m = 5$ and variable k. 50

4.1 Observed and predicted land distributions in El Salvador. 74

4.2 Observed and predicted distributions of colonial populations among the European powers, 1914. 76

6.1 Partitioning of conflicts by memory and game process. 105

6.2 Comparison of power disparities between wars occurring under memory (m) and no-memory (nm) conditions. 116

6.3 Observed and lognormally predicted power concentrations for war periods, 1820–1945. 120

9.1 Correlations between alliance entropy and years duration, 1815–1965. 165

1BP Illustrations of exponential and log-exponential (Pareto) distributions. 228

1A Observed and expected frequencies of occurrence of the pairs (n, k) of disputes between two or more major powers in the European system, 1816–1899 $(p = 0.6957)$. 232

2A Observed and expected frequencies of occurrence of the pairs (n, k) of disputes between two or more major powers and those involving central powers in the European system, 1816–1899 $(p = 0.6852)$. 232

3A Observed and expected frequencies of occurrence of the pairs (n, k) of disputes between two or more major powers and those involving any other countries in the European system, 1816–1899 $(p = 0.7231)$. 233

4A Observed and expected frequencies of occurrence of the pairs (n, k) of disputes between two or more major powers and those involving central powers in the European system, 1893–1914 $(p = 0.9474)$. 234

5A Observed and expected frequencies of occurrence of the pairs (n, k) of disputes between two or more major powers and those involving any other countries in the European system, 1946–1964 $(p = 0.7000)$. 235

6A   Findings of the empirical tests.   236

1B   Observed and expected frequencies of occurrence of the pairs (n, k) of disputes between two or more major powers, involving at least one central power, 1816–1899 ($p = 0.7000$).   237

2B   Observed and expected frequencies of occurrence of the pairs (n, k) of disputes between two or more major powers, involving at least one central power, 1893–1914 ($p = 0.5429$).   238

3B   Observed and expected frequencies of occurrence of the pairs (n, k) of disputes between two or more major powers and those involving any other countries in the European system, 1893–1908 ($p = 0.9167$).   238

4B   Wars with and without memory, 1850–1966.   238

1C   Observed and Polya-predicted values of the distribution of conflict behaviors, 1893–1914.   240

2C   Observed and Polya-predicted values of the distribution of conflict behaviors, 1893–1907.   241

3C   Observed and Polya-predicted values of the distribution of conflict behaviors, 1908–1914.   241

4C   Observed and Polya-predicted values of the distribution of conflict behaviors, 1871–1892.   241

5C   Observed and Polya-predicted values of the distribution of conflict behaviors, 1919–1939.   242

6C   Observed and Polya-predicted values of the distribution of conflict behaviors, 1919–1932.   242

7C   Observed and Polya-predicted values of the distribution of conflict behaviors, 1933–1939.   243

List of Figures

3.1   The dependence of the measure of inequality, I, upon the number of available utiles, k, for three values of m.   51

6.1   Curvilinear relationship between Ferris' power disparity ratio and the frequency of war.   113

6.2   Cumulative distribution of the logarithm of the concentration ratio.   121

10.1   Independence condition (after Rawls 1971, 76).   179

10.2   Utilitarian condition (after Rawls 1971, 77).   179

1B   Stages of sequential resource acquisition.   222

2B   Approach to infinite abundance and greater equality of the functions $g(x)$ and $h(x)$.   230

Acknowledgments

It is my pleasure to acknowledge the various agencies and persons who contributed immensely to the completion of this volume. A grant of the National Science Foundation, SES-83-09851, supported much of the research reported here, especially chapters 2, 5, 6, 8, and 9. Certain of the ideas reported in chapter 11 were developed initially in the National Endowment for the Humanities Summer Seminar for College Teachers that I directed in the summer of 1983. I will always be grateful to the participants in the seminar for their eager contributions to the discussions which made the flow of ideas so rich and compelling. An enrichment grant to the Center for International Relations of the University of Colorado, Boulder, by the office of the Vice Chancellor for Academic Affairs greatly facilitated both the research enterprise and completion of the manuscript.

Extremely able research assistance was rendered by Dale Cohen, Kun Park, and Kenneth Roberts. The excellent computer programming by Paul Buster and George Schimmel made possible the calculations reported here. The typing of the final manuscript was done by Amie Brooke, Lisa Donovan, Melinda Marquis and Cecilia Robinson at the Center for International Relations. The diligence, loyalty, and good humor of this office staff made the task of completing this volume immeasurably easier than it might have been.

Chapter 2 originally was published in revised form in the March 1986, issue of the *International Studies Quarterly*. Chapter 4 and Mathematical Appendix B include elements from an article published in a special issue of *Mathematical Modelling*, while Chapter 5 is a revision of an article that was published in the December 1984, issue of the *Journal of Conflict Resolution*.

Chapter 10 is a revised version of an article that appeared in the Winter, 1983, issue of *Polity*. I am grateful to these journals and publishers for permission to reprint the relevant materials.

My gratitude also expands to Unwin Hyman not only for publishing this volume in a timely and expeditious fashion but also for providing the series *Studies in International Conflict* for which this book is the cornerstone publication. As series editor, I hope that it is a fitting point of departure. I am indebted to Neil Richardson for his generous comments on the manuscript.

Last, but not least, the support and encouragement of my family cannot go without mention. Without their support, this book could hardly have been written; for that and many other things, they have my enduring affection.

THE ONSET OF
WORLD WAR

1

Introduction

IN RECENT YEARS, a renewed interest has emerged in the problem of nuclear war as a form of global, general, or systemic war. The arms race between the superpowers, of course, has spurred this interest, as has the specter of nuclear winter as a *deux ex machina* which can effectively terminate the existence of human civilization as we know it and, perhaps, even other life forms. Physicians, such as Helen Caldicott, have been active recently in detailing the medical consequences of radioactive fallout and other immediate by-products of a nuclear exchange. The inherent dangers of the current international system, then, have awakened a keen sense of peril in the intellectual community.

Yet for all that we have learned about the truly horrendous consequences of widespread nuclear warfare, our knowledge of the potential causes of such a holocaust is all too meager. Knowledge of the consequences of nuclear war, of course, is desirable in helping to foresee the extraordinarily bleak future that attends the end of such a war. However, these consequences, especially those of a medical nature, are pitched at the level of the individual human being. Decision makers are expected to react with such horror to these likely outcomes affecting people that they would not dare to begin a nuclear war of this type. This is the sometimes unspoken premise of campaigns such as those waged recently by Physicians for Social Responsibility.

Although decision makers clearly can be affected by the horrors of such a war, we also know that they can be influenced by the structural properties of the international system in which they find themselves. Alliances, conflict relationships, dyadic commitments, historical influences, and disparities in power all can have impacts on international outcomes which even the foreseen horrors of nuclear war may not be sufficient to overcome. As such, scholars familiar with these and other properties of international systems are obliged to analyze the potential causes of widespread conflict involving nuclear weapons in order to clearly delineate, where possible, the antecedents of general or systemic war. In this fashion, perhaps one can lessen the potentially exclusive reliance on the expected impact of concepts, such as nuclear winter, on the presumably receptive and morally sensitive decision maker.

A major question is that of the emphasis on international structure in this book.[1] What is so important about international structure that demands our attention to this extent? Surely an emphasis on the micropolitics of, say, decision making would be equal if not substantially superior as an explanatory emphasis. Without in any way derogating the utility of micropolitics, which incidentally, I believe to be important as an explanatory focus, there is considerable justification for a structural explanation.

The importance of structure lies precisely in its existence as a basis for decision making, not merely because it is a given of the international environment, but because human beings are pattern recognizers par excellence. It may even be our ability to recognize the pattern of an environment and react to it successfully that accounts for our evolutionary success as a species. Early human beings were able to sort out the differences between animals capable of being domesticated and those not, regions that were likely to be fertile and those that were not, and all manner of other pattern-dependent distinctions that lie at the root of successful decision making. Some scientists even feel that there exists evolutionary pressure toward the development of organisms which can make such macrodistinctions readily instead of being oriented to the more detailed but less patterned microworld of existence (Pagels 1982, 110). It is incumbent on us, therefore, to discover the patterns associated with the origins of systemic war precisely in order to ensure our continued existence as a species.

All of this is not to say that ideologies or people's belief systems are not important. Indeed, the intensity of beliefs will be used shortly to distinguish between two categories of warfare that are to be analyzed in this book. Nevertheless, it is a basic premise of this analysis that, at least in regard to the *outbreak* of systemic war, international structure is a decisive element.

A concise statement of the importance of focusing on the structure of the whole is given by Waltz (1979, 79). "A system is composed of a structure and of interacting units. The structure is the system-wide component that makes it possible to think of the system as a whole." As Ruggie (1986, 133–134) put it in calling on Durkheim's understanding, "Durkheim is helpful in disentangling these notions: 'Whenever certain elements combine and thereby produce, by the fact of their combination, new phenomena, it is plain that these new phenomena reside not in the original elements, but in the totality formed by their union.' A system, then, is this new totality formed by the union of parts, a totality enjoying a 'specific reality which has its own characteristics'. . . ."

Although structure is a given of international life and patterns associated with it are readily discernible,[2] there is much to discover about its workings. The fact that systemic wars of the most destructive variety have been a repetitive feature of international life suggests two observations. (1) Despite the many different decision makers that have existed at these different times, the results have been the same, namely the onset of systemic war. This pattern further suggests that it is not the decision maker in office at the time of the crisis that is necessarily decisive (although he or she can be important) but the particular structural features of international life that are critical. (2) The fact of the repetition suggests that there are hidden, perhaps even nonintuitive aspects of international structure that drive the system to war, for if the decision makers recognized the symptoms of impending systemic war with all its destructive potential, surely some if not most would have bent every effort to avoid it.

As such, the principal focus of this book is on causation, although it is causation viewed not from a monocausal perspective but from a plurality of sources. These are, in fact, the approximately 1,000 disputes which are recorded by the Correlates of War (COW) Project between 1816 and 1976. Alliances and even normative perspectives on international justice also are features of the present analysis.

Despite these diverse perspectives, there is a central motif running throughout the volume, and this is the element of international structure—not exclusively the venerable bipolar or multipolar structure of traditional international relations discourse, but also newer formulations which are based on conflict relationships among nation-states in addition to power structures in the system. A particular theoretical structure, the hierarchical equilibrium, will be put forward as a central theoretical perspective that will guide the analyses in this book. An intriguing element is the unforeseen consequence that the focus on international structure will reveal important aspects of domestic sociopolitical structure related to the onset of systemic conflicts. Indeed, the confluence between analytically similar forms in both domestic and international life will prove to be an important antecedent of the systemic war, but likely not the general war.

The particular explanatory focus of the hierarchical equilibrium and of the volume itself is the systemic war. This is a war entailing the breakdown of the international system as it existed prior to the outbreak of the war. As such, the scope of the war in terms of participant countries and the degree of civilian–military participation (leading to a large number of civilian casualties and battle deaths) must be extensive in order to yield a systemic breakdown. Essentially, the scope of the war and the widespread bloodshed (which also implies a long duration, but not necessarily the converse, for example, Vietnam) lead not only to the rise of new great powers and the decline of older ones but also to later extensive efforts to restructure the system in ways that presumably will prevent the emergence of another widespread conflict of this type (for example, Westphalia, Vienna, Versailles, or San Francisco).

The systemic war is here distinguished from the general war as an additional but related category. The concept of general war has been defined by at least one scholar (Levy 1985b) primarily in terms of hegemony and participation—that is, whether the leading power in a given time period is involved in the war and can be decisively defeated, and a majority of the remaining powers are involved in the war. Clearly, the systemic war is a more restricted version of the general war, for it involves issues of such intensity (for example, religion or nationalism) that it is likely to, and indeed does involve heavy bloodshed and civilian participation, in addition to the wide scope of participation by governments. Put another way, while the general war tends to involve a great number of powers because of issues of system leadership, the systemic war also involves a large number of powers because of issues of this type but, in addition, addresses issues of social, political, or religious organization *within* nation-states which strike at the root of a variety of belief systems. The general war casts its net wide but not necessarily deep because of the extranational aspects of hegemonic leadership (Gilpin 1981); the systemic war casts its net both wide and deep within the nation–state and even much smaller forms of human organization (church or village).

Eight wars of great duration and intensity are here categorized as systemic wars. These are the Peloponnesian War (431–404 B.C.), Macedonian War (357–336 B.C.), Thirty Years' War (1618–1648), War of the Spanish Succession (1702–1713), French Revolutionary Wars (1792–1802), the Napoleonic Wars (1803–1815), World War I (1914–1918), and World War II (1939–1945). In addition to issues of system leadership and scope of participation, these wars also were characterized by serious differences over appropriate belief systems (Thirty Years' War and World War II, in part), appropriate forms of government (Peloponnesian War, French Revolutionary Wars, Napoleonic Wars, and World War I), and emergent nationalism (World War I and Napoleonic Wars, in part). The War of the Spanish Succession is chosen for inclusion as a systemic war because issues of survival of the French polity began to arise as the French were losing badly. As a consequence, large numbers of civilians began to participate at the level of home-front military support, as in the donation of jewelry; the melting of household utensils to manufacture weapons; and, in an effort that was indeed unusual for the eighteenth century, the use of compulsory military service. It has been observed "that Louis XIV's last army was no longer a professional army, but had become a national one" (Gaxotte 1970 322).

All of these wars included civilian participation to a fairly large degree, or at least large numbers of civilians were directly affected by the war either in the form of voluntary support, sieges, or starvation.

Two general wars, the War of the Austrian Succession (1740–1748) and the Seven Years' War (1756–1763) are included as an occasional contrast to the systemic wars because, despite their broad scope of country participation and large number of battle deaths, none of them involved the depth or intensity of issues found in the systemic wars. The extent of civilian participation in these wars is the measure of intensity of feeling of the general population; most historians concur that these two wars, despite their importance, do not match the systemic variant on this dimension. However, at the structural level it will be seen that certain of the causes (although not conduct) of both types of war are the same.

The categorization of these wars as general or systemic is, of course, a matter of judgment and, more importantly, really represents the construction of a continuum of intensity of feeling and participation. Whereas it is clear that World War I or World War II stand poles apart from the War of the Austrian Succession, the War of the Spanish Succession may stand closer to the Seven Years' War on this continuum. Nevertheless, of these last two wars, the former war, here categorized as systemic, was of longer duration and incurred more bloodshed. Whether one chooses to categorize the War of the Spanish Succession as general or systemic probably is not crucial; what is critical is the realization that such a continuum of intensity and participation exists and lends understanding to the nature of widespread warfare. Dichotomization is necessary, however, in order to gain explanatory perspective on major differences between the modal instances of each type (for example, contrast World Wars I or II with the War of the Austrian Succession). Because of the remoteness in time of the earlier wars, especially the Peloponnesian for which we have few reliable sources, the analysis will concentrate on the later wars. Certainly, the use of systematic dispute data will have to be confined to the origins of World Wars I and II because of the absence of these data in earlier time periods.

The Hierarchical Equilibrium

The hierarchical equilibrium framework will inform much of the subsequent analyses. This formulation shares certain similarities with both balance-of-power theory (Morgenthau 1973) and hierarchical structures (Organski 1968, Organski and Kugler 1980); it emerges, however, with significant differences from both. In its genesis, the theory emerges from consideration of dispute length and likelihood of dispute buildup over time in the system. The theoretical construction which emerges from these initial considerations, then, is related to theories of balance and hierarchy in the system.

More specifically, an initial requirement for the absence of systemic war is the avoidance of an accumulation of serious disputes. There are several reasons for this requirement. Given the existence of such a series of disputes accumulating over time, there exists an increased probability that additional countries will become involved in these disputes, thus widening the scope of the conflict if and when it erupts. Several mechanisms exist for such a widening process. First, two or more disputes which initially had no connection with one another (such as Austria-Hungary's Balkan controversies, on the one hand, with Germany's conflicts with other great powers, on the other) could then be connected via some perceived common interest by two or more of these protagonists. Such common interests could emerge merely from the realization that "the enemy of my enemy is my friend." Additionally, the existence of protracted disputes can provide models for imitative behavior by governments which identify with each other. For example, if dictatorial elites observe other dictators profiting from aggressive policies, then the longer such a model or series of disputes of this type persists, the greater the likelihood of some form of imitative behavior.

There are, especially, three forms of imitative behavior which can follow from a series of disputes. All can lead to the joining of disparate conflicts into one and the consequent onset of a systemic war. They are detailed in chapter 2 as a basis for the development of the hierarchical equilibrium model. An additional source of systemic conflict upon the accumulation of a series of disputes is a multiplicative element wherein the sheer number of disputes detracts from the ability of great power decision makers to successfully resolve each of them, and the probability increases that any one of the disputes may escalate into a systemic conflict. These mechanisms also are detailed in chapter 2.

The basic postulate of the hierarchical equilibrium model, then, is the absence of conflict accumulation, or an average equality in beginnings and endings of disputes. For every dispute that begins, on the average, another should terminate within some constant time interval. In order to achieve this level of equality, the hierarchical equilibrium structure is developed which specifies (1) two or more hierarchies (alliances or loosely knit empires) with large power disparities between great and small powers within each hierarchy, and (2) a large number of small powers not permanently attached to any of the great powers. The existence of the large power disparities ensures that great power–small power conflicts will be short, and the numerous independent unaffiliated small powers further mitigate against the unwanted involvement by a great power in a war essentially begun by a smaller country. These arguments are further developed in the theoretical treatments of chapter 2.

Hierarchy and Minimum Entropy

There are several interesting properties of the hierarchical equilibrium structure and, specifically, the hierarchy associated with it. First, it is the only structure that internationally will meet the minimum entropy requirement that has been discovered as an essential property of stable and durable domestic political coalitions. Entropy has been associated with the concepts of uncertainty or disorder. The greater the entropy of the system, the greater the uncertainty or disorder of that system. It is clear that if a coalition, whether domestic or international, is hierarchically organized, then it can provide the clarity associated with "speaking with one voice" that would be largely absent in a less hierarchical setting. The association between very large political parties and very small ones demonstrates both minimum entropy and cabinet durability in Western-style democracies (Midlarsky 1984a). There exists a theoretical basis for the expectation of coalition durability and, at the same time, the absence of systemic war for minimum entropy coalitions. The hierarchical equilibrium model specifies the minimum entropy condition of stable coalitions which also display an absence of potential for systemic war, as we shall see, often for different reasons. Two coalitions will now be compared in anticipation of a more complete development of the hierarchical minimum entropy condition in chapters 2, 9 and 11.

For initial purposes of exposition, the entropy is maximized when there is equality in the proportions of capability in an alliance and minimized when there is a preponderance of capability in one power with very little in the remaining powers. (For a formal description of the properties of the entropy, see Mathematical Appendix A.) Thus, the minimum entropy requirement is satisfied when there exists one very large power in association with a small power. Conversely, the entropy is maximized when the two powers are of approximately equal capability. Although these concepts will be developed more systematically later in this volume, for now the utility of these concepts can be illustrated by the contrast between outcomes in the 1914 summer crisis and the 1962 Cuban missile crisis.

In the former instance, Germany and Austria-Hungary were allied in the Dual Alliance which soon became the basis for the Central Powers wartime coalition of World War I. As will be shown in chapters 2 and 5, the crisis unfolded very much as a consequence of the "blank check" given to Austria-Hungary by Germany to do as she wished with Serbia almost at the outset of the crisis. It was this joining of the two countries in a virtually fused political entity which lent the crisis its unique characteristics. One asks why it was that Germany would have engaged in such risk-taking behaviors.

One can, of course, attribute these behaviors to muddle headedness or excessive aggressive intent toward the Entente powers, France, Russia, and Great Britain (Fischer 1967). An interpretation which emerges from the maximum entropy formulation is not so much an aggressive posture as an excessive reliance on Austria-Hungary as Germany's only great power ally. And the emergence of Serbia in 1913 at twice her initial size prior to the Balkan wars, coupled with an aggressive and effective pan-Slavic propaganda campaign aimed at the ever-growing Slavic population within the Austro-Hungarian Empire, threatened to result in the disintegration of the Empire, as indeed occurred at the end of World War I. Thus, Germany's only reliable ally in Europe would cease to exist as a great power. To be sure, one can castigate German policy as having eventuated in this circumstance. As early as 1890, the failure to renew the Reinsurance Treaty with Russia began the process of German isolation from the Entente powers, for Russia then turned to France and the basic structure of the Triple Entente was formed. Nevertheless, it was probably difficult for policy makers at that time to foresee the forthcoming internal disintegration of the Austro-Hungarian Empire. When it began to be obvious around the time of the Bosnian crisis in 1908, the German dependence on the Austro-Hungarians was complete. This is the essential characteristic of the maximum entropy coalition, one where both powers are large and therefore essential to the continuation of the perceived security interests of both countries.

Contrast this behavior with the Cuban missile crisis of 1962 in which a minimum entropy coalition existed between the Soviet Union and Cuba. As suggested earlier, this is a coalition in which a great power predominates in association with a much smaller country. Instead of perceived mutual dependency as existed in the maximum entropy, Austro-Hungarian–German alliance, the Soviet Union was largely free of any dependence on Cuba. As such, when the crisis broke out in October of 1962, one of the first decisions Khruschev would reach was the elimination of direct Cuban influence on the conduct of the crisis. Thus, the crisis could proceed as a superpower confrontation without any of the local animosities felt by the Cubans toward the United States, in contrast to the 1914 summer crisis wherein the parochial interests of southeast Europe were allowed (via the maximum entropy alliance) to exert a truly extraordinary and disproportionate effect on the outbreak of World War I.

Positive-Sum Games

The hierarchical minimum entropy requirement for stable peaceful coalitions is to be supplemented by the necessity, or at least enormous desirability, of positive-sum games. In the case of domestic coalitions there exists a criterion for minimum winning coalitions, that is, fifty percent plus one vote. Stable national electoral systems are governed by the widely accepted presupposition that winning by at least this amount is a sufficient condition for accession to power. Obviously, no such criterion exists in the international sphere, for only the United Nations General Assembly can provide such a benchmark and, clearly, the loci of international authority and decision making do not reside in that institution. A ready possibility for fulfilling this criterion function is the positive-sum game. Here, two or more great powers can benefit simultaneously from a joint cooperative action. An example to be treated in detail later will be the Polish partitions of the late eighteenth century. Here, a maximum entropy coalition, the members of which are in potential danger of experiencing a general war (Hötzsch 1909), unite in the positive-sum game of partitioning a weak and largely defenseless state which formerly had been a major power in Eastern Europe. The positive-sum game of all concerned great powers benefiting from the joint action is played out with a vengeance.

In a circumstance such as this, the requirement for many smaller countries not in permanent association with any of the great powers comes into play. The existence of these countries makes it far less likely that positive-sum games for the great powers need be enacted upon the remains of another country. Instead, there are coincident gains by the competing powers, as in the virtually simultaneous move by Ethiopia toward the Soviet Union after deposing Haile Selassie and the movement by the Somalian government toward the West. The dynamics of these processes need not concern us here; the simple existence of these countries in fairly remote locations from both superpowers and their fairly loose ties to both make it possible for relatively peaceful changes in political association to take place. In chapter 10, these positive-sum behaviors also will be analyzed but from the perspective of criteria for justice in the sense developed by John Rawls.

Absence of Memory and of Polarization

There is a third level of generality beyond that of hierarchy, entropy, and positive-sum games, one that can be generalized to other forms of conflict in addition to that of systemic war. As we shall see in chapter 6, the systemic war will be seen to belong to a category of wars with memory in contrast to wars whose onset demonstrates no appreciable memory component. This level of generality emerges from the requirements for minimum entropy and positive-sum games, which still are at least partially pitched at the structural level. (For that reason they are termed structure based in contrast to the more generalized analytic properties.) Hierarchy and minimum entropy allow for the possibility of the minimization of memory for the leading power in a coalition. If the power disparity between it and its allies is great, then there is little need for reliance on the small power for security needs and so the past conflicts or memories of the small power need not intrude on the great powers' decision making. The Soviet elimination of Cuban influence in the Cuban missile crisis is a case in point and stands in contrast to the Austro-Hungarian influence on Germany in the onset of World War I. This property of the minimum entropy coalition will be referred to as the absence of memory.

At the same time, positive-sum games emerging from the existence of large numbers of small independent powers have a generalizable analytic counterpart. The positive-sum game of each side benefiting while not vitiating the neutrality of the remaining powers is equivalent to the absence of systemic polarization. New nations can persist in their nonaligned coalition, or there can occur an exchange of allies (for example, Somalia–Ethiopia) that does not lead to a permanent set of alliances in which virtually all countries are allied with one or another coalition. This, of course, is a definition of the polarized condition as one in which every state is on one side or the other and there are no neutrals. Precisely because of the continued existence of the nonaligned countries in the hierarchical equilibrium with the possibility of positive-sum games, there exists a core of resistance to a systemic polarization. This condition stands in contrast to the zero-sum game, which is likely an ideal candidate for polarizing tendencies in light of the required loss for a leading power upon some gain to an opponent.

The structural features and corresponding analytic counterparts of the hierarchical equilibrium are shown in Table 1.1. The analytical properties are to be treated here as consequences of the structural condition. The first of these—minimum entropy and positive-sum games—emerges directly from the structure itself but then is generalized in the form of systemic effects, or the absence of memory and of systemic polarization. Effectively, the first generalized analytical property is temporal while the second is spatial, thus encompassing the two domains of systemic behavior. It is understood, of course, that these are idealized consequences and in reality there will always be some tendency toward the influence of memory or the presence of some degree of systemic polarization, if only in the continued efforts of great powers to increase their influence on the system. What is required is that these factors do not have a serious impact on the course of international conflict behavior.

In addition to the advantages of minimum entropy (absence of memory, property *a* of the hierarchical equilibrium) and positive-sum games (absence of polarization, property *b*), the hierarchical equilibrium formulation constitutes a general description of international structure which is then susceptible to reductions to more limited structural forms. Put another way, this structure incorporates others within it which, under appropriate conditions imposed on the hierarchical equilibrium, emerge from it. For example, if the small powers are removed entirely, the classic multipolar structure of $m > 2$ powers is derived. Alternatively, limiting the structure to two hierarchies and removing the large number of neutral small powers yields a bipolar

10

Table 1.1
Hierarchical equilibrium.

Structural properties	Corresponding analytical properties	
	Structure based	Generalized
Property a: Hierarchy in the form of great power–small power coalitions	Minimum entropy	Absence of memory
Property b: Large number of independent, unaffiliated small powers	Positive-sum games	Absence of systemic polarization

structure with two great powers and allied small powers. Given the mix of great and small powers, the hierarchical equilibrium is the most general structure that can exist; only the midrange or central powers (which, as we shall see in chapters 2 and 5, are among the most dangerous for system stability) are omitted from this formulation. The addition of these powers also would vitiate the minimum entropy condition by actually yielding the possibility of maximum entropy hierarchies which, as can be shown, are exponential distributions in realistic circumstances (Jaynes 1957). This generalizability and flexibility of the hierarchical equilibrium allow it to be tested in a variety of circumstances, including the generally accepted multipolarity of the nineteenth century and bipolarity of the post-World War II era. Comparisons of these types of polarity will be found in chapters 3 and 4.

What happens, though, when the hierarchical equilibrium with its absence of memory and positive-sum games is not obeyed? It is the task of this volume to demonstrate not only the association between the presence of the hierarchical equilibrium and the absence of systemic war but also to detail the causative elements associated with such a war. Thus, we begin with the absence of a hierarchical equilibrium in a multipolar system in which not all of the protagonists have hierarchical relations with small powers and the independent small powers are largely absent. It will be shown, first, that probabilistically such a system is associated with inequalities in resource distribution (for example, colonies, small allies) among the system members. Envies and political intrigues can result in such a system, thus leading to the deterioration of interstate relations. The search for security can become intensified in such a setting as will be shown later in chapter 3, in which the failure of the *Dreikaiserbund* as the result of Russian envies of German successes leads ultimately to the Franco-Russian defensive alliance consummated in 1894.

In turn, alliance memory can be instituted in which a threatened protagonist may feel the necessity to rely on a smaller great power as in the

German strategic reliance on Austria-Hungary. Such alliances, then, can set the stage for the overlap of conflicts as in the exclusively great power conflicts (largely German) combined with great power–small power disputes (Austro-Hungarian) which then set the stage for a general or systemic war. Additionally, there will be shown to exist certain analytic similarities between this international circumstance and the domestic political condition of some of the key protagonists. The precise transition to a systemic war, then, will traverse some actual or feared impending change in the balance of power. This will be demonstrated in chapter 6. From the ending of such a structural systemic or general war, the existence of a power vacuum and/or the learning of violence leads to the rise of mobilizing leaders who then directly initiate the onset of a mobilization war. As will be seen in chapter 6, a change in the balance of power will precede not only structural wars but all wars occurring in polarized settings, including mobilization wars. This sequence is diagrammed below:

Multipolarity (in the absence of a hierarchical equilibrium) → Resource inequality → Alliance formation → Alliance memory → Overlap in conflict structures → Change in the balance of power → Structural war → Mobilization war

Varieties of Systemic War

A consequence of the applications of the hierarchical equilibrium will be the distinction between structural wars (for example, Thirty Years' War, World War I) and mobilization wars (Napoleonic Wars, World War II) that will be detailed in chapter 7 and tested systematically for World Wars I and II in chapter 8.

Here, a differential applicability of the hierarchical equilibrium model is explored. Whereas the model predicts both the onset of World Wars I and II, the results are more emphatic for World War I. The use of a "contagious" probability distribution yields a distinction between the etiologies of the two wars and further distinguishes between the structural and mobilization wars as two distinct variants of the systemic war.

In the former, conflicts among the several protagonists feed directly into the events or large-scale crisis initiating the war. Specifically, the 1914 summer crisis preceding World War I combined exclusively great power conflicts with the great power–small power disputes, as shown in chapter 5. In this sense, the structure of conflict relationships necessary to the onset of the war was completed by the crisis. Two independent strains of conflict behaviors were united prior to the war via an alliance framework, as in the instance of German disputes with other great powers and Austro-Hungarian conflicts with smaller, principally Balkan countries.

One finds similar connections between disparate conflicts in other structural wars. The Thirty Years' War, for example, began in Central Europe with the Bohemian revolt against Habsburg rule in 1618 and was immediately followed by the Netherlands' war against Habsburg Spain, in which the two conflicts were united not merely by the presence of the same dynastic house in both locations but also by the requirement for Spanish troops to pass through Central European battle zones to reach their destination in the Low Countries (Pagès 1970; Polisensky 1971). The Peloponnesian War (Thucydides 1954) is open to a similar interpretation in which the Corinthian conflict with Corcyra became united with the Athenian conflict with Potidae (both essentially colonial-type wars), soon to involve Sparta in conflict with Athens as a consequence of the alliance between Corinth and Sparta.

In the mobilization war on the other hand, no such dependence on a structure of conflict relationships need exist. The mobilization takes place internal to the nation-state, perhaps in response to earlier international conflict but not necessarily to any which takes place at the time of the onset of the war. The mobilizing polity initiates the vast majority of the conflict behaviors preceding the war. World War II is an instance of a war begun largely by a mobilizing polity, Germany (and perhaps another, Japan), which had aggressive designs on neighboring territories virtually from the earliest days of the war-prone regimes in power. The Napoleonic Wars began in a similar fashion as a consequence of the then extensive mobilization of France for war by Napoleon, as did the War of the Spanish Succession, and even to some extent, certain earlier wars of Louis XIV.

Among the general wars considered here, the War of the Austrian Succession would fall into the structural category while the Seven Years' War would fit the mobilization rubric. In the former, Britain's colonial war with Spain then embroiled her in a war with Spain's ally, France, and the desire to protect Hanover dovetailed with Prussia's quarrel with Austria over Silesia. Two conflict structures overlapped as in our two systemic structural conflicts. The Seven Years' War, on the other hand, arose from the coalition formation and consequent mobilization for war of Frederick's soon-to-be opponents—a consideration which led him also to mobilize and seize the initiative (Ritter 1968).

Table 1.2 illustrates the categorizations among the types of war considered in this volume. The systemic wars (although not the distinctions among them) are, for the modern period,[3] virtually identical to those selected by Gilpin (1981, 200) and, to a somewhat lesser extent because he excludes all of the wars of Louis XIV, Wallerstein (1984, 41–42). As before, dichotomous categorizations are introduced not to better reflect a reality that is likely continuous in nature but to increase our understanding of modal differences between wars that likely would not be otherwise appreciated.

13

Table 1.2
Types of war.

	Systemic war	General war
Structural wars	Peloponnesian War Thirty Years' War French Revolution- ary Wars World War I	War of the Austrian Succession
Mobilization wars	Macedonian War War of the Spanish Succession Napoleonic Wars World War II	Seven Years' War

Deductions from the Theory
and Related Analyses

Aside from direct tests of the hierarchical equilibrium formulation in chapter 2 and the remaining aspects of the theory in succeeding chapters, there are tests of deductions from the theory in chapters 9 and 10.

The first of these refers to the durability of coalitions obeying the minimum entropy formulation, suggested in principle *a* of the hierarchical equilibrium. As will be seen in chapter 9, peacetime alliances with one large and one small power (minimum entropy) tend to be more durable than those between countries of approximately equal power (maximum entropy). This increased durability constitutes a further confirmation of the importance of minimum entropy in alliances as also was found in domestic cabinet coalitions.

Concepts of justice in chapter 10 will be put forward in an attempt to shed light not so much now on the reasons for systemic war but on reasons for systemic peace and continuity. The nineteenth century especially will be singled out for examination as a period of systemic continuity which included small wars but none of the systemic variety that is the object of inquiry of this volume. Certain forms of justice will be found to apply to the nineteenth century balance-of-power system. Property *a* of the hierarchical equilibrium, which requires the absence of memory also characteristic of balance-of-power systems, will find a counterpart in Rawls' "veil of ignorance" required to establish a stable society at the original position. Property *b* of the hierarchical equilibrium, which allows for positive-sum games as the result of the large number of independent small powers, will find a direct counterpart in the need for abundance, which is a seldom-articulated but necessary provision of Rawls' difference principle (each gain to the most advantaged in society must be matched by a gain to the least advantaged). If we regard, as many do, the difference principle and its associated need for abundance as a bedrock of Rawls' framework, then this requirement for justice is satisfied by the existence of the large number of independent small powers available for political association both in the nineteenth century and the post-World War II period.

The Conclusion, chapter 11, contains an information-theoretic treatment of the hierarchical equilibrium that reveals it to be the only historical structure which satisfies two requisites for the effective learning of cooperation. Additionally, a historical dynamic for the emergence of mobilized great powers on the periphery of older strife-torn civilizations is put forward, contingent on the inequality analyses of chapters 3 and 4. These findings will turn out to be related to a well-attested pattern of civilized history (McNeill 1982).

Modes of Inquiry and of Presentation

A comment or two is required on the overall philosophy of inquiry which guides this study. A fundamental question that must be addressed in any scientific treatment, or even in one which merely claims to be a dispassionate approach, is the amount of detail required for the analysis. A historical study of, say, the evolution of one county in the state of Alaska within a relatively short time period may require a fair amount of detail in order to achieve the putative goal of giving the reader a clear and multidimensional sense of the county's development over time. On the other hand, a simple statement of relationship between two variables (I think here of the classic Newtonian formulation $F = ma$) requires only data on these two foci of inquiry. This volume steers a course between these two poles of legitimate study.

Clearly, given the central theoretical focus, this is not intended as a historical study. As such, much of the detail that would be highly relevant to the Alaskan county would be irrelevant to the present study, only because the theory suggests that we look for certain variables (that is, conflict behavior) and not for others (for example, fishing or trade agreements). On the other hand, the model is general enough in its specification of broad properties of international systems (for example, hierarchy) to allow for a fair amount of latitude in the inclusion of relevant historical detail. This detail is found in succeeding chapters. Given the lack of orderly behavior of political systems compared to that of physical systems (at least at the macro end of forces and accelerations), such a model, intermediate between the detail of chronology and that of abstract theorizing at the level of bivariate relationships, seems to be appropriate. Much historical material, therefore, will be relevant, but much will also be irrelevant according to the directives of the theory.

In some instances, as in chapters 2, 5, and 8, there exist systematic data on disputes in the nineteenth century. Here, we can examine in systematic detail the theoretical hypotheses. For earlier periods, this certainly is not true, thus necessitating the use of historical observation. For this reason, there will be a somewhat greater emphasis on the origins of World War I and its successor, World War II, in this volume. Increased credence in the findings naturally derives from more systematic data. Nevertheless, there exists sufficient historical material on the remaining systemic and general wars to provide detailed and accurate descriptions.

The mode of analysis throughout the volume will be probabilistic. In this kind of macroanalysis through historical time, probabilistic analyses are most appropriate because, simply put, we are seeking to ascertain the increasing or decreasing probability of the occurrence of a systemic war. In another sense, the use of probabilistic analyses arises from the author's epistomological assumptions about the nature of social reality. It is not a deterministic set of conflict relations which leads to war, but one in which the probability of systemic war increases or decreases. Only a good theory (in the sense of empirical validity) can help us understand the changing nature of these probabilistic relations.

There is an important question which needs to be answered before continuing. It concerns the role of modeling in the analysis of international phenomena. Why model? Most, if not all, of the conclusions of this volume derive from the use of models to explore political reality. As such, it is essential that I justify the use of what are often difficult and not easily understood procedures. For convenience of presentation and readability most of these are found in appendices; nevertheless, they constitute the core of the analytic approach.

In answering the question of why I chose this mode of inquiry, I will not emphasize two often-cited reasons. These are precision and esthetics. The first obviously derives from a major preoccupation of science, namely, the search for more exact means of expressing the conclusions of scientific inquiry. Many scientists, particularly those concerned with the physical world, might regard this as a sufficient reason for the use of mathematical models.

The second possible justification for the use of models—that of esthetics—is important but does not go to the heart of the matter. Certainly, the elegance of a mathematical–theoretical formulation is a point in its favor; if it is also more parsimonious than rival frameworks, then Occam's razor demands that it be given preference. The esthetic merits of a formulation obviously also give it an appeal to the reader which actually can make it used more frequently, thus yielding an important practical consequence.

But beyond these arguments exists one which is likely most compelling. This is one which goes to the heart of what a model is supposed to be, namely, to be isomorphic to elements of the reality which it purports to represent. And as Hofstadter (1985, 445) put it, "meaning emerges from and only from isomorphism." This is a strong statement and suggests that we can genuinely understand reality only if we have coded it in some fashion. (This is the context in which this statement by Hofstadter was made). It does not necessarily have to be a mathematical code, but ordinarily these are the most manipulable and tractable in application, especially when one seeks to make deductions from the initial argument. The code, of whatever form, is essentially the meaning abstracted from the reality in question. Whether it is the particular meaning that plumbs the depth of the phenomenon most deeply is, of course, another question, one that is decided frequently by empirical test. Nevertheless, the existence of meaning is reliant ultimately on the existence of some ideational construct which is suggested to be iso-morphic to the particular reality in question. Put another way, it is not the details themselves of political phenomena which are of theoretical interest (although they may be of intrinsic interest as in who wins an election) but the *critical* details suggested by that construct and abstracted from the rest that are of scientific importance. This is essentially what is meant by iso-morphism, at least as the concept is used in this volume.

A succinct statement of the theoretical orientation of this volume, to be placed in tandem with Hofstadter's statement about meaning in the preced-ing paragraph, is that of Waltz (1979, 94): "international politics is mostly about inequalities." Much of the succeeding analysis explores the impli-cations of this view, not in any way suggesting that such inequalities are desirable in a normative sense, but that they have specific international consequences. Indeed, as we shall see, inequalities among nation–states will have radically different influences on the probability of systemic war depending on whether the system structure obeys the hierarchical equilib-rium (typically but not always bipolar), or is multipolar without such an equilibrium.

The testing of models generally proceeds by means of goodness of fit according to statistical criteria adopted at the outset. A fit between model and data will be accepted or rejected at a given probability level for a goodness-of-fit statistic such as chi square. But beyond this formalism, throughout the volume where possible, the model's prediction for the occurrence of systemic war will be compared with its nonoccurrence. Even more specifically, the predictions of certain types of systemic war will be evaluated systematically. For example, whereas the absence of a hierarchi-cal equilibrium would predict the occurrence of systemic war prior to World Wars I and II, the presence of this condition in the mid-nineteenth century and post-World War II periods should be associated with the absence of systemic war. These periods will be explicitly compared in chapter 2. Chapter 5 contains a formal comparison of the onset of systemic war in 1914 with its absence in 1908 under similar crisis conditions. The model's predictions in chapter 6 for the occurrence of wars with memory are compared with the non-occurrence of such wars. Chapter 8 contains an explicit comparison of the prediction of a structural systemic conflict in 1914 with that for a mobilization war in 1939. Thus, where the data allow, comparisons of alternate predictions will be used as an important analytic supplement to the formal acceptance or rejection of a probability model.

Not only will the presence of a hierarchical equilibrium be associated with systemic continuity and its absence with the onset of systemic war, but it also can be shown how the presence of such an equilibrium can prevent the transformation of a relatively small war into one of much wider dimensions. The Crimean War initially had all the hallmarks of a conflict susceptible to rapid spread throughout Europe. It had all the potential of becoming at least a general war, but the presence of elements of the hierarchical equilibrium prevented this from happening, as will be shown in chapter 2.

All of this is not to claim that the presence of a hierarchical equilibrium is a sufficient condition for systemic continuity and its absence necessary for the onset of systemic war. These are categorical statements which seldom, if ever, can be applied to scientific inquiry. As will be argued in the concluding section of chapter 2, it will be far more profitable to view the absence of a hierarchical equilibrium as increasing the probability of a systemic war, given some existing conflict relations among major powers, and its presence as increasing the probability of systemic continuity. An issue that will be addressed in the concluding chapter is the timing of a systemic war based on the sequence of variables shown on p. 12.

A word or two on the organization of this volume is necessary. A primary consideration in writing it was continuity in presentation of the argument and its readability. As a result, large groups of equations or tables were deemed to hinder that purpose and are included in the mathematical and tabular appendices.

Conclusions and Policy Implications

This volume will close with conclusions about the origins of systemic war and the likely scenario for a future systemic war, most probably of the nuclear variety. Both properties (*a* and *b*) of the hierarchical equilibrium leading, respectively, to the minimum entropy formulation and need for positive-sum games, will eventuate in a tabular construction suggesting the combinations of memory and game conditions most likely to lead to systemic war in chapter 6. Conversely, conditions likely to result in systemic continuity and peace also will be delineated. The likely scenario for the outbreak of World War III will emerge from these considerations.

Despite (or perhaps because of?) the decidedly theoretical and empirical nature of this treatment, certain very specific policy implications will emerge from the analysis. They range from the specific types of armaments appropriate for small power defense consistent with peace to the suggested disposition of the Strategic Defense Initiative (SDI). Aspects of the international structure which actually may have a pacific effect are distinguished from those which are more likely to yield a systemic war. There are other policy implications of the analysis and they are included throughout the volume, but especially in chapter 11, the conclusion.

Notes

1 By emphasizing the structural perspective, as in any other choice of mode of inquiry, certain important perspectives are necessarily deemphasized. In this instance, they include game theoretic analyses of bargaining behavior and of international conflict generally as in Schelling (1960), Snyder and Diesing (1977), Brams (1985), and Zagare (1987); analyses of crisis behavior especially from the viewpoint of the psychology of decision makers as in Jervis (1976) and Lebow (1981); or treatments of deterrence with an emphasis on the post World War II period as in George and Smoke (1974), Morgan (1977), Mearsheimer (1983), Jervis (1984), and Hardin, Mearsheimer, Dworkin, and Goodin (1985). Excellent treatments which emphasize either the diplomacy of the contemporary period (Craig and George 1983) or strategic doctrine (Snyder 1984) also are not within the central purview of this analysis.
2 Schmookler (1984, 36) puts it this way: "The whole is the way the parts are put together. The higher level of organization is the structure in which the parts act. By determining the environment of the constituent elements, the structure shapes how the elements act. The behavior of the parts is therefore fully explicable only in terms of the surrounding whole."
3 The only instance of a "hegemonic war" named by Gilpin (1981, 200) that is not included here under the systemic rubric is the Second Punic War between Carthage and Rome (218–201 B.C.). Reasons for its exclusion are straightforward. In its essentials, it was a dyadic war which derived from the outcome of the dyadic First Punic War between these protagonists which ended some twenty-three years earlier. The only other major actor to appear in the Second Punic War was Philip V of Macedon who concluded an alliance with Hannibal one year after the earlier Roman defeats (Boak 1930, 93). Even this alliance was limited, for it did not include any promise of military support in Italy where most of the serious fighting was taking place (Scramuzza and MacKendrick 1958, 441). Other major Mediterranean actors such as the Seleucid king Antiochus III, or Ptolemy IV of Egypt remained aloof from the conflict (except to supply grain to Rome at inflated prices), not to mention the non-participating Parthians or Persians. As a result, this war does not satisfy the criterion of the inclusion of all major systemic actors.

2
A Hierarchical Equilibrium

A FUNDAMENTAL PURPOSE of this inquiry is to establish a theoretical framework that will explain the onset of systemic war[1] and, at the same time, its absence during long periods of systemic continuity. This framework is termed a hierarchical equilibrium theory of systemic war. It designates a particular structural condition of the international system that is conducive not necessarily to peace but to the absence of wars of this magnitude. Conversely, the disappearance of this structural condition makes it far more likely that such a war will occur. Empirical tests distinguish between those periods which demonstrated the hierarchical equilibrium (1816–1899, 1946–1964) and those which did not (1893–1914, 1919–1939). In turn, the latter two periods are called polarizing systems in order to suggest the polarization process which manifestly is not a property of the hierarchical equilibrium.

A unique feature of the analysis is the combination of elements of balance-of-power theory, especially as articulated by Morgenthau (1973), and the concept of hierarchy as necessary for peace, as developed by Organski (1968).

The structural condition of hierarchy, to be defined more precisely later, is deemed to be necessary for the maintenance of an equilibrium condition. This is not an equilibrium in capabilities or power but an equilibrium in the ongoing processes of the system. A power equilibrium, of course, has been claimed to be central to the peaceful functioning of international systems (Leckie 1817; Fénelon 1920; Pollard 1923; Fay 1930; Oppenheim 1947; Liska 1957; Herz 1959; Stoessinger 1964; Zinnes 1967; Russett 1968a; O. R. Holsti 1976). Here, the concept of equilibrium is akin to this fundamental theme of international relations theory but is manifested directly in the form of a stochastic equilibrium over time in conflict behavior. It was used successfully in prior analyses of alliances and conflict behavior. This equilibrium posits the average equality in beginnings and endings of disputes. For every dispute which begins in a certain time period, on the average, one must end or else there is a buildup of the simultaneous occurrence of a series of disputes. It is this accumulation of conflict behavior over time which is suggested to be destabilizing.

I next suggest reasons for the need to avoid an accumulation of unresolved disputes in order to prevent a systemic war. They are presented as, first, the inevitable difficulty in resolving important disputes if many exist simultaneously and each dispute distracts key decision makers from paying adequate attention to the remaining conflicts. The second major reason consists of the need for the independence of individual disputes from each other, or the avoidance of interdependencies in the form of the diffusion of conflict behavior, its reinforcement, or the occasioning of similar conflict responses to a widespread geographical process. Such interdependencies can lead to polarized international settings which can be easily susceptible to the onset of systemic war. Subsequently, I suggest that substantial power disparities between large and small powers, or hierarchy, can be a principal means of avoiding the accumulation of unresolved disputes with its associated international complexities and dispute interdependence.

Equilibrium and the Need for Independence

As suggested above, there are two fundamental reasons for the expectation of systemic breakdown upon the accumulation of a series of disputes. The first is the converse of the argument used in the Deutsch and Singer (1964) treatment of the increase in the number of new nation-states. In that instance, the share of attention devoted to each new protagonist is diminished because of the rapidly increasing $\{[N(N-1)]/2\}$ number of interaction opportunities between countries. Thus, there is less attention devoted to an arms race between only two nation-states and the probabilities of a dyadic superpower war are lessened. Here, in the present study, the dispute is the basic unit of analysis, not the nation-state, and the consequences differ from the Deutsch-Singer formulation. Upon an increase in the number of unresolved disputes, the share of attention devoted to each dispute by great power decision makers would be diminished, thus potentially decreasing possibilities for the peaceful resolution of each. If decision makers are overwhelmed by a succession of serious conflicts, each requiring a fair amount of attention, then possibilities for peacefully resolving each of them are diminished to this extent.

Additionally, if several disputes exist simultaneously for a sufficiently long period of time, then the simple condition of being in a state of conflict may lead to the desire for allies on the part of each protagonist. This may lead to a "conflict interaction opportunity" as in the joining of two or more disputes ("the enemy of my enemy is my friend") and the multiplicative element may be introduced for the number of dyadic disputes existing at a particular time.

The second basic reason for the onset of systemic war upon the accumulation of a series of disputes consists of a set of possibilities for interdependence among the disputes. These are three in number: (1) a diffusion effect, (2) a widespread process occasioning similar responses by geographically separate sovereign entities, and (3) a reinforcement effect. All of these, separately or together, can lead to polarized international settings which can be vulnerable to the onset of systemic war.

A diffusion effect exists whenever the behavior of one country, and in particular its success in aggressive conflict behavior, serves as a model or prototype for other countries. Countries whose governments are most similar to one another (for example, dictatorships) and, therefore, can identify with each other are most likely to imitate the model or prototype. This process likely occurred in the decade preceding World War II. The Japanese invasion of Manchuria in 1931 followed by the invasion of Ethiopia by Italy may have constituted the kind of demonstration of international politics by conquest which then led Hitler (and possibly Stalin) to adopt similar tactics toward Austria, Czechoslovakia, and, finally, Poland later in that decade. As a consequence of aggressions such as these, Europe became a polarized camp in 1939.

On the other hand, the rapid resolution of these conflicts and, especially, the absence of gain for an aggressor imply that there is no demonstration of success. There are no ongoing instances of aggressive behavior that can serve as a demonstration of success for others and, consequently, intensify a conflict-learning spiral. The probability models introduced later assume statistical independence among all of the ongoing instances of conflict behavior.

The occasioning of similar responses by countries to a geographically widespread process may be found in the period preceding World War I. The declining power of the Ottoman Empire led to expansionist tendencies on its southwestern fringes by Italy in the conquest of Libya in 1911–1912; simultaneously, there was a desire for increased territory and population in the Balkans at Turkish expense by Bulgaria, Serbia, Greece, and Montenegro, thus leading to the First and Second Balkan Wars of 1912–1913. In both cases, the precipitating agent was the same. The rise to power of the Young Turks in 1908 and the subsequent deposing of the Sultan Abdul Hamid in the following year quite possibly advertised to these interested external powers that they could gain at Turkey's expense during this period of internal instability and power interregnum. As we see later, both the Italo-Turkish War and the Balkan Wars are conflict events immediately preceding the onset of World War I and contributed to the instability of that period.

The last source of interdependence to be considered here, that of reinforcement, occurs when the later behavior of a country is conditioned by its earlier success when it engaged in a similar type of behavior. In the approach to World War II, a reinforcement effect was probably operating in that each of Hitler's successes in the late 1930s increased the likelihood that he would resort to similar behavior at a later time. In the analysis of World War I that follows, the success of the blank-check support of Austria-Hungary by Germany and the ultimatum to Russia during the Bosnian crisis of 1908 likely increased the probability that such unconditional support of Austria-Hungary and an ultimatum to Russia would appear again in the summer crisis of 1914. This second time, however, the Russians would not accede to a German ultimatum requiring the cessation of support for the smaller Slav ally. The Bosnian crisis contributed strongly to the polarization of Europe between Dual Alliance and Triple Entente, for Russia sought French and ultimately British support even more strongly, precisely in order to avoid a second humiliation of this type. Thus, the three forms of increased conflict interdependence as the number of disputes accumulate, the consequent polarization effect, and the sheer complexity and decreased attention span for each dispute argue for an increased systemic instability as the number of disputes in existence at any one point in time increases.

Hierarchy

Equally basic to the present analysis is the concept of hierarchy. By hierarchy I mean the condition of substantial capability or power differentials among nation-states such that there exists a very wide differential between the strongest and weakest state within a particular international cluster (alliance or loosely knit empire). While it may seem somewhat paradoxical to include both equilibrium and hierarchy in the same framework, the demands of an equilibrium in conflict behavior over time in fact necessitate the presence of hierarchy—and not merely some differential in size and power but very large differentials between large and small protagonists. This is so for a number of reasons. First, the absence of accumulation in conflict behavior over time specified by the equilibrium model requires that the existing disputes be relatively short ones, such that one dispute can end before another begins. This requirement clearly can be fulfilled more readily if the power differentials among the participants are substantial (for example, the intervention by the United States in Grenada). Small powers involved in disputes with great powers (either their allies or their opponents) would likely be far more amenable either to early settlement or surrender if there is no hope for a successful outcome for the small power (for example, Czechoslovakia in 1968). Indeed, under these conditions many disputes probably would be avoided at the outset.

The second reason for the existence of hierarchy is the requirement by the equilibrium model for the independence of conflict behavior and the consequent absence of polarizing tendencies. This independence requirement is stipulated precisely in order to avoid the several processes enumerated previously (diffusion, reinforcement) which can augment the interdependence of disputes and then lead to a buildup over time which violates the equilibrium condition. Systemic polarization can occur if the conflict interdependencies are especially widespread and severe. On the other hand, if the disputes are short ones as a consequence of hierarchy, then it is far less likely for other nations to become involved in the conflict than if the conflict were protracted. And even if a dispute was to continue for a while, if the smaller power is not seen to be sufficiently important because of small size or power, then it is also unlikely for other countries to become involved.

As a corollary, the independence requirement demands that a substantial number of these powers not be formally allied with or under the protection of great powers. If virtually all such powers were allied with great powers, then clearly a conflict involving one small power could possibly involve other powers, both great and small, and the independence requirement would be vitiated with a consequently greater likelihood of systemic war.

There is a third implication of the existence of hierarchy, namely, the relative security great powers can feel if they find themselves situated at the head of a hierarchy in which they are the leaders. There is not merely the presence of great influence over the small powers and the contribution of their armies but also the feeling (if not the illusion) of security which comes with the existence of such a hierarchy. This hierarchy of power may not only satisfy the defense needs of the leading country in the form of military bases in the smaller countries, or several armies added to its own, or even as buffer zones, but may yield certain status gratifications which could obviate the desire to exercise undue influence over other, perhaps more powerful states. This effort at influence, or even at times coercion, may begin the conflict process leading to systemic war. The sense of security for a great power attendant upon the existence of such a hierarchy also would likely diminish the perception of need to ally with other great or small powers, thus simultaneously diminishing the probability of conflict interdependence and, hence, systemic war. Such simultaneous hierarchies may exist in either bipolar or multipolar systems.

A capsule description of these hierarchies and of the entire hierarchical equilibrium structure includes the presence of (1) two or more alliances (or other loose hierarchies such as loosely knit empires) of varying size and composition but clearly including a great power and a number of small powers within each,[2] and (2) a relatively large number of small powers not formally associated with any of the great powers.[3] Note that great powers at the head of each hierarchy (as well as the hierarchies themselves) can be approximately equal in power to each other, or unequal as the case may be, as long as the power differentials within each hierarchy are substantial. (A good case in point is the emergence of the Soviet-dominated hierarchy at the end of World War II which was demonstrably unequal in power to the West. The stability of the consequent bipolar system was aided by the emergence of the large number of neutral smaller countries, as I shortly demonstrate.)

The absence of necessity for an absolute equality or inequality of power among great powers should be so because of the capability even of weaker great powers to inflict damage on stronger ones, thus suggesting caution in their relations. The existence of hierarchy with all of its implications for equilibria of various types also militates against the polarization associated with systemic war. However, as we shall see in chapter 6, the strong equality and gross inequality conditions will be associated with peace, with small departures from equality in polarized settings associated with the onset of war, especially of the systemic variety. What will be shown in the subsequent analysis (chapter 3) is that inequalities of resource possession, especially in the absence of hierarchies, increase the likelihood of polarization which then can yield systemic war. The existence of such hierarchies establishes at least an equality of form and structure which can militate against the polarization process.

A diagram should be helpful in summarizing the major arguments concerning the diminished probability of systemic war upon the existence of a hierarchical equilibrium:

1. Hierarchy → avoid (by great power) lengthy and therefore accumulated disputes → maximize dispute independence → minimize polarization → lower probability of systemic war

2. Independence of small powers → maximize dispute independence → minimize polarization → lower probability of systemic war

Consequences of the Hierarchical Equilibrium

The Hierarchical Structure

An extremely important property of the hierarchical structure is the ability of the great power at its head to make decisions unfettered by obligations to allies. The greater the power disparity between the hierarchy leader and the smaller allies, the greater the freedom of decision making for the great power. In the final analysis, its security dependence on any single ally is minimal. As A. J. P. Taylor (1971, 280) commented on Bismarck's use of alliances as stabilizing factors in nineteenth century Europe, "He [Bismarck] controlled his allies; he did not cooperate with them. There indeed was the deepest element. In international affairs, as in domestic politics, Bismarck disliked equals; he sought for satellites."

This power asymmetry among allies is tantamount to what may be called the absence of memory or the minimization of memory in alliances (Midlarsky 1983a). The great power is free to act as it pleases in its relations with other powers without the necessity for responsiveness to its own allies and their traditional foreign policy concerns or "memories." As described briefly in chapter 1, a striking illustration of the absence of alliance memory is found in the Cuban missile crisis of 1962 in which the Cubans were not allowed by the Soviets to influence the course of events, which easily could have included a joint Soviet–Cuban crusade against U.S. "imperialism" in the Caribbean. Thus, the crisis could proceed as a superpower confrontation without any of the past local animosities felt by the Cubans toward the United States. In contrast, the 1914 summer crisis allowed the historic parochial interests of southeast Europe to exert a truly extraordinary and disproportionate effect on the outbreak of World War I.

Here, the interests of the Austro-Hungarians in the Balkans, and especially Serbia, were allowed to influence the course of events leading to war between the Dual Alliance and Triple Entente. The main precursor of the 1914 summer crisis was the Bosnian crisis of 1908, which pitted Austria-Hungary against Serbia and Russia after the annexation of Bosnia-Herzegovina by Austria-Hungary. German support of Austria-Hungary during the crisis effectively led to its termination (Bridge and Bullen 1980, 161–163). Later, the emergence of Serbia in 1913 at twice her initial size prior to the Balkan Wars, coupled with an aggressive and effective pan-Slavic propaganda campaign aimed at the ever-growing Slavic population within the Austro-Hungarian Empire, threatened to result in the disintegration of the empire, as indeed occurred at the end of World War I. In 1914, Austria-Hungary was seen as the only reliable great power ally of Germany, and her continued existence in that role (especially in opposition to Russia) was perceived as an essential condition for Germany's effective opposition to the Triple Entente. Thus, Bismarck's earlier maxim of scattering "promises so as not to carry them out" (Taylor 1971, 278) was violated in the extreme by this later German reliance on an essentially weaker ally. The residues of Austria-Hungary's conflicts with Serbia and Russia were allowed to influence the behavior of the coalition leader, or put another way, an alliance memory was operative in 1914 which earlier, during the Bismarckian period, simply had not existed.

An instance of the stabilizing consequences of hierarchy is found in the Suez crisis of 1956. As the result of the very large power disparity between the

United States and its allies, Great Britain and France, especially in regard to strategic nuclear weapons, American security dependence on the two North Atlantic Treaty Organization (NATO) allies was relatively small. As a consequence, when the Soviet Union threatened these European powers with a nuclear confrontation after the invasion of Suez, the United States could take a fairly impartial view and not support her allies in their venture. The historic foreign policy interests of Great Britain and France in the Middle East and North Africa and the memory of the then fairly recent appeasement of Hitler (often compared to Nasser of Egypt, who had unilaterally nationalized the Suez Canal) were not allowed to influence U.S. policy in the crisis. Had the security dependence on her allies been greater, then the United States might have felt obliged to respond to the Soviet threat, with the possible onset of a superpower confrontation.

The existence of hierarchy in this instance likely prevented the onset of a superpower crisis which could have resulted in a systemic war. In the nineteenth century also, there are clear instances of outcomes such as these. One of them is the prevention of escalation to a systemic or general war during the more limited Crimean War. Here, it is hierarchy in the form of a loosely knit empire which was decisive in preventing Austrian involvement in the war, an involvement which clearly would have brought in the Prussians as well. For it was Austrian weakness in Italy in precisely those possessions granted to it by the Congress of Vienna that prevented cooperation with Russia and a provocation of France which could have resulted in French action against those territories. [See Gulick (1955, 254–255) for a listing of these territories including dependent dynasties such as Modena and Parma. Taylor (1971, 69) mentions the Austrian concern for these Italian dependencies.] Austrian neutrality, therefore, was preserved. If not for these concerns for the maintenance of the hierarchy in Italy vis-à-vis the French and, additionally, in the Balkans with respect to Russia, Austria could easily have been brought into the war with implications for more generalized war throughout the remainder of the continent. Thus, a concern for the preservation of hierarchy, where it exists, can also prevent the spread of what was initially and remained a relatively small war.

There exists an immediate theoretical consequence of the hierarchical structure, and that is the confluence with a process-oriented model called tit-for-tat by Anatol Rapoport and described by Axelrod (1984). In an iterated prisoners' dilemma game, tit-for-tat defeated all other programs submitted by experts in two rounds of tournament play. In tit-for-tat, the player cooperates on the first move and thereafter simply imitates the opponent's preceding move. Each move in the game clearly is dependent only on one earlier move (Axelrod 1984, 58) and therefore is without the memory of any prior history of play. There exists, therefore, a fundamental correspondence between tit-for-tat and the absence of memory in the hierarchical structure detailed above. Moreover, mathematically, there exists a unique correspondence between the two conditions. For equations [2.1] and [11A] – [13A] in Mathematical Appendix A implied by the hierarchical equilibrium model (see later) when combined with the exponential duration of disputes [confirmed empirically, see Midlarsky (1983a) for an exposition of this process in the case of nineteenth century alliances] are Markovian, or without memory beyond the immediately preceding state of the system. Tit-for-tat also is Markovian, by definition. Interestingly, the hierarchical structure is mentioned by Axelrod (1984, 130–131) as the one most capable of successfully operating tit-for-tat.

The Existence of Independent Small Powers

The second major theoretical component of the hierarchical equilibrium— the existence of independent small powers—leads to the possibility of positive-sum games or, what amounts to the same thing, an inducement to cooperate. [This, interestingly, resolves Axelrod's (1984, 186–187) dilemma as to how to induce a pattern of cooperation at the outset of the game which will be reciprocated thereafter. Tit-for-tat itself does not offer this remedy, for a pattern of unending defections could easily arise from this model, thus yielding what amounts to a feud.]

There exists a long history of the use of small sovereign states as vehicles of cooperation. The entire settlement at the Congress of Vienna turned on the future of the small countries in relation to the great powers. Poland, which already had been divided as of the late eighteenth century, continued under Russian, Prussian, and Austrian control. A portion of Saxony and of the left bank of the Rhine went to Prussia, and Austria received territories in Italy (Kissinger 1957, 171). The existence and disposition of these smaller entities avoided the breakdown of the Congress of Vienna and a possibly widespread war. What was perhaps even more important was the role of what were called the "secondary powers" (Kissinger 1957, 235–236) in maintaining peace in Central Europe, for Austria and Prussia were continually vying for the support of these smaller states and principalities (for example, Saxony, Hanover, Hesse-Electoral, Baden, Bavaria, Württemberg). The presence of a large number of these sovereign entities could allow one to ally, say, with Austria while another allied with Prussia. This hierarchical equilibrium in miniature in Central Europe very likely contributed to the prevention of systemic war in that region.

The contemporary international system also demonstrates the salutary role of the smaller powers. If one of these, say Ethiopia, decides to draw closer to the Eastern bloc, another, Somalia, can approach the West. While the Soviet Union sought to buttress its position in Afghanistan without major hindrance by the United States, the United States could do the same in Central America without serious Soviet opposition. Indonesia can veer from a neutralist, sometime pro-Soviet position in 1965 to a staunchly pro-Western position at the same time that the Soviets make serious inroads in Africa. Chile can cease being governed by a Marxist party while South Vietnam moves steadily toward incorporation with communist North Vietnam. None of these is a zero-sum conflict; they are situations which eventuate in a positive-sum or constant-sum game. More generally, with the rise of the new nations in the postwar era, both superpowers sought to gain new adherents, with simultaneous gains for both, principally in the Middle East, Asia, and Africa. Without the existence of these smaller powers, it is possible that more direct superpower confrontations could have occurred.

Perhaps the most striking example in the post-World War II era was the beginning of overt cooperation between the two hierarchy leaders in 1955 via the neutralization of Austria. This came well before any arms control agreements or other less tractable forms of agreement which require the cooperation of many significant domestic interests. The agreement about the neutralization of a small power which does not have significant strategic or resource advantage could proceed without the added difficulties of potential domestic opposition. Only later, when successful cooperation had already been experienced in a relatively uncontroversial setting with gains to both sides from Austrian neutrality, could more difficult forms of agreement be undertaken. This is but one of the cooperative functions of the existence of small powers.

A final and perhaps obvious, but no less important, consequence of the independent small powers is the dampening of polarization tendencies. The greater the number of such powers, the smaller the likelihood that the system will tend toward a completely polarized state. The condition of each side benefiting while not vitiating the neutrality of the remaining powers is equivalent to the absence of systemic polarization. New nations can adhere to any one of the existing coalitions or there can occur an exchange of allies (for example, Somalia–Ethiopia) that does not lead to a permanent set of alliances in which virtually all countries are allied with one or another coalition. This positive- or constant-sum condition stands in contrast to the zero-sum game, which is an ideal candidate for polarizing tendencies in light of the required loss for a leading power upon some gain to an opponent.

As the principal illustrations of the existence of hierarchy and the presence of a relatively large number of small powers, the nineteenth century and post-World War II era also demonstrate the strongest stability among those periods examined systematically, using equation [2.1] and its derivatives, equations [11A]–[13A] in Mathematical Appendix A.

Predictions

Several predictions emerge directly from the hierarchical equilibrium model. First, the presence of a relatively large number of very small powers is essential for the stability of the system because of the need for positive-sum games, and the power differentials between the great and small powers should be very large in order to minimize alliance memory. Systems with such power differentials should exhibit greater stability than those without them. Second, if the power differentials are not substantial, then a protracted conflict between a great and small power could involve others, and so systemic wars become more likely when midrange or central powers are involved in the conflicts among great powers.

These arguments lead to the additional implication that great-power conflicts alone are unlikely to lead directly to systemic war but require the presence of conflict involving these midrange or central powers. Great powers themselves would likely be so close in power to each other that substantial care would be exercised in relations between them lest some accidental happening precipitate an unwanted war.

Third, polarizing systems are more prone to the onset of systemic war because of the interdependence, largely via alliance formation, of the countries in the system. However, if the alliances are already formed, if there exist substantial numbers of very small powers in the system which are not directly included in the principal coalitions (usually two in number), then the requirements for the presence of a hierarchical equilibrium are satisfied.

A corollary to this proposition is that polarizing systems, or those in which a dynamic polarization is taking place, are more prone to systemic war than systems in which the two principal coalitions are already formed. The reason for this lies not only in Bueno de Mesquita's (1978) finding of increasing tightness of nation clusters having been associated with war, but in the structure of the hierarchical equilibrium model. In a polarizing system, changes of political association are rapidly taking place and so any country becomes a potential ally or focus for conquest for one or the other of the two coalitions. The concept of neutrality and the legitimacy of a large number of neutral small powers essential to the hierarchical equilibrium model are only sketchily formed or even rejected outright (for example, Hitler in the late 1930s or Dulles in the early 1950s). In an already formed bipolar system, on the other hand, the concept of neutrality and even its practice may have already been defined (perhaps by the rejected efforts of the two blocs to add these countries to their alliances) with the possibility of many nations existing in a state of neutrality and thus satisfying this component of the hierarchical equilibrium.

A word or two on nomenclature is useful at this juncture. The term bipolar structure or system will be used to refer to a condition of two already-formed international blocs that exist for some period of time with one major power in each and typically, but not always, small power allies. This stands in contrast to the polarizing system that can end in two opposing alliances consisting mostly of major powers who have chosen to ally with

30

one or the other coalition. Thus, the Dual Alliance versus Triple Entente would not constitute a bipolar system, but instead is an instance of a system which has undergone polarization within a multipolar context. Similarly, the Delian and Peloponnesian Leagues are also consequences of the polarization of a multipolar system in which the Greek city states existed earlier in approximate equality, but later saw Athens rise to prominence and develop her network of allies, to be followed by other city states choosing to ally with Sparta. Even at the time of the Peloponnesian War, Corinth, for example, saw herself as a bitter rival to Athens in her own right (Corinth also was a colonial power and like Athens, commercial) not merely as a vassal of Sparta in the Peloponnesian League (Thucydides 1954). The later rise of Thebes and the continual involvement of Persia in the Greek wars throughout this period suggest a continually polarizing multipolar system.

The concept of instability is here limited to the propensity toward systemic breakdown as measured by departures from the equilibrium condition and validated by the onset of systemic war. As will be shown, departures from equilibrium as specified by equations [2.1] and its derivatives will be predictive of the outbreak of systemic war.

In addition to an approximate equality in the number of disputes begun and resolved, these equations also require a fairly large proportion of countries in the system to have experienced no conflict, or if the conflict behavior throughout the system is fairly extensive, then the proportion of countries with very little conflict should be high. (The equations assume independence of conflict behavior, and interdependence among conflicts would diminish the number of uninvolved countries.) The large number of politically unaffiliated small countries would satisfy this requirement, for their small size, consequent small power, and political neutrality should remove them from the principal arenas of conflict behavior. Thus, the two basic components of the hierarchical equilibrium are expressed in these equations. The substantial power disparities between large and small countries required by the hierarchy would lead to short disputes which are easily resolved before others begin, and the large number of politically unattached small powers should lead to the large number (or proportion) of countries with little or no conflict experience.

Equilibrium is the operant condition in meeting the stipulation of an average equality in the beginnings and endings of disputes; this equilibrium condition is specified by equation [2.1] in the following section. A disequilibrium is said to exist when these equations are violated according to statistical criteria to be introduced in the following empirical tests. The condition of stability here is identified with that of equilibrium, and instability with disequilibrium. Although one clearly can distinguish between stable and unstable equilibria (in a stable equilibrium, the system remains within specified bounds after being disturbed; in an unstable equilibrium, these bounds are exceeded), this analysis is not designed to make that distinction. All that can be said here is that if the equilibrium is violated, a condition of instability exists. The degree of permanence or resilience of an equilibrium condition in the face of disturbing influences is not treated in this chapter.

Mathematical Formalisms

The initial assumption, of course, is that there exists an average equality in beginnings and endings of disputes, or

$$C_i = \langle D_i \rangle_{av} = \sum_{n=i}^{\infty} P(n)D_i \qquad [2.1]$$

where C_i and D_i are the respective probabilities of the initiation and resolution of i disputes. In order for the average equality to hold, there must be a random distribution of the number of disputes in existence over the time period t in question, hence the presence in the equation of $P(n)$, the Poisson distribution of disputes. The expression for $P(n)$ is derived from basic initial conditions in Mathematical Appendix A. Chief among these is the independent existence of all disputes from each other.[4] The various assumptions lead to the equations for the transition probabilities given in Mathematical Appendix A and used in the following empirical tests.

Empirical Tests

First one requires that there be included multipolar and bipolar systems and, in addition, that these be susceptible to the presence of substantial power differentials. The nineteenth century European system clearly included the presence of very small powers (for example, Parma, Tuscany, Baden, Saxony, Bavaria, Sardinia, Hesse-Electoral, Mecklenburg-Schwerin, and others), all of which of course coalesced in the unifications of Italy and Germany. Additionally, these were simultaneous hierarchies in the sense that virtually all of the European great powers had protective relationships toward certain of these powers (for example, Austria toward Parma and Modena, Prussia toward Baden and Württemberg), not to speak of the British and French empires as large and still-growing hierarchies during the century, but with many small powers not formally allied. Many of the midrange or central powers, such as Belgium or Holland, remained neutral in the ongoing European conflicts, and others who were to be more active, such as Rumania and Serbia, came into existence only toward the end of the century. Thus, our first system of choice is the nineteenth century system (1815–1899).[5]

Since polarizing systems are by definition those which violate the hierarchical equilibrium, especially in regard to the required existence of a large number of small neutral powers, these systems should be included to provide a comparison with systems in which the hierarchical equilibrium obtains. A polarizing system is found in the period 1893–1914 ending in war between the Dual Alliance and Triple Entente. (A small amount of overlap between systems at the end of the nineteenth century is allowed in order to accommodate the relatively slow diplomatic change in this period, beginning with the Franco-Russian alliance in the years 1891–1894, during which the alliance solidified.) Another polarizing system ending in war is that found in 1919–1939.

The bipolar system examined here exists in the period 1946–1964, beginning just before the rapid onset of the Gold War and ending just after the Cuban missile crisis and subsequent fall of Khruschev in the last year of this interval. Strong hierarchical elements are found here, too. Thus, four systems are compared, two of them terminated peacefully (the multipolar and bipolar with hierarchical elements) and two ended in systemic war (the polarizing systems).[6]

The data are the Correlates of War Militarized International Dispute Data (Gochman and Maoz 1984) for the period 1816–1964. All instances of conflict behavior are incorporated, including war, short of the systemic wars of World Wars I and II. It is argued here that the etiologies of the smaller wars are substantially different from wars of the systemic variety (see also note 7).

For each of the four systems, three analyses are carried out: (1) disputes between two or more major powers exclusively; (2) the combined set of disputes between two or more major powers, and those between two or more majors involving at least one central diplomatically active midrange power, as in Singer and Small (1968, 254); and (3) disputes between two or more majors plus centrals and very small or minor powers, that is, the total combined set of all possible disputes.[7] Thus, the range of conflict behavior for inclusion is stepped up incrementally for each of the systems under investigation in order to examine the effects of introducing successively greater hierarchical elements and disparities in power. Because of substantial changes in system scope and participation over this historical time span, the definitions of major, central (the central system is defined only through 1919), and minor powers will of necessity vary across some of these systems.

The results conform largely to the expectations of the model. For those interested in following the detailed findings, all tables are found in Tabular Appendix A. Summarizing here, we find that all nineteenth century systems reflect stability as measured by the chi-square statistic[8] between observed and predicted values of transitions (given by equations [11A]–[13A] in Mathematical Appendix A) from one state of the system to the next. Disputes between two or more major powers exclusively reflect a moderate degree of stability,[9] while incorporating disputes involving central powers along with majors and then the small powers as well[10] reflect successively greater degrees of stability. The central powers here are almost all formally neutral (Belgium, the Netherlands, Denmark, Sweden, Switzerland) or nonexistent for most of the century (Serbia, Rumania), so that the finding of greater stability upon incorporation of these powers in the dispute set is to be expected. Including disputes involving small powers as well as the others yields the greatest stability, as expected.

When we examine the period 1893–1914, however,[11] there is a serious disjuncture between the observations and predictions of the model. Now the politically active central powers have achieved sovereignty and, although the major powers reflect stability as before, inclusion of the central powers yields instability[12] (there are no still smaller powers because of their incorporation in the new unified Germany.)

A similar pattern holds for the interwar period of 1919–1939. Disputes involving major powers exclusively yield stability, but when the central powers are included the result is instability.[13] Thus, the two world wars of this century are preceded by unstable periods when disputes involving all of the European sovereign states are included. (Once again there are no smaller entities than the central powers.)

The post-World War II era of 1946–1964, ending with the Cuban missile crisis of 1962 and the fall of Khruschev in 1964, exhibits some fascinating patterns. First, in common with the analysis of earlier intervals, the great powers themselves do not yield evidence of instability in their disputes. Incorporating disputes involving only European powers in addition to the great powers now yields instability. Here, in the European powers, we have an analogue to the central powers which yield instability in the two pre-World War periods. Then, extending the scope to include all powers including even the tiniest found in the global system yields stability as one would expect given the findings thus far.

This "substitutability" phenomenon (Most and Starr 1984) of conflicts outside of Europe acting as surrogates of those in Europe, simply because of the extreme danger inherent in the latter, may be illustrated by the Cuban missile crisis occurring at the close of this time period. The Berlin crisis of 1961 and the simultaneous explosion of sizable Soviet nuclear devices may have impressed on all of the protagonists the extreme sensitivity of the European system and its inherent instability. The Cuban missile crisis, in this light, may be seen either as a surrogate or extension of the bipolar conflict away from its central and, therefore, most sensitive locus to an area (not without its own dangers) which may have been inherently more amenable to peaceful resolution than a similar crisis on the European continent. The threat to the weaker superpower, the USSR, of such a crisis near its own borders may have triggered a far less measured response from the threatened protagonist than one close to the borders of the then considerably stronger superpower, the United States.

Thus, when minor powers are included in the disputes but away from the center of bipolarity in Europe, the stability is increased. This finding argues for a rather restrictive interpretation of the presumably unstable bipolar system of the post-World War II period, for it appears to have been confined to Europe and any disputes outside of that continent actually helped stabilize the system.

There exists an additional concern in the matter of substitutability of conflict behavior. The logic of bipolarity, especially that which includes ideological confrontation as in the post-World War II period, entails some sort of conflict engagement with the opposing side. As long as the confrontation continues in one form or another, then substitutes need to be found for the ultimate confrontation—that of systemic nuclear war. Disputes and even small wars outside of the European zone of sensitivity can provide such a substitute.

Note the similarity between this process of extending the range of participants in 1946–1964 to that which occurred in the nineteenth century. In both cases, when smaller and, for the most part, weaker powers were included, the system appeared more stable. This similarity between the two systems, albeit one multipolar and the other bipolar, should be contrasted with the behavior of the two pre-World War polarizing systems which, although similar to each other, stand in stark contrast to the other two systems which ended peacefully.

But it is also clear that it is not merely the number of protagonists that matters but the distance in power between great and small powers, for the inclusion of countries such as Ethiopia or Thailand in the conflict system in 1946–1964 had the consequence of widening greatly the distance in size and power among the protagonists, much as the early inclusion of principalities such as Parma and Tuscany prior to the unification of Italy established a wide discrepancy in power between the largest and smallest protagonists. Indeed, one can assert that powers such as Great Britain and France stood in the same power relationship to these small principalities in the nineteenth century as do the United States and Soviet Union to many of the smaller countries in the post-World War II era. That is, the presence of these small countries as essentially vassalages may have been conducive to the building of hierarchy in Europe where there existed major powers and very small countries, almost principalities, which were under the tutelage of the major powers. Other middle-sized countries or central powers, such as Belgium or the Netherlands, tended to remain neutral in the ongoing alliance and conflict system. Thus, a substantial gap in power between major powers and the smaller countries likely led to a peaceful outcome, in contrast to the growing power of central powers, such as Rumania or Serbia, much later in the nineteenth century, vis-à-vis weakening major powers such as Austria-Hungary. Certainly, these smaller countries were willing to engage in serious conflict with some of the major powers at the beginning of the twentieth century.

This finding is consistent with an earlier one which found a heterogeneity in alliance formation among small powers, with the implication that there existed a "roulette wheel" type of process with the major powers at the hub of the wheel and the minor powers at the rim (Midlarsky 1981). This allowed for the possibility of major powers at various times allying with one or another of the minor powers for short or long periods of time as the case may be. This diversity or heterogeneity of the system, of course, diminished rapidly with the unification of first Italy and then Germany.

There exists one final way to test the small power–great power conflict relations implied by the hierarchical equilibrium model. This is to examine the dyadic conflicts between great and small powers in the four time periods under examination. The theory predicts that such conflict sets should be stable in the nineteenth century and post-World War II periods but unstable in the periods preceding both World Wars. This should be so because of the availability of large numbers of small powers of either neutral or powerless status relative to the great powers in the former two instances, thus satisfying the hierarchical equilibrium model, but not in the latter two cases where such availability was circumscribed.

The small powers in 1919–1939 and 1946–1964 are extra-European ones (the conflict system is now more globalized) as weak complements of the extraordinarily weak powers in Europe relative to the nineteenth century major powers. There are no small powers in Europe in 1893–1914, only central powers. For the sake of parsimony, as before, these tables are not presented (they are available on request), but the general results are found in Tabular Appendix A. The 1816–1899 and 1946–1964 periods demonstrate stability while the pre-World War polarizing systems do not, thus providing additional confirmation for the hierarchical equilibrium model.

Simultaneous Hierarchies in Bipolarity and Multipolarity

All of this leads directly to the presence of simultaneous hierarchies in both multipolar and bipolar systems. If we visualize multipolar and bipolar systems as consisting of a series of major power–minor power sets (for example, alliances), with a fairly large number of countries available for alliance, implying that not all are allied at any given time or are easily removed from their current alliance frameworks,[14] then the stable bipolar system is a subset of the stable multipolar system, albeit with certain different properties as a result of the diminished number of such sets and the presence of ideological conflict. The key term however, is *stable.* As we shall see shortly in chapter 3, the multipolar system without the associated small powers (or colonies) is inherently less stable in regard to systemic war than is the bipolar system also without the smaller powers. As long as there are minor powers within some accessible radius of the major powers, but outside of a particularly sensitive area such as Europe, then stability in conflict behavior can be achieved. It was the dynamic polarization of the late nineteenth and early twentieth century and the continuation of that process in the interwar period with, at the end, very few decidedly weaker minor powers available for alliance or conflict, that led to systemic war. (Even Poland was able to inflict a partial defeat on the Soviet Union in 1920 and Finland was nearly able to do so in 1940.)

In the 1893–1914 period, the extra-European world was by then almost entirely colonized or politically inaccessible, as in Latin America because of the Monroe Doctrine (backed by the British navy), and the same was true for the interwar period. Thus, any conflict activity outside of Europe could not seriously alleviate the systemic instability. In contrast, the emergence of new nations in the post-World War II era had the consequence of making available an entirely new set of nations for alliance formation or any other diplomatic activity. Thus, the simultaneous hierarchies of the nineteenth century multipolar system and of the mid-twentieth century bipolar system could be built upon the availability (as long as it lasted) of a substantial number of decidedly weaker minor powers—a circumstance that was not true of the periods approaching World Wars I and II.

In one limited sense, the late nineteenth–early twentieth century multipolar system, as it polarized slowly around the two principal alliances, displayed similar dynamics to that of the post-World War II bipolar system.[15] Much of the colonial activity of the European powers, especially France, during the late nineteenth century has been interpreted as a substitute for conflict in Europe (Taylor 1971, 344). After the defeat of France by Prussia in 1871 and the disappearance of many of the smaller European powers, the potential for major power war was to be found outside the European continent. Thus, during this period, virtually all of the conflicts among the Western powers occurred in colonial contexts (for example, the Kruger telegram of 1896 or Agadir in 1911), and only in 1914 was the principal locus to be shifted to the European continent. And even here, the conflict did not occur *sui generis*, but had to be "imported" via the Balkans.

The existence of small, relatively powerless colonies to be fought over may have served the same function for the European powers in this time period as has the emergence of the new nation-states during the post-World War II era. However, the instability of the European system prior to World War I was not seriously attenuated by this conflict activity outside of Europe, probably because of the already acquired colonial territories which could engender more serious conflict among the great powers if "trespassed" upon, in contrast to the post-World War II system in which the new nation-states were not yet committed, if at all.

Table 2.1 summarizes the findings of the empirical tests of the theory. The first three columns connoting stability or instability are to be read as summations of columns to the left, with the exception of the furthest column on the right-hand side of the table. Thus, the greatest stability for the nineteenth century is to be found in disputes which include major, central, and minor powers. The table with chi-square values in the various cells is reproduced in Tabular Appendix A.

Table 2.1
Findings of the empirical tests.

Time period	Disputes between			
	Two or more major powers +	Central (midrange) +	Minor (smaller)	One Major one minor[a]
1816–1899	Stability	Greater stability	Greatest stability	Stability
1893–1914	Stability	Instability	(No smaller powers in Europe)	Instability
1919–1939	Stability	Instability	(No smaller powers in Europe)	Instability
1946–1964	Stability	Instability (European)	Stability (global)	Stability

[a] For 1893–1914, central powers only.

Conclusion

Research Findings

A hierarchical equilibrium theory of systemic war has been largely confirmed and has led to a series of empirical findings. The first and most striking of these is that, in all of the time periods studied, the great power conflicts alone demonstrated stability and it was only in conjunction with other conflict sets that instability was discovered. This suggests that great powers, if left to their own diplomatic devices, can establish stable relations regardless of system structure, be it multipolar as in the nineteenth century, or bipolar as in the post-World War II era.[16] However, this finding will be tempered by the results of chapters 3 and 4, which suggest that inequalities can develop among the major powers in the allocation of international resources, some of these, of course, concerning the allegiance of small powers.

The results here suggest the essential role of the small powers in relation to the onset of systemic war, for if they exist in a substantial power differential with the great powers and the hierarchical equilibrium is obeyed, then systemic war becomes even less likely than if the great powers are left to their own devices. However, if these very small powers are absent and there exists a large number of midrange powers, then systemic war becomes more probable.

A fundamental difference between the nineteenth century and post-World War II systems, on the one hand, and the polarizing systems approaching World Wars I and II, on the other, is that the addition of smaller powers to the conflict sets in the former instances led to more stable systems, whereas in the latter two cases the addition of conflicts involving mostly midrange powers led to instability. This finding constituted a confirmation of the hierarchical equilibrium theory and the hypothesized tendency of polarizing systems to be the most unstable in regard to systemic war.

It is under conditions of polarization and the absence of hierarchical equilibrium that war becomes more likely, as in the two pre-World War periods. Most important, the equilibrium model of equation [2.1], with its implications of severe hierarchy, was able to distinguish between periods ending in systemic war and those which did not.

What differentiates bipolar major power conflicts from multipolar ones is the existence of a region of sensitivity in the bipolar 1946–1964 period in Europe. Here, very small neutral powers are absent and the hierarchical equilibrium is violated. When conflicts external to Europe are included in the analysis of 1946–1964, the system demonstrates stability, as it should under conditions of a large number of small neutral countries.

Interpretations

These findings must now be placed in the proper perspective. One can speak of necessary and sufficient conditions for the onset of systemic war. The violation of the hierarchical equilibrium as expressed in equations [2.1] and equations [11A]–[13A] of Mathematical Appendix A may be thought of as necessary for the onset of systemic war although certainly not sufficient, for a crisis along the lines of the summer crisis of 1914 is likely also to be necessary for the onset of such a war (Midlarsky 1984b). The presence of a hierarchical equilibrium may be thought of as sufficient (although perhaps not necessary) for the prevention of such a war, although this would be difficult to demonstrate conclusively, for all that would be required to vitiate this argument is one instance when systemic war erupted under conditions of such an equilibrium.

In place of necessity and sufficiency as conceptual benchmarks, a still more profitable way to view these findings, one that is wholly consistent with the epistemology of this inquiry, is from the perspective of probabilities. The violation of a hierarchical equilibrium can be thought of as strongly increasing the probability of systemic war, while obeying it substantially decreases that probability. Indeed, there may be other consequences of a violation of that equilibrium, such that certain severe domestic rather than international consequences may follow. The analysis of chapter 8 suggests that the 1919–1932 period may actually have been more unstable internationally than the 1933–1939 period, but the domestic consequence of the rise of Hitler led later, in a time-lagged effect, directly to the mobilization war of World War II. This finding, and the distinction between structural and mobilization wars (see chapters 7 and 8), may account for the very strong instability demonstrated by the 1893–1914 period, as well as the somewhat less emphatic results for 1919–1939 (see Tabular Appendix A).

Theoretically, a contribution of the hierarchical equilibrium formulation is the synthesis of an equilibrium component of balance-of-power theory (for example, Morgenthau 1973) with that of hierarchy (Organski 1968) and the unique requirement of a large number of small powers not permanently allied with any of the great powers. The element of equilibrium or equality among great powers is introduced in that all of them are situated at the head of hierarchies which include much smaller powers, even if the great powers and the hierarchies themselves are not demonstrably equal in power. The hierarchical element, of course, is manifest in the power differentials within each of the coalitions. The differences between the present framework and the previous two theories appear in the notion of hierarchy, which is essentially foreign to balance-of-power theory, and the absence of a necessity for substantial power differential between the leading power and the challenger, as in the Organski formulation.

An important theoretical component is found in the strong confluence between the element of hierarchy, with its implied absence of memory, and tit-for-tat (Axelrod 1984) in which such a condition also is present. Additionally, the positive-sum games associated with the independent small powers imply the greater likelihood of cooperation at the outset, which can establish, on a firm footing, the desired pattern of reciprocal cooperation in tit-for-tat.

The present theory is largely consistent in its implications with those of the long cycle (Modelski 1983; Thompson 1983) and of the power cycle (Doran and Parsons 1980).[17] Changes in power relations between large countries and midrange powers during the long-term decay of a hierarchical equilibrium, as occurred prior to World War I and during the interwar period, are equivalent to the "deconcentration" of power prior to a global war, as predicted by the long cycle. Additionally, because of the changes in hierarchical relationships during such periods, the probabilities of misperceiving and miscalculating the force capabilities required for victory increase dramatically; therefore, the probability of precipitating a systemic war during this period of maximum change increases accordingly as suggested by power cycle theory.

It should be noted that the hierarchical equilibrium theory may be substitutable for, or at least coextensive with, the theory of deterrence as another explanation for the absence of systemic war in the post-World War II era. Indeed, deterrence processes have received most of the credit for the absence of nuclear war, when in fact this relative peace may have been at least as much, or perhaps even more, the consequence of stable structural hierarchies of widespread power disparities among nations, and a global system extensive enough in the number of its small sovereign entities to allow for the existence of conflict behavior away from the major zone of sensitivity on the continent of Europe. Normative implications of this circumstance will be treated in the concluding chapter.

Notes

1 In this analysis, the concept of systemic war is identified completely with the breakdown of the international system or global war. However, it is possible to define a much smaller system, as in a region such as the Middle East, and carry out an analysis similar to the one found here.

2 This coalition pattern is virtually identical to that of stable cabinet coalitions with long duration (Midlarsky 1984a) in which a large, predominant party with a high percentage of votes leads a coalition of much smaller parties which have each obtained a small percentage of the vote. Both the international hierarchy identified in this study and this type of domestic coalition meet the minimum entropy requirement for durability identified in that analysis.

3 Dehio (1962) argues the need for colonial territories (in a sense a functional equivalent of small powers) in association with the European balance–of–power system because of the ever-present need to equilibrate the system with new territorial additions to the great powers. Chatterjee (1975) adopts a similar view but from a game-theoretic perspective. Midlarsky (1983c) previously argued for the necessity of such extra-systemic territorial additions to the balance-of-power system in order to maintain in operation certain elementary criteria of justice, especially a version of Rawls' (1971) difference principle. Each gain to the most advantaged great power must also be matched with a gain to the least advantaged (for example, the Polish partitions). New territorial additions, or the dismemberment of older ones, clearly are needed for this process to occur.

4 Obviously, countries can influence each other, but if the specific terms of various disputes are kept independent of each other, then stochastic independence can be achieved for the disputes themselves (for example, the Soviet intervention in Afghanistan being largely independent of the U.S. involvement in Central America) despite the influence that individual great powers can have on each other.

5 The use of the 1899 ending for the nineteenth century not only conforms to standard usages but also facilitates comparison with other studies (for example, Midlarsky 1981); See also note 12.

6   Although the Concert of Europe dominated the international scene in the post-Vienna period, its fragility and transformation into a classical balance-of-power system was signaled as early as 1823, and certainly by 1828, in the disputes between Great Britain and other Concert powers over the future of Greece. The post-1946 period did not have a large number of neutral nations, but as the conflict arena expanded outside of Europe (as early as 1948), aligned or only weakly allied countries such as Egypt, Thailand, or Ethiopia (the latter two in the Korean War) had the consequence of quickly meeting this stipulation of the hierarchical equilibrium until the great increase in the number of new nations began in the mid to late 1950s.

7   The conflict behaviors analyzed here include all instances of serious disputes involving two or more major powers in the time periods under investigation. The major powers are Austria-Hungary, France, Germany (Prussia), Great Britain, and Russia throughout the entire nineteenth century. Italy joins this set after her unification, while the United States and Japan became great powers in the very late nineteenth century. The major powers in the post-World War II period are those defined by the United Nations Security Council as in the Correlates of War project. A listing of the central powers is found in Singer and Small (1968, 254) and includes countries such as Belgium, the Netherlands, Serbia, Bulgaria, and Rumania. The disputes range from minimal conflict behaviors, at the lower end of a five-point hostility scale, to the outbreak of war at the upper end of the scale. However, none of the time periods investigated here includes instances of systemic war (World Wars I and II), and it is suggested that, both theoretically and empirically, systemic wars of this magnitude demonstrate fundamentally different properties from nonsystemic wars such as the Austro-Prussian or Balkan Wars. Not only does the scope of the conflict in the form of the number of protagonists differ widely in the two instances, but the number of battle deaths in a systemic war (nine and fifteen million, respectively, in World Wars I and II) vastly exceeds that found in any of the nonsystemic variety. Removing the instances of war from the data sets and repeating the analyses made no difference in the conclusions of stability or instability for each of the systems analyzed here.

8   A fit between observation and theoretical prediction is rejected at $p < 0.10$. The choice of $p < 0.10$ is arbitrary, of course, as is any other choice of significance level. The overriding concern here is that we do not readily accept the proposed equilibrium model (or any other such model), and so $p < 0.10$ would allow us to reject it somewhat more frequently than, say, $p < 0.05$. Here, the chi-square statistic is used as a goodness-of-fit measure, and so the choice of a higher probability level for rejection implies rejection of the model with greater frequency. For the chi-square test, adjacent categories were combined until a minimum expected value of 1.5 was obtained. In this process of summing across rows, values greater than 1.5 were skipped in order to maximize the number of available degrees of freedom (see Gibbons 1971, 72).

9   Use of somewhat different criteria, such as a requirement that a major power exist in that state for at least half of the time period under consideration, gives a more impressive fit between observation and prediction (Midlarsky 1983a, 783). However, these criteria led to the absence in the data set of certain major powers such as Italy in the latter portion of the nineteenth century, and these powers are included here.

10 In order to include all possible European countries, the smaller European (noncentral) countries are included here (for example, Baden, Bavaria, Parma, Modena), although they are absent from the 1893–1914 period because these countries either became central powers later in the century or were absorbed in

the unifications of Italy and Germany. The criterion governing both the nineteenth century and 1893–1914 analyses is that all possible sovereign European entities be included.

11 In chapter 5, the period 1893–1908 will be found to be stable. This finding then leads to certain conclusions regarding the importance of the summer crisis in precipitating war in the unstable system of 1914 in comparison with the failure of the very similar Bosnian crisis to precipitate war in the stable system of 1908.

12 The period 1816–1870, prior to the unification of Germany, also demonstrated stability [χ^2 = 6.344, degrees of freedom (df) = 7, $p < 0.70$]. There are at least two substantive reasons (aside from comparability with prior findings) for the treatment here of the entire 1816–1899 period instead of reliance solely on the 1816–1870 interval prior to the unification of Germany and the disappearance of many small actors. If, over a period of years, decision makers such as Bismarck viewed the environment as one which contained many heterogeneous participants, then even after the objective disappearance of these actors some inclination toward stability and alliance fluidity, that is, balance-of-power politics, very likely remained. For twenty years after the formation of the German Empire, this flexibility appears to have existed [for additional detailed arguments, see Midlarsky (1981, 290)]. Second, Germany, after its unification, sought to build a new hierarchy, this time in the form of empire, and it was only after being largely frustrated in these efforts that much of the aggressive behavior of the late nineteenth and early twentieth centuries emerged. As long as these efforts were still ongoing, there could be the expectation of peace. In this connection, see also note 14.

13 The present analysis which combines two sets of disputes—(1) those between two or more major powers exclusively, and (2) those between two or more major powers involving at least one central power—should be distinguished from an analysis which treats only the latter set [part (2)]. This set of disputes alone can evidence stability, as in fact was demonstrated in Midlarsky (1984b). However, when the two sets [(1) and (2)] are combined, serious instability is discovered.

14 Although the number of strictly neutral European countries in the nineteenth century was not as large as that of the post-World War II period, it is precisely the randomness of alliance formation and partner choice with its implied absence of fixed associations which leads to a functional equivalence with neutrality. In the final analysis, it may make little difference whether a country is perpetually neutral but available to the "highest bidder" as it were, as in the contemporary period, or perpetually alternating alliances as in the nineteenth century, thus suggesting that it could be easily removed from its current alliance framework. In both cases, there is the absence of fixedness and the suggestion of fluidity which can make bargaining, instead of the use of deadly force, a central feature of international politics.

15 I am indebted to Professor Pat McGowan for suggesting this similarity between the two time periods.

16 This set of findings is consistent with that of Bueno de Mesquita (1978), in which polarity as a static structural variable had little impact on the occurrence of war. It is also consistent with the arguments of Most and Starr (1983, 1984) concerning the importance of decision-making variables in the onset of war, as will be developed in the subsequent distinction between structural and mobilization wars.

17 For a further development of long cycle theory, see Thompson and Zuk (1982) and Rasler and Thompson (1983).

3

The Long-Run Instability of Multipolar Systems

THE ANALYSIS OF the hierarchical equilibrium in the preceding chapter demonstrated the salutary effects of the existence of such an equilibrium. Although wars theoretically can occur under the stipulation of these conditions, and in fact do at times occur as in the post-World War II era, they are not of the systemic variety. The data used to test the theory of course were limited to the nineteenth and twentieth centuries because of the unavailability of dispute data for earlier periods. We can, however, probe analytically and historically for the validity (or absence of same) of other elements of the theory, as in the consequences of multipolarity for inequality among the units comprising the system. In the following discussion, multipolarity is taken to mean the "pure" condition of major powers ($m \geq 3$) existing simultaneously in a recognized community of nations. All of the major powers must be aware of each others' existence as part of this community.

Most important, the simultaneous hierarchies of the hierarchical equilibrium are absent within the confines of this community. Thus, the pure condition of multipolarity would not exist in the early portion of the nineteenth century especially in Central Europe. As we saw in the preceding chapter there were, in fact, simultaneous hierarchies in Central Europe with some of the German states or principalities allied with Prussia, some with Austria, and others remaining largely independent politically vis-à-vis the two leading German powers. This, of course, disappeared with the unification of Germany under essentially a Prussian hegemony. Formerly existing hierarchies in Italy under Austrian tutelage disappeared with the unification of Italy during the previous decade or so. Thus, as of 1871 on the continent of Europe, there existed a condition of pure multipolarity with the consequences to be detailed below in the approach to World War I.

Prior to that analysis, however, we will consider the problem of polarity in general, followed by some of the historical evidence for the consequences of multipolarity in various systems. As will be seen, although hierarchical equilibria with m major power ($m \geq 2$) demonstrate superior stability when compared with major powers without the associated small powers (absence of hierarchy and positive-sum games), the bipolar condition of two major powers alone will turn out to be superior in this regard to the multipolar structure. As a consequence of the arguments in the chapter, one will be able to posit the following order in regard to diminishing probability of systemic war. The greater than sign (>) used here means superior stability in regard to the absence of this type of war.

$$\text{Hierarchical equilibrium } (m \geq 2) > \text{Bipolarity } (m = 2) > \text{Multipolarity } (m > 3)$$

Arguments Concerning Polarity

The question of polarity in international politics indeed has once again become a concern for students of international conflict. Although unresolved in its entirety after the debates of the 1960s and 1970s, the question of the supremacy of bipolar or multipolar systems in regard to stability has recently become a major focus of inquiry. This is not surprising in light of the emergence of recent concerns over the effective use of historical materials, especially over long cycles of economic and political behavior in relation to major power wars. Clearly, system structure should bear some relation to the onset of a global or systemic war, for it is the system itself that is undergoing some purposive transformation by concerned powers which in the end likely will yield a transformation of its structural contours. The extensive use of historical materials in connection with this research enterprise likely has sensitized the scholarly community to the matter of system structure in relation to global war.

Perhaps it was the very indecisiveness of the debate's early outcome which led to a hiatus followed by a revival of recent research on polarity. Although Rosecrance (1966) provided a synthesis of the Deutsch and Singer (1964) preference for multipolarity and Waltz's (1979) preference for bipolarity in suggesting that multipolarity was associated with a higher frequency of war and bipolarity with greater severity, and M. Haas (1970) gave some empirical confirmation for this view, the matter did not rest there. In what has emerged as probably the most extensive and well-known statement of a position, Waltz argued forcefully that bipolarity in virtually all cases is associated with peace, while multipolarity contains inherent instabilities which are war prone, likely including very severe wars.

Waltz's arguments are compelling. With only two powers, there can be continuous political adjustments between the two powers. A "fine tuning" of international practice can occur which can obviate much of the uncertainty associated with multipolar systems which, by definition, contain more than two major actors, frequently as many as six or seven. Even crises can have a pacific effect, for each of them can serve as an arena for testing and communication of political intent. In the end, such crises can leave the two actors with a much clearer understanding of the opponent's perspective.

Several recent studies provide support for this view. In particular, Thompson (1986) found that significantly less global warfare was associated with bipolarity than with multipolarity, while Levy (1985a) carried out extensive historical analyses which yielded bipolarity as the more stable system for eight of nine indicators of stability involving great-power war. Of greatest interest here is the incidence of general war which can be system destroying. Bipolarity was found to be decisively more stable than multipolarity. We shall have more to say on this point later.

Despite Waltz's arguments and the empirical evidence for them, the proponents of multipolarity have much to say for their position. As Morgenthau (1973) and Gulick (1955) suggest, the existence of many different coalition possibilities, not to mention the salutary role of the balancer, can be stabilizing influences in multipolar systems. Deutsch and Singer argue for the stabilizing effect of many different interaction opportunities, especially for the diminution in hostile attention each of the superpowers can devote to the other. The share of attention that one country can give to another in these circumstances can only be a fairly small fraction of the total.[1] In this fashion, arms races and other manifestations of dyadic hostilities are dampened with an associated decrease in the probability of superpower or global war. The proponents of multipolarity also would argue that peace by crisis in bipolar structures is at best a dubious, and perhaps very dangerous, manner of conducting policy in the nuclear era. Only one failure in such crisis management can end the existence of civilization as we know it. Bipolar systems also are inherently zero sum in nature (what you gain I must necessarily lose) and, therefore, are more conflict prone than the non-zero-sum activity in multipolar systems.

Arguments for multipolarity, then, have a considerable force and logic of their own, yet the evidence is running strongly counter to this theoretical position. When one is confronted with two theories of approximately equal analytic content and persuasiveness, and one is more strongly supported empirically than the other, then it is likely that one of two conditions holds. Either both theories are in some sense true and they should be synthesized in some fashion, or, failing that alternative, there exists an additional non-obvious theoretical perspective which can shed light on the debate. Given

46

bipolarity and multipolarity as power structures with inherently different attributes (as are two-party and multiparty systems) as well as the different empirical findings, it is highly unlikely that a synthesis can be accomplished satisfactorily. Far more likely is the existence of the hidden and, perhaps, even nonintuitive perspective which can distinguish theoretically between the two conditions. Such a perspective is called for not only by the preceding arguments but by the need to account for the existence of an important apparent exception to the pattern of the superior stability of bipolar systems. This is the multipolar nineteenth century which experienced an almost unparalleled history of stability, especially in comparison with the eighteenth century with its many conflicts among European powers.[2] This fairly recent historical experience would suggest that multipolarity may be peaceful in regard to both the frequency and severity of war and would seem to belie the arguments of Waltz and Rosecrance and the related empirical findings.

As we shall see shortly, such is not the case. Multipolarity (in the absence of hierarchical equilibria) will be shown to be inherently unstable under certain basic assumptions, while bipolarity will demonstrate a fair degree of stability. The late nineteenth century European experience will be shown to be somewhat exceptional in giving what appeared to be all the indications of stability and durability which, in reality, existed under ephemeral conditions. Multipolarity now will be linked with the emergence of inequality, with three case studies of structural systemic wars and one of general war presented in support of this relationship. The only structural systemic war not treated here is that of the French Revolutionary Wars, for their origin was almost exclusively internal. However, as we shall see in a separate discussion of this instance, there is a strong parallel between the internal class divisions of French society and associated scarcities, on the one hand, and the international scenario that is now examined, on the other.

Multipolarity and Inequality

I begin the analysis with three basic assumptions. (1) What we generally regard as multipolarity (or bipolarity for that matter) was situated historically within European and world systems of some fairly widely accepted scope and definition. That is, the units or countries within the setting constituted a system in which the actors were aware of each other as system members and openly acknowledged that membership. (2) Inequalities among system members are more destabilizing than equalities. Envies and political intrigues which can result in war are far more likely under the former circumstance. (3) In the absence of a centralized administration, the system is subject to random processes which impact on the system members.

The first assumption derives from treatments, such as Gulick's (1955), which posit the historical balance of power as one existing within a common cultural frame of reference. For most of the period under examination here, this was the political culture of post-Reformation Christian Europe. A secular political culture, but one based on fairly widely accepted norms of behavior, emerged in the post-Westphalia period. The Abbé de Pradt (1800, 86–87) found that Europe formed "a single social body which one might rightly call the European Republic." Vattel (1870, 251) declared that the practices of balance-of-power politics "make of modern Europe a sort of Republic," and Gentz (1806, 69) called it a "European commonwealth." The shared experience of the European states led to the emergence of common norms which were established within what was commonly held to be a balance-of-power framework. As Martens (1795) summarized it, "the resemblance in manners and religion, the intercourse of commerce, the frequency of treaties of all sorts, and the ties of blood between sovereigns, have so multiplied the relations between each particular state and the rest, that one may consider Europe (particularly the Christian states of it) as a society of nations and states. . . ."[3] Kaplan's (1957, 23) rules of the balance-of-power system are a precise articulation of these norms of system behavior which are generally acknowledged by all of the system participants (for example, "Treat all essential actors as acceptable role partners").

The second assumption follows from the current and still widely accepted observation that equality is more conducive to political stability than inequality. We find the virtual equation of justice with equality in Artistotle's *Politics* as we do in Rawls' (1971) second principle of justice, which demands equal access to all social and economic opportunities. Even more directly, entire theories of instability and their empirical confirmation have been based on the premise of severe inequalities. Included among these are theories based on relative deprivation, rapidly declining economic circumstances, and scarcity of valued commodities.[4] It is the last of these which will directly concern us in evaluating the relevant properties of multipolar systems. Given a particular society of states, equalities among the members are more likely to yield stability in the long run than are inequalities. The particular dynamics by which occur the inequality-induced conflicts among states will be treated later. For now, we will simply observe that in the modern period the most stable societies by far are those with industrialized economies and their associated equalities, in comparison with the severe inequalities found in the instability-prone, largely agrarian countries.

The last assumption is almost axiomatic in international politics.[5] Without a central administration, the only other significant system forces which can exist, *ceteris paribus*, are random ones.

Formal Distinctions

A bipolar system composed of two major powers now will be formally compared with a multipolar one consisting of three or more major powers.

All major powers initially will have no small powers associated with them. The number of powers in the multipolar system will be taken to be five initially in order to conform to the existence of five major powers throughout much of eighteenth and nineteenth century Europe. The case of three major powers also will be treated but will be shown to demonstrate essentially the same dynamics.

Consider now the existence of k utiles to be distributed among m major powers ($m = 5$ shortly). The utiles are international desiderata or resources, and can be allies, which generally are smaller powers to be associated politically with the great powers, or colonies to be absorbed politically by the great powers. There could also be other international utiles (for example, access to natural resources).

If k items (utiles) are distributed randomly among m recipients (countries) with equal probability for each recipient, then n_r, the number of recipients with r items in the long run after a steady state has been reached, is given by the following distribution:[6]

$$n_r = m \binom{k}{r} \left(\frac{1}{m}\right)^r \left(1 - \frac{1}{m}\right)^{k-r} \qquad r = 0, 1, 2, \ldots, k$$

[3.1]

With $m = 5$ and allowing r to assume successively larger values, we obtain the number of powers, n_r, with r utiles. Table 3.1 presents these values. For example, with $k = 15$, the table shows one country with one utile and one with five utiles; for $k = 30$, one country has four and another has eight. Additional calculations were made with $m = 3$ and $k = 15, 30, 60, 120,$ and 180 as well as with $m = 7$ and associated values of k. Thus, we see in Table 3.1 that, with only 15 utiles to be distributed (left-hand column), a random result is that one of the five countries will receive one utile while another receives 2 utiles, and so forth through the fifth country that receives 5 utiles. Compare this with the distribution to be expected when 180 utiles are randomly distributed (right-hand column). Again, there is a disparity to be expected among adjacent recipient countries of one utile difference among them, but now with each receiving between 32 and 36 utiles. These calculations will be used in the later construction of Figure 3.1.

What is required now is·a measure of inequality to reflect the disparities in random allocation of the k utiles. This is suggested by the prior use in studies of inequality of the difference between allocations to the upper and lower proportions of a society.[7] This measure also has shown strong correlation with the Gini index of inequality which is a fairly standard measure.[8] Using the top and bottom 20% for $m = 5$, the country which is lowest in distributed resources or utiles would be compared with that which is highest. The difference between the two is treated as a percentage of the amount held by the least-favored country recipient. Thus, for $k = 15$, the measure is $I = [(5 - 1)/1] \times 100 = 4 \times 100$, or there is a 400% difference between the top and bottom countries in possession of resources. For $k = 30$, the difference is $[(8 - 4)/4] \times 100 = 1 \times 100$ or 100%, while for $k = 180$, the difference declines dramatically to 11.76% or approximately 12%.

Table 3.1

The number of countries with r utiles (n_r) with $m = 5$ and variable k.

			k		
r	15	30	60	120	180
1	1[a]				
2	1				
3	1				
4	1	1			
5	1	1			
6		1			
7		1			
8		1			
9					
10			1		
11			1		
12			1		
13			1		
14			1		
⋮					
20				1	
21				1	
22				1	
23				1	
24				1	
⋮					
32					1
33					1
34					1
35					1
36					1

[a] All values less than 0.5 are treated as zero; all greater than or equal to 0.5 are shown as 1.

Thus the relationship between k available utiles and I, the inequality between least- and most-favored recipient, clearly is curvilinear and of an exponential form. The inequality is greatest for a small available number of resources and diminishes rapidly in extent as the number of available resources increases in the lower right-hand portion of the table. This relationship is plotted in Figure 3.1 for values of $m = 3$, 5, and 7, leading to the three curves shown. The value $m = 5$ is chosen to correspond to the existence of five great powers during much of eighteenth and nineteenth century Europe, while $m = 7$ corresponds to the emergence of a wider global system at the beginning of the twentieth century with the addition of three great powers, the United States, Italy, and Japan, and the decline of an older one, Austria-Hungary. The value $m = 3$ will correspond to a much older instance of emerging tripolarity to be explored shortly.

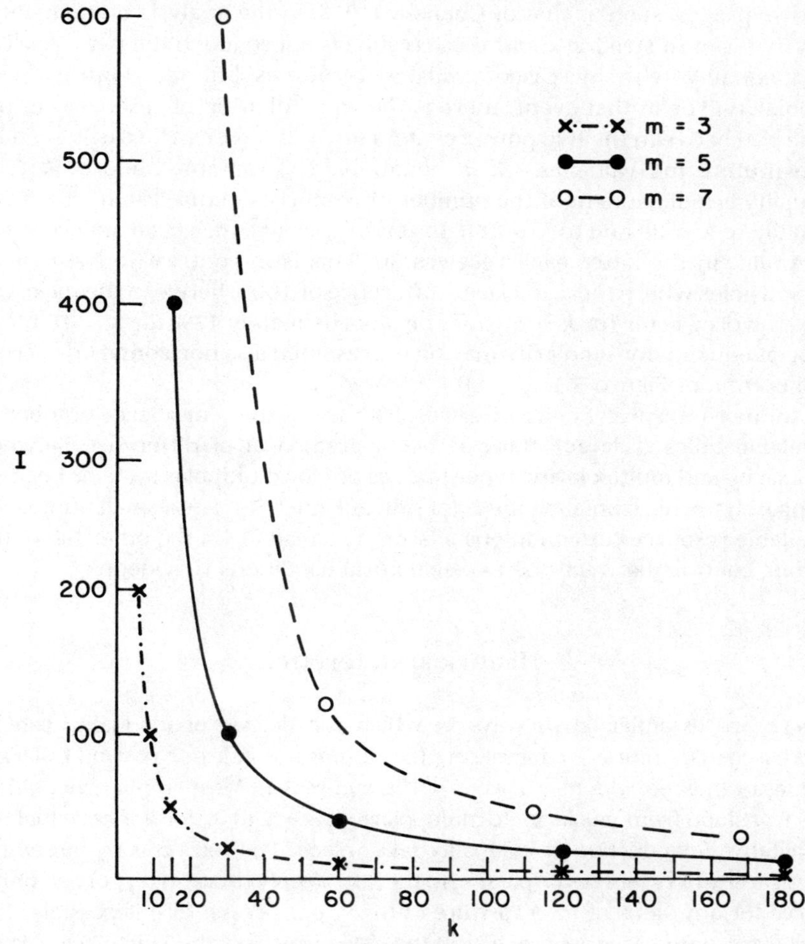

Figure 3.1

The dependence of the measure of inequality, I, upon the number of available utiles, k, for three values of m [x , m = 3; ●, m = 5; O, m = 7].

It turns out that the relationship indicated here is a special case of a more general relationship between scarcity and inequality identified in an earlier treatment.[9] The exponential approach to greater equality under increased abundance emerged from a general mathematical–theoretical treatment. Here, the approach is more specific but yields an additional dividend. Whereas in that study, the exponential formula was of a general nature and only in an abstract way could be identified as a measure of inequality, here this is no longer true. The exponential inequality measure, I, has a very specific meaning of difference between best and worst off in the context of several international seats of power and, moreover, is consistent with earlier usages, such as that of Chenery (1975) in the analysis of inequality.

What is most striking about these results is not so much the rapid decline of inequality with increased available resources but the contrast with bipolarity. For in that event, there is the equal division of resources in the long run between the two power centers ($m = 2$). This can be easily seen by substituting the value $m = 2$ in equation [3.1] for any value of k. The equality is independent of the number of resources in the system; it applies equally to $k = 30$ and to $k = 180$. In the former instance each side receives 15 utiles, in the latter each receives 90. This is in contrast to the case of $m = 5$ poles where there is a large difference of 100% between the most and least favored actor for $k = 30$ but only approximately 12% for $k = 180$. The case of equality for bipolarity may be represented as a horizontal line across the bottom of Figure 3.1 at $I = 0$.

Another interpretation of these results, then, is that, for a large number of available utiles (k large), there is not a great deal of difference between bipolarity and multipolarity, where values of I for multipolar systems begin to approach the horizontal on the right side of Figure 3.1. For a small number of available resources or conditions of scarcity (small k), on the other hand, the strong contrast between the two structural conditions is evident.

Historical Referents

There are essentially two ways in which the degree of inequality can be increased. The first is by increasing the number of poles or passing to larger values of m (say, from $m = 3$ to $m = 7$ in Figure 3.1). Most emphatic would be the transition from bipolarity to multipolarity ($m = 2$ to 3), for it is here that the qualitative introduction of inequality takes place. The second is by increasing the scarcity of resources or passing to the left, steeply descending portion of the curve for any value of m. A mixture of the two processes also is possible. The first great systemic or general war of the modern period, the Thirty Years' War, began after the transition from bipolarity to tripolarity. The first global war of this century, World War I, and its likely continuation in World War II began after a process of the second type, although mixed with some moderate increase in the value of m, the number of great powers emerging at the end of the nineteenth century. Our first example to be treated briefly, the Peloponnesian War, will illustrate generally the relationships expressed in Figure 3.1, especially the important role of colonies as international desiderata.

The importance of the Peloponnesian War resides in its constituting a prototypical instance of the highly destructive systemic war. Nor should the importance of the other cases be minimized for they constitute several of the most widespread and destructive wars of the modern period. Only World War II (not to be treated in this chapter) could compete effectively with the Thirty Years' War in the degree of human annihilation and bestial conduct, especially toward civilians, but as we shall see in chapter 7 this latest systemic war is more properly understood as an outgrowth of World War I instead of a systemic war *sui generis*. All four of our historical instances of structural systemic war now will be examined in some detail, although with a greater emphasis on the origins of World War I. Additionally, the one instance of a structural general war also will be examined. The abundance of available materials for the most recent example, World War I, coupled with detailed analysis by contemporary historians make it an almost ideal test case.

The Peloponnesian War

The beginnings of the Peloponnesian War can be found in processes similar to those suggested in Figure 3.1. A multipolar system traditionally had existed in Hellas with each of the Greek city-states maintaining its autonomy, insofar as possible, or allying with somewhat larger city-states to form regional alliances for mutual protection. Many of the future allies actually were colonies spurred by overpopulation in the older Greek cities. This colonization process was in a very advanced stage by the time of Pericles and the onset of the Peloponnesian War. Thucydides (1954, 14), by far the principal source of our knowledge about the war, refers to the fact that "Attica became too small for her inhabitants and colonies were sent out to Ionia." This colonization process was widespread in Hellas and its environs and involved many cities, such as Corinth and Corcyra. The fact that there were many of these colonies, now outside of Hellas and repeatedly fought over, suggests a scarcity condition. Indeed, the Peloponnesian War began in precisely this manner where Epidamnus, originally a colony of Corcyra, was being absorbed by Corinth, thus leading to conflict between the two colonial powers. Almost immediately thereafter, Potidae, a colony of Corinth originally but now paying tribute to Athens, revolted against the Athenian overlordship. It was these two colonial conflicts which ultimately drew Sparta and her Peloponnesian allies into a systemic war with Athens and her allies. Corcyra asked for Athenian intervention against the more powerful Corinth, and Athens assented, defeating the Corinthians at sea and also defeating the Potidaeans and their Peloponnesian allies on land. Sparta was now asked by Corinth and Potidae to intervene against Athens, which she reluctantly did (Kagan 1969).

The concept of independence of the small states, central to the hierarchical equilibrium, is essentially absent here. Each of the larger cities which gave rise to the smaller colonies laid claim to a tributary status for the smaller colony. Only long struggles between the two could lead to independence for the smaller colony, and even this generally was not permanent.

An earlier equality among the larger Greek city-states was now being violated chiefly by the growth in Athenian power. The analysis of Figure 3.1 suggests this eventual outcome, for at least one of the power centers in such a multipolar setting will stand out from the remainder, especially in comparison with the weaker system members. And as Pericles remarked in his last speech justifying his war policy even in the light of two recent destructive invasions of Attica by the Peloponnesians which led to talk of relinquishing the empire, "No doubt all this will be disparaged by people who are politically apathetic; but those who, like us, prefer a life of action will try to imitate us, and, if they fail to secure what we have secured, they will envy us. All who have taken it upon themselves to rule over others have incurred hatred and unpopularity for a time; but if one has a great aim to pursue, *this burden of envy must be accepted*, and it is wise to accept it" (italics added).[10] The fact that it is Pericles who makes these judgments is significant in that Thucydides regards Pericles as a superb ruler whose decisions were largely correct,[11] especially in comparison with the demagogues who succeeded him (Finley 1972, 25–28).

The Thirty Years' War

The Thirty Years' War began with the famous defenestration of Prague in 1618 and ended with the Peace of Westphalia in 1648. Two regents of Prague and a secretary were hurled from a window in 1618, which was the start of the Protestant rebellion against Catholic rule in Prague. The majority of Bohemia at that time was Protestant but under the rule of the Catholic Habsburgs. At this time, the Habsburg dynasty controlled Austria, Hungary, the Tyrol, Silesia, Moravia, and, of course, Bohemia as well as other territories in Central Europe. The other branch of the dynasty, in Madrid, governed Spain, Portugal, the Low Countries, and much of Italy. Clearly, the Habsburgs were the dominant power in Europe. They were staunchly Catholic and committed to the restoration of Catholicism as the universal Christian church. The fact that the head of the Habsburgs also was the Holy Roman Emperor and, thus, officially entrusted with the counter-reforming crusade, legitimated the nexus between the Habsburg dynasty and absolutist Catholicism.

Arranged against the Habsburgs were the Protestant states in central and north Germany and, in particular, the United Provinces of the Netherlands which had won a kind of independence from the Spanish Habsburgs in 1609 but only in the form of a truce which was to last until 1621. It was expected at that point that war between the Protestant Netherlands and Catholic Spain would be renewed. Eventually, the Protestant states of Denmark, Sweden, and even England (albeit never fully) intervened. Virtually all of the

54

German Catholic states and Poland (via the conflict with Gustavus Adolphus) were involved in the war on the Habsburg side, but Catholic France and even the Papacy ultimately fought against the Habsburgs. This rather surprising turn of events will later assume significance for our understanding of the onset of mobilization wars.

It is acknowledged that it was the rise of Calvinism in the sixteenth century that helped spark the onset of the Thirty Years' War in 1618. As Pagès (1970, 39–40) has remarked

> Two facts above all must be borne in mind, for they were to make this crisis inevitable. The first was a direct consequence of the way in which the peace [of Augsburg, 1555] was drawn up. . . . The second fact was the ever-increasing growth of Calvinism, which continued to spread in the Rhineland, in southern Germany, in Upper and Lower Austria and in Hungary. . . . Now the Calvinists had not been included in the peace and the new confession which for the most part spread to the principalities whose prince was a Catholic, could only do so in violation of the principle "cuius regio, eius religio." The members of the Calvinist Church thus formed within the Empire an extraneous body outside the protection of the imperial laws. . . . Consequently, the Calvinist princes took steps to defend themselves, either by uniting or by seeking alliances with foreign princes. They were to be the first to take up arms against the emperor.

It was the "ever-increasing growth" of Calvinism as an "extraneous body" not included within the Peace of Augsburg which makes it an illustration of the processes outlined previously. The Peace of Augsburg was a treaty directly incorporating bipolarity in recognizing (1) the legitimacy of only two types of states, Catholic and Lutheran, and (2) the principle of *cuius regio, eius religio* wherein the population of a principality was required to be of the same religion as its ruler.[12] Calvinism, of course, was not included within this bipolar arrangement and yet continued to spread throughout the regions enumerated by Pagès.

Most important was the recognition that Calvinism was not only a religious form gaining increasing numbers of new adherents but was also represented by powerful states. In particular, Holland was about to embark on an illustrious commercial and naval hegemony in mid-century. The enormous difficulties experienced by the then strongest power in Europe, Habsburg Spain, in subjugating the United Provinces late in the sixteenth century gave evidence of this soon-to-be-achieved stature. In addition, as early as 1591, the largely Calvinist German Protestant League of Torgau was formed under Christian I of Saxony, John Casimir of the Palatinate, and Christian of Anhalt. This organization was to find a later counterpart in the mainly Calvinist Protestant Union of 1608.[13]

"The liberated Netherlands had already become, by the end of the old century, the potential organizer of an opposition to the Habsburgs since their political and economic interest were diametrically at odds with those of

Spain." According to Polisensky (1971, 22) the author of the previous quote, the conflict between the Netherlands and Spain was one of the two major axes of conflict in Europe (the other being the Turkish question), one which had already "been draining the life-blood of Spain since 1566 and had been the root cause of Spanish bankruptcies in 1557, 1575, and 1596 as it was to be again in 1607" (Polisensky 1971, 21). Thompson (1986) even treats the years preceding and including the outbreak of the Thirty Years' War (1608–1620) as unipolar with the Netherlands as the leading global power. Although this assessment is based principally on sea power, nevertheless the threat from this Calvinist state to the Spanish Habsburgs, also a sea power and militantly Catholic, must have been pronounced. Additionally, much of Switzerland already was Calvinist with the then strong reputation of the Swiss for military prowess.

It is also clear that much of Europe viewed the Bohemian activities, as well as the activities in certain German cities, in comparison with the Calvinist Dutch and Swiss as a point of reference. For example, Sir Dudley Carleton wrote from the Hague in 1619, "It is doubtful whether the Bohemians and their allies would follow the example of these [the Dutch] provinces, or of the Swiss, by forming a union of cantons . . . And I have all the more support for my view from reading the letters of some of the Directors, written shortly before the election of the Palatine Prince [Frederick]. I find in their breasts not so much arrogance, but that they were thinking of how to unite in confederation with this state [the United Netherlands] and the Hanseatic cities. . ." (quoted in Polisensky 1978, 60). ˙

Thus, the increasing spread of the new religious form in Habsburg Austria and the subsequent Bohemian revolt could only be viewed by the Empire as a threat to its existence by this emerging third pole of European loyalty. The consequent election of a Calvinist King of Bohemia (Frederick) in the heart of the Austrian Habsburg domains (the weaker of the two Habsburg houses) must have been intolerable (Polisensky 1971, 22).

The adherence of each of the principalities to either Catholicism or Lutheranism meant, of course, a zero-sum condition for each of them upon a significant gain to the Calvinists. This is clearly a condition of scarcity wherein Calvinist gains could only be made upon losses to Lutherans and Catholics. Upon the death of Christian I of Saxony in 1591, for example, the earlier Calvinist gains in Saxony were uprooted by the Elector of Brandenburg, the guardian of the new eight-year-old monarch; upon the death of the Elector seven years later, a staunch Calvinist, Joachim Frederick, succeeded to that position and made significant Calvinist inroads in Brandenburg. In 1608, Calvinism was firmly established by John Sigismund in that principality (Williams 1969, 204, 218, 238).

An approximate correspondence to the conditions of Figure 3.1 exists because after the Reformation the foundations of the Catholic church were so shaken that large numbers of persons were "up for grabs" religiously, as it were. A kind of theological vacuum existed wherein the Reformation could proceed largely in its Lutheran manifestation, the counter-Reformation could gain vigor thus enhancing the Catholic cause, or yet different forms of Christian faith could gain adherents as in the instance of Calvinism. The requirement for a uniformity in faith between a prince and his subjects made the tension more acute, for as increasing numbers of persons became, say, Calvinist, the emergent demand for a change of faith by the prince or his physical replacement, meant also a change in the political configuration of the region. An emerging inequality, mainly between Catholic and Calvinist principalities, was occurring in precisely those areas that historically had been Catholic (as had actually all of Christian Europe) but were dislodged from those moorings during the previous century. In Bohemia itself "nine-tenths of the population, a large majority of the nobility and nearly all the townspeople were Protestant of different shades" (Polisensky 1972, 67). This was the tripolar tension which existed at the time of the defenestration in Prague which began the Thirty Years' War in 1618.

Although Calvinists and Lutherans (as well as certain other Protestants) eventually fought battles together during the war, at the outset of the conflict the Lutherans functioned as a separate entity, for the most part remaining neutral in the conflict. [According to Pagès, they "had perhaps even less sympathy for the Calvinists than they had for the Catholics" (Pagès 1970, 66). Wedgwood (1972, 26) quotes a Lutheran writer who declares that "The Calvinist dragon is pregnant with all the horrors of Mohammedanism."] Further, "the election of a Calvinist as king of Bohemia caused them [the Lutherans] considerable anxiety and deterred them from intervening" (Pagès 1970, 66). John George of Saxony, probably the single most important Lutheran neighbor of Bohemia, actually sided with the Catholic emperor against the insurgents. The envy of the rising Calvinist power is here discernible. The tripolar nature of early seventeenth century Central Europe and, especially, the need for any expanding seat of power (pole) to gain at the expense of another, thus reinforcing the scarcity condition, made the conflict more likely to occur.

An additional reinforcement of the scarcity condition in Bohemia occurred domestically in the poor agricultural situation consequent upon a high population density and the peasant revolts of the previous century (Wedgwood 1972, 28). Indeed, a Protestant peasant revolt against the Habsburgs occurred in 1604 in neighboring Hungary which had important international repercussions. The Turks recognized the legitimacy of the new leadership under Stephen Bocskai (Williams 1969, 230), thus threatening to bring a fourth seat of international power into the prevailing tripolarity, with the potential consequences suggested by Figure 3.1. This process was reinforced in 1613 by the refusal of the Protestant princes of the German Diet in Ratisbon (with the exception of the Elector of Saxony) to agree to the Emperor Matthias' request for aid against the Turks. All of the Catholic princes, of course, acceded (Williams 1969, 248). The two major axes of

European conflict—that among the three contending forms of Christianity and that between the Empire and Turkey—were being united as one. Thus, superimposed upon the tottering international tripolarity of Central Europe was not only the threat of an important fourth pole in that environment but a domestic agricultural scarcity with all of its own implications for instability. The fact that many of the wealthiest and most influential (in Vienna) Bohemian nobility were Catholic, likely aggravated the already tense situation (Polisensky 1972, 101).

The fact that most of Central Europe was identified as Catholic, Lutheran, or Calvinist meant that such a war also was likely to be a general or systemic war. In the final analysis, Bohemia, "the economic backbone of the power of the Austrian Habsburgs" which "paid more taxes and sent more soldiers against the Turks than any other possessions of the Habsburgs" (Polisensky 1972, 65, 67), with a population approaching three million, simply could not be allowed to become a Calvinist resource, in the language of this study.

The Approach to World War I

Because of the remoteness in historical time and absence of detailed historical materials, the preceding discussion of the emergence of tripolarity and the onset of the Thirty Years' War could only be approximate, as indeed was the discussion of the origin of the Peloponnesian War. In the more recent nineteenth century period approaching World War I, we can be more exact even in pinpointing the precise envies and jealousies and their timing consequent upon the emergence of inequality within a multipolar setting. Although the number of great powers increased after the unification of Italy and the later emergence of the United States and Japan, this is not the principal avenue for the emergence of inequality in this instance. Instead, it is the increasing scarcity of colonies or other resources to aggrandize which characterized the end of the nineteenth century. It is sufficient to mention the Kruger telegram of 1896 as indicating the first serious conflict between Britain and Germany over southern Africa prior to World War I, or the Franco-German rivalry in North Africa leading to the three Moroccan crises of 1906, 1908, and 1911.[14] The first of these was to lead to the Algeciras Conference, which was to have grave consequences for the onset of World War I. It was here that Germany was nearly isolated internationally, for Italy went her own way and, in the end, even Austria-Hungary gave only weak support to her closest ally (Taylor 1971, 450–451). Germany's resolve never again to leave herself in that position may have led to the unconditional support she gave Austria-Hungary in 1908, during the Bosnian crisis, and again in 1914.

These events followed from an initial confrontation in a colonial context under conditions of rapidly closing colonial opportunities, especially for Germany. One can view the German aggressiveness in the first decade of the twentieth century as, in part, a consequence of the envies of the colonially more favored France and, especially, Britain. ("if we are bled to death," said Kaiser Wilhelm II on the eve of World War I, then "England shall at least lose India.")[15] We shall have more to say about the antecedents of the colonial crises of the early eighteenth century in the succeeding chapter.

In the east, another scenario was being enacted with equally grave consequences, at least according to George F. Kennan (1979) in his magisterial *The Decline of Bismarck's European Order*. He begins his inquiry with certain of the same concerns that originated the present study, namely, "a long-standing preoccupation with the First World War—as a phenomenon in history and as a fact in the life of our own time. . . . Why, I was obliged to ask, had some eight million men, most of them young and on the very threshold of the fruition of life, been obliged to renounce the privilege of leading out their lives, to abandon those lives in horror, agony, and hopelessness . . ." (Kennan 1979, 3). The major line of his inquiry explores the reasons for the breakup of the *Dreikaiserbund* which united Austria-Hungary, Germany, and Prussia in an alliance, first in 1881, and then renewed in 1884 for another three years. It was the disintegration of this alliance which ultimately opened the way for the Franco-Russian negotiations culminating in the defensive alliance of 1894. It is this alliance which is explored by Kennan (1984) later in his *The Fateful Alliance: France, Russia, and the Coming of the First World War*. The Triple Entente, of course, was built up from these foundations.

The *Dreikaiserbund* essentially provided for the benevolent neutrality of each of the powers if they should find themselves at war with a fourth power. This pact was a cornerstone of Bismarck's European policy, for it united the three powers in such a way as to isolate France diplomatically. Austria-Hungary was provided assurance that Russia would not attack her in the Balkans. Russia was assured against combined Austro-German aggression and, in addition, any aid from these quarters to England in the event of a repeat of a Crimean-like venture. Most important from Bismarck's perspective was that, in the event of a Franco-German conflict, Russia would be forced to remain neutral. In this fashion, French hopes of a successful *revanche* would be small indeed.

Much of Kennan's volume explores reasons for the breakup of the *Dreikaiserbund*, which ultimately led to the signing of the Franco-Russian alliance in 1891 and again in 1894 in full defensive form. Fully one of four parts of the book (220 pages) is devoted the Bulgarian *gâchis*, as Kennan (1979, 103ff) calls it. It is in this episode that he discerns "the moment of inner commitment to the eventual abandonment of the agreement with the Austro-Hungarian and German Empires which for five years had constituted the cornerstone of Russia's international position; in its place, embarkation on the long and gradual slope that would lead to the signing, some six years later, of the Franco-Russian alliance" (Kennan 1979, 204).

The problem of Bulgaria arose as a consequence of the Russo-Turkish War of 1877–1878, eventuating in the Congress of Berlin in 1878. As a result of that meeting, a near-independent Bulgaria was created, to be a Russian satellite if that power so wished. In addition, the southeastern part known as Eastern Rumelia was to remain, at least in theory, a Turkish province, albeit with a Christian governor approved by the European powers.

A German, Prince Battenberg of the House of Hesse-Darmstadt, was elected to the Bulgarian throne with the consent of Tsar Alexander II (Kennan 1979, 104). Although Battenberg's relations with the Russian ruling house were at times unsteady, they were to be far worse after the assassination of Alexander II and the accession to the throne of Alexander III. At an early stage in his reign, sometime in 1883, the new tsar vowed to be rid of the Bulgarian monarch largely because of the latter's intent to rule his country without undue Russian influence, especially the two Russian generals sent by Alexander III to oversee matters.

After a period of some intense diplomatic conflict between the two countries, matters came to a head in 1885 with a fairly spontaneous uprising in Eastern Rumelia in favor of unification with Bulgaria. All of the major powers were surprised by the event, and Battenberg rose to the occasion and assumed leadership of both halves of Bulgaria even to the point of defending Bulgaria successfully against an invading Serb army.

It was clear to the tsar however, that the emergence of a united Bulgaria under a new national hero would not exactly wed the new country to any great power, including Russia. Indeed, Austrian power was being felt in the region, particularly in the ultimatum to Battenberg to cease his pursuit of the now defeated Serbian army. This was in addition to the already evident Austrian domination of Serbia, which presumably also had been arrogated to the Russian sphere after the Congress of Berlin.

Thus, Russian policy in the Balkans was perceived to have been a grand failure. One of Russia's ostensible satellites in the region was lost to Austria and the other, Bulgaria, was proceeding in the same direction.

It was in December of 1885, just at the end of the brief Serbo-Bulgarian hostilities, that the first open dissatisfaction over the *Dreikaiserbund* appeared in the conservative nationalist press. M. N. Katkov, the extremely influential editor of *Moskovskie Vyedomosti* accused Battenberg of being a tool of England and identified the Three Emperors' alliance as a vehicle for that implementation (Kennan 1979, 144). By the following summer, in 1886, Katkov was ready for a fuller statement of his position. This was an editorial in *Moskovskie Vyedomosti* published on July 30 in which he effectively urged the abandonment of the *Dreikaiserbund* (Kennan devotes a full chapter to this editorial). Although Austria-Hungary was perceived as the principal opponent, it was Bismarck and German power in back of Austria which was the real limitation on Russia's greatness. The editorial opened with, "The German Chancellor has acquired, together with his deserved fame, a certain mythological quality. His hand is suspected in all the events of our time; he is viewed as the possessor of the talisman before which all obstacles dissolve and all locks open. Without his agreement, one is given to understand, one may neither lie down nor stand up; he runs the whole world" (quoted in Kennan 1979, 177). It was due to the German chancellor's machinations that Russia was being squeezed out of the Balkans. Only independently of the limitations of the *Dreikaiserbund* could Russia really achieve her true stature as a great power.

In the following January, Katkov followed up these initial arguments with a private letter to the tsar, nearly of book length (Kennan believes that it ranks among the basic political documents of the period), in which once again the *Dreikaiserbund* is inveighed against. Katkov subsequently was received by the tsar in a personal interview. "The tsar (sic) came away from the reading of it [the letter] persuaded that Katkov's view reflected the passionate feelings of great and influential portions of Russian society—feelings of such importance that they deserved deference regardless of how well or ill founded they were" (Kennan 1979, 261). Further editorials in *Moskovskie Vyedomosti* on March 18, 1887, again attacked existing Russian policy toward Austria, finally sealing the fate of the *Dreikaiserbund*. The "long and gradual slope" toward the Franco-Russian alliance had begun.

That these allegations of Bismarck's intentions toward Russia were largely false and had little or no basis in fact turned out to be irrelevant. Bismarck actually wanted to give Russia something of a free hand in Bulgaria, but Austria was reluctant.[16] Being convinced of the widespread belief in Bismarck's perfidy, the tsar's own inclinations in that direction were sufficient to doom the *Dreikaiserbund* by Tsar Alexander III.

Kennan (1979, 184) summarizes Katkov's position thusly, "It was the combination of these two things—the ignominy of Russia and the success of her German partner—that was intolerable to him. Possibly he could have endured Bismarck's successes if Russia had had fewer failures. He might, conversely, have endured Russia's failures if Bismarck had had fewer successes. *The combination of the two was unendurable*" (italics added). It is clearly the inequality in international resource distribution that Kennan indicates was "unendurable" to Katkov. The range of social comparison within the European multipolar environment allowed, if not encouraged, the making of such comparative assessments by Katkov.[17] In his later volume, Kennan (1984, 33) remarks that Bismarck had been a "formidable rival figure whose successes had aroused in Russia that peculiar form of resentment that only envy can arouse."

Envy may not only have a direct impact on the rupture of alliances, such as the *Dreikaiserbund*, but may have important indirect consequences as well. It is clear from the foregoing that the Russians badly misperceived Bismarck's intensions regarding Russia and the Balkans. The level of envy may have been sufficient to yield considerable misperception of the German position. Thus, misperception[18] may play an important intervening role between the consequences of inequality such as envy and the deterioration of interstate relations.

What were some of the successes that Katkov and Kennan allude to that had aroused Russian envy? Obviously, one was the "honest broker" played by Bismarck in Berlin in 1878. But this was eight years before, and much had happened since then. In particular, in late 1884 a conference of fourteen nations had been convened in Berlin concerning the colonization of Africa. As a result of the Treaty of Berlin in the following year, the same year as the uprising in Eastern Rumelia, the European powers, among other things, agreed to respect each other's incursions into Africa. This, in fact, began in earnest the scramble for Africa.[19]

It is hardly possible that Katkov could have been unaware of this signal event in the history of colonialism with Berlin and Bismarck at its center. Germany briefly had begun to acquire colonies in Africa and the Pacific; this treaty was now the legitimator and precipitator of such new acquisitions. These were new "successes" for Bismarck to contrast with Russian "failures" in a similar arena. This is precisely the language of the distribution (3.1) in which "successes" and "failures" are distributed randomly among the recipients.

I have dwelt at considerable length on Kennan's recounting of these events not only because of his eminence as both diplomat and historian and the similarity of his explanatory purposes to my own but because, of all of the students of the onset of World War I (for example, Albertini, Fay, Schmitt, Fischer), Kennan alone chose to focus in such great detail on the decaying bases of the old order upon which late nineteenth century European stability was based. Theoretically, it is the slow erosion in the bases of cooperation over time which is suggested by the emerging inequality in resource distribution indicated in Figure 3.1.

Note that an important assumption embodied in equation [3.1], although not always satisifed (this will be treated at some length momentarily), is satisfied in this instance. This is the independence of the onset of each of these events from the other. Clearly, events in Eastern Rumelia, which precipitated the Bulgarian crisis, were independent from the race for colonies in Africa, which was associated with the Congress of Berlin of 1884. Although the *consequences* of the latter were to affect Russian nationalists such as Katkov, the onset of each of these events was, nevertheless, independent of the others. This is all that is required by equation [3.1].

A further requirement of equation [3.1], randomness, is satisfied by these events. Kennan (1979, 120–137) goes to great lengths to show how the rebellion in Eastern Rumelia was not planned by the great powers nor were they even aware of its forthcoming occurrence. The Russians, the Bulgarian government (although likely not elements of the nationalist population), the Austrians, and the Germans had no knowledge of its planning or execution until the event occurred. This is the kind of random even which can set into motion processes which eventuate in the inequalities of Figure 3.1.

Other Illustrations

The French Revolution, in its origins, interestingly conforms to the classic model of scarcity engendering inequality between peasant and landlord as outlined in the formal model found in Midlarsky (1982). As Lefebvre (1947, 113) put it, "The situation had grown worse since the middle of the eighteenth century, for the population had increased perceptibly, probably by three million. The number of proletarians [land workers] had risen, while through the division of inheritances, the shares of property owners had become smaller. There was, therefore, at the end of the Old Regime, an agrarian crisis." According to Young (1792, 397), "I have more than once, seen division carried to such excess, that a single fruit tree, standing in about ten perch of ground has constituted a farm, and the local situation of a family decided by the possession." Furthermore, there is the rapid growth of a new class, the bourgeoisie, which is a direct analogue of the growth of a new religious pole (Calvinism) in early nineteenth century Europe. Given the acute scarcities just now cited, the growth of still new demands for resources by this new class actor must have exacerbated the already tense situation between landlord and peasant. The French Revolutionary Wars were to follow almost immediately upon the start of the French Revolution.

In this sense, the French Revolution reflects the beginning of the modern period for the onset of systemic war as well as for its other consequences (mobilized populations, etc.). For now, scarcities and the other progenitors largely internal to the nation-state were to impact first on the state, via a species of class warfare, and then on the surrounding international system. A new societal unit has been added to the international system in this period—social class—that was to have profound consequences for international conflict. The Bolshevik, Nazi, Iranian, and Cuban revolutions were to have similar consequences. The fact is that the French Revolution was the first of these, and its unexpected characteristics—especially its loathing of monarchy—likely contributed to the intensity of the conflict in the French Revolutionary Wars and the later mobilization variant of the Napoleonic period.

Our example of a general (nonsystemic) structural war also exhibits many of these properties. The zero-sum nature of scarce desiderata appears here as well. Frederick the Great initiated the War of the Austrian Succession by conquering Silesia, an extremely wealthy province of Austria. And according to Ritter (1968, 75),

From the first day his foreign policy sought to make it quite clear to the world that a new epoch had begun in the history of Prussia, that with Frederick's accession a new and disturbing power had joined the concert of Europe. Frederick was convinced that above all Prussia lacked reputation—the respect due to a state which needed to be feared. He was well aware that Vienna had considered his father as nothing more than a poltroon, whose threats and outbursts of anger need not be taken too seriously.

Thus, envy of the until then more favored Austrians was a major component of his decision calculus which included, of course, the addition of desirable resources to his domain.

Note that in a bipolar structure these processes would have been greatly transformed. In the approach to World War I, without the possibility of German support for her activities in the Balkans, it is likely that the Austrians would have readily agreed to a Russian predominance in Bulgaria while securing their own presence in Serbia. This is an illustration of the equality of distribution in bipolar systems, also specified by equation [3.1]. There can be an alternation over time in gaining access to available resources, or it can occur simultaneously with both gaining access at approximately the same time.

Illustrations of the successful operation of bipolarity along these lines abound. An early instance is the Treaty of Tordesillas of 1494 between Spain and Portugal sponsored by the pope.[20] At his encouragement, these two colonial powers were to divide their activities between East and West. In this fashion, Brazil became a Portuguese colony while all of South America to the west fell to Spain. An equality àcceptable to both sides ensued, thus ensuring that future conflict over these territories would be minimal.

More recently, of course, we have the post-World War II bipolar system that, with the availability of new nations for political competition, has demonstrated a considerable stability, likely more than would be warranted by the nuclear deterrence process alone (see chapter 2). A country, such as Ethiopia, can leave the Western orbit and join the Soviet bloc while another, such as Somalia, does the exact opposite. Chile can cease being governed by a Marxist government as South Vietnam moves steadily toward incorporation by North Vietnam. It is constant-sum or positive-sum processes such as these which allow for an approximate equality in political access for each of the superpowers as suggested by the dynamics of equation [3.1].

Envy can also arise in bipolar systems, but the mechanisms for moderating its effects are far more direct. It is clear, for example, that the East Germans and, especially, the Soviets were envious of the West German economic and political success in the post-World War II period which, in concert with East Germany's own dismal performance at that time, led so many East Germans to escape to West Germany. The response, the building of the Berlin Wall, was surely an imperfect solution by the Soviets and East Germans but, nevertheless, worked as a means of maintaining intact East Germany's societal infrastructure. Although the West lost easy access and refugees, the propaganda coup of a wall needing to be built in order to keep a captive population intact was welcomed. Subsequently, without a massive drain of professional talent, the performance of the East German system improved greatly. In this sense, a kind of equality of competitive advantage was achieved in this bipolar confrontation as suggested by the results of the analysis using equation [3.1]. In contrast, as we have seen, there was no direct means for responding to the misperceptions and distortions occasioned by the immense differences between German and Russian successes and failures in the 1880s, especially in the acquisition of colonies and satellites. The decline of Bismarck's foundations for peace may be dated from that time.

Comparison with the Parable of the Tribes

This analytical approach meshes nicely with that developed recently by Schmookler (1984, 42–54) in his parable of the tribes. The basic argument is as follows: Given several tribes living in close proximity to one another but acting independently of each other, if only one of them takes it into its collective mind to behave aggressively toward one or more of the others, then some kind of power-oriented behavior including the possibility of violence is inevitable for *all* of the tribes. The first several might be destroyed and/or absorbed into the growing empire of the first. Any who desire to remain free would have to learn the ways of power in order to remain in that condition. There are four possible reactions for the threatened tribes: (1) withdrawal, (2) destruction, (3) transformation, and (4) imitation.

In the first of these, the threatened tribes simply withdraw into a geographic isolation. Failing that alternative the targeted tribe(s) can be destroyed by the aggressor, which, of course, is the second alternative. Incorporation within the political boundaries of the aggressor or some other massive changes within the corpus of the victim to make it more palatable to the aggressor constitutes the third alternative. Finally, as a defense against the threatening attributes of the aggressor, a targeted tribe can assume some of these same attributes and mount a successful defense. Clearly, the first alternative is unavailable to a modern, settled nation-state, and so the remaining three involving some sort of violence or coercion constitute the remaining alternatives. Schmookler's point is that the learning of power is necessary for survival for those who seek to maintain their own culture relatively intact even in the face of only one assailant initially. A societal evolution for power along the lines of a "survival of the fittest" is a logical outcome of the parable of the tribes.

Whatever the merits or deficiencies of the evolutionary argument, the parable itself neatly summarizes the instability of a multipolar system. If only one of the nation-states within the system appears to behave aggressively and another perceives itself to be the victim of that behavior as measured, say, by inequality in resource distribution, all of the nation-states will be forced to react one way or another. This is one way of viewing Kennan's "long and gradual slope" leading to World War I. Only Russia had to feel somehow outdone by Germany for the tsar's government to gradually loose itself from its former allies in the *Dreikaiserbund* and begin the long path to the Franco-Russian alliance and, from there, to completing alliances among all of the major European powers, thus eventually making the occurrence of war more probable.

What is even more compelling about the argument here in comparison with the parable of the tribes is that the first "aggressor" nation does not even have to behave aggressively in order to bring the system eventually to ruin. All that is required is that there be the semblance of aggressive behavior (perhaps even misinterpreted by wary observers) in order for one or more of the threatened nation-states to take counter action in the form, say, of alliance rupture and/or initiation. The parable of the tribes can be seen as an "overt or crude" form of the argument of this chapter with many subtler and perhaps even more insidious processes made possible by the structure of a multipolar system. Certain of these ideas are developed further in the section on a historical dynamic in chapter 11.

Conclusion

Probabilistically, I have shown that multipolar systems engender serious inequalities under conditions of scarce international desiderata. Bipolar systems do not suffer from this limitation, allowing for equality of distribution under all conditions. Historically, there exist counterparts of these theoretical circumstances, in some cases strikingly conforming to the theoretical conditions. However, I do not claim that the conditions of equation [3.1] are duplicated in the international environment. There are too many instances where nations watch each other closely, thus vitiating the independence assumption (although there are derivations of these random distributions which explicitly violate independence).[21] In addition, many events in the international arena are non-random, having been generated by some central direction as, say, at the United Nations. Nevertheless, we have seen that important instances such as the Bulgarian *gâchis* do satisfy these requirements.

Whatever the exceptions or direct satisfactions of the initial assumptions, the consequences still likely would be systemic instability. The underlying tendencies toward inequality driven by equation [3.1] would be present at least to some degree for the great powers to overcome in their search for stability. Many important historical processes, such as the Polish partitions (by conference) of the late eighteenth century, came about precisely in order to avoid serious inequalities, as in an uncoordinated division of Poland, which appeared to the great powers to verge on anarchy, and a consequent dismemberment by the great powers individually. One of the most famous aphorisms concerning great power behavior in the partitions explicitly highlights this aspect of equality as in "they confused the equity of the action with the equality of shares" (Lewitter 1965, 335).

Dehio (1962) argues that an ever-widening balance-of-power process was needed in order to avoid serious conflict in Europe. The nineteenth century colonial process was a case in point. The principal argument here is that inequalities attendant upon multipolarity required the seeking of new territories, either in colonies or in partitions, in order to compensate for these inequalities. It is no accident that the eighteenth century, in the absence of widespread colonialism, not only experienced the Polish partitions but other partitions were widely and sometimes openly discussed, including that of the Ottoman Empire and, surprisingly, those of Sweden and Holland.[22] Russia, after the Bulgarian episode, turned eastward to the abundant lands of Siberia and easier access to loosely governed central Asian and Chinese territories, thus seeking her compensation in these more available and abundant territories. It was this process that would embroil her in conflict with yet another rising power of the now-expanding multipolar system, Japan.

A major difference between bipolarity and multipolarity that now emerges is one that is emphasized here because of the dynamic aspects of this approach. Bipolarity as a structure generally is found at the outset of a particular period, as in fact occurred at the end of World War II. Each of the two blocs rises up fairly quickly in response to the other's threatening activities. Equality, or at least a near-equality or equity, is maintained over time as suggested by the probabilistic analysis. Changes may occur *within* blocs, but the parity condition between them is seldom altered dramatically. Thus, the structural condition can be maintained in approximately the same form for a fairly long period of time.

In contrast, the multipolar system is continually changing in response to changes in equality, or, more accurately, inequality in response to increasing scarcity. The emergence of inequality in resource possession between the most advantaged and disadvantaged powers in the multipolar system almost inevitably leads to efforts to redress the advantage in the form of alliance formation among the more disadvantaged, which then would be countered by alliance formation initiated by the more advantaged. Sometimes the process can be reversed; in either case, the inequalities lead to structural changes of the most important variety. Instead of a bipolar structure maintained more or less intact over time, the multipolar condition yields new structures which may beget additional structures in order to redress imbalances. It is these fluctuations in the form of Delian and Peloponnesian League, Protestant Union and Catholic League, or Dual Alliance and Triple Entente that ultimately find the protagonists in some sort of confrontation which could easily lead to systemic war.

A final caveat is in order. I do not claim that the nexus between inequality and political violence is indisputable. The findings of other studies are, properly, much too mixed to make any such assertion,[23] although there does now exist evidence for a fairly robust relationship between land inequality and political violence in Latin American and certain Middle Eastern countries (Midlarsky 1988b). What I do claim is that through long and involved processes as detailed masterfully by Kennan, the "long and gradual slope" can be reached which can lay the foundations for the later onset of political violence. This likely is the sort of long-run, indirect process found in most relationships between inequality and political violence.

Notes

1   Deutsch and Singer (1964) base their arguments on the existence of $N(N-1)/2$ possible interactions among the N countries in the system. As N increases the number of possible interactions increases disproportionately, thus diminishing the share of attention each country can devote to a dyadic conflict. Deutsch and Singer (1964, 406) do argue in the end for the long-run instability of multipolar systems in absolute terms, but in comparison with bipolar systems, multipolar systems still are suggested to be more stable, whether in the short or long run.

2   For the evidence on the large number of wars in the eighteenth century and associated casualties, see Levy (1983b).

3   Quoted in Gulick (1955, 10–11).

4   Probably the best known recent exponent of relative deprivation as a source of political violence is Gurr (1970), while rapidly declining economic circumstances as progenitors of instability are found in Davies (1962). Scarcities and consequent inequalities in the etiology of revolution are explored in Midlarsky (1982).

5   Raymond Aron (1968, 160), for example, asserted that "The interstate order has always been anarchical and oligarchical: anarchical because of the absence of a monopoly of legitimate violence, oligarchical (or hierarchic) in that, without civil society, rights depend largely on might." On the other hand, theorists of the long cycle, such as George Modelski (1983), assert that there are periods of global order with a hegemonic power at the head of the hierarchy. Robert Gilpin (1981) argues for the existence of hegemonies and the periodicity of hegemonic wars.

6   This distribution is given for precisely this type of problem in Johnson and Kotz (1977, 114). Also see Feller (1968, 35).

7   For the use of such a measure, see Chenery (1975).

8   See, for example, Park (1986).

9   Midlarsky (1982, 25–30). The equal probability for each recipient creates what can be called a maximum entropy distribution which yields the exponential distribution after the imposition of the scarcity constraint. Thus, the circumstances here are in all important respects identical to those of the earlier analysis.

10   See Thucydides (1954, 133).

11   See Brunt (1963, XXVI–XXVIII).

12   See Pagès (1970, 35).

13   See Williams (1969, 204, 238) for notations of these historical events.

14   For descriptions of these crises see Thomson (1966, 483–487).

15   Quoted in Zinnes, North, and Koch (1961, 476).

16   As Kennan (1979, 241) put it, "The urgings he [Bismarck] had given to the Austrians to respect Russian interests in Bulgaria were too numerous to count."

17   The range of social comparison as a variable of importance in understanding people's comparisons of their own rewards with those of others is found in Brickman and Campbell (1971).

18   Relationships between misperception and international conflict are treated by Jervis (1976) and Levy (1983a).

19   These events are recounted in Thomson (1966, 465–466).

20   See Blum, Cameron, and Barnes (1966, 52).

21   Some of these possibilities are discussed in Chatterji (1963). In one instance, the distribution of x conditional upon $x + y$ is binomial, as in equation [3.1], if x and y are Poisson. Other, more applied examples can be found in the operations research literature.

22   See Hötzsch (1909, 668–670).

23   For a review of some of these findings, see Park (1986).

4

A Distribution of Extreme Inequality

MY ANALYSIS OF the inequalities inherent in multipolarity depends on the random operation of a stochastic process which, in turn, is dependent on the equal probability of each country getting a particular desidaratum, as shown in the preceding chapter. Given the frequent sequential arrivals of countries to the various locations, particularly as they acquire colonies, this equiprobability assumption obviously is not always valid. What, then, is the relationship between bipolarity and multipolarity under the condition of sequential arrivals? I will derive a "new" distribution which turns out to be identical to the Pareto distribution. As will be seen, the first two poles are no longer equal in this circumstance, but the inequality between the first and second arrivals (bipolarity) is far less extreme than between these two and much later arrivals (multipolarity). In other words, if the particular resource universe is divided by only two actors, the inequality between them will be shown to be far less than if there are other actors in the resource system (for example, the acquisition of colonies). I will turn shortly to the general problem of sequential resource acquisitions in the case of land distributions in general and then apply the same model to colonial holdings in 1914, as an end product of the processes outlined here.

In one sense, the following can be seen as a digression, for much of it is not directly concerned with the onset of systemic war in our historical instances. On the other hand, we are laying the foundation for a systematic analysis of colonial possessions leading up to World War I. Given the nineteenth century as the only one of our time periods which offers systematic data, this opportunity for a systematic analysis should not be overlooked.

The sequential aspect of colonial acquisition later will be shown to operate in the context of the approach to World War I. The distribution of land in a colonial context, as in Latin America, will be studied as a general process, and later the distribution of colonial populations governed by European powers will be detailed as a separate process specifically related to the onset of World War I. Thus, whether the random processes of the preceding chapter hold true or the sequential acquisition to be described shortly is operative, serious inequalities will be found to emerge in a multipolar setting. As will be shown in connection with colonial populations preceding World War I, these inequalities will have significant impact on the processes antecedent to the war's onset. More generally, the following treatment can be applied to any sequential acquisition.

Suppose that there is a programmed inequality. Instead of the equiprobability of resource distribution and the scarcity induced inequality as in the preceding treatment, the inequality is inherent in the distribution at the outset. There are processes which exhibit such severe inequalities. Any sequestering of a scarce resource which also requires a surrounding "cushion" or margin of safety is a case in point. Those who enter the process later must defer to the earlier arrivals who already have established their control with the accompanying margin of safety to ensure continued control. An example might be the founder of a corporation who takes all the reins of power required to operate effectively and, at the same time, remain in that position indefinitely. Those who enter the corporation later clearly will receive only some proportion of the resources initially allocated to himself by the founder. Or consider the colonial process wherein the early colonial powers will arrogate to themselves as much territory and population as is required to ensure continued political and economic control over the chosen colony. Frequently, this means including the extra margin of safety to prevent other colonial powers from competing effectively or to prevent the indigenous population from revolting effectively.

Access to resources (for example, water, as in rivers) and an infrastructure of political and economic control also may require such expanded sovereignty over a large territory. The history of British expansion in India to the northwest frontier is a case in point. Later, the French in Asia could colonize only on the fringes of the large British holdings. Still later the Germans, especially in Africa, could colonize only on the fringes of the British and French holdings. In successive stages each of the arrivals determines the smaller proportionate share of the later arrivals in contrast to the equiprobability of initial access assumed in ordinary stochastic models.

Land distribution is another variable likely to be modeled successfully by this sequential process. As in the sequence of colonial acquisitions, the first arrivals to a sparsely settled area will have first choice, or at least will be in the best position to oust the indigenous population. Proximal land with required resources, such as water, also will likely be taken by the first arrivals. Later arrivals will be able to take only some (smaller) proportion of the remaining area. Land distribution in Latin America as territory settled by the Iberian arrivals after the fifteenth century is one case in point, as we shall see shortly.

An Expository Geometric Approach to the Pareto Distribution

The following argument represents sequential arrivals of colonists or acquisitors of various kinds. Instead of the equal opportunity or equiprobable scenario found at the outset in the geometric–exponential form (Midlarsky 1982), this distribution of extreme inequality is derived by the explicit inequality of sequential arrivals. In the former instance each actor, at least initially, has the probability of having as much of a scarce resource (for example, land) as any neighbor, only later to be subdivided geometrically as the result of the absence of primogeniture. A random process over time eventually results in an inequality in land holdings. Here, the inequality is explicit at the outset. Sequentially, each actor arrives and by successful competition, war, or other aggressive behavior takes some large (random) proportion of what is available. In turn, the next arrival (for example, a loser in the first round) takes a large random proportion of what is left. This procedure is repeated with the sequential arrival of N actors until even a large proportion of the remainder is not worth taking. Although each proportion taken is random, one can, as in any random variable, calculate a mean or some other measure of central tendency as a descriptor of the proportion taken in the overall process. Mathematical Appendix B contains a geometric derivation of the Pareto distribution. A more complete account can be found in Midlarsky (1988a).

Two forms of the Pareto distribution are its log–exponential form

$$f(x) = A_1 e^{-k \log_e x} \qquad k>0, \ 1 \leq x < \infty \qquad [4.1]$$

where k is a constant and A_1 is a normalization constant designed to make the sum of the probabilities equal unity. In turn, the function $\log_e x$ transforms the ordinary exponential distribution into the Pareto distribution (Gumbel 1958, 151; Johnson and Kotz 1970, 240),

$$f(x) = Ax^{-k-1} \qquad k>0, \ 1 \leq x < \infty \qquad [4.2]$$

Equations [4.1] and [4.2] are identical. The constant k here is the familiar Paretian exponent, α.

A property of the Pareto distribution is that no matter how much you add to the available resource pool, the extent of inequality still will be severe. As we shall see shortly in an application of this distribution, no matter how much the colonial resources of the late nineteenth century were opened to additional European colonization, as in the opening of Africa as a consequence of the Treaty of Berlin of 1885, the inequality in colonial holdings among the great powers would still be extreme. It was German recognition of this unpleasant reality, especially vis-à-vis Britain and France at the end of the scramble for Africa, which likely hastened the colonial crises of the early twentieth century and the coming of World War I.

Political Implications and Two Applications

The invariance property of the Pareto distribution suggests that once the initial sequestering has occurred, as in Figure 1B (see Mathematical Appendix B), there is little one can do to alter the form of the distribution (although not its parameters). Redistribution is likely the only way this can be done, but in most societies this is generally done at the lower levels of income where the Pareto distribution does not apply to begin with. Thus, the persistence of this distributional form is to be expected in most, if not all capitalist societies as, in fact, has been found until the present.

Another implication follows from the infinite variance implied by the infinite regression of the triangles in Figure 1B and found in the Pareto–Lévy distribution (Johnson and Kotz 1970, 245). For those in the later stages of arrival to any such process, the leavings are small and keep getting smaller as time proceeds. In domestic politics such potentially explosive processes are alleviated by the growth of income usually in the form of wage increases at the lower income levels or by explicitly redistributive programs. In international politics, there are no such palliatives and, as we shall see shortly, the log–exponential–Pareto distribution will closely model at least two important acquisitive processes.

Consider first land distribution as one such sequential process of resource acquisition as implied in the earlier discussion. The exponential distribution itself has been used to successfully model land distributions in prior revolutionary situations, especially for the poorer sectors of the population (Midlarsky 1982; Midlarsky and Roberts 1985). In this instance it is more than likely that the equiprobability of land holdings occurred at least initially for the forebearers of the current peasantry, but with population growth, a steadily growing inequality prevailed. And indeed the exponential distribution did fit remarkably well to the landholdings of the poorer 87% of the distribution with land holdings up to and including 4.99 hectares. But what of the much larger holdings of 50 hectares and above which comprise 1.9%

of the holdings? Theoretically, given the scarcity assumption (El Salvador is extremely land poor in relation to population size) and sequential arrivals, one would expect the log–exponential–Pareto distribution to hold. As before, I will continue to refer to this distribution solely as log–exponential to emphasize its connection with the exponential distribution of scarce resources. The exponential distribution (in discrete form, for purpose of empirical application) is given by

$$p_i^0 = A_1^0 e^{-k_1 x_i} \qquad\qquad [4.3]$$

where as before k_1 is a constant and A_1^0 is another constant designed to ensure that the sum of the probabilities equals unity.

Table 4.1 gives the observed land distribution above 50 hectares in El Salvador and the predicted distributions both by the log–exponential and exponential distributions. The latter theoretical distribution is calculated in order to provide a contrast, if any, with the hypothesized log–exponential distribution. The theoretical values are calculated by first linearizing the probability distributions as a consequence of taking logarithms of both sides of the equations [4.1] (in discrete form) and [4.3]. This leads to

$$\log_e p_i = \log_e A_1 - k \log_e x_i$$

for the log–exponential distribution and

$$\log_e p_i^0 = \log_e A_1^0 - k_1 x_i$$

for the exponential distribution. The values of k and k_1 are estimated by regressing $\log_e p_i$ and $\log_e p_i^0$ on the independent variables, and the regression coefficients serve as least-squares estimates. The values of A_1 and A_1^0 are chosen to normalize the equations so that the sum of the proportions equals unity, or

$$A_1 = 1 \Big/ \left(\sum_{i=1}^{n} -k \log x_i \right)$$

and

$$A_1^0 = 1 \Big/ \left(\sum_{i=1}^{n} e^{-k_1 x_i} \right)$$

Table 4.1
Observed and predicted land distributions in El Salvador.

Size of holding (hectares)[a]	Observed number of holdings	Observed proportion of holdings ($\times 100$)	Predicted proportion of holdings ($\times 100$)	
			Log–Exponential[b] $k = 1.0318, A_1 = 47.1698$	Exponential[c] $k_1 = 1.772 \times 10^{-3}, A_1{}^\circ = 0.4017$
50.00–99.99	2214	51.16	54.81	35.17
100.00–199.99	1121	25.90	26.79	30.79
200.00–499.99	713	16.47	11.18	21.60
500.00–999.99	189	4.37	5.09	10.63
1000.00–2499.99	91	2.10	2.12	1.81

[a]Category ranges are the same as those presented in the source (Wilkie and Haber 1983, 58–59). Data are for 1960 to maintain consistency with the earlier treatment of the lower ranges for El Salvador. Values of x_i were estimated by the midpoints of each of the category ranges, or $x_1 = 75$, $x_2 = 150$, etc.

[b]$\chi^2 = 2.878$, df $= 3$, $p < 0.50$

[c]$\chi^2 = 12.998$, df $= 3$, $p < 0.01$

As can be seen, the log–exponential distribution provides an acceptable fit with a value of the chi-square goodness-of-fit statistic having a probability of occurring less than 50 times in 100 chances. Therefore, it can be taken as nonsignificant. The exponential distribution, on the other hand, can be rejected at $p < 0.01$. Here the chi-square statistic is used as a measure of goodness of fit and so higher probability levels imply acceptance of the model while lower probabilities imply rejection. It should be noted that the exponential distribution itself was found to be an almost perfect descriptor of the landholdings in the range 0–4.99 hectares with a chi-square value having a probability of occurring less than 90 times in 100 chances (Midlarsky and Roberts 1985, 175–176). Thus, the inapplicability of the exponential distribution here to the higher ranges but the applicability of the log–exponential distribution is all the more striking.

Our second application is to the acquisition of colonies by the European powers. It was largely sequential throughout the past several centuries and led to a particular distribution of colonies prior to World War I. Here, I will use colonial population as the variable to be modeled; the only other alternative, area, is too inhomogeneous because of the extreme variation of colonial holdings from desert to fertile river valleys. The data on colonial populations are taken from the *Statesman's Year Book, 1914*. Because of the concern here with the onset of systemic war as a potentially explosive outcome of serious inequalities in the international system, only European powers are included and, of these, only those territories which are explicitly and separately listed in the data source as being of colonial status contribute to the data compilation. This led to the inclusion of the dependencies of twelve European countries. Four ranges of colonial population were found and the averages for each are given in Table 4.2. As before, the log–exponential and exponential distributions each are calculated as rival theoretical models, using the same estimation procedures as in the land distribution illustration. Although the fit between model and data is not perfect, it does conform largely to the log–exponential form as suggested by the value of the chi-square goodness-of-fit statistic. Once again, the exponential can be rejected as a potential model for this observed distribution.

Conclusion

Whereas in domestic politics there are various remedies for inequalities of the Pareto sort, as in increased wages at the lower income levels or redistribution, none of these exists in international politics. Only upon the imminent outbreak of World War I could Kaiser Wilhelm II of Germany (in the second category of Table 4.2) declare that "if we are bled to death, England shall at least lose India", as we saw in chapter 3 (p. 59). This is a redistribution to be brought about (or hoped to be) in the international arena. Scarcities of

Table 4.2

Observed and predicted distributions of colonial populations among the European powers, 1914.

Colonial population size (mean)	Observed number of countries	Observed proportion of countries ($\times 100$)	Predicted proportion of countries ($\times 100$)	
			Log–Exponential[b] $k = 0.2642, A_1 = 17.2414$	Exponential[c] $k_1 = 3.596 \times 10^{-9}, A_1^{\circ} = 0.3237$
691,560	5[a]	41.67	49.40	32.28
9,754,540	4	33.33	24.55	31.25
39,493,121	2	16.67	16.97	28.08
375,710,827	1	8.33	9.09	8.38

[a]The source is the *Statesman's Year-Book, 1914*. The countries represented in the four categories are from top to bottom (1) Austria-Hungary, Denmark, Italy, Spain, and Sweden; (2) Belgium, Germany, Portugal, and Russia; (3) France and the Netherlands; and (4) Great Britain.

[b]$\chi^2 = 4.418$, df $= 2$, $p < 0.20$

[c]$\chi^2 = 7.507$, df $= 2$, $p < 0.05$

colonies as international resources of their time, especially in the latter stages of the colonial process and the sequential arrivals of colonizers are emphasized by the geometric derivation of Mathematical Appendix B. A similar process likely occurred in the acquisition of large land tracts in the early colonization of El Salvador. (Even today in El Salvador, one speaks of the "fourteen families" who hold much of the economic and political power (LaFeber 1983)). The preceding derivation of the log–exponential–Pareto distribution clarifies how such unattenuated processes can come about in international and domestic politics.

As a consequence of these findings, it is possible to generate certain hypotheses about the onset of political violence. These take the form of three categories. (1) Where growth processes at the lower levels of income exist as reflected, say, by the lognormal distribution, it is likely that political violence will be avoided even if the log–exponential distribution holds at the higher income levels. (2) However, where there is a subdivision process of holdings at the lower levels instead of growth as reflected by the exponential distribution, in addition to the log–exponential at the higher levels, then political violence is far more likely. This is the pattern that was found in El Salvador. Here there is no attenuation of the extreme wealth seen at the upper income levels, only a continuous subdivision over time for the peasantry which gradually depresses the income level. (3) The final pattern is that of the log–exponential distribution alone as seen in the colonial process. Here, throughout the range of holdings, the inequality is extreme. This is probably the most violence-prone distribution. Indeed, it has been claimed to be inherently unstable if it holds throughout the range of potential applicability as is found here (Ord, Patil, and Taillie 1981, 197–198). The destruction of empires, either directly as the result of war or indirectly as a result of systemic wars such as World War I, is likely a consequence, at least in part, of this unremitting feature of international political life.

It is no accident that two distributions which are no longer Paretian—the distributions of income in Eastern Europe and of colonial possessions internationally—came about as the result of either direct or indirect violent redistribution, the former as the result of Soviet troops in Eastern Europe and the latter as a consequence of the two World Wars and anticolonial activities. The early sequestering of scarce resources and the invariance property of the Pareto distribution suggest that where this distribution is dominant throughout the entire range of income or holdings, political violence of a redistributive sort is more likely than in other possible circumstances.

An exacerbating factor likely is the presence of upward mobility as the result of competition. It is a well-known property of the Pareto distribution that for any value of resource holding x, the average of all holdings above x varies directly with it (Chipman 1976, 145–147). This means that the ratio of the mean greater than x, or $M(x)$, to x is a constant throughout the range of Paretian applicability, or "The constancy of the ratios $M(x)/x$ for all values of x in a society at a given time appears to mean simply that the sociological equilibrium that is established is such that at each income level the sentiment of inequality is independent of this income" (Allais 1973, 79). Put another way, wherever one is situated on the resource possessions scale, "looking upward" one will see the same thing.

Now, if a particular great power is competitive with others who have larger colonial holdings and, at the same time, is increasing its own acquisitions (as Germany did in the late nineteenth century) yet "looking upward" sees the same thing, then it may feel as if all its efforts were for naught. If its "inequality sentiments" were strong at the outset, then they would still be there, even after the expenditure of moneys and effort, likely with an added touch of bitterness. Moreover, there would be at best only an incomplete understanding of the reasons for the apparent "spinning of the wheels" despite the formidable efforts and expenditures of money. As a consequence, other countries, especially system leaders such as Britain or France, could be targeted by the aspiring polity as intentional frustrators of those aspirations. This is one more expression of the invariance properties of the Pareto distribution, one that is likely to be far more dangerous in a dynamic circumstance such as the late nineteenth century colonial process than in more static situations without the aspiration of mobility to higher levels.

As we shall see later in chapter 10, the existence of these extreme inequalities is normatively unacceptable from the perspective of a prominent and persuasive theory of justice.

Finally, I have shown that the condition of only two international aspirants or poles differs markedly from that of three or more. Although the inequality between the first two arrivals is substantial, it becomes far worse as additional actors are added to the resource universe. While the inequality between England and France in colonial population (see Table 4.2) was on the order of magnitude of 9 (the ratio between richer to poorer), that between Germany and England was an order of magnitude of 40 while the lowest category was of an order of magnitude of 500 times poorer in colonial population than the richest.

In light of these results, one might establish the Pareto distribution as an upper boundary for the inequality of resource holdings, and the exponential distribution, implied by the analysis of the preceding chapter and earlier treatments, as a lower boundary. This is because of the equiprobability of resource distribution at the outset. The actual inequality in resource holdings experienced by international and domestic actors likely would vary between these two limits. Wherever one is situated on this continuum, there will be found the inequality of resource distribution in multipolar systems.

5

Conflict Overlap in Systemic Wars*

THUS FAR, WE HAVE treated the hierarchical equilibrium and emergent inequalities among major powers in a multipolar system. Given the sequential model in the introductory chapter, it is time now to consider the presence of overlapping conflicts as a basis for the spread of systemic war. As before, the presence of detailed and, in some cases, systematic data prior to World War I allows for a more systematic analysis of the origins of that war than for the earlier instances. Additionally, the overlap in two different forms of *international* conflict behavior also will be found to overlap with *domestic* conflicts which derive from entropy concerns outlined in chapter 1.

The international systems to be compared are the nineteenth century (1816–1899) system of conflict behavior and the period of 1893–1914, which is that preceding World War I. (As in chapter 2, a small amount of overlap is allowed in order to accommodate the relatively slow diplomatic change in this period beginning with the Franco-Russian alliance in the years 1891–1894, during which the alliance solidified and formed the basis for the Triple Entente, which was soon to oppose the Dual Alliance in the summer crisis of 1914.) The former period is well known for its historic stability; here, that stability will have to be demonstrated analytically. The second of

*Much of the material in this chapter is reprinted from Manus I. Midlarsky, "Preventing Systemic War," *Journal of Conflict Resolution*, Vol. 28, No. 4 (December 1984), pp. 563–584. Copyright © 1984 Sage Publications, Inc. Reprinted by permission of Sage Publications, Inc.

the two periods, of course, will have to demonstrate properties that are substantially different and, in addition, that have a structural correspondence with the summer crisis of 1914. This crisis has been studied perhaps more than any other and, therefore, provides an excellent referent for the present study. A principal question, as before, is why was there widespread systemic warfare at the termination of one of these periods (1893–1914) but no such war in the other (1816–1899)? Also, what are the distinguishing features of each that lead to the different outcomes?

As in chapter 2, the data used here also are the Correlates of War Militarized Dispute Data for the period 1816–1914. For each of the two systems, (1) disputes between two or more major powers will be examined, followed by (2) disputes between two or more major powers that involve at least one central power (that is, diplomatically active midrange power) as defined in Singer and Small (1968, 254), and (3) the set of disputes combining the first two cases. Only European disputes are included because of the centrality of Europe in the onset of World War I.

The systematic analysis is of the same form as that used in chapter 2 with the same equations ([2.1] and [11A]–[13A]) in Mathematical Appendix A. Here we are once again concerned with the stability of a system of disputes, and the arguments of that chapter pertain here as well. The complexity for decision makers of many disputes occurring at once, as well as the interdependence among them as a result of conflict diffusion, reinforcement, and similar responses to geographically widespread processes, can yield instability in the form of a greater probability of systemic war. The analysis here differs from that of chapter 2 in that the third category, although identical empirically to that of chapter 2, is conceptualized as the combination of the first two instead of as the result of incremental additions of country categories to the disputes. In chapter 2, what was sought was the consequence of hierarchy for dispute stability, hence the incremental additions. In the analysis to come in this chapter, we are concerned with overlapping (1) great power disputes and (2) those between the great powers which involve at least one central power. It is principally the overlap which is of concern here, as indicated in the specification of the overall model of the origins of systemic war in the introductory chapter.

The disputes involving only two or more great powers in 1816–1899 already have been analyzed in chapter 2 and were found to be stable (see Tabular Appendix A). The disputes between two or more great powers involving at least one central power have not yet been analyzed; the analysis is shown in Tabular Appendix B. Here, the stability is even greater as evidenced by the excellent fit between observation and prediction. When we combine these with the disputes solely among the great powers, once again stability is achieved, as shown in Table 3A of Tabular Appendix A.

In the 1893–1914 period, as we saw, disputes solely among the great powers reflected stability. We can now examine the disputes between two or more major powers which involve at least one central power and, once again, stability is achieved, as shown in Tabular Appendix B. Finally, the combination or overlap between the two dispute sets is analyzed and found to be unstable. The fit between observation and prediction is very poor, as can be seen in Table 4A.

Substantively, we can say that the absence of equilibrium for this system was a consequence of the combined set of major power disputes alone and major power disputes involving at least one central power. (Use of the year 1913 as an end point for this interval also led to the finding of instability.)

Aside from the finding of an unstable system and its implications for the predictability of systemic war, this pattern suggests an understanding of the onset of World War I that differs substantially from more traditional interpretations (for example, Albertini 1967; Fay 1928). In these, conflicts among the major powers were the principal or nomothetic causes of the war, while the conflict between Austria-Hungary and Serbia was simply the "spark" or proximal cause of the war. Here, the two patterns of causation have equal status, in the sense that neither the pattern of great power conflicts involving a central power nor that confined exclusively to great powers is demonstrably unstable. Only when the two are combined in a joint set is instability demonstrated. This finding should be contrasted with that of the nineteenth century where the joint set of the two conflict varieties demonstrates greater stability than that of the major powers alone. This fundamental difference will be discussed in more detail at a later point. For now, the equality of the two modes of explanation—that is, great power conflicts and great power conflicts involving central powers—suggests that both patterns existed in the period approaching World War I and contributed to its onset. This conclusion is further supported by the existence of a pattern of major–central power conflicts of at least twenty years duration prior to 1914 (Midlarsky 1983b).

Isomorphism to the
Summer Crisis

When asked at the start of World War I how all this could have happened, Bethmann Hollweg, the German chancellor, is said to have replied, "Oh, if I only knew" (Nomikos and North 1976, 7). Although this quote is often used in Germany to exculpate the German government from responsibility for the war's onset, there is a wider meaning to be found here. The joint occurrences of great power conflicts, on the one hand, and small power–great power conflicts, on the other, may be sufficiently complex so that few decision makers in a crisis could foresee the outcome. (Hereafter, the term small or smaller power will be used frequently as a generic category to include all countries—both central and minor—that are substantially smaller in power than the major powers. Although central or mid-range powers are by far the most likely to be involved in conflict with major powers leading to systemic war, once overt conflict has erupted for whatever reason, it is the *overlap* with solely great power disputes that is of importance, not the precise power status of the smaller country. It is also difficult to gauge the central or minor power status for actors in earlier systemic wars as in the instances of Corcyra and Potidae).

This is the first destabilizing consequence of the accumulation of disputes noted earlier. Individually, each of these sets of equilibrated disputes was manageable, but the simultaneous occurrence of both conflicts may have preoccupied decision makers with the one type to the point where they were unaware of the dangers of the other. For example, although Germany and Russia could resolve their fundamental differences without reference to third powers, the escalation of the Austro-Serbian dispute introduced an element of small power–great power conflict to which decision makers concerned solely with great power differences would most likely not lend much credence. It was this complexity of the overall system of conflict that may have led decision makers either to err or to grossly underestimate the consequences of the crisis at its outset. It probably led directly to the loss of control over events in the crisis noted by Snyder and Diesing (1977). In addition, the failure to realize that the small power–great power disputes had actually formed a discernible and dangerous pattern of conflict behavior also likely increased the propensity toward inadequate decision making in the crisis.

But there is a deeper sense in which the structure of the conflict process preceding the war conditioned the pattern by which the crisis unfolded. Recall that this instability is the result of the fusion or combination of sets of conflicts analyzed separately. If that fusion had not taken place, then the preceding analysis implies that each of the two conflict sets could have been resolved peacefully. Thus, *any decision or action that provided such unification can be cited as a principal contributor to the unstable outcome of international warfare.*

There is, in fact, one such decision that unified the two conflict sets: the famous blank check given to the Austro-Hungarian diplomats by the kaiser at the outset of the crisis that had been used so successfully in the prior Bosnian crisis of 1908. As noted earlier in this chapter, the preceding successful use of the blank check by Germany likely constituted a basis for the reinforcement of this type of behavior. The kaiser, in 1914, explicitly indicated his express support for any actions Austria-Hungary might contemplate against Serbia, including the possibility that the Serbs "be disposed of *and* that right *soon*" (quoted in Nomikos and North 1976, 37). This was intended as a reprimand for the German ambassador to Vienna, who was counseling restraint to the Austrians. As a result of this policy of complete support, the Austrians could be seriously emboldened in their policy toward

Serbia, with consequences that we now know. From the perspective of this study, however, this was not simply an invitation to boldness by Germany but the effecting of a juncture between two sets of disputes—those involving major powers exclusively and those that had central power (that is, Serbian) involvement as well.

It was Germany, of course, that tended to have the greatest number of disputes with other major powers, France, Russia, and Great Britain. Although Austria-Hungary also experienced conflict with Russia, the major share of its disputes were with the Balkan powers, such as Bulgaria, Serbia, and Turkey. Thus, the promise of complete support by Germany affected the union between predominantly major power disputes, such as those experienced by Germany, and disputes involving central powers that were the main preoccupation of Austria-Hungary. Without that juncture, the crisis could not have followed the pattern that did indeed evolve, and it likely would have had a peaceful outcome.

There is one further way to test this structural correspondence between precrisis conflict processes and crisis behavior. This can be done by examining a crisis similar in characteristics to that of 1914 but with a peaceful outcome: the Bosnian crisis of 1908 (Sabrosky 1975). Here, all of the initial protagonists are involved at the outset, with Russia supporting the strong Serb protest of the annexation of Bosnia-Herzegovina by Austria-Hungary, and Germany fully supporting the Austro-Hungarians. A blank check between Germany and Austria-Hungary is found here, too, and yet a war did not develop, the crisis ending peacefully. But if the structure of the conflict process is substantially different such that a conjunction between two sets of conflict events is *not* inherently unstable, then a blank check of this type would have little consequence. If the system resulting from the combination of the two forms of conflict is not an unstable system, then complete support of the type given to Austria-Hungary by Germany would have no major impact. Was such a system unstable at the time of the Bosnian Crisis?

The entire set of disputes (Table 3B, Tabular Appendix B) from 1893 until 1908 is analyzed. There is an excellent fit between observation and prediction, suggesting that a fundamental difference in the structure of conflict relationships existed between the time of the Bosnian crisis and the time of the summer crisis of 1914. Thus, despite the existence of a blank check in both instances, these differences in conflict behavior preceding both crises apparently led to the different outcomes.

Implications for the Study of Crisis

The first clear implication of this analysis is that structure does matter for the outcome of international crisis, but it does not necessarily mean that system structure as measured by alliances, polarity, or other forms of structural cohesion determines the outcome. Here, the structure of conflict relationships has been found to be important. By focusing on conflict relationships or, more specifically, the equilibrium or disequilibrium of the structure of conflict relationships, we can approach more closely the dynamics of the conflict process itself that will be resolved one way or another during the crisis period. This is not to say that the conflict structure is in any way deterministic, but simply that, given the instability of the set of conflict relationships, the probabilities are higher that war will be an outcome of the crisis.

The second implication is that surprise may be a less important component of the crisis than had been considered until now, at least in the World War I instance (Brecher 1980; Hermann 1972). This is simply because the juncture between the two conflict sets occurred very early in the crisis; in fact, it occurred on July 4–5, only one week after the crisis began. The remaining four weeks of the crisis may have been the consequence of working out the implications of that early decision and, indeed, the perceptual distortions—such as the excessive amount of hostility versus capability perceptions (Zinnes *et al.* 1961)—may actually have been a consequence not so much of the surprise element or excessive stress but of a self-justification or rationalization mechanism. After all, once the blank check had been issued and the two conflict sets joined, how else could one justify what may have been a hasty and unwarranted decision except by reference to perceptions of threat and hostility from the potential enemy? By perceiving the enemy as a monolithic hostile coalition, the decision to forge one's own coalition as an inseparable entity (the direct consequence of the blank check) becomes justified.

Seeing the opposing coalition as excessively hostile or "frustrating" in intent (Holsti, North, and Brody 1968) is attributing a nonrational set of motivations to the potential enemy and, therefore, that enemy would be much less amenable to rational discourse in negotiation. This is an almost ideal way to justify and rationalize one's own behaviors that, in the instance of strong support for Austria-Hungary's aggressive behaviors toward Serbia, have a high hostility component at the outset. This excessive perception of hostility by the Dual Alliance at the beginning of the crisis is mirrored by the fact that, in the first month of the crisis, there were 171 perceptions of hostility on the part of the Dual Alliance decision makers but only 40 for the Triple Entente (Holsti *et al.* 1968, 152). The tendency for the Dual Alliance decision makers to magnify or "overperceive" the actions of the Triple Entente countries (Holsti *et al.* 1968, 158) is consistent with this hypothetical justification of past hostile decisions. Only if the opponents are seen as truly acting in a hostile and vindictive fashion can such early hostile action be justified. Viewed from this perspective, the decision making during the crisis becomes an ex post facto process designed to provide justification for what had already occurred.

84

This interpretation of crisis dynamics provides a reasonably straight-forward explanation for the finding by Holsti (1972b, 67) that Germany, of all of the Dual Alliance and Triple Entente protagonists, had the highest number of perceptions of "necessity" for its own actions (110), even more than Austria-Hungary (80), which in many ways was the single major power originator of the crisis. In addition, the chi-square comparison between "necessity" and "choice" for "self" and "enemies" for Germany was by far the highest ($\chi^2 = 85.8$, $p < 0.001$) of any of the protagonists. Although Austria-Hungary reacted very strongly to the assassination, it still was in the nature of a reaction, whereas Germany made the early and, in many ways, self-conscious decision to support its ally fully. Thus, a decision of this kind would require more justification than a reactive one, and the concept of a necessity for action in the sense of being compelled in a certain direction would provide that justification.

At the same time, this is not to say that stress, time constraints, and perceptions of threat are not salient aspects of international crises (Holsti 1972b). Rather, the preceding analysis suggests that, just as there exists an interaction process among many decision makers in which these elements indeed are induced in the interactive process, there also can exist a priori rationalization processes that can augment these properties of crisis in order to justify past hostile behavior. Indeed, both processes are likely present, but it is the hostile behavior at the outset conditioning later responses that has received little, if any, systematic attention in the crisis literature.

Comparison with crises that had been resolved peacefully reveals the absence of such a juncture of conflict relationships. The explicit rejection by the Soviet Union of any influence by Castro in the Cuban missile crisis (Holsti, Brody, and North 1964; Holsti 1972a) had the consequence not only of removing a potentially erratic source of decision making but also of preventing the set of conflicts between the United States and other Latin American nations from intruding into the crisis. The then fairly recent U.S. influence in the removal of Jacobo Arbenz from leadership in Guatemala or the memory of other more overt interventions in Central America, such as that in Nicaragua, might have provided material for Cuban propaganda and possibly excited some anti-American feeling in the form of protests or demonstrations that could have diverted the attention of American decision makers from the goal of resolving the crisis peacefully. If the Soviet Union had allowed Castro a public opportunity to declare the crisis a joint Soviet–Cuban venture against "American imperialism," then the complexity of the crisis would have increased accordingly. In the "minicrises" between the United States and the Soviet Union at the end of both Middle East wars of 1967 and 1973, neither of the superpowers allowed their Middle East allies to influence policy unduly, thus preventing the joining of the regional conflict sets to the global ones (Brecher 1980, 225, 285).

Turning to our other systemic wars, in the Thirty Years' War we also find this overlap of two distinct types of disputes. The coming together of events in the west, particularly in the Low Countries with the expiration of the truce between the Netherlands and Spain in 1621, coincided with the ongoing revolt in Bohemia, which had begun only three years earlier. Indeed, the defeat of the Protestants at the Battle of the White Mountain in the autumn of 1620 occurred only months before the expiration of the truce between the Habsburgs and the Netherlands. The fact that the Habsburgs were in both places (Spain and Austria) is a structural condition of the war which lent not only a geographical dispersion and overlap but likely gave it a longer duration, with a consequent greater bloodletting, because of the weakening effect on a single actor exposed to these several ongoing engagements. In 1608, a Protestant Union of German Princes was formed, to be followed in 1609 by a Catholic League. War nearly erupted between the two alliances in 1614 in the crisis of the Jülich Succession, which was, in a sense, a precursor of the onset of the Thirty Years' War (Hayes, Baldwin, and Cole 1967; Pagès 1970).

The Peloponnesian War began with a structural nexus between the dispute between Corinth and Corcyra, on the one hand, and the conflict between Athens and Potidae, on the other. Corcyra had been a colony of Corinth but was now proposing to be allied with Athens after war broke out between Corinth and her former colony over control of Epidamnus. The Athenians accepted the alliance with Corcyra and they fought together against Corinth (Thucydides 1954).

In the second conflict, Potidae, although a colony of Corinth, was paying tribute to Athens. When the Potidaeans revolted against Athens, the Corinthians aided them. Corinth now sent delegations to Sparta to urge the Spartans to enter the conflict on her side. Thus, the Peloponnesian War began with overlapping disputes, much as in the case of the Thirty Years' War and World War I.

The structural nexus in the French Revolutionary Wars was not only the sister (Marie Antoinette) of the Austrian Emperor on the French throne at the time of the Revolution but the already ongoing revolution in the Austrian Netherlands (today Belgium) which threatened to make common cause with the French Revolution (Palmer 1971). This was in addition to the large number of aristocratic French emigrés, largely in Austria, who, now residing in proximity to the Austrian court, counseled war against revolutionary France.

Our instance of a structural general war (not systemic) also exhibits these structural overlappings. The War of Jenkins' Ear between Britain and Spain (largely a naval war), which began in 1738, quickly became a war between France and Britain as the result of the alliance between France and Spain and became a general war on the continent upon Frederick the Great's invasion of Silesia (Ritter 1968). This event touched off the War of the

Austrian Succession in 1740, which was to bring France to Prussia's aid and Britain to Austria's. The concern for Hanover, near to Prussia, by the Hanoverian British King was also to do much to bring Britain into the War of the Austrian Succession on the side of Austria against France and Prussia.

Confluence with Domestic Conflicts

These international disputes also overlapped considerably with domestic conflicts at the time of the outbreaks of the systemic wars. In the instance of World War I, we can detail the domestic condition with considerable accuracy by examining the distribution of legislative seats in both Austria-Hungary and Germany, especially in the former as the initial locus of aggressive activity toward Serbia, and even more particularly in the Austrian portion of the Dual Monarchy as the more influential and, as it happens, the more threatened domestically.

One can observe at least two important dimensions of conflict in Austria prior to World War I. The first concerns nothing less than the continued hegemony of the German-speaking population within imperial Austria as had persisted for several hundred years prior to the twentieth century. Probably the greatest shock to the German-speaking leadership occurred upon perceiving the results of the elections to the Reichsrath after the widening of the suffrage in 1907. Based on documented predictions of this legislature, we know that the German-speaking portion expected to retain approximately 45% of the seats (Beaumont 1907, 633), a 3% reduction from the 48% held as a result of the 1901 election, which was apparently acceptable. In actuality, the results of the election gave them 35%, a 13% reduction instead of the predicted 3%.

This scenario has additional implications in light of the entropy considerations raised theoretically at the outset of this volume. Maximum entropies in alliances or coalitions, based on relatively equal partners, create additional uncertainties which have greater conflict potential than minimum entropies associated with strong hierarchies. This conceptualization, which has been applied to international alliances, now can be applied to the domestic coalition problem.

A striking feature of the 45% (actually 45.15%; Beaumont 1907, 633) expected seats for the German-speaking population is that it just barely exceeds the limit set for achieving cabinet durabilities in multiparty systems along the lines of two-party systems. In other words, the highest realistically attainable durability (roughly equivalent to stability) of cabinet coalitions for multiparty systems is that attained by two-party systems, and the necessary value for first parties, calculated on the basis of theoretical entropy considerations pertaining to legislative distributions, is 44–45% (Midlarsky 1984a). The value *expected* by the Austrian legislators just barely exceeded this level, which would have insured stability for their (German-speaking) governance; in fact, it was missed by 10%.

It is not that the German-speaking cohort made the kind of mathematical calculation here that led to the 44–45% finding, but in keeping with the empirical foundations of that calculation made on the basis of already existing distributions, it is likely that their parliamentary experience led them to choose this value as an attainable assurance of continued dominance. This expectation, as we see, was violated to a considerable extent and, of course, had the additional consequence of raising the entropy of the overall distribution. (The greater the equality of proportional contributions of legislative seats, the greater the entropy).

In addition to this loss of hegemony and concomitant increased uncertainty which was perpetuated in the later 1911 election (Ogg 1913, 482–483), there was a second source of uncertainty and potential conflict. This was the dramatic rise of the Social Democrats from 2.8% of the seats in the previous (1901) election to 17.4% in 1907. This was an unexpected rise, a rise which was, to some extent, approached by their rivals, the Christian Socialists, a mostly reactionary party. But in 1911, this party, too, was defeated by the Social Democrats, especially in Vienna, where the latter raised their quota of deputies from 10 to 19, while the former was reduced from 20 to 4 (Ogg 1913, 483). Thus, the spectacular rise of the Social Democrats, with their egalitarian and antiaristocratic platform pertaining to virtually all important arenas within Austrian political life, was to further compound the uncertainty engendered by the loss of legislative hegemony by the German-speaking population.

In Germany, too, we see the spectacular rise of the Social Democrats from 13.4% at the time of the dissolution of the 1907 Reichstag to 27.7% at the election of 1912 (Ogg 1913, 237). Although Germany did not have the extraordinarily difficult nationalities problem of Austria-Hungary (at least not to the same extent), this parallel rise to power of the Social Democrats in the two close allies must have reinforced the sense of uncertainty and impending conflict experienced by both governments. Historians, such as Mayer (1967, 1969) and Kennedy (1980), have pointed to the domestic sources of international uncertainty and conflict in the time period prior to World War I. The preceding analysis gives it an analytically similar perspective to that adopted in the entropy-based international systemic sources of the war. Just as the Austro-Hungarian-German alliance was said to be a maximum entropy coalition because of the absence of a vast power disparity between the two signators, so, too, the increased entropy in the two legislatures reflecting the absence of clear dominance by any single social or political grouping constitutes a virtual domestic isomorph to the international condition. In addition, there exists the simultaneous overlap of three distinct conflict dimensions, two of them external—the great power and great power involving small powers—and the domestic.

In our other structural systemic wars, one can find similar confluences, although obviously not susceptible to being detailed to the same extent. Nevertheless, the parallels can be seen, at least in rough outline. It is clear that both the Thirty Years' War and French Revolutionary Wars found their beginnings in internal conflict which took the form of revolution. The French Revolutionary Wars, of course, followed immediately after the French Revolution itself, as did the Thirty Years' War after the Bohemian revolt.

It is less clear what the role of internal conflict was in the Peloponnesian War. Yet we know that Sparta always was in a precarious position vis-à-vis her helot (largely Messenian) population. Indeed, prior to the outbreak of the First Peloponnesian War in 460 B.C., there occurred a serious Messenian revolt (465–462 B.C.), which likely pointed to the Spartan vulnerability in that area, especially in light of the small number of Spartan males and the need for Athenian troops to help the Spartans put down the revolt (Ste. Croix 1972, 172–173). There exists a parallel here between the Spartan vulnerability of numbers, especially relative to these frequently rebelling subject populations [Ste. Croix (1972, 331) suggests a decline of 5,000 existing Spartan males to 1,000 between 479 and 371 B.C.], and the declining proportion of the German-speaking population in the Austro-Hungarian Empire relative to the remainder.

Of course, we cannot apportion precisely the responsibility for the outbreak of systemic war between internal and external conflict factors.[1] Here, I am merely noting the overlap between them, which incidentally does not occur to anywhere near the same extent in our one structural general war. The most that can be said is that Frederick the Great saw in the accession of the young Maria Theresa to the Austrian throne an opportunity for Prussian aggrandizement. Neither the basic organizational structure nor the power relations among major domestic societal groups was at issue, as in all our cases of structural systemic war. Here again, we see a distinction between the two types of war, not so much in extensity of participation by sovereign entities but in the depth to which the systemic conflict reaches into the bowels of domestic society.

Creating Disjoint Sets

The findings here and the preceding arguments have clear implications for crisis management. The prevention of the juncture between two or more sets of international disputes should be a principal goal of policy makers, as should awareness of the possible confluence of these disputes with domestic conflicts. Similarly, creating what may, in a formal sense, be called disjoint sets of conflict relationships should also be a goal of policy makers. These would be two or more sets of conflicts in which no conflict element would be found in more than one set. The probability of a widespread systemic war resulting from a crisis is likely proportional to the extent to which such sets are created. The desirability of this strategy may not only be true of policy in the midst of crisis but also may be a vehicle for overall conflict resolution. Henry Kissinger's Middle East policy of separating the Egyptian–Israeli conflict from the remainder of the Middle East controversies had the result not only of eventually yielding the peace treaty between the two countries but also of possibly preventing a future widespread war in the Middle East. Interestingly, Syrian support of the effort to destroy the Palestine Liberation Organization (PLO) as an independent political force may have had similar consequences, for the organized Palestinian armed conflict with Israel could now be controlled by Syria, thus creating to the north of Israel a single set of conflicts not joined to any others.

From this perspective, Soviet support of Cuban military activities in Africa had the opposite consequence, for it joined a regional set of African conflicts with Caribbean ones involving a great power—the United States—which potentially could have involved the Soviet Union itself in some crisis far removed from its borders as a result of this mixed and conjoint set of conflict relationships.

Conclusion

The analysis has demonstrated significant analytic differences between the nineteenth century pattern of conflict behavior, which did not lead to widespread war, and the early twentieth century pattern, which did. The finding of the presence of an overall equilibrium in conflict behavior in the former but not in the latter emerges from theories of international politics that emphasize equilibrium as a fundamental property of peaceful systems. Additionally, the absence of war as an outcome of the Bosnian crisis but its presence after Sarajevo can be understood as a consequence of the essential instability of the pre-1914 period compared to the relative stability of the pre-1908 period (it is likely that the domestic instability had not yet reached its full international impact) despite the presence, in both instances, of a juncture between two sets of conflict relationships. If the 1908 system had been equally unstable, then similar decision-making processes in both instances might have had the same outcome. Perhaps it was the increased strength of the Triple Entente relative to the Dual Alliance after 1908 (Sabrosky 1975) that led to an increased willingness on the part of the Entente partners to engage the Dual Alliance in various system-destabilizing conflicts prior to 1914.[2] Whatever its source, however, the 1914 system demonstrates an instability in conflict relationships not shared by its temporal predecessors.

These findings also shed a somewhat different light on the dynamics of the 1914 crisis. In addition to the consequences of interactions among decision makers, which have been studied carefully and at length, the outcome of the crisis also may have been strongly conditioned by the need for German decision makers to justify their early hostile behaviors in providing unconditional support for the proposed Austro-Hungarian action against Serbia. Later perceptions of hostility and the necessity for aggressive action may have been direct consequences of the need to justify the earlier decision.

There are clear implications of these findings for crisis management such that even if a system is unstable, decision-making procedures can minimize the probability of war as an outcome of crisis. Chief among these is the prevention of conjoint sets of conflict relationships or even, as a precrisis strategy, the creation of disjoint sets. In this fashion, instabilities can be localized such that widespread systemic war becomes much less likely.

Notes

1 This may be an important instance of the limitations of a structural approach. As Waltz (1986, 343) comments on the apportioning of causation in structural theories, "one cannot say for sure whether the structural or the unit-level cause is the stronger".

2 The major strengthening of the British navy occurred after 1908 with the passage of the Naval Bill in the following year. There may have been a curious and unfortunate coalescence of several events in 1908. The rise to power of the Young Turks and the consequent power interregnum (which likely invited the later aggressive actions of Italy and the Balkan countries), the Bosnian crisis with its potential for the later reinforcement of Germany's successful aggressive behavior in supporting Austria-Hungary against Russia, and the failure of the London Naval Conference to regulate conditions of naval warfare that led to the 1909 English Naval Bill all occurred in 1908. This suggests that 1908 be used as the year to date the onset of instability in this time period. However, there are insufficient data in the seven years from 1908 until 1914 to test this hypothesis. Further, the critical variable is the stability or instability evident at the end of a period rather than the choice of a year to begin it. What must be avoided is the inclusion of too many years preceding the onset of instability so that an essentially stable earlier period could mask the emergence of instability at a later point. Since this did not happen in the 1893–1914 analysis, the selection of the historically suggested year of the consummation of the Franco-Russian defensive alliance (end of 1893, beginning of 1894) in opposition to the Dual Alliance is an appropriate choice.

6

The Balance of Power, Preponderance, and the Onset of War in Polarized Settings

IN PROCEEDING THROUGH the various stages of the model developed in chapter 1, we now have arrived at the point of change in the balance of power as a progenitor of a polarized conflict system tending toward structural systemic war. We have seen how multipolarity as a form of international system structure yields inequalities which, via the consequent envies and intrigues as well as diminished resources vis-à-vis rivals, can yield alliance formation. The influence of memory in alliances, such as that between Austria-Hungary and Germany or between Athens and Corcyra, can generate the overlap in dispute sets which increases the probability of systemic war. In this chapter we will explore how a change in the balance of power between the opposing coalitions can precipitate such a war and at the same time develop a more systematic treatment of alliance memory which really has not received a terribly thorough examination as yet. As an approach to the consideration of these factors, we will treat an issue that has developed in the international relations literature.

One of the basic unresolved issues confronting the study of international conflict is the question of whether power parity or power preponderance leads to war. This issue has moved to the forefront of international conflict theory because of the centrality of one of the theories critically concerned with the debate, namely, that of the balance of power. According to one of its principal proponents (Morgenthau 1973) the balance of power is presumed to lead to peace, whereas according to one of its leading critics

(Organski 1968) it is likely to lead to war. On the other hand, power preponderance is presumed to lead to peace by Organski. It is the fundamental counterposition of these two perspectives which has framed the contours of this debate.

The importance of this issue derives not only from the dependent variable of concern, namely, the onset of international war, but also from the logic of the two theories. Both are eminently plausible. The notion that a balance or equilibrium between two states or coalitions will lead to peace certainly is reasonable. If both sides are apparently equal in power, then each side will presumably be satisfied with the arrangement. There will be no major efforts to outstrip the opponent in military production or some other manifestations of power. Equilibrium further connotes fairness or equity. Under these circumstances, intuitively we would expect that a balance between the opposing actors could persist.

Arguments in favor of preponderance have a similar ring of plausibility if not authenticity. If two powers are sufficiently remote from each other in power or force capability, there is a diminished likelihood of war. The more powerful nation will not be threatened by the much smaller actor, whereas the smaller power, for its part, will hesitate to initiate a serious conflict with the far more powerful country in recognition of the disastrous military consequences that could follow. The absence of threat, on the one hand, and the possibility of quick military defeat, on the other, likely would foster peace between these two nation-states.

Despite these eminently reasonable arguments for the validity of both theories yielding peace, various empirical studies taken together have confirmed neither approach. While Garnham (1976a,b), Weede (1976), and Organski and Kugler (1980) found in favor of power preponderance, Ferris (1973) and, with certain important qualifications having to do with alliance formation, Siverson and Tennefoss (1984) found in favor of the balance of power. Singer, Bremer, and Stuckey (1972) discovered that the balance of power led to peace in the nineteenth century, whereas preponderance had that consequence in the twentieth century. Bueno de Mesquita (1981a) found that neither formulation was true.

It is this problem or anomaly that frames the research questions to be asked and answered here. The first of these, of course, is that of the superiority of power preponderance or parity as a progenitor of peace. Interestingly, neither will be found to be superior but both will be associated with peace, while small departures from parity, or changes in the balance, will be associated with war. A skewed curvilinear function will be found to embody this finding and to fit the data. In order to arrive at this finding, however, we first require some conceptual clarifications. In the literature, the balance of power is treated both as a static condition (polarization or polarized condition) and as a dynamic process (alliance fluidity). Changes in the former but not the latter will be found to be associated with war. Indeed, the balance of power as a dynamic process will be associated with the prevention of systemic war. The distinction between the static and dynamic variables will find support in an interpretation of earlier findings by Singer *et al.* (1972).

A second step in the argument is to introduce the hierarchical equilibrium, which synthesizes elements of both power parity and power preponderance, and has as its major analytic properties the absence of memory and positive-sum games. The violation of these two properties in the form of memory retentions and the onset of zero-sum games will be shown to be associated with the onset of wars with memory which includes systemic war as a principal focus. The origins of World War I as a case in point will be treated analytically using this approach. The twin violations of the hierarchical equilibrium will yield the answer to the initial question of whether power parity or power preponderance is superior as a stabilizing condition. That answer will be found in the small departures from parity or balance that are associated with polarized international settings which lead to war.

This chapter, then, follows the following format. First, the balance of power as condition will be distinguished from the balance of power as process. The Singer *et al.* (1972) findings will be introduced in support of this distinction. Analytic properties of the hierarchical equilibrium theory of systemic war—absence of memory and presence of positive–sum games—will be used to trace a path to the onset of World War I. Violation of these two conditions and a clustering of wars with memory around a small change in the balance of power will be demonstrated in two data sets.

A policy-related consequence of the analysis is the ability to reflect on possible outcomes of major technical strategic breakthroughs, such as the Strategic Defense Initiative (SDI) proposed by the Reagan administration, armaments reductions, and the kind of repertoire of responses needed for crisis decision making in the modern period.

The Balance of Power
as Condition and as Process

Consider first a fundamental distinction between the balance of power as a static condition of international relations and as an ongoing dynamic process.[1] The former, generally, is associated with equilibrium or equality between individual powers or international coalitions (Haas 1953; Zinnes 1967). As E. B. Haas (1953, 448) puts it, "An imposing array of politicians and political scientists has urged that the term 'balance of power' means what it seems to imply to the uninitiated layman: an exact equilibrium of power between two or more contending parties." The balance of power as process, on the other hand, is an ongoing set of relationships subject to certain rules or regulations. Chief among these is the following requirement: "Permit defeated or constrained essential national actors to re-enter the system as acceptable role partners or act to bring some previously inessential actor within the essential actor classification. Treat all essential actors as acceptable role partners" (Kaplan 1957, 23).

This, effectively, is a requirement for the absence of alliance memory. The finding of the absence of alliance memory in nineteenth century European alliance systems (Midlarsky 1983a) emerges from earlier stochastic treatments of the randomness of alliance formation and partner choice (McGowan and Rood 1975; Job 1976; Li and Thompson 1978; Midlarsky 1981; and Duncan and Siverson 1982). All national actors are acceptable role partners regardless of past friendships or enmities. This postulate further implies that there can be random and even rapid turnovers in alliance partners, for the past friendship of an alliance partner is no indication of its future reliability in that role (the absence of memory requirement). Under certain conditions, this requirement is inconsistent with the balance of power as an international political condition, for the latter static condition can be satisfied with the same two coalitions persisting in a state of opposition for a fairly long period of time. As long as there exists a relative equality between the two alliances, then the condition of being in a state of balance is satisfied. However, such a stasis condition manifestly would not satisfy the balance of power as a process, for clearly an alliance which persists over a fairly long time interval has a core of memory, which, in fact, may make it less likely that the alliance will be broken in the future. The alliance between Austria-Hungary and Germany prior to World War I is a case in point.

The balance of power as a persistent, relatively unchanging condition can be tantamount to international polarization. To connote its static nature, I shall use the term polarized condition. If the two coalitions (for example, Dual Alliance, Triple Entente) confront each other for a fairly long period of time and, in addition, are coalitions which include virtually all major international actors, then this is exactly what is meant by polarization or a polarized condition. There exist two poles of international allegiance which differentially command the loyalties of all major actors. If these relatively equal coalitions, which stand in opposition to each other, include virtually all major actors, then the balance of power as a condition is entirely equivalent to a state of international polarization.

Here, we find a major confusion in the lexicon of international politics, for hardly anyone in the field of international relations would consider the balance of power to be ipso facto a progenitor of systemic war. Yet most scholars likely would consider a polarized condition to be a prime candidate for that dubious distinction. Nonetheless, we have just seen that under certain circumstances these two international conditions are entirely equivalent. It is perhaps this confusion in terminology which has laid the foundation for our failure to specify the precise consequences of the balance of power.

We ought to examine now the available alternatives when such a condition of balance or, more precisely, polarization under conditions of approximately equal power exists. Either the two coalitions can persist in their state of relative power equality or one can gain a power advantage over the other. Here, we see the advisability of the directive to maintain or keep the balance, for if the two approximately equal coalitions have persisted in the polarized state for a while, then the balance will perforce have been assumed to be the normal state of affairs. Any effort to seriously alter this condition or, alternatively, to take advantage of some fortuitous circumstance which leads to a distinct power advantage likely would be viewed as enormously destabilizing. The "normal" state of affairs will have been disrupted with very grave suspicions as to the motives of the newly advantaged coalition. Thus, when confronted with a major change in the balance that implies predominance for one side or the other, maintaining the balance would appear to be the decidedly preferred alternative. This, in fact, is what is generally borne in mind when the balance is advocated (Kissinger 1957). It is far preferable to maintain such a balance, even qua polarization, than to risk a sudden change in the balance of power which could lead to war initiation by the threatened coalition. Thus, even more than the balance of power as a form of polarization, *changes* in the balance carry with it a strong likelihood of systemic war.[2]

To fix ideas now, the balance of power as a *condition* of international relations is equivalent to polarization or a polarized condition. The balance of power as a *process* is the same as the fluidity of alliance association. Later, we will have occasion to examine polarized dyads in which the countries are at odds with each other for some period of time, in analogy with polarized coalitions, in which the alliances exist in that hostile state during some time interval.

World War I as a Case in Point

The onset of World War I as a systemic war conforms to this understanding. A balance of power as a condition existed for some time prior to the onset of the war.[3] Beginning in the early 1890s with the Franco-Russian Entente and continuing on into the first decade of the twentieth century, the balance of power was divided between the Triple Alliance of Austria-Hungary, Germany, and Italy versus the Triple Entente of Great Britain, France, and Russia. After the Italo-Turkish War of 1911–1912, Italy effectively left the Triple Alliance, leaving the Dual Alliance of Austria-Hungary and Germany to fight in World War I.

Although this condition of balance appeared to be precarious, it did, nevertheless survive the various crises of the late nineteenth and early twentieth centuries. The Moroccan crises, Algeciras, the Kruger telegram, and Berlin–Baghdad railway episodes all were weathered effectively by the European great powers. Indeed, according to Sir Edward Grey (1925), the British Foreign Minister in 1914, Europe had entered a period of genuine rapprochement among the great powers, chief among these being Great Britain and Germany, especially after the agreement between these powers concerning the Berlin–Baghdad railway which was signed, ironically, in June of 1914. In order to understand the outbreak of war, the balance of power itself as a polarized condition then, clearly is insufficient as a predictor of the war's onset. In order to understand this event we must look to changes in the balance of power immediately preceding 1914 and those that were threatened by the summer crisis itself. As Morgenthau put it,

> In the years immediately preceding the First World War, the balance of power in the Balkans increased in importance; for, since the Triple Alliance between Austria, Germany, and Italy seemed approximately to balance the Triple Entente between France, Russia, and Great Britain, the power combination that gained a decisive advantage in the Balkans might easily gain a decisive advantage in the over-all European balance of power. It was this fear that motivated Austria in July 1914 to try to settle its accounts with Serbia once and for all, and that induced Germany to support Austria unconditionally (Morgenthau and Thompson 1985, 212).

At the end of the Second Balkan War, in 1913, Serbia was twice its previous size in both territory and population. Although still small relative to Austria-Hungary, the implications of this doubling in size were profound for the future stability of the Austro-Hungarian Empire. The rapidly growing Slavic population in the Empire was increasingly restive at the absence of direct governmental representation in the reigning monarchy. Pan-Slavic propaganda emanating from both Russia and Serbia added a further element of instability for it implied that this population in the Empire, which was exceeding the other two in rate of growth, did not belong under the same political aegis as the Teutonic and Magyar peoples.

From the German point of view, the potential disintegration of the Empire, as did indeed occur in 1919, had profound geopolitical significance. First, Germany's only great power ally would cease to exist. Germany would then be virtually isolated in the international arena. Second, and perhaps even more important, there would be no great power ally of Germany on Russia's border to provide additional defense against the enormous Russian land forces. It was not so much that German decision makers were fearful of the quality of these forces but that their sheer numbers could threaten to overrun the Dual Alliance's eastern defenses unless there were some correspondingly large number of troops to oppose them; this, Austria-Hungary as a great power could provide. As a result, when the internal stability of the empire was threatened by the assassination of the Archduke Francis Ferdinand, heir to the throne of an aged and ailing monarch, by the hand of a pan-Slavist, Germany was fearful of a disintegration of her eastern defenses (Taylor 1971). This debility, of course, would be added to the already resurgent armies of France and Russia, who had both added significant new numbers of troops as the result of lengthened army service.

Even if the assassination did not spell instantaneous disintegration of the Dual Monarchy, the less-than-total support for Austria-Hungary in the summer crisis might mean her eventual loss to Germany. Already, at Algeciras in 1906, Austria-Hungary had shown less than complete solidarity with Germany to the point that the demonstration of German isolation even from her two principal allies, Austria-Hungary and Italy, was a principal outcome of the conference. After Italy's effective departure from the Triple Alliance shortly before the summer crisis, German isolation would have been complete if not for Austria-Hungary (Crankshaw 1963, 327).

Here is a change in the balance of power (qua polarization) which was undoubtedly disadvantageous to Germany. After the assassination, for the first time in her history, it appeared as if Germany would be seriously threatened by the potential loss of her only great power ally. It is this impending unfavorable change in the balance of power that we can pinpoint as the principal justification for Germany's blank check to Austria-Hungary to do as she wished with Serbia. The systematic studies of threat in the crisis (Zinnes *et al.* 1961; Midlarsky 1984b) support this interpretation of the crisis dynamics. The perceived threat and hostility to Germany now appeared so great as to justify even the most extreme measures of support to her weaker ally.

In another systemic war, the Thirty Years' War, we encounter a similar process (Pagès 1970; Polisensky 1971). The Peace of Augsburg in 1555 had divided Europe between Protestant (mostly Lutheran) and Catholic. This division persisted, but the rise of Calvinism, largely in Catholic areas, began to increase the religious divisions and tensions. This, in turn, led to the formation of the Protestant Union in 1608 followed by the Catholic League in 1609. These coalitions persisted until the Protestant revolt of 1618 in Bohemia threatened to result in the permanent loss of Bohemia to the Catholic cause. With a population of 3,000,000 (about that of England in the seventeenth century) and a strong economy, this loss would have amounted to a substantial change in the balance of power in favor of the Protestant states. [The phrase, "who holds Bohemia holds Central Europe" was attributed to Bismarck (Henderson 1940, 220).] It was this revolt in Bohemia, with its strong implications for change in the balance of power, that began the Thirty Years' War.[4]

In the onset of the Napoleonic Wars, Switzerland, then threatened by Napoleon, loomed very large as a gateway to the continent of Europe in addition to the deserved reputation her soldiers had for military quality. By adding Switzerland to his camp, Napoleon effectively was opening the gateway to all of Europe, including Italy and the various German states. The significance of Switzerland can be measured by the unwillingness of the English to give up Malta, key to the Mediterranean, as specified in the Treaty of Amiens, if the French were to retain the Swiss advantage.

The origins of World War II also follow this pattern of a change in the balance generally involving a smaller country, here two countries, Czechoslovakia and Poland. First, war was nearly precipitated over the Sudetenland in 1938 and was only prevented by appeasement at Munich along the lines of the Treaty of Amiens. Then, one year later war did, in fact, occur over the issue of Poland. Czechoslovakia, or at least its Bohemian portion, looms very large in two of our systemic wars.

Both Czechoslovakia and Poland were not merely central powers of some significance geographically and economically but also had demonstrated military significance during World War I. The Czech Legion, consisting of freed prisoners of the Austro-Hungarian army in Russia and armed by the British, was, early in the Russian civil war, the only truly effective fighting force in Siberia opposed to the Bolsheviks (Pipes 1957). In 1938, the Czechoslovak army was well trained, well equipped, and fully prepared to fight if any support had been forthcoming from the British and French. Similarly, the Poles had demonstrated considerable prowess in inflicting a defeat on the Soviet forces in 1920 upon their invasion of Poland. In a real sense, the Poles may have been overrated militarily as a result of this success, as later events in 1939 were to demonstrate. However, there was no way to determine this prior to the onset of the war.

In the Peloponnesian War, the adherence of Corcyra to the Delian League coupled with the investment and impending fall of Potidaea to the Athenians suggested a strong change in the balance of power favoring Athens versus the Peloponnesians.

The War of the Spanish Succession proceeded from a deep concern over the consequences of the impending union between France and Spain. A Bourbon on the Spanish throne might indeed imply that "the Pyrenees no longer exist," as the Spanish ambassador to Versailles put it (Hayes 1932, 309), and that Spanish power, then considered still formidable, would thoroughly upset the European balance in favor of the Franco-Spanish union.

In the French Revolutionary Wars, the revolution in the Austrian Netherlands (today Belgium) was of deep concern to Austria and did much to occasion her entry against revolutionary France, which might be strengthened by this new revolutionary entity on her borders. Indeed, the Austrian Netherlands had been a traditional locus of conflict between Austria and France at least since the War of the Spanish Succession.

Similarly, in a general war, we find in Frederick the Great's invasion of Silesia, a wealthy and, for that time period, industrialized portion of the Austrian Empire, a change in the balance of power far too favorable to Prussia. The War of the Austrian Succession was immediately precipitated, to be succeeded by the bloodier Seven Years' War which resulted from the coalition building against Prussia during the eight intervening years between the two wars. Prussia's retention of this territory after the War of the Austrian Succession was to prove far too favorable a change in the balance vis-à-vis Austria and, ultimately, France and Russia.

An Interpretation of Earlier Findings

Does the available systematic evidence support this interpretation that the balance of power as (polarized) condition is associated with war, and especially systemic war after a change in the balance as in the twentieth century, but that the balance of power as (fluid) process is associated with peace as in the nineteenth century? There exists at least one comprehensive study which does indeed provide such support. Singer *et al.* (1972) studied the effect of power concentration (CON) on the nation-months of war in the international system between 1820 and 1965 and found that power parity was associated with peace in the nineteenth century but with war in the twentieth century. Of the major studies of power parity or preponderance noted earlier, this is the only one which measures war in nation-months with at least one major power participant in the war. Clearly, nation-months as a variable, in contrast, say, to the onset of war, taps the dimensions of systemic war, for the larger the number of nations and the longer the conflict, the greater the approach to a systemic conflict or, at least, one occurring within a polarized international setting.

Once viewed in this light, then, these findings begin to be immediately interpretable, for the twentieth century with two systemic wars is instantly distinguishable from the nineteenth with no such wars. The nation-months data, in fact, reveal a fairly even quality to the war experience of the half decades of the nineteenth century but an uneven quality as to the twentieth century with World Wars I and II predominating in the nation-months of war for the half decades beginning in 1913 and 1938 (Singer *et al.* 1972, 29).

Most important is the role of the variable "change in power concentration." Whereas the change in the concentration of power correlated at $r = -0.41$ with nation-months of war in the twentieth century, the variable

100

concentration itself correlated at $r = -0.23$. (The signs are negative because declining concentration values are associated with increasing nation-months of war.) This is an exact reversal from the nineteenth century, wherein change in the concentration of power correlated at $r = 0.19$ and concentration itself at $r = 0.81$ with nation-months of war; here, a positive association was found between concentration or hierarchy and increasing nation-months of war. Thus, preponderance is associated with war in the nineteenth century but with peace in the twentieth century. A multivariate analysis supported the importance of changes in concentration for the twentieth but not for the nineteenth century, with concentration itself being far more important in the nineteenth than in the twentieth centuries with the same sign reversals. Indeed, a multiplicative model including change in concentration showed that this variable was able to explain 46% of the variance in nation-months of war in the twentieth century, which is by far the strongest of any of the predictors in this century.[5] Concentration alone still was strongest for the nineteenth century, with 72% of the variance explained, but, of course, in the opposite direction.

Thus, for the predominance of systemic war in the twentieth century, change in concentration is the most potent predictor. In the absence of this type of war, concentration itself was most important in the nineteenth century, but in the opposite direction. Translated into the vocabulary of this study, this means that change in the balance of power as a condition (or a polarized condition) is most strongly associated with systemic war (nation-months in the twentieth century), but that the balance of power as a process implying a fluid parity is most strongly correlated with peace (nineteenth century). Fluidity of association is, of course, a property of the balance of power as process in the nineteenth century which is absent from the balance of power as a condition in the twentieth century period examined here.

These findings now can be seen as a strong confirmation of one version of balance-of-power theory, wherein parity is associated with peace and, especially, the absence of systemic war, but only under conditions of fluidity of association. This was lost in the twentieth century, largely due to the rise of nationalism and mass society and the consequent inability of leaders to sever alliances and make new ones at will. Under the balance of power as a condition, and small departures from it, systemic war becomes more probable; in particular, changes in concentration which bode ill for one or another of the protagonists are most clearly associated with the onset of systemic war. These latter findings are consistent with the distinction between *condition* and *process* and the general theoretical framework offered here.

Thus far, we have understood the origins of the systemic war as rooted in the approach to the balance of power as a polarized condition. This we have seen operative in the various systemic wars, with special emphasis on the modern period. A principal question to be asked is how the system moved from the balance of power as process in the nineteenth century, with its fluidity of association, to the balance of power as a condition and progenitor of war early in this century. The hierarchical equilibrium, with its properties of absence of memory and positive-sum games, will be used to inform our understanding of this process. Subsequently, the transition to war from the polarized condition will be examined systematically. In so doing, the issue of parity versus preponderance will be addressed by means of a formal model.

A Formal Model

The hierarchical equilibrium, as we have seen, embodies the principles of absence of alliance memory (although not necessarily of individual country memories) and positive-sum games. It was confirmed empirically for the nineteenth century conflict system and for the post-World War II period when, obviously, no such systemic wars occurred (see chapter 2) using the Militarized International Dispute Data (Gochman and Maoz 1984) and a set of stochastic equations implied by the hierarchical equilibrium model. The model was obeyed in the periods 1816–1899 and 1946–1964 but not in the years immediately preceding World War I and during the interwar period.

More generally, memory here refers to the tendency for past conflicts to be institutionalized in the country's contemporary foreign policy decision making. This particular concept of memory does not rely on the recollections of earlier conflicts by particular individual decision makers (although other perspectives certainly do) but on structural constraints, generally but not always, of a geopolitical nature. For example, the Austro-Hungarian conflicts with several Balkan countries derived from the gradual breakup of the Ottoman Empire on Austria-Hungary's borders over a long period of time and the consequent emergence of these independent powers to be repeatedly fought over as satellites or allies. The existence of an irredentist claim on the borders of a country, as in the French desire to regain Alsace-Lorraine in 1914, is another illustration of memory. Royal houses with members in common among two or more countries also constitute a constraint which can function as a memory. The death of Marie Antoinette, the French Queen but also the sister of the Austrian Emperor, constituted a particularly egregious memory of the Austrian monarchy and a goad to the onset of war with revolutionary France.

In technical terms, the absence of memory implies the existence of a Markovian process in which only the present state of the system influences the next state. Geopolitical circumstances, which clearly persist over time, or familial connections, which can last generations, violate this notion of the absence of memory. In treating two or more states now, a dyadic memory exists when only two states are involved, an *N*-adic memory exists when there are more than two but with no significant political interdependencies among them, and an alliance memory exists when the particular memories of an ally become those of another power as the result of a firm alliance commitment.

It is the memory of past friendships and enmities built into alliance formation combined with the onset of zero-sum processes that is suggested to lead to systemic war. In symbols we can say that

$$P(W_s) = f(M, Z) \qquad [6.1]$$

where $P(W_s)$ is equal to the probability of systemic war, M is the extent of memory (*N*-adic and alliance), and Z is the onset of zero-sum processes. It remains now to define the relationship more precisely. It is suggested that it is the simultaneous presence of both factors which yields a systemic war specifically via the balance of power as a constant-sum condition, C_s, which then, upon some actual or impending change in the balance, yields the zero-sum state. Thus,

$$(M \times C_s) \rightarrow \textit{(balance of power condition)} \qquad [6.2]$$
$$\Delta\textit{(balance of power condition)} \rightarrow (M \times Z) \rightarrow P(W_s) \qquad [6.3]$$

The balance of power as a condition arises from the tendency to limit the flexibility of alliance formation as the result of memory processes, along with the simultaneous tendency for virtually all major actors to be associated with one or another of the polarized coalitions. It is the change in the balance-of-power condition (impending or having recently occurred) which then can lead to general or systemic wars. The arrows between variables are to be read as "increases the probability of" and in no way are intended to be deterministic.

By analogy, a similar but not identical set of equations can be written for the polarized dyad or any other polarized international setting short of the systemic conflict. Here, the theory is being extended to the nonsystemic war which occurs in a polarized setting. In symbols here, the probability of war (nonsystemic) as a consequence of polarization, $P(w_m)$, also is a function of memory (*m*) but not of the alliance-related variety. Nor does it have to be *N*-adic. Zero-sum processes also can be entered into by the dyad as the result of some internal change, as in a technological breakthrough or addition of military units. Here, the zero-sum process is not the same as in the systemic case for, as argued previously, the degree of balance or parity is very close in the polarization process leading to systemic war. This is because of the lengthy polarization time and balance mechanisms, both of an external (alliance process) and internal nature. The constant-sum process, therefore, in the systemic case entails a fair degree of equality between the two coalitions. Any change, then, leading to the zero-sum process and, equivalently, a change in the balance of power will likely be some very large percentage of the existing power disparity between the two sides or at least larger than, say, in the dyadic case. This is because the balancing mechanisms are fewer in the latter instance, thus leading to less "fine tuning" in the dyadic case. The smaller impact of a zero-sum change in the nonsystemic condition leads once again to the use of the lowercase, in this instance the letter z. The fact that there are fewer possibilities for change in the nonsystemic war necessitates a statement of lesser probability of some change and the use of a dashed arrow. Thus

$$P(w_m) = f(m, z) \qquad [6.4]$$
$$(m \times c) -----> (balance\ of\ power\ condition) \qquad [6.5]$$
$$\Delta(balance\ of\ power\ condition) ------> (m \times z) ------> P(w_m)$$
$$[6.6]$$

The Partitioning of Conflicts

Essentially, the processes approaching the onset of wars with memory can be explored in a fairly straightforward fashion. The simultaneous occurrence of various memory and game–theoretic conditions can be represented in a bivariate table (Table 6.1). Elements of the theory are now being extended analytically. The "zero point" for memory should be its absence as in a classic balance-of-power process in which past enmities and friendships are irrelevant to current situations. From here one can successively introduce the memory of a dyad, as in the influence of a past war, or several simultaneous memories, as in an N-adic condition. Finally, an ongoing alliance memory can be introduced in addition to the N-adic memories.

The game-theoretic circumstance proceeds similarly in incremental fashion. Positive-sum games, in which two or more powers or coalitions benefit, can become constant-sum games, in which there are no gains and no losses, to be followed by the zero-sum game, in which one side gains at the other's expense. A special case is the negative-sum condition, in which there are no winners and no losers. In the context of international warfare this is somewhat exceptional for, by definition, someone wins in such an encounter. Nonetheless, in the context of potential for nuclear war, this will prove to be important; however, one should keep in mind its tentative nature. Effectively then, on the horizontal axis "resources" are subtracted to achieve finally a negative-sum condition and, on the vertical, memory is expanded to include additional actors with memories of past grievances and structural configurations which involve these actors. A move horizontally to the right increases the likelihood of war and, if such a war occurs, a

Table 6.1

Partitioning of conflicts by memory and game process.

Memory	Game process[a,b]			
	Positive sum	Constant sum	Zero sum	Negative sum[c]
Absence of memory	Balance-of-power process plus hierarchical equilibrium (nineteenth century Europe prior to the unifications of Italy and Germany)	Balance-of-power process (Bismarckian diplomacy)	Territorial war; [Central American War (1885); Chaco War (1932–1935)]	Territorial war after widespread diffusion of nuclear weapons
Dyadic memory	Hierarchical equilibrium (post-World War II bipolarity, especially after the emergence of new nations)	Current relations between USSR–China, Egypt–Israel, China–Vietnam	Russo-Turkish War (1877–1878)	War potential of a Cuban missile crisis; potential destabilization of SDI
N-adic memory	Polish partitions of the late eighteenth century	Post-Westphalia (1648) period	War of the Spanish Succession (1702–1713); Napoleonic Wars (1803–1815); World War II	Middle East War after nuclear weapons diffusion
Alliance memory	Balance-of-power condition beginning with firm Austro-German alliance and failure of the Reinsurance Treaty with Russia (colonialism of late nineteenth century)	Balance-of-power condition in the early twentieth century; no rampant colonialism but crises in confrontations between great powers in colonial contexts (for example, Moroccan crises, Algeciras)	Thirty Years War; World War I	Crisis-induced World War III between East and West generally involving smaller ally in the initial phases

[a]Moving from left to right increases the likelihood of war.

[b]If war occurs, moving from top to bottom indicates increasing likelihood of systemic involvement.

[c]All entries in this column are hypothetical in nature.

downward vertical move increases the likelihood that it will be a systemic war. The historical entries in the table are not to be seen as "absolutes" but only as illustrations of a particular combination of memory and game process. Other instances also could be found for the various categories.

In the first cell, the balance of power as a fluid process connotes the absence of memory. In addition, the positive-sum process of unaffiliated small powers available for alliance yields a hierarchical equilibrium if the larger powers also have small power allies, which they almost always did in this period. Thus, we have a picture of (1) two or more coalitions between large and small powers and (2) a fairly sizable number of independent small powers (unique to the hierarchical equilibrium) in which the large powers are free to ally with whomever they choose. There are two sources of the absence of memory here: the balance-of-power process, in which there are no restrictions on the alliance process among major powers, and the individual hierarchy itself, which disallows the possibility of the very small powers seriously influencing the larger one and, thus, pulling the larger one into war. Much of the nineteenth century prior to the unifications of Germany and Italy conformed to the model of alternating alliances and hierarchies between large and very small powers in Central Europe and Italy (for example, Bavaria, Baden, Tuscany, Parma, Modena).

In the second cell in the first column, the fluidity of the great powers is removed and there can exist a dyadic hostility, but the hierarchies between great and small powers and the large number of small powers are preserved. This is the hierarchical equilibrium configuration without the fluidity of association between the great powers themselves. The post-World War II period conforms to this image, with large coalitions between great and small powers, the ongoing grievances between the great powers themselves, and a large number of unaffiliated small powers.

The third cell of the first column yields the somewhat unusual condition of an N-adic memory in a positive-sum situation in which, as an illustration, the former combatants in the Seven Years War ending in 1763, Prussia and Russia along with Austria, partitioned Poland three times between 1772 and 1795. Here, the positive-sum process of all gaining simultaneously is made possible only by the availability of a weaker power which can be partitioned. The latent hostilities or memories from the Seven Years' War and new issues arising in relation to the Ottoman Empire made the positive-sum process, although perverse, nevertheless essential to the maintenance of peace in Europe (Hötzsch 1909).

Finally, in the fourth cell of the first column, the balance-of-power condition emerges with N-adic memories manifested now in alliances largely among equals. Generally, it is two such alliances which exist as in the Triple Alliance and Triple Entente. It was the positive-sum process of late nineteenth century and early twentieth century colonialism, especially in

Africa, that likely prevented any major changes in the balance of power as a condition which could have led to systemic war.

Taking the cells one at a time in the second column, the restriction to a constant-sum process removes the many small powers or colonies (1) available for addition to one or another coalition or (2) to be fought over. Here, only the alternations in alliances without the past friendships or enmities are important. The period between the formation of the German Empire and the rapid colonization of Africa beginning in the mid-1880s conforms to this model. There were no smaller powers in Europe and rapid colonization by all the powers had not yet begun (Taylor 1971). The shifting and simultaneous alliances of this period, especially masterminded by Bismarck, provide an instance of the balance of power as a process with no excessive reliance on any single power and without the positive-sum process including the smaller powers.

Instances of dyadic memory abound in which there are no changes in territory, thus yielding a constant-sum condition, but the condition of some hostility remains. An illustration is provided by current relations between Egypt and Israel after the signing of the peace treaty in 1979, especially the controversies over small pieces of territory but, as yet, no military engagements. *N*-adic memory of a constant-sum nature likely was achieved in the immediate post-Westphalia period wherein the memories of the Protestant–Catholic wars were rife but no serious efforts were made to undermine the general peace.

In the last cell of this column, we find the stasis of the polarized balance-of-power condition. The alliance structure has been formed as a political manifestation of the international memory and there is little, if any, change in this structure one way or another. The early twentieth century prior to World War I is a case in point. The Dual Alliance and Triple Entente were formed and neither side experienced any change in the acquisition of territory or the like. A constant-sum process was maintained or, more accurately in this instance, a condition of stasis, for there was virtually no change to speak of in the alliance structures. As Crankshaw (1963, 371) put it, there was a "strange paralysis" to the diplomacy of this period. The only important change would appear external to the two major alliances—in the Balkans and in the threat now emanating from an enlarged Serbia.

The third column details the entry into zero-sum activity. Here we see the quick move on the part of one nation or another to implement a territorial grab. This can occur without any substantial prior history of conflicting territorial claims which led to war; the Central American War of 1885 is an example of this type. These wars ordinarily are of short duration and of little consequence except, of course, for the protagonists themselves. The Chaco War between Bolivia and Paraguay may be another case in point. Farther down the column is the dyadic memory which can result in war. The Russo-Turkish War of 1877–1878 is an example, for it was the memories of victories and defeats in earlier wars, especially of the nineteenth century, which fueled the onset of this conflict.

The *N*-adic memory, for the first time, brings us to a species of general or systemic war, namely, the mobilization war. Here we have the simultaneous occurrences of zero-sum processes and *N*-adic memories. An excellent case in point is the War of the Spanish Succession (1702–1713) after the memories of the previous wars of Louis XIV, namely, the War of Devolution, the Dutch War, and the War of the League of Augsburg. The zero-sum condition of Spain effectively becoming fused as one with France and not available to traditional allies such as Austria was intolerable to the remainder of Europe. Similarly, the Napoleonic Wars arose from the bitter memories of the preceding French Revolutionary Wars and the zero-sum aspects of Napoleon's incursions into Switzerland, Holland, and Italy. World War II—with its many memories of hostilities during and after World War I and with the zero–sum acquisitions of Austria, Czechoslovakia, and, finally, the largest country in Eastern Europe, Poland, by Germany—also is a good case in point.

In the lowest cell of the table, we now have the structural systemic war arising now not from many separate dyadic conflicts, as in the preceding cell, but from a structural joining of several protagonists and their principal conflicts.[6] Here, for example, the Spanish Habsburgs, already in a state of conflict with Protestant Holland, join the Austrian Habsburgs in the quelling of the Bohemian Protestant revolt. The presence of the same ruling house in the two staunchest supporters of Catholicism lent the initial strong structural element to this war in addition to the Protestant Union and Catholic League. At least two alliance memories were operative in the joining of one country's (Spain's) conflict memories to another's (Austria's) contemporary active conflicts. The threatened "Protestantizing" of Bohemia was, of course, an intolerable zero-sum loss to the Habsburgs. In the case of World War I, we not only have the Dual Alliance and Triple Entente as by now relatively long-term structural coalitions but the existence of a strong alliance memory. The past Balkan conflicts of Austria-Hungary, especially with Serbia, constituted a memory of conflicts which were to bind Germany irrevocably to the onset of World War I, as Austria-Hungary plunged deeper into the Balkan morass. As argued previously, in each of these instances the change in the balance of power was perceived to be substantial and war was begun.

The last column is perhaps the most interesting, for it has the fewest empirical referents yet may be most salient for our collective future. Here, both sides must lose in any conflict arising under these circumstances. Clearly, the obvious referent is the possession of nuclear weapons by both sides of any controversy. Only in the second and fourth cells do we have a clear notion of what a likely confrontation will entail. In the second cell, the Cuban missile crisis of 1962 is a noteworthy illustration. The possibility of a negative-sum outcome, that is, nuclear war, had arisen after the dyadic nuclear arms race (a salient memory form) led to the circumstances of 1962. Here, a constant-sum condition of approximate parity in nuclear armaments gave way to a zero-sum condition of a strategic missile gap very much in favor of the United States. Indeed, so extreme was the disparity that the decision to place missiles in Cuba, with all of its dangers, was taken by the Soviet Presidium as a way of redressing the strategic imbalance (Allison 1971, 54–55). It was the potential negative-sum outcome that ultimately led to withdrawal of the missiles and a return to the more manageable zero-sum and, ultimately, constant-sum conditions.

Here for the first time, one party's gain and another's loss is defined in terms of armaments instead of the traditional territorial or alliance adherence. This points to the importance of memories and zero- or negative-sum processes not only on one salient dimension but on several. In the technologically oriented era in which we find ourselves, this becomes especially important. Thus, a quantitative or qualitative breakthrough in the arms race can yield a zero-sum condition in vulnerability for one or the other side which can be just as destabilizing as a major loss in territory or the loss of an ally.

In this regard, the current SDI can serve the same function as a missile gap or the threatened disintegration of an ally, as in World War I. The perception of vulnerability in the near future by the disadvantaged power can be dramatically increased, with a consequent increased likelihood of entry into the negative-sum process of a nuclear exchange as a way of forestalling an even greater potential destruction in the future by the power that will soon enjoy the invulnerability of a successful SDI.

The fourth cell represents the more "traditional" fear of a nuclear war beginning as the consequence of some regional crisis escalating into a confrontation between the superpowers. Each of them comes to the support of its threatened smaller ally, thus initiating the potential nuclear crisis.

The first cell in this column can be taken to represent a hypothetical universe in which all powers have the capability to destroy one another but have no specific conflict memories. More realistic is the third cell, which envisions the spread of nuclear weapons throughout a region, such as the Middle East, with its numerous *N*-adic conflict memories.

From Fluidity to Polarization

This completes the partitioning of conflicts based on simultaneity of occurrence of these two principal variables. There remains now the discussion of process for, since each of the variables is categorized incrementally along the horizontal and vertical, one can examine the likely consequence of moving one cell at a time in any given direction. Put another way, we will now be exploring the transition from the balance of power as process to that of condition, or as Liddell Hart (1930, 17) remarked on the situation in Europe after 1907, "The new grouping of Europe was not the old balance of power but merely a barrier between powers."

Note that the first cell representing the absence of memory and positive-sum games is virtually at the opposite end of the matrix from the onset of structural wars such as World War I or the Thirty Years' War. Is it possible to trace a path, say, to World War I from the balance-of-power and hierarchical equilibrium processes at the upper left through various stages to the lower right?

First, the number of small independent nations decreased, thus violating a basic tenet of the hierarchical equilibrium. This occurred after the unifications of Italy and Germany and is expressed in a move to the right from the first cell of the first column to the first cell of the second column. Subsequent to the suitability of any power to be a potential ally in the Bismarckian period, this tendency to ally with virtually any country became very restrictive toward the end of the century with the failure to renew the Reinsurance Treaty between Germany and Russia.

By the mid-1880s only colonialism existed as an option for positive-sum processes, mainly in Africa. The rise of this accelerated colonial process can be interpreted as an effort to restore the positive-sum process of the earlier era, especially now with the more restricted alliance potential. By the end of the century even that was foreclosed by the dearth of available territories to colonize. These transitions are shown in the move diagonally to the first and second cells of the bottom row of the table. At this point the Z-shaped process moves horizontally into a constant-sum column with both major coalitions already formed; the balance-of-power condition now obtains under constant-sum circumstances. Only the move into the zero-sum category with the rise of Serbia and the subsequent assassination would remain.

The overall theoretical treatment here has a particularly interesting confluence with that of Arnold Toynbee (1946) on the disintegrations of civilizations, which, of course, can and frequently do entail the onset of systemic war. Civilizations disintegrate as there appear societal schisms in which (1) a dominant minority declines in power, (2) an internal proletariat increases in number and power, and (3) an external proletariat also experiences a power increase (Toynbee 1946, 582–583). The definition of proletariat here is extremely broad and includes those who feel themselves "'in' but not 'of' the society" (Toynbee 1946, 583).

Clearly, the disintegration of the Austro-Hungarian Empire around the turn of the century as an old but decaying society fits this model. The Austrian ruling minority was barely 25% (23.6%) of the total population of 50.88 million (Crankshaw 1963, 422) and the rate of growth of the Slavic population ("internal proletariat") was greater than that of the Austrian. The "external proletariat" of slavophils in Serbia and elsewhere in Southeast Europe also was growing, not only in population but in dedication to the new nationalism.

The characteristics of a declining civilization identified by Toynbee also have strong implications for a change in the balance of power as a condition. As argued earlier, if the two contending forces have existed in a stable condition of balance for a while, then any serious change in the balance could precipitate war; the massive decline of a bulwark of one of the two coalitions is undeniably a candidate for such change.

The actual or potential disintegration of a society in connection with the origin of systemic war brings up the possibility of an obverse process. If the disintegration of a country can bring on a structural war, then the buildup of a neighboring and contending power can have similar consequences. In two instances of structural wars, the "external proletariat" essentially was busy with state building, both in the case of Serbia, which doubled in size after the Second Balkan War, and in Bohemia, which established a Protestant leadership largely independent of the Austrian Empire.

A focus on state building also can help understand the origins of other systemic or general wars. The War of the Austrian Succession began as part of Frederick the Great's state building of Prussia. He especially wanted to connect the scattered territorial holdings of the Hohenzollern dynasty and the "grab" for Silesia was one such effort touching off this war. The Seven Years' War in Central Europe was an almost immediate consequence of the dissatisfaction with Prussia's gains in the War of the Austrian Succession and Frederick the Great's determination to hold or perhaps even expand these holdings. The Napoleonic Wars and World War II occurred after the completion of various state building efforts by France and Germany, respectively. Later, these considerations will be important within a formal model of the onset of war.

It is possible to understand elements of the table and especially the Z process leading to World War I as resulting from substitutability phenomena (Most and Starr 1984). The diagonal transition from the second cell of the first row to the first cell of the last row may be seen in this light. The colonial process of the late 1880s until the end of the century was likely a search for substitutes for the earlier fluidity of the alliance process and the presence of small powers on the European continent. Certainly, at least in A. J. P. Taylor's view (1971, 344), this colonial process was a substitute for the conflict that would inevitably have been enacted on the continent of Europe, especially by France, if not for this process of "exporting" the conflict behavior away from that continent.

An earlier process of this type occurred after the end of the Seven Years' War in 1763 when three of the former antagonists, still dissatisfied over certain of the outcomes of that war (as after the later Franco-Prussian War), transported the conflict in an easterly direction in the creation of an earlier version of a positive-sum game in the Polish partitions of the late eighteenth century. In the creation of a positive-sum game on the remains of a formerly sovereign entity, these partitions, away from the center of conflict activity in

Europe, presaged the coming of more extensive processes of this type in Africa and Asia at the end of the following century. A historian, Hötzsch (1909, 668), saw the Polish partitions as preventing the onset of another great European war.

Tests of Change in the
Balance of Power

For polarized coalitions or hostile-country dyads as in the second column of Table 6.1, rows 2 through 4, a change in the balance of power is most likely to be associated with the onset of war. The balance initially does not have to be manifested in absolute power equality but in some state of power distribution which is moderately acceptable to both sides, most likely in the vicinity of the parity condition. However, if the steady-state balance is based on some power inequality more-or-less acceptable to both sides, then any change either toward or further away from equality could be destabilizing, (for example, the growing American missile preponderance just before the Cuban missile crisis); similarly, any departure from a state of balance as equality also could be destabilizing).

There exists one way to test the hypothesis of change in the balance of power as a progenitor of war expressed in the transition from the second to the third columns of Table 6.1. This test also will reflect on the debate concerning whether power parity or preponderance is a condition of peace. As it turns out, both conditions will be associated with a more pacific state while a change in the balance of power as a condition will be associated with a greater likelihood of war.

General Power Disparities

In order to first test the hypothesis of change in the balance, we require data on the incidence of wars and power differences between nation-states and coalitions. Ferris (1973) analyzed all of the types of war indicated in the third column of the table and, in addition, constructed power ratios for the participants. The theory embodied in Table 6.1 predicts that war should be more likely under conditions of a change in the balance of power and, in particular, that systemic wars should originate in this manner.

Because of the specification of the balance of power as a condition, or polarization in the second column prior to the onset of war, it will not do to examine all possible changes in the balance of power among all countries, including those not hostile to each other, for the second column specifies an already polarized or, in the case of only two countries, an already hostile relationship. Therefore, in the absence of data on which are hostile relationships and which are not (for example, United States–Canada) we will focus on wars that already occurred as overt expressions of hostility. The power conditions under which the wars occurred then can be examined. If the framework here is accurate, the greatest frequency of war should be found upon some change in the balance of power (1) around the vicinity of power balance or parity and (2) within a short time interval prior to the war's onset. Later, we shall have occasion to introduce explicit comparisons between various power conditions and the absence of war.

The first of these questions can be answered by examining the distribution of wars over differences in power disparity or concentration. Small departures from power parity should be overrepresented in such a distribution, for the small changes in the balance should be most likely to result in war. This distribution is plotted in Figure 6.1, with four points aggregated

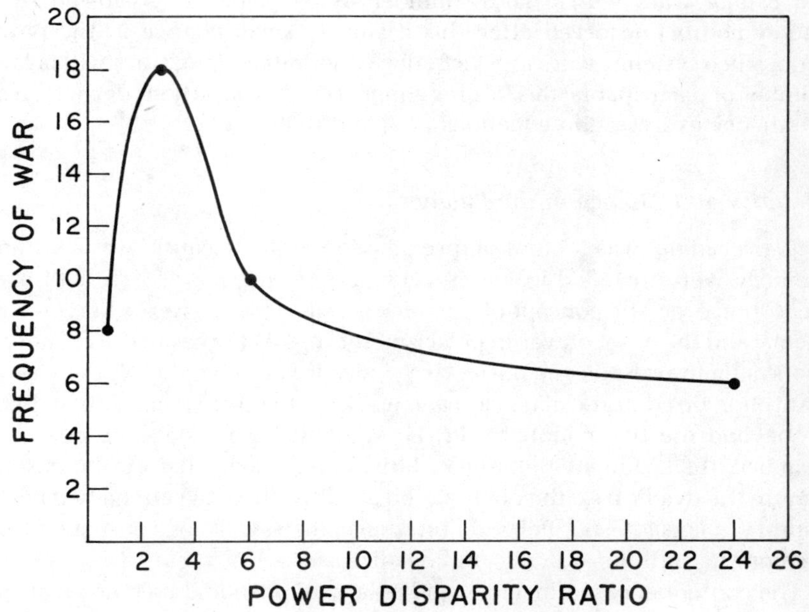

Figure 6.1
Curvilinear relationship between Ferris' power disparity ratio
and the frequency of war.

from data in Ferris (1973), who analyzed all instances of war between 1850 and 1965. This is a first approximation only, because wars without memory, which will be removed shortly in the next analysis, are included in Ferris' findings.

It is clear that the single largest value is found immediately to the right of the power parity condition. Smaller values are found further to the right. This finding is in accord with the expectation that when there exists power parity, the greatest frequency of war should be found in the first change from the parity condition, with successively lower values thereafter. As Ferris (1973, 76) comments, "Few wars are seen to occur when the two sides to the conflict approach equality in power capabilities below the ratio level of 1.45. Once that threshold is exceeded, however, the number of war events increases markedly."

In regard to our second concern, that these wars and especially systemic wars should occur within a short time interval after the small change in power distribution, again some of Ferris' findings are relevant. Specifically, he found that the majority of the wars in his study broke out after a 0–20% (his maximum is 80%) change in the power ratios had occurred within three years prior to the war's outbreak. More importantly, 6 out of the 8 long wars with a large number of participants (greater than 30 nation-months) occurred after this relatively small change in the power ratio. Since systemic wars are, virtually by definition, long wars with a large number of participants, this finding supports the expectations deriving from the theory expressed in equations [6.2] and [6.3].

Memory and Change in the Balance

The preceding was a first approximation only because wars without memory were included in Ferris' findings. As equations [6.1]–[6.6] make clear, however, the concept of memory is critical to the nexus between the theory and the onset of war in polarized settings. Whereas in the instance of the systemic war the memories are widespread as in the *N*-adic case or institutionalized in the alliance framework, in the dyad clearly they do not go beyond the two countries. In the systemic case, as a consequence of memory, the coalitions themselves ultimately polarize before the onset of war; in the dyadic case the polarization occurs only between the two hostile country protagonists. Polarization, nevertheless, is a consequence of memory in both the systemic and dyadic cases.

The consequences of memory and polarization should include an awareness of each side's military preparations by the other, especially in comparison with the no-memory condition. Here, in the latter instance, there is no history of serious violence between the two sides and, as such, conflict memory is minimal or nonexistent. Colonial wars by the European powers against non-European states during the last century perhaps best exemplify this circumstance, although there are other examples, such as the first of the Central American wars of the last century or, more generally, the first serious violence occurring between any two contiguous powers or coalitions.

As can be seen by inspecting equations [6.1]–[6.6], it is the conjunction of memory and zero-sum process which gives rise to the onset of wars in polarized international settings. These are the wars with the greatest likelihood of occurring as the result of small changes in the balance. By implication, then, wars occurring as a consequence of this conjunction should demonstrate (1) the right-skewed form for power disparities in comparison with its absence in the no-memory condition, (2) a significantly lower mean for power disparities in the memory (m) condition because the bunching of values at the lower end of the near-balance condition for conflicts with memory should yield a lower mean for that group in comparison with the no-memory (nm) condition, (or, in symbols, $\overline{N}_m < \overline{N}_{nm}$), and (3) a lower variance for the memory group because of the reasoning invoked in connection with item 2 above and the related consequence of a fairly flat distribution of values for the no-memory condition (or $s_m^2 < s_{nm}^2$).

Ferris' data and histories of wars in the period 1850–1966 for which Ferris did his analysis allow a test of the three implications of the theory. Coding rules for the absence of memory versus memory conditions were as follows. (1) If a war occurred within fifty years after the end of a previous war with the same combatants, then it was treated as a conflict with memory.[7] (2) If a war occurred within twenty-five years after the end of a previous war in the same region (for example, Central America, Western Europe), but with only one of the earlier combatants, then it was treated as one with memory.[8] (3) If violence broke out between protagonists within a five-year period prior to the official outbreak of war, then it was treated as part of the same conflict.

These criteria were derived from an examination of the histories of the conflicts themselves. For example, it is well known that irredentist sentiments for the recovery of Alsace-Lorraine were still high in France in 1914, some 43 years after the loss of these territories. The Central American War of 1885 laid the foundations for the later conflict of 1906 in that region, despite the fact that not all of the protagonists were the same. In the case of the Chaco War, despite an earlier outbreak of hostilities in 1928, the onset of war is officially dated from 1932 and so the earlier instance is simply included within the overall Chaco conflict. These criteria are admittedly somewhat crude but do allow for the retention within the memory category of only those conflicts with readily observable conflict antecedents within some reasonable time period.

Table 6.2 presents the frequency distributions of war in the memory and no-memory conditions. Effectively, equations [6.1]–[6.6] are combined for this test because although equations [6.1]–[6.3] should lead to a more peaked distribution, one with different central tendencies than equations [6.4]–[6.6], these differences do not prevent a single test from being applied. It is clear, first, that the frequency distribution of conflicts with memory conforms to the right-skewed model seen in Figure 6.1 (giving that appearance because of the larger number of conflicts with memory), whereas that for the no-memory condition does not. Tabular Appendix B (Table 4B) contains the lists of conflicts found in each category. The means and standard deviations are found below the distributions. A *t* test[9] for differences between means yielded $t = 1.821$, df $= 24$, $p < 0.05$, while an *F* test ($F = 3.203$, $df_1 = 15$, $df_2 = 25$) for difference between variances was significant at $p < 0.01$. Thus, all three propositions are supported by the data. Memory is a distinctive characteristic of conflicts which occur in the vicinity of relatively small departures from power parity, because of a likely preparation on both sides prior to the conflict. Those without memory exhibit no such regularity of behavior. These latter conflicts "smear" across the entire range of power disparity ratios instead of bunching around values close to parity, as in the memory condition.

Table 6.2

Comparison of power disparities between wars occurring under memory (*m*) and no-memory (*nm*) conditions.

Power disparities	Number of wars (*m*)[a]	Number of wars (*nm*)[b]
0–1.25	2	2
1.26–1.99	8	3
2.00–3.99	8	3
4.00–7.99	7	3
>8.00	1 (19.274)[c]	5 (15.599)[c]

[a]$n = 26$, $\bar{x} = 3.580$, $\sigma = 3.717$.

[b]$n = 16$, $\bar{x} = 6.887$, $\sigma = 6.653$.

[c]Power disparity averages are given here as additional information for this category because it is open ended. These averages enable one to see the extent of right skewness of the distribution of wars in the memory condition.

The confluence of memory and zero-sum processes associated with changes in the balance of power is characteristic of our polarized conflicts. What distinguishes the systemic conflict from the merely polarized one between two nation-states is the movement into *N*-adic memory and, ultimately for the structural systemic war, the alliance-related memory.

An implication of the model, although not tested here directly, is that the onset of systemic war as the result of *N*-adic or alliance memory is more likely than the onset of its dyadic counterpart. This is because there are any number of possible changes in the balance occurring among the *N* potential participants, or among the allies, in addition to the individual countries' own internal power circumstances characteristic of the dyadic case. Thus, once a polarized international condition evolves systemically, the potential sources of some change in the balance are greater, thus yielding an increased probability of war relative to the dyadic case.

This is one more distinguishing feature of wars of the systemic variety—an increased sensitivity to change in the balance as the result of the manifold possibilities for its occurrence after the polarization process has occurred. Of course, the polarization process itself is a lengthy one as Table 6.1 and the associated Z process amply demonstrate; this is one reason, among others, for the relative rarity of systemic war. As we shall see shortly, both World Wars I and II as systemic wars of the modern period appear in power concentration categories close to parity, as they do in Ferris' power disparity ratios. This state of power "fine tuning," then, ironically is susceptible to many different possible impacts, each of which could alter the balance sufficiently to precipitate war.

The Lognormal Model

We can, however, go farther and indeed specify a mathematical model for changes in the balance of power prior to a polarized conflict. This is the lognormal distribution. Consider what is essentially a unique isomorphism between the bases of the lognormal distribution and the present theory. According to equation [6.3] or [6.6], the change in the balance of power is effected by some zero-sum process, the memory condition, of course, carrying over from the previous state. Clearly, the entry into the zero-sum condition amounts to a power change which would likely be reflected in changes in power disparity or power concentration. Further, as shown in equations [6.2] and [6.3] (or [6.5] and [6.6]) and in the second and third columns of Table 6.1, that change would be proportionate to the existing state of balance, or

$$C_t - C_{t-1} = kC_{t-1} \qquad [6.7]$$

where the left-hand side of equation [6.7] connotes some change in the balance of power as a condition, from C_{t-1} to C_t, or concentration at times t and $t-1$, respectively, and k is some random variable independent of any of the power conditions. The probability of war in a polarized setting,[10] $P(W_m)$, then, is some function of the change or

$$P(W_m) = f(C_t - C_{t-1}) = f(kC_{t-1}) \qquad [6.8]$$

The terms in the parentheses are the fundamental assumption of proportionate effect underlying the lognormal distribution. Furthermore, it is a small change from the existing state of balance which is the critical

117

element both substantively here and in the derivation of the lognormal distribution (Aitchison and Brown 1957, 22). It is also stated as, upon rearranging equation [6.7]

$$(C_t - C_{t-1})/C_t = k \qquad\qquad [6.9]$$

which is the independence of proportionate change in power disparity from any particular category. When the central limit theorem is adduced, $\log C$ is normally distributed according to the equation

$$f(C) = \frac{1}{C\sigma\,(2\pi)^{1/2}}\,exp\left[-\tfrac{1}{2}\left(\frac{\log C - \bar{x}}{\sigma}\right)^2\right] \qquad C>0 \qquad [6.10]$$

where $\bar{x}$ and σ are, respectively, the mean and standard deviation. Thus the lognormal model, in addition to embodying the skew property, also has a unique correspondence to the transition from equations [6.2] to [6.3] and from [6.5] to [6.6], or the onset of war in polarized settings.

There is a fortunate convergence between the substantive theory of a change in the balance increasing the likelihood of war and the mathematical assumption of a proportionate effect as shown in equation [6.7] leading directly to the lognormal distribution. Both types of reasoning lead to the prediction of a right-skewed distribution with a disproportionately higher frequency of war in the lower categories of power disparity or concentration.

An additional confluence between the substantive theory and the bases of the lognormal model is that processes of growth and decline are inherent in both. State building as a process, inevitably entailing the growth of national power and the disintegration of civilizations indicating a power decline, has been singled out as especially important in understanding the origins of systemic war. Clearly, such processes impact strongly on values of power disparity or power concentration. At the same time, the lognormal distribution has been successful at modeling processes of growth, such as business-firm size (Simon and Bonini 1958; Ijiri and Simon 1964, 1977), economic growth (Tintner and Sengupta 1972), per capita income (Lazear and Michael 1980), or comminution processes akin to disintegration (Hatch and Choute 1929; Herdan 1960). The growth of populations internationally (Russett 1968b) and number of arrests as a growth process in the urban disorders of the late 1960s also were successfully modeled by the lognormal distribution (Midlarsky 1978).

Another aspect of the model also deserves comment. As can be seen in equation [6.7], it is Markovian, or the future state of the system is dependent only on its current state. Put another way, it is a memoryless process in regard to power considerations, one in which past memory beyond the

118

current state of the system has no influence on the transition to the future state.[11] This is precisely what is hypothesized in the transition from equations [6.2] to [6.3] (or [6.5] to [6.6]) in which only the game process has any influence with conflict memory held constant. Clearly, the conflict memory process brought the system to the polarized state of hostile dyads or coalitions, but once having formed into the balance of power as a condition, only the game process is relevant in carrying the already balanced opponents into war.

Thus far, temporal patterns of causality could not be explored effectively; the Singer *et al.* (1972) study, however, does allow for such exploration. It allows for a strong contrast to be shown, if it exists, between the theoretically suggested skew relationship and other possibilities. Because of the research design and its consequent even distribution of concentration values over time, the lognormal model can be put to a precise test of goodness of fit. The fact that the wars included are limited to major power wars and the concentration values are calculated only for the major powers suggests an applicability to the polarized conflicts identified in equations [6.1]–[6.6].

Table 6.3 in the first three columns shows the distribution of power concentration over the incidence of major power wars in the period 1820–1945. The concentration of power is noted at t_0 and the onset of war at $t_1 - t_2$, during the next five-year interval as tested by Singer *et al.* (1972). This is exactly the same time lag used in their study.

If no war was begun during $t_1 - t_2$, then the concentration at t_0 was not counted. A dichotomous variable is used for the war outcome because changes in concentration at the systemic level involving all of the major powers theoretically are not suggested to predict to any given frequency of war. One cannot know from the concentration values themselves how many countries were involved and their interrelationships, which, of course, would bear on the frequency variable. Additionally, certain of these wars can be related, as in the wars of German or Italian unification, and not be the required discrete phenomena. The time period is 1820–1945 primarily because the post-World War II period reflects very different power concentration values, likely reflective of the new bipolarity (all are higher than the maximum value for 1820–1945) which effectively constitute data outliers relative to the remainder.

The lognormal distribution is applied to the data in Table 6.3. The fit is excellent as indicated by the chi-square goodness-of-fit statistic between observed and predicted values. The lower the magnitude of chi-square and the higher the probability level, the better the fit between model and data. These values indicate that the departures of model from observation as reflected by the chi-square statistic could have occurred by chance with a probability of less than 90 times in a hundred opportunities.[12] It is also known (Simon and Bonini 1958; Midlarsky 1978) that the cumulative

Table 6.3

Observed and lognormally predicted power concentrations for war periods, 1820–1945.[a]

Concentration interval[b] at t_0 (C)	$\mathrm{Log}_{10}(1 + C)$	Observed frequency of five–year intervals with war initiation $(t_1 - t_2)$	Predicted frequency of five–year intervals with war initiation $(t_1 - t_2,$ $\bar{x} = 0.09376^c$ $\sigma = 0.00752)$	No war $(t_1 - t_2)$
0.200–0.209	0.0723[d]	1	1.08	4
0.210–0.219	0.0903	1	1.35	1
0.220–0.229	0.1417	3	2.13	1
0.230–0.239	0.1777	2	2.67	1
0.240–0.249	0.1804	3	2.71	2
0.250–0.259	0.1482	2	2.22	0
0.260–0.269	0.0986	1	1.48[e]	0
0.270–0.279	0.0541	1	0.81	0
0.280–0.289	0.0242	1	0.36	0[f]

$\chi^2 = 0.699$, df $= 3$, $p < 0.90$

[a]The source is Singer, Bremer, and Stuckey (1972, 29).

[b]Lower limit of the next interval is used to calculate logarithms as in Derman, Gleser, and Olkin (1973, 342–344).

[c]Mean and standard deviation are based on individual values, not the grouped data shown here.

[d]In order to avoid negative values throughout this column, the number 1 is added to each value in the first column.

[e]Neighboring values for the chi-square test are combined until a minimum of 1.5 is obtained as suggested in Gibbons (1971, 72).

[f]There is an additional value in the range 0.370–0.379.

distribution of the logarithms of the concentration values over time should approximate a straight line. This is shown in Figure 6.2.

Because of the measurements over time, the data allow for the exploration of causality. What is the pattern of power concentration at t_0 and *no* war at $t_1 - t_2$? This is seen in the farthest column to the right of Table 6.3 and clearly is a different pattern approximating the exponential distribution. The largest frequency is found at the parity condition. This agrees with Ferris' (1973) [as represented by Sullivan (1975, 183)] approximate exponential pattern of power disparity values for nonconflictual dyads and the concomitant maximum at parity. It is known (Good 1963; Jaynes 1957) that, in the absence of additional information (say, theory or other findings), the random pattern of the exponential distribution is the one most likely to be found. Thus, the skewed lognormal distribution with maximum frequency of war at lower levels of departure from parity suggested theoretically by equations [6.2]–[6.10] is found only at the one period lag between power concentration and war as sensibly employed previously by Singer *et al.* (1972).

Note that the second, third, and fourth categories from the top, which should be most sensitive to the change in the balance as a departure from parity, also represent the onset of the most intense conflicts of this period. World War I, World War II, and the Russo-Turkish War of 1877–1878 (after which occurred the Congress of Berlin) all are associated with concentration values in these categories. The presence of the two systemic wars of this period in these categories is especially important, for the state of balance as polarization between coalitions should be particularly sensitive to any changes in the balance of power. Thus, an examination of the categories of Table 6.3 close to parity supports the basic theoretical proposition of the greater likelihood of systemic war under conditions of a change in the balance near parity.

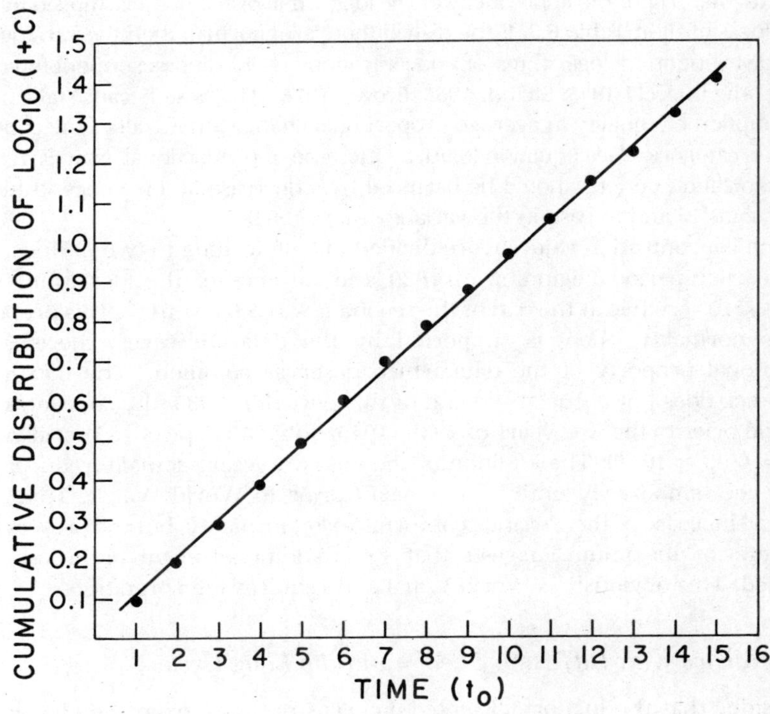

Figure 6.2
Cumulative distribution of the logarithm of the concentration ratio.

As a further assessment of similarities and differences, we can compare the distribution of concentration values associated with war and those associated with no war, or columns three and five in Table 6.3. This can be done for the first four concentration categories not only because of the required equality in total number of cases (the total Ns change immediately upon entering the fifth category) but also because of the theoretical significance of the parity category and immediate departures from it, as we have just seen. A value of $\chi^2 = 6.337$, df $= 2$, $p < 0.05$ was calculated, thus allowing a formal rejection of equality between the two distributions for these concentration values at a fairly widely accepted level of significance.[13]

The implication of this finding, of course, is that in comparison with the likely random generation of the exponential-like distribution of concentrations for no war (Good, 1963; Jaynes, 1957), the lognormal distribution for the onset of war is a consequence of transformations of the exponential by substantive political forces.[14] In Ferris' (1973) data we also find the right-skewed form (see Figure 6.1) for power disparities associated with war, but the exponential form for nonconflictual dyads (Sullivan 1975, 183).

A further test of the applicability of the lognormal distribution is implied by the goodness of fit in Table 6.3. If the distribution is lognormal, then the variance of the distribution of logarithms of concentrations should increase monotonically over time (Kalecki 1945; Steindl 1965; Brown 1976). This is so because, given the assumption of equality in average proportional change among all of the concentration categories [see equation (6.9)], an increase of proportional growth in high concentration periods should be balanced by a decrease in low concentrations. This leads to an increase in the variance (Hart 1962).

The concentration values were divided in half, leading to two periods. For the earlier period beginning in 1820, the variance of the logarithms was 3.55×10^{-5}, while at the end of the second it was 5.65×10^{-5}. This property of lognormality, then, is supported by the data. However, there is an additional property of the data which deserves comment. The maximum variance does not occur at the end of this period in 1935 (the concentration period prior to the war years of 1939–1945) but in 1910 prior to World War I ($\sigma^2 = 6.96 \times 10^{-5}$). The addition of the interwar years actually reduces the variance temporarily until it rises again prior to World War II. Thus, the overall increase of the variance conforms to lognormality, but the presence of an interior maximum suggests that some additional event or process occurred. This obviously is World War I and requires interpretation.

Confluence with Diffusion Theory and the Long Cycle

Consider that the lognormal model emerges not only from the concept of proportionate change as evoked in equation [6.7] but from diffusion theory. The Kolmogorov diffusion equations include the proportionate effect of equation [6.7] and the consequent lognormal distribution (Bharucha-Reid 1960; Midlarsky 1978). Increasing variance over time is, of course, a property of the diffusion process. Thus, if after the Congress of Vienna, as

122

after Versailles, the concentration values were moderately high, then an increasing variance implies that the concentration values should be lower at a later point in time. These points in time, in fact, are found during the periods prior to World Wars I and II. The diffusion of power, then, is reflected by the lognormal model applied to these data. World War I becomes in this interpretation an effort to raise the power concentration—or, what is the same thing, reverse the diffusion process—and restore some order to the system. The decline of the variance in concentration values after World War I is once again a property of the data, as it is after World War II.

This interpretation finds agreement with theorists of the long cycle (Modelski 1983; Modelski and Morgan 1985; Thompson 1983; Rasler and Thompson 1983), for it is their contention that it is the "deconcentration" of power at some lengthy time period following a systemic war which then leads to another such war followed by attempts to reconstitute some acceptable authority structure. In turn, another deconcentration process occurs followed by another systemic war. It is the diffusion of power which is identified here as the dynamic of such a long cycle with, particularly, the proportionate effect process of equation [6.7] as the basis of such diffusion. Simple equality of average proportionate growth across power concentration categories yields this diffusion as an increase in the variance over time. The power cycle (Doran and Parsons 1980) as a reflection of the growth and decline of national power over time clearly is a contributor to the concentration values.

The increase in the variance and, by implication, diffusion of power prior to the onset of a systemic war is suggested by the failure of a hierarchical equilibrium and the Z pattern of Table 6.1. The decline of large power disparities between large and small countries and the disappearance of the very small countries in Europe (as well as colonial opportunities elsewhere) is equivalent to the diffusion or deconcentration of power. Countries which formerly were either nonexistent or far too weak to challenge great powers now can do so as Serbia did in 1914.

A modern variation of this scenario is the recent confrontation between Libya and the United States. Twenty years ago such a small country, barely independent, would hardly have been in a position to confront the United States; now, heavily armed and with great power support, she can do so. It is dynamics such as these which are suggested by the increase in the variance over time of the distribution of concentrations.

Conclusion

Theory and Findings

We can now state a principal conclusion of this analysis, namely, that the debate between preponderance and parity as progenitors of interstate violence should not be stated in these terms. Instead, extreme parity and overwhelming preponderance are associated with the relative absence of war, with immediate departures from parity and moderate preponderance associated with the onset of war. Indeed, these categories approximate a continuous ordering of violence propensity as expressed in the lognormal distribution, with extreme parity and overwhelming preponderance approximately equal in their tendency toward peace, with the most violent being the near departures from parity followed, in order, by moderate disparities. The dynamics in each of these cases, of course, likely differ. In parity there is the probable hostile standoff or simply a satisfaction in the state of equality. In the small discrepancy there is the possibility of some small change in the balance precipitating war, while moderate levels of disparity or preponderance allow for the possibility of the illusion of success even when the odds weigh against the success of the venture. The case of overwhelming preponderance allows for few such illusions to enter the decision-making calculus (Weede 1976).

These results follow from the theoretical framework suggested in equations [6.1]–[6.2] and expressed in Table 6.1. Although changes in the balance are associated with the onset of all types of war, still one must be careful to distinguish between systemic war and other types of war. The differences between various types of war can be seen at a glance in Table 6.1 as the result of partitioning by the absence of memory and game process variables. Table 6.1 in its Z shaped process gives an analytical account of the transition from the balance of power as a process to the balance of power as a condition preceding the onset of World War I.

The Z process gives a fairly accurate and, at the same time, complex analytic account of the approach to World War I. This is not surprising in light of the puzzlement so many scholars have expressed on the descent of Europe into war in 1914 after the relative peace of the nineteenth century. At the same time, the last transition into the zero-sum column and the onset of war is a simple move as equations [6.2]–[6.3] suggest. The fact that it could be modeled successfully in Table 6.3 by a two-parameter distribution function is evidence of that simplicity.

There are several implications which derive now from the juxtaposition of the simple and the complex. The first, deriving from the element of simplicity is that the transition into war is not inevitable and, by adroit decision making, can be avoided. Equation [6.7] is Markovian and, therefore, not dependent on a previous state of the system. Thus, the decisions of the moment during a crisis in the transition from the second to the third column in Table 6.1 can carry the day for war or peace.

At the same time, the latitude of decision makers in the crisis is circumscribed by the existence of the balance of power as a condition, or a polarized state in column two. Precisely because of the polarization, the alternatives are few and, if the threatened disintegration of a weaker and

124

only great power ally or the international isolation as the result of the defection of that ally is a possible outcome of the crisis without war, then the war outcome is made more likely. This points clearly to the unwise German policy of reliance on Austria-Hungary as the sole great-power ally after 1890, Italy in the Triple Alliance almost always having been peripheral in the German calculations. At the moment of crisis, the options can be extremely limited by the long-term processes leading to the crisis.

This is precisely what O. R. Holsti (1972b, 67) found in his analysis of the 1914 crisis. German decision makers were distinguished from all of the others, even the Austro-Hungarian, by the extraordinary extent to which they felt bound by constraints of "necessity" in comparison with the wide range of choices open to their adversaries. Indeed, the effort to maintain or increase the available options is one interpretation of the Z process identified in Table 6.1.

Bismarckian diplomacy was an effort to maintain open options in the face of declining opportunities as a consequence of the decline in the number of small powers and the hostility of France after 1871. Colonialism was an additional effort in that direction after the European option began to close with the failure to renew the Reinsurance Treaty between Germany and Russia in 1890. Finally, internal and external processes, largely nationalistic, began to hasten the disintegration of the only great-power bulwark of German diplomacy. It was perceived by German decision makers in 1914 that there were few available options. Yet the crisis still does not have to carry with it an aura of inevitability. Decision makers still can save the situation, but with far fewer available options than in a nonpolarized condition.

As a result of the presence of World Wars I and II in the concentration categories close to parity in both data sets examined here (in Ferris' data they appear in the second and third categories) and the increasing variance of the logarithmic concentrations prior to the two systemic wars suggesting power diffusion, a principal conclusion of this analysis is that, whereas changes in the balance are associated, generally, with the later onset of war in polarized settings, it is changes in the balance very close to parity which presage the coming of a systemic war.

An additional implication of these findings concerns distinctions among different types of war in regard to etiology. Although we have suggested that the origins of the systemic war are distinguishable from those of the polarized dyadic war by the increased sensitivity to change in the balance, the wide range of participants, and the lengthy polarization time, still another new category of warfare emerges from this treatment. This is the polarized dyad as the result of conflict memories. This instance, too, is responsive to changes in the balance, but likely not as much as in the systemic variety. Both the dyadic and systemic polarized cases should be treated separately from the no-memory condition in which polarization is largely absent, as is any apparent sensitivity to changes in the balance of power.

The findings here agree with Most and Starr's (1987) analysis of the logical structure of the parity-preponderance problem, wherein they argue that both conditions logically must be consistent with peace. The findings also agree with Sullivan's (1975) earlier conjecture of a curvilinear relationship of this type, stated largely in connection with Ferris' data, although Sullivan did not anchor this relationship within a general theoretical framework.

What is perhaps most important about these findings is not only that they derive from a very old and, until recently, time-honored tradition of international politics (namely, balance-of-power theory) but that they synthesize elements of the theory (for example, Morgenthau and Thompson 1985) with its critics (for example, Organski 1968). Both extreme parity and extreme preponderance can lead to peace as expressed respectively by these theorists. What this analysis has shown is not only that these conditions hold in two sets of data, with small disparities most strongly associated with systemic war, but that the relationship is strong enough to be susceptible to formal modeling.

It is important to note in the model that the change in the concentration of power is some random proportion of the existing concentration, as embodied in the values of k. Given the earlier arguments concerning the subjectivity of what is an acceptable or unacceptable change (for example, the Cuban missile crisis), the changes themselves clearly should be a random variable across incidents of war in the third column of Table 6.1. Nevertheless, the onset of systemic wars should uniformly reflect some potential or actual departure from near parity because of the prior history of balanced coalitions during the polarization process.

The centrality of power and its change are emphasized here in contrast to the exponential distribution which is a consequence of purely random influences without any central variable of importance. It is the stochastic element which is a major departure from earlier theories of the balance of power, for it suggests that, despite the centrality of changes in the balance of power, they essentially vary randomly across cases as specified by equations [6.7]–[6.10], thus disallowing the possibility of specifying a uniform quantitative condition of the balance and its change required for peace or war.

Policy Implications

A clear policy implication is that, in closely balanced systems such as that between the United States and the Soviet Union, any major technological or other breakthrough implying a serious change in the balance is potentially destabilizing. It is possible that President Reagan's amiable personality in dealing with leaders such as Chairman Gorbachev could temporarily mitigate the destabilizing effects of a successful Strategic Defense Initiative (SDI), but with the inevitable passage of the current presidency and the possibility of less competent personal leadership, the destabilization may become manifest with a desperation on the part of the Soviets to counter this technical advantage.

In a somewhat different form, this was seen in the Cuban missile crisis of 1962 with all of its potential dangers. In the approach to a missile preponderance by the United States in 1962, one may find a hint as to a possible outcome of the SDI venture during the window of vulnerability for the United States, before the system is completely in place. There is no inevitability of the war outcome in such a circumstance, but there is a severe narrowing of options for the threatened non-SDI power such that war becomes more likely before the system is operative. Here, one sees the analogy with the theoretical disintegration of a sole great-power ally and the increased likelihood of war prior to the occurrence of that event. This is but one of the policy implications of the preceding analysis.

A prior unbounded increase in the variance preceding the two systemic wars of this century also suggests that contemporary changes in the balance should be small in order to minimize variance changes and keep the power concentrations within some bounds, albeit unspecified. Although increases in power seldom follow such a controlled procedure [the Strategic Arms Limitation Talks (SALT) treaties and Washington Treaty for the Limitation of Naval Armaments being somewhat exceptional], power decreases can be made in such a fashion. Reductions in nuclear armaments, therefore, where agreed upon, should follow a small proportional decrease whereby the principals decrease their armaments simultaneously and in small proportion to their current states. Unilateral nuclear disarmaments or some other dramatic changes in armaments possession clearly are not suggested by the findings of this study.

The finding of a Markovian diffusion of power prior to the onset of the two systemic wars of this century has strong implications for the conduct of policy in response to this process. It is clear that the response of the European powers, especially Germany, was the precise opposite of what was desirable. It is known that the most effective response of a system to a variety of random disturbances, such as a diffusion process, is to increase its own variety of responses. Indeed, this has been defined as the essence of systemic regulation (Ashby 1963, 206–207) and was obeyed in the Markovian alliance processes of the nineteenth century through the Bismarckian period (Midlarsky 1983b). Yet, the downward movement in Table 6.1 from the first to the fourth rows preceding World War I constituted a serious limitation of possible responses, with alliance memory ultimately stipulating the outcome of systemic war.

In effect, a dichotomous choice of systemic war or no systemic war was found in 1914. Without the alliance memory, the choices would have been at least three in number with a small war in southeast Europe or Serbian accession to the Austro-Hungarian demands added to that of systemic war.

Other responses also could have been generated, such as an international conference as proposed by the British but rejected by Germany likely because of the fear of being once again isolated internationally, even by her Austro-Hungarian ally, as at Algeciras in 1906.

Perhaps the human psyche requires an early imposition of certainty on an uncertain environment, hence the growing alliance structure of the end of the late nineteenth century. The League of Nations, which formed as an outgrowth of the Allied victory in World War I, may have been a similar response, but with equal inflexibility and perhaps equally tragic consequences. This may be the ultimate paradox out of which arose the transition from the fluidity of the balance of power as a process to the polarization of the balance of power as a condition. The human need to greet an increasingly uncertain environment with the trappings of certainty (for example, fixed alliances) is precisely the opposite from that which is required for systemic continuity, as Bismarck so clearly saw. (As A. J. P. Taylor (1971, 278) put it, "He scattered promises so as not to carry them out.")

If the history of recent systemic wars is any guide, an effective response set to environmental stimuli is a multifaceted one. Simply put, an increasingly diffuse system of power concentration requires a repertory of increasingly diffuse responses (for example, Libya versus the United States). Whether policy makers can effectively generate such responses as time proceeds is, of course an open question, but one critical to the prevention of systemic war.

Notes

1 Claude (1962, 13–25) probably comes closest to this distinction in distinguishing between the balance of power as a situation, often connoting equilibrium, and the balance of power as a system. However, the meaning he imparts to the term "system" is not the same as Kaplan's usage adopted here, namely, that of the random choice of alliance partners without the memory of past friendships or enmities. One of the earliest modern efforts at explicit distinctions among the meanings of the balance of power is by the economic historian Polanyi (1944, 259–262), although he too did not make the particular distinction found here.

2 A basic difference between this approach and that of the power transition as developed in Organski and Kugler (1980, 19–27) is that changes in the balance here can arise equally from alliance processes, from fundamental changes within nation-states, or some combination of the two. The power transition emphasizes internal change, and it does not treat the concept of polarization as it is developed here.

3 Commenting on the condition of stasis in Europe prior to 1914, Sir Edward Grey (1925, 291), the British Foreign Minister, noted that "the failure to arrest expenditure in armaments was but a negative feature, and there was nothing new about it. Europe had grown used to such expenditure, and to failures to arrest its growth. There seemed no reason to suppose that it would cause a crisis this year any more than it had done in previous years."

4 The condition of balance can be so finely tuned that but a small change in its structure can precipitate a war. An interesting illustration is provided by a sequel to the Dutch War between France and the United Provinces ending in 1679. In November 1681, Louis XIV, laid siege to the city of Luxemburg, then as now a small city, and not of terribly significant strategic importance. Yet, so antagonistic were the Dutch to the idea of Luxemburg falling into the hands of the French, that, despite the possibility of the outbreak of a new European war, William of Orange was ordered to move to the relief of the city when it appeared that it would fall to the French forces. As a consequence of this stand, Louis XIV raised the siege of Luxemburg early in 1682 (Hassall 1907, 48).

5 This percentage variance explained was found with all other variables in the equation controlled (Singer *et al.* 1972, 39).

6 Elsewhere in this volume, I have termed these structural wars to connote the structural condition of two or more political entities joined by a political coalition which also joins their heretofore separate conflict axes. An example is the Dual Alliance of 1914, which joined the exclusively great power conflicts of Germany with the great power–small power conflicts of Austria-Hungary. The simultaneous presence of the Habsburg Monarchy in both Spain and Austria and the joining of the two in the Catholic war against the Protestant states of Holland and Bohemia constitute another case in point. A mobilization war, on the other hand, proceeds largely as the result of one power's mobilizing resources for war in an *N*-adic setting as in the Napoleonic Wars, World War II, or Louis XIV's War of the Spanish Succession.

7 If there was a continuous history of some conflict but no overt violence in the past, then war between the two countries was treated as one without memory. The Russo-Finnish War of 1939–1940 is a case in point, for despite a history of Russian colonial rule in Finland dating from 1743 with the cession of Finland to Russia by Sweden, there was little, if any violence. Beginning in the nineteenth century, Finland was allowed a fair degree of autonomy by the tsarist government. Although there was violence in 1917–1918, it was more in the nature of a civil war with German and Russian involvement than a war with the Soviet government which had granted independence to Finland on January 1, 1918 (Jutikkala 1962; Smith 1958). If the protagonists earlier had fought within the required time period but if one or more were colonized at the time and, as a result, were not included in the war data compilation, the later conflict occurring when independence was achieved is treated as one with memory. The War of Italian Unification in 1859 and the Palestine War of 1948–1949 are cases in point. Each of these wars followed earlier conflicts which included among the combatants not-yet-sovereign entities. If a war occurred within fifty years of the ending of an earlier one with the same combatants, but with an ally added now to one or another side, it was treated as one with memory, as in the First Balkan War.

8 Although these are fairly clear-cut criteria, they require some refinement in practice. For example, despite the formal participation of Hungary in World War II on the Axis side clearly within the fifty-year time interval of the Russo-Hungarian war of 1956, which would invoke the first memory criterion, and the presence of Russia as a combatant within the twenty-five-year interval, which would invoke the second, the Russo-Hungarian War still is treated as one without memory. This is because of the more pro forma nature of the Hungarian participation and the efforts of Admiral Horthy, the Hungarian Regent, to withdraw Hungary from the Axis cause just prior to the German occupation in late 1944 (Seton-Watson 1957, 15). The principal battles in this region in 1944–1945, then, were fought between the Soviets and Germans almost to the

total exclusion of the Hungarians. Moreover, in 1956 it was precisely those with the strongest memories of Soviet tanks in World War II who refused to fight the Russians, while the fighting was carried on by much younger people without such memories (Kecskemeti 1961, 112–113). The issues involved in this war (often called the Hungarian Revolution) also differed from those typically involved in a regional conflict. The onset of this war contains strong elements of revolutionary behavior as in the deep cleavage within the native communist elite paving the way for the mass revolt, which would place this conflict clearly in the category of domestic revolution (Skocpol 1979), until the Russian intervention on the side of the pro-Soviet elements in Hungary. Put another way, the issues initially giving rise to the revolution were not centrally related to those of World War II and arose more as the result of the Soviets seizing "targets of opportunity" as they installed native communists in power subsequent to deciding the central issue of victory over Nazi Germany. In contrast, the Korean War is treated as one with memory because of the continuity of regional concerns of the Chinese for the safety of Manchuria and its neighbor, North Korea, as they had earlier fought the Japanese during the preceding two decades for control of this region.

9 Because of the absence of homogeneity of variance, the variances could not be pooled. As a consequence, the t test used was that for unequal variances and the degrees of freedom estimated as in Walker and Lev (1953, 157–158).

10 The general category W_m includes both systemic wars, W_s, and nonsystemic wars with memory, w_m, or $W_m = W_s + w_m$.

11 Here, it is important to distinguish between conflict memory, as it influences the values of M and m in equations [6.1]–[6.6], and power memory, as it influences the future change in the balance of power in equations [6.7]–[6.10]. In the former case it is the memories of past conflicts which influence the future and, in the latter instance, it is the earlier power considerations (at t influencing $t + 1$) which carry such impact.

12 Normally, the basis of the requirement for large expected frequencies is the desire to avoid small numbers in the denominator of the expression for chi square, for then the value of chi square would be inflated and the null hypothesis of equality between two groups would be rejected with greater frequency than it actually should. Here, on the other hand, one seeks to accept the null hypothesis of equality between the theoretical and observed distributions and so any additional factors, such as small expected frequencies which lead to more likely rejection, actually are desirable in the sense of yielding more conservative outcomes. From this perspective, when the categories in Table 6.3 are disaggregated leaving only the bottom two combined, the value is $\chi^2 = 1.418$, df $= 5$, $p < 0.95$. Thus, risking an even greater likelihood of rejection of the null hypothesis leads to an even better fit between observed and predicted values.

13 The concentration values associated with war were treated as the "theoretical" distribution to be compared with the "observed" exponential. This was done principally to preserve degrees of freedom as the result of minimizing the aggregation of categories. The first two categories were combined for the chi-square test.

14 An interesting parallel from another discipline is found in neurocybernetics, in which the researcher remarks (Tolkunov 1975, 27), "Thus, the different forms of interval histogram may be regarded as the result of deformation of the simplest Poisson flow, due to the influence of physiological processes. If this assumption is valid, any deviation of the empirical interval histograms from the exponential distribution should reflect physiological properties of the neuron under investigation and of the part of the neural network to which it belongs."

7

Structural and Mobilization Wars

THE GENERAL OR systemic war is distinguished from other types of war, mainly dyadic, by the extent of participation. Here, as we have seen, we do not find the single two- or three-party war with fairly limited casualties and short duration. Instead, the wars of central concern here range over a wide expanse of territory and number of sovereign entities with a much larger number of casualties and duration (although as we saw in chapters 1 and 2, duration is a less reliable indicator than casualties). Our task here, as before, is to inquire into the dynamics by which this comes about. Why do these wars take on the dimension they do and not remain limited to much smaller confines? The answer, initially, will be given in the form of a distinction between two basic types of systemic war. In making this distinction, certain reasons for the emergence of widespread warfare should become apparent.

Basically, there are two types of general or systemic war, and I have termed these structural and mobilization wars. The structural war primarily connotes the structural condition of two or more political entities joined by a political circumstance (coalition, geopolitical dispersion, or dynastic connection) which also happens to simultaneously join two conflict axes. This circumstance then leads to a change in the balance of power immediately prior to the onset of war. Examples are the Dual Alliance of 1914, which joined the exclusively great power and small power–great power conflicts, and the simultaneous presence of the Habsburg monarchy in both Austria and Spain in 1618 and the consequent joining of the two in the Catholic war against the two Protestant states (Holland and Bohemia). The joining of Athens' support of Corcyra against Corinth (Sparta's ally) with her conflict with Potidae is another case in point. So too is the joining of the ongoing revolution in the Austrian Netherlands with the Austrian, Prussian, and English concerns for the preservation of monarchy. In our one instance of a general war it was the ongoing War of Jenkins' Ear between Britain and Spain as well as British concerns for Hanover that were to overlap with the Prussian attack on Silesia. The Franco-Spanish and Franco-Prussian alliances were to complete the circle.

A mobilization war, on the other hand, proceeds largely as the result of one power's mobilizing resources for war as in the Napoleonic Wars, World War II, or Louis XIV's War of the Spanish Succession. Here, too, a change on the salient power dimension is seen to be unacceptable by one or more of the protagonists. However, in the mobilization instance, the salient dimension is the power of the mobilizing state.[1] In the case of Napoleon I and Louis XIV in the War of the Spanish Succession, it was the power of France; in World War II, it was the power of Germany that was at issue. The Seven Years' War proceeded largely from the increase in Prussian power as the result of the earlier War of the Austrian Succession.

Another and more remote source of the structural war, as we have seen, is the emergent inequality in a multipolar setting. Since all of these wars began in a multipolar environment, they would be subject to the probabilistic contrasts identified in chapters 3 and 4. This is another meaning of the term structural used in this context. It is not the particular desires for aggression and conflict that motivate the decision makers initially (although that may come later). Instead, it is the structure of multipolarity and its attendant inequalities which give the initial impetus, in contrast to the mobilization war which proceeds directly from aggressive intent.

Origins of the Structural and Mobilization Wars

Structural circumstances made it fairly easy for widespread wars to occur in the eighteenth century. First, major states such as Prussia were still in the process of state building. At the time of the outbreak of the War of the Austrian Succession, for example, Hohenzollern holdings were scattered from the Rhine to East Prussia, with serious territorial gaps between them. The War of the Austrian Succession, in fact, began with the invasion of Silesia by the forces of Frederick the Great in an effort to increase his territorial holdings and, at the same time, place a wedge between two of his potential enemies, Saxony and Poland (McKay and Scott 1983, 166). Second, the scattered holdings of the various monarchs, even those of united countries such as England, made it far more likely that a relatively small war could involve a geographically remote protagonist. It was the danger to Hanover, home of the English dynasty's George II, that made it more likely that Britain would oppose France and her German allies in the War of the Austrian Succession (McKay and Scott 1983, 166). Not only was the British navy required to oppose the French, but subsidies to Austria's land forces were needed to pursue the war to some kind of acceptable outcome.

It must be recalled that the concept of the state, in the modern sense of geographically contiguous territories usually associated with a nation, did not yet exist in the eighteenth century. The territories of what are today called states were actually holdings of monarchies to be treated more or less as fiefdoms. As time progressed, of course, these territories were treated less as fiefdoms and more as components of nation-states. Nevertheless, this process was hardly complete in the mid-eighteenth century.

An interesting asymmetry exists between the two varieties of systemic war. Whereas each of the structural systemic wars—the Peloponnesian War, Thirty Years' War, French Revolutionary Wars, and World War I—began as the result of coalitions and political interconnections between the protagonists and were followed by some actual or impending change in the balance of power, this is not true of the origins of the mobilizing wars: the Macedonian War, the War of the Spanish Succession, the Napoleonic Wars, and World War II. In these latter cases it was the aggressive (diplomatic or military) acquisition of additional territory which sparked the conflict. And these territories were considerable in size and importance. Spain added to France, of course, was a near doubling in size. Napoleon was simultaneously infringing on the sovereignties of Holland, Switzerland, and Italy. Hitler incorporated Austria, Czechoslovakia, and, finally, Poland into his empire before the European powers were willing to oppose him militarily. It is this perceived direct accretion of power which contrasts with the simple enmeshing of all the relevant powers (if not immediately in military form then in diplomatic support which later would eventuate in military support) at virtually one stroke. As such, there is a fundamentally different dynamic to the origins of the mobilization war which makes it, perhaps, more amenable to prevention at the outset.

Consider the successive aggressive moves by Hitler in Central Europe. If he had stopped after any of the acquisitions before Poland, the Second World War might have been prevented. In this sense, Neville Chamberlain fundamentally misperceived the nature of the coming world war in supposing it to be similar to the first, and therefore preventable by extraordinary policy "flexibility", in place of the firmness that was necessary. The British were accused of committing a similar error in signing the Treaty of Amiens in 1802, which was ruptured upon Napoleon's simultaneous incursions in three directions. If the Napoleonic impulse had been constrained to only one of the three countries or Hitler's to only one, say, Austria or Czechoslovakia, or Spain had been a less prized territory at the time of Louis XIV, then it is possible that none of these wars would have erupted.

The major difference between the structural and mobilization war in this regard is the presence of salient conflicts not involving a mobilizing power but concerning a weaker ally in the former instance. In the Peloponnesian War the conflicts between Corinth and Corcyra (Athens' ally), on the one hand, and Athens and Potidae, on the other, gave rise to the war. Sparta, as Corinth's ally and presumed protector, could not allow herself to remain outside the conflict arena (Ste. Croix 1972).

In the case of World War I, it was conflicts peripheral to the seat of power in Berlin which became of central concern. As a consequence of the Balkan Wars and the doubling of Serbia in size, the salience of pan-Slavism had been brought home with a vengeance to the Austro-Hungarians. The structural nexus with Germany then involved Berlin in the war. Similarly, the threatened secession of a Protestant-dominated Bohemia brought the Spanish Habsburgs into full support of the Austrian branch, the structural nexus, of course, being the same hereditary House and militant Catholicism. The steady growth of Calvinism in that region and its already ensconced status in nearby Switzerland made it all the more threatening. In particular, the War of the Jülich Succession between Catholic and Protestant states in neighboring Bavaria led to the formation of a military alliance, the Protestant Union, among Protestant states, in 1608, and a corresponding Catholic counterpart, the Catholic League, in 1609. It was these polarized factions which did much to lay the groundwork for the Protestant rebellion of 1618 and the attendant secession of the Bohemian Crown from Habsburg dominion. In the French Revolutionary Wars, the structural nexus comprised the French emigrés (now outside of French borders), the ongoing revolution in the Austrian Netherlands, and the common support for monarchy of Austria, Prussia, and even England (Palmer 1971).

Territorial dispersions that were so common prior to the premodern era made the incidence of a structural war more likely. So, too, did the density of interfamilial connections among the ruling dynasties of this era. Territories were consolidated under the rule of single monarchies as much by duly arranged marriage as by other processes, such as conquest. Each of these marriages was arranged with great care with the goal of maximizing the territory added to the royal house. As a consequence, it was said of families such as the Habsburgs that they married their way to power. Indeed, at the height of Habsburg power in the sixteenth century, Charles V of Spain was Holy Roman Emperor, King of Spain, and ruler of all of the Habsburg localities in Central Europe, the Netherlands, and much of Italy, especially after the Battle of Pavia in 1525 (Grant 1932, 70). The onset of the French Revolutionary Wars, of course, was strongly influenced by this structural attribute of European politics because of Marie Antoinette's simultaneous status as French queen and sister of the Austrian Emperor.

Coalition formation, geophysical dispersions, and dynastic connections, then, can strongly increase the probability that when a war breaks out it will almost automatically involve more than two sovereign participants. The mobilization war of one or more sovereign entities individually mobilizing for war, of course, does not involve such explicit structural considerations. Nevertheless there is a relationship between the structural and mobilization war, that of precedence in time.

Power Interregna

If we examine each of the structural wars considered here, namely, the Peloponnesian War, the Thirty Years' War, the War of the Austrian Succession, French Revolutionary Wars and World War I, we see that each was followed either by a single mobilization war or a series of smaller wars culminating in a large-scale mobilization war. In the first of these, the Peloponnesian War, at its end (in 404 B.C.) it was Sparta which sought hegemony not only in the Peloponnese but in the entire Greek world. With Persia's help, Sparta now was able to be master of Greece itself although the Asian colonies had to be given up to Persia. It was the military stalemate between the anti-Spartan coalition and Sparta and her allies which sparked the Persian diplomatic intervention, especially the struggle for Corinth (395–387 B.C.) as the chief indication of the military impasse.

The rise of Thebes now signaled the end of the brief Spartan hegemony in Greece. In the famous battle of Leuctra (371 B.C.) the Spartan military tactics failed for the first time in the face of the Theban revolutionary phalanx, and Spartan predominance in Greek affairs was at an end. Theban ascendancy, however, was short lived. Theban imperial ambitions were countered by a grand coalition of Athenians, Spartans, and other states. In 362 B.C., the anti-Theban coalition was defeated, but the death of Epaminondas, the Theban leader of genius, spelled the end of Theban ambitions. With the exhaustion of all these powers, the stage was set for the defeat of all of them separately or together by Philip of Macedon and the successor empire of Alexander the Great (Scramuzza and MacKendrick 1958).

In the events following the Thirty Years' War, the process is similar although the protagonists and outcomes differ. As at the end of the Peloponnesian War and its sequels, the exhaustion of the principals led to the testing of power and force capabilities by a rising power, France. Although a combatant in the Thirty Years' War, France was not especially weakened by it, having entered it seriously only in the latter stages. Indeed, France, emerges as the most powerful continental land power in 1648. The continuing Franco-Spanish War until 1659 as an outgrowth of the Thirty Years' War further confirmed the rise of French power.

With the rise of Louis XIV, the mobilization process begins in earnest. In 1667–1668 another war against Spain was waged, this time the War of Devolution. This was followed by the more destructive Dutch War of

1672–1679. But now after seeing the humbling of the Dutch and Spanish in the first two of Louis XIV's Wars, the English, formerly neutral, now chose to intervene in what was to be called the War of the League of Augsburg (1688–1697). Here, the conflict was widened from the relatively few participants of the Dutch War—Spain and some German rulers, such as the Elector of Brandenburg in support of Holland—to a larger great power array of Austria, Spain, and now England under the leadership of William of Orange, the implacable foe of Louis XIV (Hayes, Baldwin, and Cole 1967).

This widening sphere of war was to be followed by the longest and most intense war of all, the War of the Spanish Succession (1702–1713). Louis XIV welcomed the terms of the will of Charles II of Spain which specified that, upon his death, the grandson of Louis XIV would become King of Spain. This prospect that "the Pyrenees no longer exist" (Hayes 1932, 309) was obviously deeply unsettling to the European powers. A grand alliance of England, Holland, Austria, Brandenburg-Prussia, Hanover, and, later, even Portugal was assembled against France and Spain. This was to be the mobilization war of France against Europe (excepting Spain) which was to dwarf the mobilization properties of the War of the League of Augsburg. Whereas in the earlier wars Louis XIV sought territorial gains for France and increases to Bourbon glory, here the combination of France and Spain, with all of the Spanish colonial territories in Europe (for example, Belgium) and America, would be tantamount to hegemony.[2]

It is this seeking after hegemony, as Louis XIV did in the War of the Spanish Succession, which distinguishes this war both from the previous wars of Louis XIV and from the structural systemic wars. Here, the attempt at hegemony parallels the Spartan, Theban, and, most notably and successfully, Macedonian efforts consequent upon the Peloponnesian War. A major difference, of course, is the fact that the major protagonists in the intervening wars differed in the former instance but were the same in the case of Louis XIV. Sparta and Thebes unsuccessfully sought a long-term hegemony after the defeat of Athens in 404 B.C., while it was Louis himself who fought the intervening wars and the final War of the Spanish Succession.

In outcome as well as in process, there are differences. Philip II of Macedon was successful in achieving hegemony. Louis XIV was barely able to maintain some earlier French gains and prevent a massive French defeat. Yet despite these differences in process and outcome, basic similarities are found in the outcome of a power vacuum after the end of the structural war which can serve as a magnet for would-be hegemonic contenders. Unresolved issues remaining from the preceding wars also could impact on the later conflict. Additionally, there can exist a learning process wherein the experience or observation of violence can serve as an accelerator or precipitator of later violence. More will be said on this later.

A final characteristic of the interregnum period is the presence of turmoil internal to some states in question. This conflict allowed disaffected groups or classes within the several states to make common cause with the mobilizing polity. Probably the most famous of these historically is the likely collaboration of Greek upper classes with the Macedoneans as Philip II pursued his goal of hegemony over all of Hellas (Mann 1986, 220–221; Rostovtzeff 1941). The interwar period of the twentieth century witnessed the rise of strong fascist movements in both Britain and France which were favorable to the mobilizing leaders, Hitler and Mussolini. Indeed, it was said in many French banking and high army and clerical circles that "better the German Hitler on the Champs Elysées than the Socialist Jew, Blum." It was this basic hostility to the French state personified at that time by its Prime Minister, Léon Blum, that likely contributed to the French sociopolitical paralysis prior to the Second World War and rapid military defeat when the war began in earnest.

Our remaining two interregna between systemic wars exhibit similar properties. In the period immediately prior to the War of the Spanish Succession, not only were significant elements within Spanish society favorable to union with the French monarchy but the government itself ultimately adopted that view. At the end of the French Revolutionary Wars and before the start of the Napoleonic Wars in 1803, there was internal ferment throughout Europe as the concepts of equality and self-determination spread throughout the empires of Europe and undermined their very foundations.

It is here that we find an additional distinction between the systemic and general war, although certain of the circumstances at the outset of both wars are the same. General wars do not rely on the presence of internal conflict for their onset and propagation, although systemic wars, likely do. Certainly, whatever domestic turmoil existed within the European powers between 1748 and 1756, the end of the War of the Austrian Succession (a general war) and beginning of the Seven Years' War, was at a low level and unrelated to the onset of the later mobilizing conflict.

General Wars

The war of the Austrian Succession, although not a systemic war by our reckoning here, exhibits some of the same properties (although surely not the domestic ones), principally because of its structural origins. The combining of the Anglo-Spanish War of Jenkins' Ear with the Austro-Prussian conflict over Silesia came about essentially via France's alliance with both Spain and Prussia. The Spanish monarch hoped to gain more lands in Italy and, thus, sided strongly with his fellow Bourbon, Louis XV of France. In addition to the now hostile relationship with France, Spain's ally, British fears for Hanover's safety after the demonstrably aggressive conquest of

Silesia by Frederick II led the British to support the Austrians (Ritter 1968). Smaller countries also joined the conflict. Essentially, the House of Bourbon in both France and Spain provided the structural link to make this a general although not a systemic war. The indecisiveness of the outcome, however, and the absence of clear power superiorities and inferiorities was to make more likely the more destructive mobilization war of 1756–1763: the Seven Years' War.

As in the Peloponnesian War (and its sequels), the Thirty Years' War, the French Revolutionary Wars, and World War I, a major outcome of the War of the Austrian Succession was to not clearly specify a power or group of powers as decidedly superior. Although Austria lost Silesia, the power of Austrian arms was not so inferior to Prussian that Maria Theresa would not seek another round. Moreover, the colonial fighting between the British and French was very indecisive. Thus, when Maria Theresa sought to regain Silesia, first by diplomatic maneuvers which included the "diplomatic revolution" of alliance with France (a measure of her determination to even ally with the traditional Austrian enemy), and war broke out in 1754 between French and English colonists in America, the new mobilization war was begun shortly thereafter.

Here, it was Austria which had bent every diplomatic and military effort to regain Silesia (Hayes *et al.* 1967). It was a war with a particular purpose that would, in addition to the restoration of territory, once and for all deal effectively with the rising power of Prussia. The mobilization efforts were not restricted to Austria, but Russia too sought to deal a blow to the upstart Frederick. Although Frederick struck first in Saxony, it was only after becoming aware of the war preparations against him.

Modernity

Our final two instances of mobilization wars consequent upon structural predecessors reflect more of a modern component. The Napoleonic Wars (1803–1815) followed the French Revolutionary Wars (1792–1802) and World War II followed World War I. The modernity of both is reflected in the sources of the first set of wars and the role of modern armaments in the second.

The French Revolution, which began in 1789, was to have one very important international consequence in addition to its frightening portent for the monarchs of Europe. The emigration of frightened French nobility to safer havens, such as those of Austria and Prussia, was to augment the already internationalized European nobility. Thus, in addition to the fact that Marie Antoinette was the sister of the Austrian Emperor, many emigrés, especially those centered in Coblenz, were to agitate for foreign intervention in the French Revolution (Palmer 1971). Out of these structural

138

nexi were to come the French Revolutionary Wars of the First and Second Coalition, ending only after the Peace of Amiens. Although extremely favorable to Napoleon, this settlement did not stop his appetite for conquest. The earlier French Revolutionary Wars had revealed the weakness of France's opponents. Napoleon, after 1803 and the failure of the Peace of Amiens, would proceed with the next twelve years of war.

The modernity of this sequence of wars can be seen in its origins in the French Revolution. Here, no longer was the whim of the monarch sufficient to at least begin preparations for war (he also had to get sufficient funds to pay troops); now the populace for the first time was involved. And it was a dramatic upheaval which led directly to the onset of the first of these wars, a condition hardly realized in all of European dynastic history until that time. The popular mobilization for revolution against the monarchy also made possible the later mobilization of the population for the Napoleonic Wars. An army of 400,000 was assembled for the invasion of Russia in 1812, an unheard of figure for that period.

Modernity also appears in the final sequence that we will consider, namely the First and Second World Wars. The structural properties of World War I have been made clear enough in chapter 5 in the overlap between solely great power disputes and those involving smaller powers as well. The inequality attendant upon the multipolar situation also contributes to this circumstance. We will have occasion, later in the next chapter, to examine in greater detail the distinction between World War I and World War II as, respectively, structural and mobilization wars. For now, we can observe that the structural properties of World War I are not duplicated in World War II. Instead, the power interregnum of the interwar period became particularly apparent as Hitler began to probe for the strengths and weaknesses of the Allies. In so doing and observing the essential weakness of the Anglo-French coalition, the mobilization for war by Germany accelerated during the late 1930s.

It is opportune here to consider some essential differences between the systemic wars we have identified and the nonsystemic general wars for, in so doing, some aspects of modernity will appear in the systemic nature of World War I. All of the structural systemic wars—the Peloponnesian War, the Thirty Years' War, the wars of the French Revolution, and World War I—share a property that distinguishes them from the remainder, namely, the existence of strong religious, ideological, or domestic structural conflicts. Put another way, the appropriate way of living one's life was at issue in these wars, in contrast to the War of the Austrian Succession or the Seven Years' War, in which such an issue was not at stake.

Thus, in addition to the concern over who wins or loses in the structural systemic war, there exists at least one additional axis of conflict in these wars which makes the stakes incomparably higher. In the Peloponnesian War, it was democracy or oligarchy which, as a direct system of government, depended heavily on who won or lost, Athens or Sparta. Clearly, the everyday life of the ordinary citizen was to be affected by the outcome. The Thirty Years' War witnessed the great clashes between Protestant and Catholic (at the outset, more properly Calvinist, Lutheran, and Catholic) which did nothing less than specify whether or not salvation and grace were to ensue and in what form. Clearly, these were burning issues of the period for all people. The French Revolutionary Wars introduced the then momentous issue of the replacement of monarchies by republics—of course a direct threat to the divine right of monarchs. And in World War I the issue of dictatorship or at least unpleasant autocratic rule versus democracy was introduced, first with the violation of Belgian neutrality by Germany and then, soon after, by the brutality of the early phase of the occupation of Belgium. Clearly, these were all fundamental issues of governance or ideography of a very basic sort.

It is this second conflict axis, in addition to who wins or loses, which intensifies the conflict. One can understand these systemic wars with all their intensity and bloodshed as in part a consequence of these fundamental issues. Certainly, issues of this type were not present in the two general wars considered here: the War of the Austrian Succession or the Seven Years' War.

Yet in World War I, even after the occupation of Belgium, the distance between autocrats and democrats was not that great. Tsar Nicholas II had as his principal title "Autocrat of all the Russias" and, of course, Russia fought on the side of the Allies. Here, the element of modernity enters with the introduction of new weapons of offense and defense (Quester 1977), which in itself was to prolong the conflict. One can understand the brutality of German rule in Belgium in 1914 and its claimed (by the Allies) confluence with autocracy as a consequence, in part, of the frustration experienced by the German leaders at the failure of the timetable of the Schlieffen plan as the result of the stubborn Belgian resistance. Without that resistance, made possible not only by Belgian bravery but also by the fortresses and defensive weapons used to good effect by the Belgians, the Schlieffen plan might well have succeeded. Thus, whereas the Germans expected a short, immediate breakthrough of the Belgian lines to Paris, they were held up over ten days, thus allowing the French to bring reinforcements to the Marne and preventing the early collapse of France as demanded by the Schlieffen Plan.

The war carried on in its condition of stalemate (very much by artillery and machine gun), thus increasing immeasurably the number of casualties but also fueling the accusations of German barbarism and its confluence with German autocracy. Later, unrestricted submarine warfare and the sinking of passenger ships, such as the Lusitania, were to continue to propel the ideographic aspect of the war in this direction. It was a complex mix of technology and ideas which ultimately was to make of World War I a modern systemic war.

Timing

The timing between the end of the structural war and the onset of its mobilization successor can be variable and, indeed, can go through various stages which differ from one instance to the next. In the sequels to both the Peloponnesian War and the Thirty Years' War there occurred a series of smaller wars which demonstrated the weakness of the various single opponents and even coalitions in the face of a determined mobilizer. The end result in one case was enforced hegemony by Philip of Macedon; in the other it was the War of the Spanish Succession between Louis XIV and virtually the rest of Europe. The period between the two World Wars of this century was not very different in that the Spanish Civil War and Sino-Japanese War, as well as the Italo-Ethiopian War, demonstrated the lack of resistance to determined mobilized aggression.

In other circumstances, there can exist a very short period between the end of one form of general or systemic war and the onset of the other, as in the eight years between the end of the War of the Austrian Succession and the onset of the Seven Years' War (1756) or the one year between the signing of the Peace of Amiens and its failure in 1803. In both instances, the issues were fairly clear at the end of the structural war. In the former it was the success of Frederick II, which the Austrians needed some seven years to build a coalition against. In the latter instance, it was the power of Napoleon that was evident already at the end of the French Revolutionary Wars that took only a very short time to be demonstrated anew in his violations of the Treaty of Amiens.

Despite these processual differences among our instances of structural–mobilization pairs, the outcome in all instances is the same. The rise of a great mobilizing leader with clear aggressive intent seeking to fill the power vacuum by means of force and using the already acclimated, perhaps even violence-acculturated population to his own advantage, is a hallmark of the mobilization war. The ease with which the German population marched off to war in 1939 attendant upon the mobilization process is one case in point, as was the willingness of France to equip Napoleon with yet another army in 1814 after his escape from Elba. It is the person of Philip of Macedon, Louis XIV, Frederick the Great, Napoleon, or Hitler which stands at the center of the mobilizing polity, in contrast to the structural war in which there is no central figure of note initiating the conflict.[3]

The salient features of all of these conflicts series are the virtually uninterrupted, somewhat episodic violence between the end of the structural and beginning of the mobilization wars, and the rise of the mobilizing leader as the central figure in the initiation of the later mobilization conflict.

At the end of the mobilization variant of the structural mobilization pair with its turmoil between the two wars, there generally is a long period of peace begun either by the victory or decisive defeat of the mobilizing leader, at least within the region in question. Philip's victories, followed by those of Alexander, ended the long period of violence and power interregnum begun by the Peloponnesian War in Hellas. The War of the Spanish Succession ended the long series of wars begun even before the end of the Thirty Years' War (The Franco-Spanish conflict) and which continued unabated after the accession of Louis XIV to the French throne. Of course, his impact and ambitions also were at an end. The Napoleonic Wars finally ended the period of international violence begun shortly after the French Revolution, and World War II, with the decisive defeat of Hitler, clearly closed the chapter on European turmoil begun in 1914.

Distinctions between the Systemic and General War

At bottom in each of these pairs is an issue of overriding importance which requires widespread violence to resolve successfully. In all of these wars, of course, hegemonic issues intruded forcefully, but beyond these are issues concerning the political and social organization of human society. Underlying the conflict between Athens and Sparta were important issues of democracy versus oligarchy which were of overriding importance to the Greek city-states, as were religious issues to the participants in the Thirty Years' War, at least at the outset. The French Revolution, of course, raised issues of transcending political importance to the monarchies of the day, as did German behavior early in World War I (particularly in Belgium) and, of course, in World War II. Sometimes the early issues, which were so important at the outset of the war, tend to be transformed into others, as in the later secularization of the Thirty Years' War and the rise of the issue of French preponderance. That issue was to be transformed still later into one of the virtual survival of the centralized French polity during the War of the Spanish Succession.

We now see the distinction between the systemic and general war developed in bolder relief. Initially, the distinction between the two rested on the extent of civilian participation, but now we can ask the more fundamental question of why that participation comes about in one case and not (or much less so) in the other. The answer resides essentially in the nature of the conflict issues. Whereas we have just seen that the issues generated in connection with our systemic wars are of fundamental importance to both polity and society, this is not the case with our one general structural–mobilization pair. Here, at the outset of both wars, the territory of Silesia conquered by Frederick the Great at the onset of the War of the Austrian Succession was at issue. If Frederick was to disgorge Silesia—the most bloody and intense locus of both the War of the Austrian Succession and the Seven Years' War—Prussia would have been disengaged from the war. All that Maria Theresa wanted was the return of Silesia to Austria, and she quickly would have made peace if that territory had been returned (Blum, Cameron, and Barnes 1966). As the central continental opponent of Frederick, of course, Austria's continued participation in the war was most critical. Although Elizabeth I of Russia hated Frederick personally and, perhaps, had more ambitious war aims, nevertheless they were not of the same dimension as those found in the War of the Spanish Succession, our closest point of comparison to a general war. In this war, territory was no longer at issue as it was throughout the Seven Years' War. Whatever territorial issues might have been outstanding already had been resolved fairly early in the conflict. The territories of Belgium and formerly held French possessions along the Rhine had been conquered by the victorious Allied powers fairly early in the war. Now it was France herself and the future survival of the centralized French polity and society as had evolved under Louis XIV which were at stake.

Thus, we can summarize the principal characteristics of our structural–mobilization pairs of systemic wars: (1) The structural war originates as a consequence of overlapping conflicts among the several protagonists which, in turn, has important implications for the balance of power; (2) there exists a virtually uninterrupted series of conflict behaviors or turmoil between the end of the structural war and the onset of the mobilization variant; (3) the mobilization war is characterized by the rise of a strong leader who is either fairly decisively victorious or defeated in that war; and (4) the issues governing both the systemic structural and mobilization wars are of transcending importance, as can be seen by a comparison between perhaps the most "doubtful" of our systemic wars (the War of the Spanish Succession) to that of a superficially similar but, at bottom, substantially distinct general war (the Seven Years' War).

War Aims in
the Structural Context

Before turning away from this topic, an issue that should be addressed concerns the implications of these findings for the literature that has accumulated around the issue of Germany's aims in World War I. In treating this issue, differences will emerge between the behavior of major powers in the structural and mobilization instances. I shall not address the matter of war blame or guilt, for such a cavil is not likely to yield a productive outcome. More to the point is the relevance of the distinction between structural and mobilization wars for the argument claiming Germany's aggressive intent in World War I, as exemplified by Fischer (1967).

First, a necessary distinction, and one that is too frequently overlooked, is that between processes relevant to the onset of the war and those that take place after its beginning. Although the blank check given to Austria-Hungary by Germany clearly increased the probability of the war's onset, there was no inevitability that it would lead to that consequence. After all, the same blank check issued to Austria-Hungary in 1908 yielded a very different outcome. The Kaiser, however, did not know (perhaps could not know) that the conflict system in 1914 was an unstable one upon joining the great power and small power disputes, in contrast to the stability evidenced in 1908 under conditions of the same overlap as seen in chapter 5. Thus, the same blank check could have utterly different results in the two instances. Here, the emphasis on subjective motivation in the matter of war "blame" is at issue, for the outcome of war or peace was dependent far more on the objective characteristics of the conflict system in 1914 in contrast with, say, 1908, than on intentions of decision makers.

Another perspective is supplied by the fact that fully five-sixths of Fischer's treatment (roughly 500 out of 600 pages) contains evidence and argumentation drawn from the period *after* the war's onset. These were goals of conquest and annexation in Eastern and Western Europe that obviously were in the minds of German decision makers before the war, but could only be seriously implemented when it appeared as if victory in the West was imminent in the very early stages of the war (for example, Bethmann-Hollweg's September plan for German disposition of conquered territory as described by Kagan (1987)). Reasoning by analogy, as does Kagan in his analysis of this problem as related to a possible World War III, a plan to dispose of certain territories in Eastern Europe or even in the Soviet Union in a specified manner favorable to the West after a "victory" in nuclear war does not imply that such a war is made substantially more likely. Contingency plans always exist for the eventualities of victory or defeat against a potential enemy. Again, we see that the time span before and after the war's onset must be kept analytically distinct in our understanding of the war's etiology.

A third perspective is suggested by the term structural war itself. It has been taken to mean a war whose antecedents include significant international structural influences such as alliances, especially as they affect the eventual overlap between the two kinds of disputes—great power and great power-small powers—just prior to the war. Here the various alliance formations of the late nineteenth and early twentieth centuries gave rise to a clear sense of political paranoia and defensiveness among both German civilian and military decision makers as exemplified by Moltke, Chief of the German General Staff, who stated that Germany was "in a condition of hopeless isolation which was growing ever more hopeless" (quoted in Fischer 1967, 50).

This defensive posture is a vastly different matter from the clearly aggressive mode adopted by Hitler in World War II, or for that matter, Napoleon, Louis XIV, or Philip of Macedon in our remaining mobilization

144

wars. Thus even Fischer, perhaps the foremost proponent of German aggressive intent in World War I, concedes that there was a fundamentally defensive core to Germany's policies prior to the war's onset, differentiating that war from the later mobilization variant of World War II.

Germany's defensive posture and international isolation very likely developed out of wrong-headed aggressive policies that would have given Bismarck cold chills had he been alive, yet the lack of foresighted behavior on the part of German decision makers in causing this isolation between 1891 (the Franco-Russian Entente) and 1908 (the Bosnian crisis and the onset of the naval arms race in earnest) cannot be used to attribute to them deliberate intent to precipitate war in the midst of the later crisis in 1914. On the other hand, one could make such attributions in comparable circumstances in the instances of Hitler and our other mobilizing leaders.

It is fair to say that one or more of the major powers behaves aggressively during the long time period preceding a structural systemic war, especially in colonial or quasi-colonial contexts, but this behavior differs substantially from a deliberate policy of conquest and/or annexation within the systemic core practiced by all of our mobilizing leaders prior to and during the mobilization variant.

Conclusion

A failure to perceive the differences between the structural and mobilization variants of the systemic war can have fatal consequences. At Munich in 1938, Neville Chamberlain obviously was committed to the prevention of another systemic war on the order of World War I, yet by demonstrating the extreme willingness to compromise, if not appease, he actually hastened the coming of World War II. The onset of a structural war such as the Thirty Years' War or World War I implies a defensive posture by one or more of the protagonists, principally as the result of overlapping conflicts and threatened changes in the balance of power. In the Thirty Years' War, it was the Empire in Central Europe and, in particular, the Habsburg domains which were on the defensive against the Protestant inroads, especially in the important Kingdom of Bohemia (Trevor-Roper 1970, 270). In the onset of World War I, the perceptions (although perhaps not the actuality) of threat and hostility by their enemies directed against the Dual Alliance (Zinnes *et al.* 1961; O. R. Holsti 1972b) revealed a similar dynamic. Any increase in threat obviously could worsen the situation and make the onset of war a more likely outcome. The perceived need to support Austria-Hungary, by German decision makers, or at least prevent its defection of course, was pronounced.

The mobilization dynamics in Germany during the late 1930s on the other hand, revealed an intention to at least employ military force against neighboring countries (in contrast to aggressive policies in colonial contexts prior

145

to World War I), if not to initiate a global conflict. Given the already existing forceful intent, the threat of a military confrontation in 1938 could have diminished the probability of war, especially with the German General Staff's growing doubts about the wisdom of the entire aggressive enterprise. Thus, a much less accommodating posture and a demonstration of resolve on the part of Chamberlain might have had the desired result of "peace in our time," or at least a diminution in the extent of the conflict.

The pairing of structural and mobilization systemic wars in this manner enables us to understand what might otherwise be viewed as anomalous findings. Doran and Parsons (1980, 956–957), for example, found that Germany experienced the most rapid decline in relative capability[4] of any major power prior to World War II, yet still initiated its ill-fated *revanche* against the Allied powers. Only in the context of the preceding structural war, its residue of embitterment and, perhaps more important, its legacy of an apparent power interregnum on the European continent can we understand this impulse of *revanche* with its near certainty of defeat.

Another set of findings explained, at least in part, by the structural-mobilization pair and differences in the origins of the two forms of systemic war is that of Richardson (1960). He found that his model of the arms race between two international coalitions provided an excellent fit to the data preceding World War I but needed major alterations, particularly in requiring an *N*-adic treatment, in order to fit the World War II arms race. (This, incidentally, is consistent with the distinction between alliance and *N*-adic memories used to distinguish between structural and mobilization wars in Table 6.1.) Finally, theories concerned with the timing of the long cycle (Modelski 1978; Thompson 1983; Väyrynen 1983; Goldstein 1985) appear to have greater empirical validity when World War II is paired with World War I.

A further development of the overall theme of this chapter within a broader historical context will be found in the discussion of a historical dynamic in the Conclusion, chapter 11.

Notes

1   Although it was the fear of Athenian power which was an issue in the Peloponnesian War, it is clear from virtually all accounts of the war (Thucydides 1954; Kagan 1969; Ste. Croix 1972) that neither Athens nor Sparta wanted the war and even made an interim peace as soon as was diplomatically feasible to do so. It is this reluctance to wage war by the principals that distinguishes the structural variant from the mobilization wars in which Philip of Macedon, Louis XIV, Napoleon I, and Hitler clearly did not shrink from the waging of aggressive warfare.
2   For treatments of the wars of Louis XIV, see Tanner (1934), Atkinson, (1934), G. Clark (1970), and Veenendaal (1970).

3   Pericles, of course, was the Athenian leader at the outbreak of the Peloponne-
     sian War, but Athens was warred upon instead of the converse (at least initially),
     and Frederick as a political–military leader had not yet emerged as central to the
     conflict in the War of the Austrian Succession, having just assumed the throne.
     In any event, Frederick hoped to annex Silesia without a major war, given the
     recent accession of the seemingly passive young Maria Theresa to the Austrian
     Throne. It was even unclear whether she would keep the throne, given the
     uncertainty of the Austrian succession at that time.
4   As Doran and Parsons (1980, 957) put it: "To the extent that relative capability is
     accurately depicted by these curves, the German *revanche* under Hitler was
     remarkable not for its proximity to victory but for its recklessness and high
     probability of defeat . . . in the face of overwhelming latent military capability
     elsewhere in the system."

8

A Comparison between Two Systemic Wars

STRUCTURAL WARS, as we have seen, and mobilization wars are suggested as distinct categories of systemic war. In the former instance, the conflicts among the several protagonists feed directly into the events or large-scale crisis initiating the war. Specifically, the 1914 summer crisis preceding World War I combined exclusively great power conflicts with the great power–small power disputes.

In chapter 5, the conflict system of the great powers exclusively demonstrated stability, as did the great power–small power system. It was only upon combining the two systems that instability was discovered. The great power–small power conflict system included, of course, conflicts between Austria-Hungary and Serbia, which were then combined with the exclusively great power conflicts, such as those between France and Germany or between Germany and Russia. The critical event was the blank check given by Germany to Austria-Hungary to do, with full German support, as she pleased with Serbia in the crisis. This unconditional support by Germany of the proposed Austro-Hungarian action against Serbia was the effective nexus between the great power conflict system and that composed of great power–small power disputes. It was Austria-Hungary among the great powers which experienced the majority of conflicts with small powers such as Bulgaria, Serbia, Montenegro, or Rumania, while Germany was involved principally in conflict with other great powers such as France or Russia. As such, the crisis (and especially this aspect of it) was a direct reflection of the conflict processes preceding the war, which included the intense hostility between Austria-Hungary and Serbia concerning pan-Slavic appeals emanating from the latter, and, of course, the ongoing great power rivalries.

In this sense, the structure of conflict relationships necessary to the onset of the war was completed by the crisis. Two independent strains of conflict behavior, exclusively great power conflicts and great power–small power disputes, were united prior to the war, as in the previous illustrations of German disputes with other great powers and Austro–Hungarian conflicts with smaller, principally Balkan countries.

One finds similar connections between disparate conflicts in other structural wars. The Thirty Years' War, for example, began in Central Europe with the Bohemian Revolt against Habsburg rule in 1618, and then was followed by the Netherlands' war against Habsburg Spain, in which the two conflicts were united not merely by the presence of the same dynastic house in both locations but also because of the requirement for Spanish troops to pass though Central European battle zones to reach their destination in the Low Countries (Pagès 1970; Polisensky 1971). The Peloponnesian War, in which the Corinthian conflict with Corcyra became united with the Athenian conflict with Potidaea (both essentially colonial-type wars) and was soon to involve Sparta in the conflict with Athens as a consequence of the alliance between Corinth and Sparta, is open to a similar interpretation. The revolution in the Austrian Netherlands threatened to join with that of France in the early 1790s, and this nexus plus the royalist French emigrés in Austria gave impetus to the onset of the French Revolutionary Wars.

In the mobilization war, on the other hand, no such dependence on an overlapping structure of conflict relationships need exist. The mobilization takes place internal to the nation-state, perhaps in response to earlier international conflicts but not necessarily to any which take place at the time of the onset of the war. The mobilizing polity initiates the vast majority of the conflict behaviors preceding the war. World War II is an instance of a war begun largely by a mobilizing polity, Germany (and perhaps another, Japan), which had aggressive designs on neighboring territories virtually from the earliest days of the war-prone regimes in power. Here, there is no clear instance of a crisis occurring immediately prior to the onset of the war. Although Munich did occur one year earlier, the issues of that crisis and Sudeten territory were resolved, however unhappily for the Czechs, in that conference. The invasion of Poland as the immediate event of concern in the onset of World War II was not associated with a crisis of major proportions, essentially having emerged from Hitler's aggressive intent. The Napoleonic Wars began in a similar fashion as a consequence of the then extensive mobilization of France for war, as did the wars of Louis XIV, especially the War of the Spanish Succession. Philip of Macedon, of course, mobilized and planned carefully for the eventual conquest of all of Greece.

The question now is whether we can detect any empirical differences in the patterns of conflict behavior preceding each of the two modern instances of systemic war in response to these theoretical distinctions. Data of this kind simply are not available for the analysis of earlier systemic wars, and so we will have to rest content with a systematic examination of the contemporary period. If the structural and mobilization wars indeed are different forms of systemic war, then the conflict behaviors preceding each should reflect this distinction. Specifically, the structural war as exemplified by World War I should be far more sensitive to the disputes between nations which occur just prior to the war than should the mobilization war. The pattern of conflict relationships and, especially, their overlap prior to the war's outbreak is the essential ingredient in the structural case; there should exist a fair degree of independence from this concern in the mobilization instance.

Although the equilibrium equations attendant upon the hierarchical equilibrium distinguished between peaceful periods and those ending in systemic war, a first empirical clue to some differences between the two systemic war periods emerges. The application of the equilibrium equations [2.1] and [11A]–[13A] yielded a chi-square value for goodness of fit between observation and prediction of 16.505, df = 5, $p < 0.01$ for the 1893–1914 period, and one of 14.706, df = 8, $p < 0.10$ for 1919–1939 (see pp. 234–235). It is clear that the departure of theory from observation is more emphatic for 1893–1914 because of the lower probability level for the chi-square statistic. This is our first empirical distinction between the two wars. However, for the establishment of firm distinctions we require a model now which allows for a detailed empirical examination of these disputes.

The equilibrium relations which gave rise to the somewhat different (in detail) but essentially similar conclusion of instability for both the 1893–1914 and 1919–1939 periods required a time period of some length (approximately twenty years) in order to accumulate sufficient data for a reliable conclusion. It would be impossible to use these equations for the analysis of short time periods just prior to the war as is required here. As such, we seek an alternative model which can demonstrate a sensitivity and responsiveness to conflict behavior, here the disputes among nation-states.

A model of diffusion or contagion can provide such a measuring instrument for the detection and display of sensitivities of this type.[1] This is because a first-order response to the observation of conflict can be a contagious response in which certain countries enter into the conflict system and others remain outside of it. Generally, the number of countries responding to the contagious conflict system will increase over time preceding a structural war, while no such requirement should exist for the mobilization war, principally because of the internal dynamics of the mobilization process. A primary difference between the structural and mobilization war is the sensitivity of the former to the structure of conflict relationships in the international system, while the latter should exhibit no such sensitivity, at least at the time that the war is initiated. The principal feature of overlapping conflicts in the structural case implies the increased involvement of a larger number of conflicts and, hence, countries in this instance in comparison with the mobilization war.

Well-known models of diffusion or contagion are, however, notorious for their susceptibility to different and even contradictory interpretations of their outcomes (Feller 1968; Midlarsky 1978). Such is the case with the negative binomial distribution which can be interpreted as a model of diffusion or, alternatively, as a model of heterogeneity. Diffusion is defined as the increased probability of a particular event occurring elsewhere in the system after the prior occurrence of a similar event and should be contrasted with heterogeneity as simply differential (for example, policy-based) propensities on the part of countries to experience the phenomenon in question (Feller 1968, 1970; Midlarsky 1970; Job 1976; Siverson and Duncan 1976). Bivariate distributions (Midlarsky 1983a,b), which divide the time period in two, can provide the necessary distinctions, but again, a fairly large amount of data is required over a considerable length of time.

There exists, however, a model of diffusion which is not susceptible to differing interpretations (Feller 1971, 57; von Mises 1957, 143).[2] This is the Polya (or Polya–Eggenberger) distribution which, in fact has the negative binomial as a limiting case (Johnson and Kotz 1977) but can be used in its pristine form to realistically approximate the diffusion condition.

The Polya Distribution

The Polya distribution arises from an urn model in which there exist b black balls and r red balls in an urn. After each withdrawal, s balls of the same color as the one just withdrawn are placed in the urn. For example, if a black ball was chosen, then s black balls are introduced into the urn, prior to the next withdrawal. Thus, there exists an increased probability of a black ball being chosen on the next withdrawal. It can be seen that this is an approximate model of diffusion, for after each event of a certain type, say a dispute, there exists an increased probability of a like event as in another dispute occurring in the next time interval.

This increased probability can occur as the result of new issues arising from the settlement of the earlier dispute (for example, the Serbian hostility toward Austria-Hungary intensifying after the Austro-Hungarian annexation of Bosnia-Herzegovina in 1908). The new level of international antagonism then implies an increased likelihood of another such dispute occurring in the foreseeable future, as indeed occurred in 1914. The likelihood of new countries entering the later conflict also is increased because of the diplomatic maneuvering during the interval between the two disputes and the consequent polarization of the system in that time period.

Indeed, the diffusion process captures certain of the dynamics identified in the overall model of chapter 1. Inequalities among great powers, as in the disputes between Russia and the Dual Alliance powers over the Balkans, yield ultimately the Bosnian crisis which then sets the stage for further disputes among the great powers that now include additional small powers as well. All that remains, then, is an overlap among several disputes occurring just prior to the onset of the war.

The probability function of the Polya distribution is, for n repetitions of the procedure and s number of balls of the color just withdrawn replaced in the urn, with b and r defined as above (Johnson and Kotz 1977, 371).

$$P\left[x = j\right] = \binom{n}{j} \frac{\left(\frac{b}{s}\right)^{j} \left(\frac{r}{s}\right)^{n-j}}{\left(\frac{b+r}{s}\right)^{n}} \qquad (j = 0, 1, \ldots, n) \qquad [8.1]$$

where

$$\binom{n}{j} = \frac{n!}{j! \, (n - j)!}$$

Tables of the Polya distribution are published in Johnson and Kotz (1977, 218–237). For each value of the maximum number of disputes, n, experienced by the most conflict-prone countries in a given time period, the tables are entered; by inspection, the parameter values providing the best goodness of fit are selected. Theoretical values corresponding to these parameters are then used to calculate the predicted numbers in the tables. Neighboring parameters (for example, $s = 3$ instead of $s = 4$) are inspected in order to verify that the tabled values chosen give the best correspondence between theory and observation.

Time periods of concern are those preceding the two world wars. The data utilized are the Correlates of War Militarized Dispute Data (Gochman and Maoz 1984), as in our prior analyses. Disputes are those involving two or more major powers and at least one central power (mostly European; Singer and Small 1968, 254) for the nineteenth century until World War I and a circumscribed international system thereafter which approximates the contours of the older central system.[3]

First, we consider the period prior to our example of a structural war, World War I. Here, the Polya distribution is applied to all of the conflicts enumerated above during 1893–1914. This period is chosen because of the consummation of the Franco-Russian alliance at this time. Parameters of the theoretical distribution are given in Table 1C (see Tabular Appendix C). The fit is a good one, as can be seen from the chi-square goodness-of-fit test; the predicted values reproduce the observed numbers to a fair degree of precision.

It would be useful now to divide the interval in two in order to see if there are any substantial differences between the conflict behaviors in each of the two portions of the interval. Here, 1908 is chosen as the cutoff in order to evaluate the extent of change upon the onset of the naval arms race in 1908 [Richardson (1960) chose this year as well] with the failure of the Naval Conference of that year to set limits on such armaments.[4] The six-year interval prior to the war also will provide an equal time period to that which will be analyzed in 1933–1939. The results for 1893–1907 and 1908–1914 are entirely equivalent.[5] The chi-square values have the same probabilities of chance occurrence. Indeed, the applicability of the Polya distribution in the 1908–1914 interval is very good, with a clear correspondence between prediction and observation.

An intriguing question is the extent to which the earlier 1871–1892 period also reflects these patterns, for if the diffusion of conflict behavior began immediately after the formation of the German Empire, then the 1893 cutoff is much too late and one can attribute the development of these conflict processes to the formation of the German Empire and an attendant political destabilization of the European system.

In fact, we find that the Polya model fails to predict the observed values. This is the first departure from prediction for the model and suggests a differential applicability based on theoretical expectation, for the period immediately subsequent to the formation of the German Empire was not historically one of the unbridled spread of conflict throughout the system. Instead, the efforts of Bismarck to create countervailing power coalitions tended to approximate the earlier balance-of-power system that emerged shortly after the still earlier breakdown of the Concert system (Langer 1966; Midlarsky 1981). The analysis of this period supports this historical understanding of the post-1871 period.

It is when we turn to the 1919–1939 period, that we find more emphatic rejection of the diffusion model. The chi-square goodness-of-fit statistic now is significant at $p < 0.05$. The Polya diffusion model is no longer capable of analytically describing the conflict behavior in this period.

This finding conforms to the theoretical expectation put forward in this study concerning the distinction between structural and mobilization wars. Whereas the former, over time, engages increasing numbers of countries in a conflict spiral which can end in war as shown in analyses of the 1893–1914 period, the latter does not exhibit such a pattern over time but, instead, primarily is a consequence of mobilization efforts internal to the mobilizing nation-state.

However, these mobilization efforts may be, in part, a consequence of the conflict behavior diffusing in the system at an earlier point in time which, then, later conditions the mobilization response. As such, there should exist a distinction between an earlier international conflict-prone period, which might indeed exhibit the diffusion of conflict behavior, and a later period during which the conflict propensity had been internalized within the mobilizing polity. The cutoff in this case is chosen to be 1933, when Hitler came to power in Germany and the mobilization for war began in earnest within the mobilizing polity. Thus, the 1919–1932 period is examined followed by 1933–1939 as the immediate prewar interval.

The Polya distribution is applied to the earlier of the two periods; the fit, although not perfect, is acceptable as an analytic descriptor of this period. Conflict emanating initially from World War I and fueled by the Great Depression spread throughout the system. It is when one examines the 1933–1939 period alone[6] (as we did in 1908–1914) that the departure from the Polya distribution is readily apparent. Here, this distribution fits the data not at all, thus confirming the failure of the Polya diffusion model to effectively describe the period approaching the onset of a mobilization war. Although the international conflict of the earlier (1919–1932) period does likely affect the onset of the mobilization war, it is through the time-lagged intermediary of the mobilization process in at least one country that this occurs, instead of the direct impact of conflict diffusion as in the structural conflict of World War I. The contrast between the results for 1908–1914 (shown in Table 3C) and those for 1933–1939 (given in Table 7C) is striking.

It is instructive to reflect on particular reasons for the failure of the diffusion model in the approach to World War II. An important source of failure becomes apparent when one observes that the majority of the conflict events is found in the tail of the distribution where the six great powers—Germany, Italy, Japan, France, the USSR, and Great Britain—are found. These powers, of course, will soon be at war. By the same token, the remaining countries are found in the upper portion of the distribution with far fewer conflict behaviors.

In contrast, during the period preceding World War I, there is a fairly even spread of conflict behavior over the countries in the system. Although a fair proportion of the countries are heavily involved in the conflict behavior, a large portion are not or are only moderately involved and experience only a few disputes. The prototypical model for this applicability would appear to be the period 1908–1914 (shown in Table 3C) where, with the exception of only one category (four disputes), all are almost perfectly predicted by the Polya model with a fairly even spread of conflict behavior over countries in the system. This, of course, conforms to the image of the structural war in which many countries, both great powers and small powers, contribute to the onset of the conflict in contrast to the mobilization war which would likely be centered on great powers. This conclusion does not obviate the important role of a small power in the onset of a mobilization war. Czechoslovakia and Poland, for example, were critical small powers in the onset of World War II. However, these smaller countries were targeted by the mobilizing power (here Germany) instead of being drawn into a generalized, diffusing, and widespread conflict process as in the approach to World War I.

The notion of intent is critical to our understanding of the initiation of these wars. In the instance of the mobilization war, there exists an aggressive intent on the part of the mobilizing power. Although both Napoleon and Hitler as mobilizing leaders sought to avoid systemic conflicts at the time that their respective wars broke out, their postures and ultimate ambitions nevertheless entailed aggressive actions toward other countries.

No such claims can necessarily be made in the case of the structural war. Here, a crisis of some major proportions erupts, which in the instance of World War I coalesced several conflicts into one, namely, that between Austria-Hungary and Serbia, on the one hand, and Germany with other great powers on the other. The crisis then becomes a necessary condition for the onset of the war, which in the mobilization instance does not require a precipitating crisis for its onset.

Conclusion

A hierarchical equilibrium theory of systemic war had been earlier suggested and distinguished between periods ending in systemic war and those which did not. In turn, certain distinctions have now been found between the two contemporaneous systemic wars, World War I and World War II.

The structural property of a diffusing conflict system involving both great and small powers is exhibited in the approach to World War I. This diffusion property was not demonstrated in the approach to World War II, thus suggesting the status of a mobilization war for this conflict. The Polya distribution as a genuine model of diffusion or contagion was capable of making this distinction.

It is useful to reflect now on the likely contours of a future systemic war, most likely the last of its kind, if it ever occurs. Clearly, both great and small powers have been brought into the current conflict system via the two great alliances of both East and West. Thus, there is the potential for a considerable diffusion of conflict behavior among a wide variety of powers. Further, and perhaps more important, there does not now exist a great power that is clearly mobilizing for war as was the case prior to World War II. Although armaments increases are occurring, none of the superpowers has specific territorial or other potentially inflammatory claims against the other.[7] As such, it is likely via some unexpected turn of events in a smaller, but nevertheless important, country that will likely lead the superpowers to an unwanted war much as occurred in the case of World War I. The origins of the Second World War, then, likely do not provide an adequate model for the onset of a future unexpected conflict, but it is to the initiation of the First World War that we should look for guidance.[8]

These arguments lead to clear implications for precrisis strategies or, at least, policies pertaining to crisis management. Given the juncture between exclusively great power disputes and small power–great power conflicts in the structural conflict of World War I, along with additional parallels found in other structural wars (Thirty Years' War, Peloponnesian War, French Revolutionary Wars), the various dispute sets should be kept operationally distinct from each other. The prevention of the juncture between two or more sets of conflict relationships should be a principal goal of policy makers. Similarly, creating what may, in a formal sense, be called disjoint sets of conflict relationships (see chapter 5) should also be a goal of policy makers. These would be two or more sets of conflicts in which no conflict element would be found in more than one set. The probability of widespread systemic war resulting from a crisis is likely proportional to the extent to which such sets are created. The elimination of serious Cuban influence from the 1962 Cuban missile crisis between the United States and Soviet Union is a case in point, perhaps one to be emulated if a crisis of this magnitude were to be repeated.

Notes

1   In earlier work (Midlarsky 1978), I distinguished between diffusion as imitative behavior, which requires an independent precipitant for its occurrence (for example, an urban disorder occurring only after a police action against a youth gang), and contagion as imitative behavior, which results solely from observation and does not require any precipitating event. In conflict behavior between nation-states, seldom do decision makers act solely upon observation of other behavior, and so precipitants of some sort generally are required. (For example, the Bosnian crisis of 1908, which included Austria-Hungary, Germany, Russia, and Serbia, emerged from the precipitant of the Buchlau agreement between Austria-Hungary and Russia earlier in that year.) As such, the term diffusion is appropriate in this context.

2   Feller (1971, 57) remarks that "The Polya urn model and the Polya process . . . are models for true contagion where every accident effectively increases the probability of future accidents."

3   The disputes here are between the central powers (until 1918) and any other countries in the international system. These disputes also must have involved at least two major powers (also central) in the conflict. The central powers are Austria-Hungary, Denmark, England, France, Holland, Portugal, Prussia (Germany), Russia, Sardinia (Italy), Spain, Sweden, Switzerland, Turkey, Greece, Belgium, Serbia, Rumania, China, Japan, the United States, Norway, Bulgaria, Albania, Czechoslovakia, Poland, and Finland. Between 1919 and 1939 the central system is expanded to include all countries in the world with the exception of Canada and the countries of Latin America. These countries remained largely outside of the major conflict systems of this period to join later only after the onset of World War II.

156

4   There may have been a curious and unfortunate coalescence of several events in 1908. The rise to power of the Young Turks and the consequent power interregnum (which likely invited the later aggressive actions of Italy and the Balkan countries), the Bosnian crisis (with its potential for the later reinforcement of Germany's successful aggressive behavior in supporting Austria-Hungary against Russia), and the failure of the London Naval Conference to regulate conditions of naval warfare that led to the 1909 English Naval Bill, all occurred in 1908.

5   This equivalency does not imply that the 1893–1907 interval demonstrates the same degree of instability as does 1908–1914. Indeed, the continuing diffusion of conflict behavior throughout the overall combined period implies that the addition of the later interval should reflect increased instability over the earlier one alone, as shown in chapter 5.

6   When we restrict the conflict behaviors to those involving European countries only, the same conclusion emerges. Here the chi-square goodness-of-fit statistic between observation and prediction is 4.940, df = 1, $p < 0.05$.

7   China still has outstanding territorial claims on the Soviet Union in the Amur River region and Vladivostok. However, the contemporary evidence suggests that the Chinese have largely abandoned the forcible pursuit of these claims since the late 1960s.

8   Kagan (1987) and Kahler (1979) reach similar conclusions, although from different perspectives than the dispute-based theoretical framework offered here. In this context, also see Aron (1966), Beer (1981), Howard (1983), and Miller (1985).

9

Alliance Durability

THUS FAR, THROUGHOUT this volume the impact of a hierarchical equilibrium or its absence has been explored. The particular dependent variable of concern has been the onset of systemic war or, put another way, system stability. Now, as implied in chapter 1, we turn to some parallel consequences of the existence of hierarchy and explore the impact of this equilibrium on alliance durability. If the existence of this equilibrium leads to system stability in the form of the absence of systemic war, then it is possible that some additional forms of stability might also follow from the presence of this equilibrium. While the existence of hierarchy and positive-sum processes has been found to be related to the absence of systemic war, it is likely that these components of the hierarchical equilibrium have an impact on alliance durability as another form of system stability. Any parallel consequences of the hierarchical equilibrium which yield additional stabilizing influences should, of course, be explored.

Consider first the effects of hierarchy. In a coalition between the weak and very strong, the latter can be controlling.[1] If some political difference should arise within the alliance framework, it is unlikely to eventuate in some rupture of the alliance because of the great disproportion in capabilities which would make it unwise for the small power to accentuate the rift and possibly incur the hostility of the great power. Generally, such mutual dependencies strongly favor the great power, for the small power is most frequently dependent on it for protection and could ill afford to lose it if war were to break out.

Alliances between relative equals, on the other hand, contain structural symmetries which can have the opposite consequence. Larger countries may feel that they can "go it alone" or may not be averse to offending their former ally and seeking new ones for some designated political purpose. Such alliances would end more readily than those with significant asymmetries.

The question of asymmetric resources focuses on one additional important reason for the greater expected longevity of alliances with substantial hierarchies. Large powers at the head of such hierarchies may simply have greater resources at their disposal in attempting to influence the smaller power. The effective use of those resources may yield dividends in the form of political loyalty, if not quiescence within the alliance framework.

In addition to these arguments emerging directly from structural considerations, there is yet another which is more analytically focused. The specification of substantial disparities in capabilities between large and small powers, as in the hierarchical equilibrium, yields what is called a minimum entropy coalition. In such a structure, the degree of disorder or uncertainty is minimized. The entropy in capabilities for a coalition is maximized when there are two powers of roughly equal capabilities and is minimized when the power disparity between the two countries is very large (the formula for the entropy is given in equation [9.1]; values of $p_1 = p_2$ signify maximum entropy, whereas $p_1 \ll p_2$ represents minimum entropy). One need not merely refer to capabilities in the sense of meaning essentially national power; one can also analyze votes for parties in national elections as signifying another form of capability. Here, where durability was measured by longevity of cabinet governments (Midlarsky 1984a), the minimum entropy coalition was found to be more durable than the maximum entropy coalition.

Analytically, a clear analogue exists between the international and domestic counterparts. Minimum entropy for one coalition, if it implies increased durability, should also imply increased durability for its counterpart in another setting. The entropy is sufficiently abstract as a concept and measure to allow generalization across different types of coalitions. It also has been found to have unique properties as a measure of system characteristics that allow for such inter-system comparisons (Ornstein 1973; Sinai 1976).

An additional reason for the stability of the hierarchical coalition arises from the consequences of change. If, as the result of industrialization processes or other internal dynamics, there occur changes in the power relations between two allies, the hierarchical alliance would be far better able to absorb and be tolerant of such changes. In the event that power disparities between great and small powers are sufficiently large, then increments in power to a small country or changes in the power condition of the large country should minimally affect the alliance arrangement. Any such changes would be a small proportion of the total distance in power between the two countries.

In an alliance among equals, on the other hand, small changes in power relations could seriously disturb the coalition framework. The country which is gaining in power could find that it no longer requires the additional security provided by its ally. Alternatively, the less dynamic power could feel threatened by such changes in the power relationship. Rather than endure an emerging domination by its now more powerful ally, the threatened power could seek security in some other coalition which does not carry with it this particular liability.

Finally, if the coalition is sufficiently hierarchical, there exists the possibility of reciprocity. In the game of tit-for-tat [analyzed by Robert Axelrod (1984)], the player cooperates on the first move and then simply imitates the response of the other player in an iterated prisoner's dilemma game. The possibilities for reciprocity are very strong here if the second player reciprocates the first cooperative move—then a series of repeated cooperations can occur. Tit-for-tat defeated all other computer programs in two separate rounds of tournament play.

The greater the extent of hierarchy, the greater the possibilities for reciprocation. First, there would be increased clarity as to the principal source of the cooperation to be reciprocated. In a minimum entropy coalition, the greater the disparity in capability between the large power and small power(s), the greater the likelihood of attributing policy decisions to the leading power. Strong patterns of reciprocity can then develop which would be less likely in the less organized environment of a maximum entropy alliance between approximate equals in power. The clarity of policy sources would be less, and the combined policy of the coalition toward another may contain "mixed signals" arising from the compromise necessitated by the bargaining between equals. Thus, cooperation with a potential enemy defined by a high degree of clarity would be less likely in this maximum entropy alliance, and when it occurs might have diminished probability of reciprocation because of the compromise nature of its appearance.

The issue of clarity or certainty in the signaling process points to an advantage to the use of the entropy measure in addition to its prior successful use in the analysis of domestic coalitions. This is the meaning often attributed to the entropy as a measure of uncertainty (Shannon 1948; Khinchin 1957).[2] The greater the entropy, the greater the uncertainty of the overall configuration, whereas the smaller the entropy, the greater the certainty. Given the concern with clarity both of policy development within the coalition and of signaling to a potential adversary, the entropy interpreted as a measure of uncertainty is, perhaps, uniquely suited to the task of measurement in this instance.

To summarize, the effect of hierarchy within the alliance structure is to (1) introduce a substantial resource base in the great power for the reward of continued cooperation by the small power, (2) provide a comfortable "cushion" against changes in power relationships which could be destabilizing in the absence of such a resource base, (3) yield a minimum entropy coalition with its implied absence of uncertainty, and (4) maximize the potential cooperation of an opposing coalition due to clear reciprocal signaling. All of these factors can yield stability within alliances as well as between opposing alliances which otherwise could be terminated simply as the result of the onset of war.

Thus far, we have considered the effects of the hierarchical component of the hierarchical equilibrium on coalition stability. What of the positive-sum component earlier associated with the independent small powers? Here, the positive-sum aspect is to be found directly within the coalition itself for both the great power leader and its small power ally. As indicated earlier in the discussion of hierarchy, the great power, virtually by definition, has resources at its disposal with which to influence the small power. This influence does not have to be for insidious purposes internationally but can have benign purposes and outcomes in which both the great power and small power benefit from the relationship. Technical assistance or, even more specifically, the activities of agencies such as the Peace Corps have benefited both the great and small power without the threat value that can come from the presence of political representatives of the great power within the borders of the small ally. Relations between these powers can be cemented by such positive-sum processes in the absence of threat, which can further add to the durability of the alliance. The great power gains the further support of the small power, while the latter gains the benefits of the expertise brought by the foreign nationals. The additional individual benefits to both the foreign and domestic nationals wrought by these personal relationships forged over time are, of course, outside the confines of this treatment.

Turning now to the question of alliance durability per se, there has existed, on the whole, a dearth of studies of this phenomenon. A substantial proportion of the systematic empirical studies of alliances have been in relation to war experience (for example, Singer and Small 1966; Singer and Associates 1979; Bueno de Mesquita 1978, 1981b; Wallace 1973; Ostrom and Hoole 1978; Thompson, Duval, and Dia 1979). Many, of course, have focused on alliance formation, as in the Poisson-based studies (McGowan and Rood 1975; Job 1976; Siverson and Duncan 1976; Midlarsky 1981). Alliance cohesion, of course, has been a major focus (Holsti, Hopmann, and Sullivan 1973), with threat perception emerging as a major determinant of cohesion. But this is likely as close as it gets; alliance durability per se has received but scant attention.[3] As Ward (1982, 60) has remarked in his extensive review of the literature and identification of gaps therein, "Considerable examination of the topic of alliance maintenance needs to be undertaken. Despite the lip service paid to this notion, its role in alliance dynamics is virgin territory." If the durability of alliances is properly understood as a form of alliance maintenance, then a study of the type proposed here is required.

Alliance durations, of course, have been measured as empirical quantities (Job 1976; Midlarsky 1983a), but the factors that have contributed to their variations over time (as distinct from cohesion, as a measure of integration) have generally escaped attention. This is perhaps because of the alliance–war nexus; many alliances end at the time a war is begun or are honored during wartime. Examples of the former are the Dual Alliance or Triple Entente ending in 1914 or the alliances between Prussia and various small German principalities ending in 1870. The alliance among the Axis powers (Germany, Italy, Japan, Hungary, Rumania, and Bulgaria) was consummated in 1940–1941. Certain alliances, it can be argued, are begun solely in relation to some impending or ongoing hostilities. Given the presence or possibility of war, then, as a clear factor affecting the formation and duration of alliances, it is understandable why durability in and of itself has not received the attention it deserves. The variable being measured can all too quickly be terminated by an exogenous factor, that is, war.

It is proposed here to examine alliance durability excluding the impact of this exogenous variable. There may indeed be structural elements of alliance organization which can impact on alliance duration without the influence of war. It is to these factors that this chapter is directed.

Procedures

All alliances listed in the Correlates of War (COW) data files between 1816 and 1965 were analyzed. The year 1965 was chosen as the end point for alliance formation during this period instead of 1980 (the last year of data availability) in order to allow for the possibility of recent alliances terminating.[4] If 1980 were used, then little such possibility would exist.

Alliances ending in war or those formed during a war were excluded. This was done, first, in order to minimize the impact of events wholly extraneous to the alliance. A war involving one of the parties to the alliance but having nothing to do with the alliance itself still could end the alliance. Second, as indicated earlier, alliances ending in war could have been formed shortly before the war itself with that end in mind. Sensing the coming of a war, one or another of the future partners might have initiated the proceedings leading to the alliance for immediate security purposes. Thus, it is not the alliance per se that would be the object of inquiry but, essentially, one of the processes leading to war. These considerations apply even more strongly to alliances begun during a war (for example, the signing of the first Axis treaty in 1940).

Of the 190 alliances listed in the COW data, 89 were excluded as a result of these rules of procedure. The remaining 101, then, constituted the data set for the analysis. The basic hypothesis to be tested is that the minimum entropy alliance is more durable then the maximum entropy variety. A fairly stringent test of the hypothesis is that there is a covariation between entropy and durability. The greater the entropy, the smaller the durability of the alliance as measured in years of duration; of course, the converse is hypothesized as well.

There are several possible methods of investigation. First, all dyadic associations could be analyzed. In this format each alliance organization (for example, NATO), no matter how large, would be decomposed into all of the individual dyadic commitments. Formally, this would imply all of the $[N(N-1)]/2$ dyadic possibilities, which is an unrealistic circumstance. The major purpose of such aggregate alliance organizations generally is the protective "umbrella" of the great power (as in NATO), but clearly the adherence of the smaller powers is desired by the great power for security reasons. There is, therefore, an asymmetry in association between small and great powers within the alliance which leads to a far different interpretation for the protective nature of, say, the American–Norwegian association in comparison with the Danish–Norwegian. To treat both as equivalent dyads would be unfortunate.

Another possibility is to examine only the great power–small power dyads. However, here a bias clearly would be introduced in favor of the hypothesis. If one disaggregates the great power–small power dyads and treats each one separately, then the total N would be inflated in favor of individual small power–great power associations. The length of existence of alliances, such as NATO, the Warsaw Pact, or the Rio Treaty, would immediately impart a bias in favor of the durability of the small power–great power or minimum entropy coalitions.

It was therefore decided to treat each alliance organization (for example, NATO) as a separate unit and avoid disaggregation into dyads. The question of appropriate forms of measurement then arose. The entropy is defined as

$$H = -\sum_{i=1}^{N} p_i \log_e p_i \qquad [9.1]$$

where p_i is the proportion of capability of each country in the alliance framework, there are N countries, and the logarithm is taken to the base e. One can, in the measurement of the alliance entropy, include all N countries but, as in the previous discussion of a possible dyadic analysis, this too would be misleading. Because of the additive nature of the entropy, each country, however small its capability, adds to the total value. The sum of those individual values might be quite large, and even if the alliance is solely between the great power and several much smaller powers (for example, NATO, Warsaw Pact), the overall entropy still might be quite high and even, in fact, higher than a dyadic alliance between two great powers exclusively (for example, Austria-Hungary and Germany). Treating the two forms of alliance as approximately equivalent would be misleading.

Two expedients were adopted in response to this problem of measurement. The first was to concentrate on only two countries—(1) the alliance leader, that is, the country with the largest capability; and (2) the smallest power in the alliance—and sum only these two proportions of capability in equation [9.1]. If the alliance was of the hierarchical variety, then it would have a minimum entropy corresponding to that hierarchy. If it was not strongly hierarchical and the only powers in the coalition were approximately equal in capability, then the smallest and largest power would sum to a much higher entropy value and accurately reflect the essential absence of hierarchy. Thus, in this mode of measurement, the largest and smallest proportions of capability in the alliance were entered into equation [9.1] in order to assess the extent of coalition hierarchy.

The second measurement mode was more conservative and analyzed only dyadic alliance organizations (omitting all N-adic cases) under the supposition that there might be some bias in the first mode introduced as the result of including in the entropy calculation only largest and smallest country capabilities from the N-adic alliance. If the hypothesis was still confirmed using only dyadic alliances, omitting such clearly favorable (for the hypothesis) instances as NATO or the Warsaw Pact, then there would be added confidence in the findings. In this second analysis, N also is set equal to two in equation [9.1] as in the first analysis, but only strictly dyadic alliances are included from the data set.

There remains now the matter of the choice of measures of capability. This is complicated by the length of time of the analysis. The only ones which clearly carry across the time period are total population and number of military personnel. Others, such as energy consumption or gross national product (GNP), are collected for most countries only in the later portion of the overall period and so, to a significant degree, a lack of comparability across time would be introduced by the use of such measures.

One possibility is steel production, for which data exist until almost the beginning of the time period of analysis, and this variable is included as a measure of industrial capacity. Probably even more suitable as measures of capability which have operational meaning across the entire time span are the total population and number of military personnel. Early in the nineteenth century, industrial capacity was not yet widely understood to be related to force capability, for military capacity did not yet turn on industrial production. Only later in that century, especially with the Prussian victory in the Franco-Prussian War, was industrial capacity clearly linked to military prowess. Thus, all three measures [size of the total population, number of military personnel, and quantity of steel production (in metric tons)] are included.

Entropy values were calculated using all three measures in separate analyses. For example, in the calculation of entropy values for total population, the proportion of total population in the alliance was calculated for the power with the largest population (p_1) and the proportion for the country with the lowest (p_2). The entropy was then calculated using equation [9.1],

$$H = -(p_1 \log_e p_1 + p_2 \log_e p_2) = 0.119$$

for the first alliance in the set, that emerging directly from the Congress of Vienna in 1815. Values such as these were calculated for all 101 alliances where data were available in the COW capability data set and then correlated with years duration both for the entire set and for the dyadic alliances exclusively. The same procedures were repeated three times for each of the capability measures as the basis of the entropy calculation. (Obviously, no choice of largest or smallest capability need be made in the dyadic analysis because there are only two countries per alliance.)

Results and Discussion

These results yield a 3 × 2 table of correlation coefficients, as shown in Table 9.1. As can be seen from the table, all of the correlation coefficients are significant at least at p < 0.01 for all of the measures of capability used in the entropy calculations. Percentages of variance explained range from 41%, or nearly half of the variance in the case of total population, for the entire set (and nearly that for military personnel), to 11% for steel production in the dyadic analysis. It is clear that the hypothesis is confirmed in all instances. There is a negative relationship between alliance entropy and durability, or put another way, the greater the hierarchical relationship in the alliance, the greater the durability of that alliance.

Table 9.1
Correlations between alliance entropy and years duration, 1815–1965.

Entropy	Total population	Military personnel	Steel production
Total set	-0.64^a $N = 101$	-0.62^a $N = 94$	-0.37^b $N = 98$
Dyadic only	-0.54^a $N = 74$	-0.54^a $N = 67$	-0.33^b $N = 71$

[a] p < 0.001.
[b] p < 0.01.

Differences in the findings deserve mention. Although the dyadic analysis explained a smaller proportion of the variance than did the total data set including the *N*-adic alliances, the differences are not substantial. Given the dyadic treatment as a conservative test which avoids any of the potential positive biases of the total set, there can be a fair degree of confidence in the findings concerning the hypothesized relationship between hierarchy and durability.

Of additional interest is the similarity in findings between the use of total population and military personnel, on the one hand, and the differences between these variables and steel production, on the other. Apparently, steel production is tapping a somewhat different capability dimension than are total population and military personnel. The last of these variables is, perhaps, the most direct measure of capability imaginable. It specifies the number of troops which can be put into the field at a moment's notice, thus suggesting potentialities for the immedate application of force, if necessary. Total population is not quite as direct a measure, but still certainly is not remote as a measure of capability. It suggests the manpower resources immediately available if the number of military personnel needs to be augmented. This measure can be seen as one step removed from the immediacy of application of the number of military personnel.

Steel production, on the other hand, is several steps removed from the application of force. Decisions need to be made as to whether this production will be put to military use and, if so, how quickly this will occur, whereas the size of armies or their immediate potential in the form of available population to be mobilized, is directly relevant. There are many modern instances of heavy steel producers whose production does not primarily have military uses. Sweden, West Germany, Japan, and Canada are cases in point.

Policy Implications

There are two important policy implications which follow from this treatment. First, in the context of alliances, which are immediate policy instruments for mutual protection especially in time of war, the direct instruments of force capability are more relevant than some more remote expression of capability. Put another way, allies (and likely potential antagonists) will trust in a more immediate expression of the use of force than those which are less directly relevant. The greater the degree of trust, especially of a small power dependent on a larger one, the greater the likely duration of the alliance. To this extent, both the United States and USSR have enhanced the durability of their respective hierarchical alliance structures by placing large numbers of military personnel and instruments of war on the territory of smaller powers. Although there would appear to be an element of coercion—especially of countries who, if left to their own devices might not adhere to the alliance (for example, Poland)—for most countries, especially in alliances such as NATO, the presence of these troops serves to increase the durability of the alliance. Reliance on U.S. steel production, if not immediately translated into weapons of war, would be a far weaker reed to rely upon and likely would not enhance alliance durability.

The second implication concerns the stability of the system as a whole. To the extent that the long duration of alliances enhances system stability, the alliance relationships between large and small powers are vastly preferable to those between powers of approximately equal magnitude. In addition to the specific increased potential for war as the result of the policy interests and memories of one partner more heavily influencing the other if both powers are large, there now is the general finding of decreased durability of these alliances in comparison with those exhibiting substantial hierarchies, or minimum entropies. If alliances remain stable over time, there exists a greater clarity in the system than if such alliances were to be repeatedly ruptured. Expectations of behavior, generally, are clearer when there exist alliances of long duration. For example, a Soviet attack on Western Europe elicits a fairly clear understanding of the likely use of force by the West to counter such a move. If alliances, say between France and West Germany alone or between any of these countries and Britain, were to shift perceptibly over time as would be expected in the maximum entropy case (as in the discarding of one ally and increased emphasis on the other), then the clarity of a response by one of the partners to a Soviet attack on the other would be less predictable.

This absence of clarity of expectation, in fact, was true of much of the period of the balance of power, especially in the eighteenth century when countries such as Prussia and, for that matter Britain, had reputations as "perfidious Albions," or the most unfaithful of allies. At the same time, the eighteenth century was replete with long wars (Levy 1983b), principally general wars although, of course, not of the same intensity in bloodshed and political consequence associated with systemic wars such as the Thirty Years' War or the two world wars of this century. However, given the presence of nuclear weapons as agents of immeasurable added destruction, the absence of clarity in maximum entropy alliances could yield a miscalculation which could have consequences approaching those associated with earlier systemic wars. Put another way, nation-states may no longer be able to afford the ambiguity associated with the ever-shifting alliances of the classical balance-of-power period (especially in the eighteenth century with its many wars—the nineteenth century already demonstrated the presence of hierarchy both in Europe, especially Central Europe, and in colonial possessions).

Whereas in that earlier time, the random alliance formation of the balance-of-power period resulted in war, but not of the systemic variety, the nature of nuclear weaponry makes such a luxury untenable. Even dyadic wars or *N*-adic ones short of the systemic variety can yield such human and material destruction with the use of but a single weapon that escalation to systemic war may require the use of only one missile. Thus, coalition durability may be a desirable structural feature of the international system if only for the clarity it lends to international discourse which in itself may be necessary for the prevention of systemic war. To the extent that nuclear proliferation may diminish the extent of hierarchy in capabilities between nuclear and nonnuclear powers (for example, The Suez invasion by Britain and France, without consulting the United States, after successful nuclear weapons testing by both countries), it could also decrease alliance durability, with implications for the destabilization of the system as a whole.

Notes

1   A study which did not seek to explicitly investigate the effects of hierarchy on alliance cohesion is that of Brody and Benham (1969). In investigating the spread of nuclear weapons through an internation simulation using local (American) surrogates for international decision makers, these investigators found that when nuclear parity was introduced throughout the two blocs comprising the system "(a) threat external to the bloc was reduced, (b) threat internal to the bloc was increased, (c) the cohesiveness of the blocs was reduced, and (d) the bipolarity was fragmented" (Brody and Benham 1969, 173).

2   The entropy also is used as a measure of information. This essential equivalence between information and uncertainty can be understood as the consequence of the reduction in uncertainty which follows from the receipt of bits of information.

3   An exception to this pattern is the review of alliance behavior by Bueno de Mesquita and Singer (1973).

4   Alliances which did not end by 1984, the year this study was carried out, were treated as terminating in that year.

10

Normative Justifications

A QUESTION THAT was implied by the preceding analyses is essentially a normative one, namely, why is a system oriented to power parity, the existence of hierarchical relationships with small powers and flexibility of alliance partners (at least until the end of the nineteenth century) essentially stable in regard to the onset of systemic and even general wars? An answer frequently given for the absence of such wars is the hegemonic position of England during the nineteenth century and its pacific effect on European politics. Yet England's military hegemony was only naval, not land based, and, therefore, not directly applicable to the prevention of widespread warfare on the European continent. Indeed, the Crimean War occurred even with England as a combatant and was prevented, in part, from becoming general or systemic by considerations of the maintenance of hierarchy in Italy and the Balkans by Austria and her consequent neutrality in this war, as we saw in chapter 2.

There must, then, be additional considerations which impacted on the stability of the nineteenth century system at least until the unification of Germany in 1871. The findings concerning the hierarchical equilibrium in chapter 2, the association between power parity and peace in this century noted in chapter 6 in connection with the Singer *et al.* (1972) findings, and the general fluidity of alliance behavior (absence of memory) associated with nineteenth century alliances speak to these aspects of nineteenth century international behaviors as progenitors of peace.

This conclusion is reinforced by the analyses of chapters 3 and 4, which support an association between international resource inequality and systemic war as well as the association between parity and peace found in chapter 6. Of course, the hierarchical equilibrium itself suggests at least an approximate equality among two or more major powers in their simultaneous leadership of international hierarchies. Moreover, it shares with the balance of power the absence of memory requirement. And the nineteenth century exhibited elements of both processes not only in the absence of memory for alliance formation but in the positive-sum (for the great powers) aspects of great power–small power (and colonial) relationships, solely characteristic of the hierarchical equilibrium.

What are the normative components of parity or equality and of positive-sum processes which are so compelling as antecedents of peace or, at least, the absence of systemic war? To understand these components of the analysis we must turn to a major normative theorist and assess the degree of correspondence between his theory and the components of the balance-of-power system identified here. Because there exists no theory of the hierarchical equilibrium prior to the present analysis, the various theories initially will refer to the balance of power to be followed later by the contribution of the hierarchical equilibrium.

For all the interest John Rawls' work, *A Theory of Justice* (1971), has inspired in the social sciences, including a recent emphasis on distributive justice within international relations theory,[1] his thought would not seem to have any significant influence on the study of traditional *Realpolitik*. This is all the more surprising because there is a unique and important nexus between his theory and a necessary condition for balance-of-power politics, namely, the primacy of studied self-interest. Indeed, Rawls is perhaps the only major modern philosopher whose theory derives from positivist traditions which are mostly, if not entirely, applicable to the international system. Human beings, as sovereign entities, come together to make their own fundamentally simple rules and then presumably abide by them.

In this sense, the international system may be one of the few political systems which has a direct counterpart in the "original position"—a special feature of Rawls' theory that I will soon explain. International relations theorists have assumed that a direct concern for justice did not apply in the world of *Realpolitik*, but as I shall argue shortly, Rawls' treatment of the issues of justice in the real world does make his theory relevant to the understanding of international politics, especially during the period of the historical balance of power and existence of a hierarchical equilibrium. This period I take to be coterminous with the nineteenth century following the Congress of Vienna, but many of my observations also apply to preceding periods.

Unlike earlier theories of justice, such as that of Augustine or Aquinas' versions of the "just war,"[2] Rawls has formulated a positive theory that emanates directly from his version of the social contract in which he posits the famous "original position" that constitutes both chronologically and theoretically the foundation of his argument. I shall examine this aspect of Rawls' theory before discussing the application of his principles of justice to our historical system. I will then analyze the centrality of the concept of equilibrium in Rawls' thinking as well as in balance-of-power and hierarchical equilibrium systems. I will argue that the Rawlsian concern for justice includes strong emphasis upon stability which has consequences similar to those deriving from the explicit concern for stability inherent in the historical development of balance-of-power theory.

Rawls' Theory

In a hypothetical but extremely useful version of the social contract, Rawls set forth the "original position" which means that persons come together in a convention, as it were, to decide the nature of their future relations. None of them has any knowledge of the others' past histories, current social positions, or personal strengths and weaknesses such as intelligence or determination to succeed. Thus, a "veil of ignorance" operates to prevent individuals from maximizing their own future positions by manipulating the terms of the social contract to their own advantage. The express purpose of this meeting is to make a social contract that is seen to be just by all. A corollary purpose, as we shall see shortly, is the establishment of a just and equilibrated society.

Rawls (1971, 302) hypothesizes two fundamental principles of justice that may plausibly be deemed to have been incorporated in the social contract. These are the general principles of maximum liberty and equal opportunity:

1 Each person is to have an equal right to the most extensive total system of equal basic liberties compatible with a similar system of liberty for all.

2 Social and economic inequalities are to be arranged so that they are both

   a to the greatest benefit of the least advantaged, consistent with the just savings principle; and

   b attached to offices and positions open to all under conditions of fair equality of opportunity.

Rawls regards the first rule of maximum liberty as lexically prior to the second, and within the second rule, he holds 2b, the fair opportunity principle, to be lexically prior to 2a, the difference principle.

These rules form the core of Rawls' theory. He argues that they are the logical consequences of the deliberations in the original position. Given its veil of ignorance, implying the absence of known advantage for any of the participants, these are the likely principles that would have been chosen. Freedom is the obvious first choice for those concerned with procedural guarantees so that arbitrary and wanton constraints are not imposed upon the protagonists. Having established these guarantees, parties to the social contract can now require that all shall have equal access to the rewards of the political and economic system, acting once again on the basis that none has knowledge of one another's talents, inheritances, or abilities so that none would wish to deny access to any, lest they themselves be somehow excluded.

It is the difference principle which sets Rawls apart from other liberal theorists. He proposes to compensate the least-advantaged members of society for the advances of the most successful; a gain to the more fortunate must be matched by some gain to the least fortunate. The worst off in society must gain along with the most advantaged if Rawls' criteria for the existence of a just society are to be met. It is this addition to the basic corpus of liberal thought which distinguishes him from utilitarians such as Bentham and Sidgwick and makes possible the application of his theory to the balance of power and even more importantly, to the hierarchical equilibrium.

The Balance of Power

Balance-of-power theory is less clearly articulated, for it has had numerous exponents who have set forth the assumptions and basic operations of this process.[3] Nevertheless, one of its fundamental assumptions is that a system composed of independent neighboring states of more-or-less equal power, or at least a sufficiently large subset of states with approximately equal power, exists. Member states are independent but, at the same time, they share elements of a common culture and related values. The geographical limitation of the system to Europe and the defined membership—all sovereign European states—further imply the existence of common understandings. As noted previously, the Abbé de Pradt (1800, 86–87) found that Europe formed "a single social body which one might rightly call the European Republic." Vattel (1870, 251) declared that the practices of balance-of-power politics "make of modern Europe a sort of Republic," and Gentz (1806, 69) called it a "European commonwealth." In other words, the shared experience of the European states, in contrast to other countries and other regions, led to the emergence of common norms to be established within a balance-of-power framework.

One must assume the exercise of rational judgment in operating a balance-of-power system. The power of individual states must be calculated. Populations, territories, and finances were all subject to assessment and estimation if not to precise measurement. Talleyrand's rather specific advice to Napoleon on the balancing of French versus Austrian power, the precise calculations of the monarchs in the partitions of Poland (each receiving parts of Poland in rough proportion to existing sizes of territory and population), and the entire calculation efforts of Castlereagh and Talleyrand at the Congress of Vienna indicate the operation of explicit estimating procedures. At a time when the power of a country depended significantly on the

172

number of muskets available (rather than on weaponry of immense sophistication and an attendant industrial establishment), such calculations were made and put to use by statesmen.

It is in the principal aim of the balancing process that we can also draw valuable parallels. The avowed goal, of course, is that no single state shall dominate. None should benefit so completely that its rise to power would overshadow and endanger the others. It will be seen that this maxim is relevant to the preservation of both the individual states and the state system. Further, the survival of individual states depended on the survival of the framework. "Self-interest, according to this line of reasoning," says Gulick (1955, 31), "could best be pursued by attention to group interest. By preserving the state system you would preserve the parts thereof." Or, as Metternich,[4] an ardent supporter of the balance of power, put it,

> *Politics* is the science of the vital interest of States in its widest meaning. Since, however, an isolated state no longer exists, and is found only in the annals of the heathen world . . . we must always view the *society* of states as the essential condition of the modern world. . . . The great axioms of political science proceed from the knowledge of the true political interests of *all states*; it is upon these general interests that rests the guarantee of their existence.

Thus, the three components mentioned previously—opposition to preponderance, maintenance of state independence, and that of the state system itself—were all part of the same interdependent process of the balance of power. They led almost inevitably to the system's one overriding concern: the search for equilibrium. In his correspondence and speeches, at or pertaining to Vienna, Castlereagh continually referred to a "just equilibrium" among the powers of Europe (Webster 1921). Talleyrand also spoke of it, and Metternich, we know, tried to achieve it. This was not an equilibrium in the sense that all members of the state system would be exactly, or even roughly, equal in strength. Rather, it was the equilibrium of weight and counterweight in power juxtaposition so that power inequalities, such as they were, would be placed in equilibrium by an alliance with one or another of the great powers. The balance of power depended on an intricate system of alliance and counteralliance such that no state would gain a preponderance.[5]

Rawls' Theory Applied

The concept of equilibrium in Rawls' analysis is expressed as a concern with persistence. A system, he observes (Rawls 1971, 456), "is in equilibrium . . . when it has reached a state that persists indefinitely over time." A stable equilibrium exists when the system returns to its original state after external forces have impinged upon it, and it is unstable if these forces succeed in changing it permanently. Given Rawls' analysis in terms of the least or most advantaged, we must ask how stable or unstable the equilibrium is with regard to the advantaged or disadvantaged sectors. Clearly, the difference principle, providing that the least advantaged gain as a result of gain to the most advantaged, is intended to serve as a stabilizing factor. Here, it is the second principle of the hierarchical equilibrium in its emphasis on independent small powers that is suggested by this essentially positive-sum process.

Rawls' reference to equilibrium is reminiscent of the convening of a major international conference (Rawls 1971, 119–120).

> Equilibrium is the result of agreements freely struck between willing traders. For each person it is the best situation that he can reach by free exchange consistent with the right and freedom of others to further their interests in the same way. It is for this reason that this state of affairs is an equilibrium, one that will persist in the absence of further changes in the circumstances. No one has any incentive to alter it.

If the term "person" were to be changed to "nation-state," and the pronoun "he" to "it," this description would just as easily apply to the negotiation process at major international conferences such as the Congress of Vienna.

The preceding elements, suggested to be components of the balance-of-power system, are also found in the Rawlsian scenario. Rationality, a common framework, and shared cultural principles are explicit assumptions in Rawls' formulation of the original position, whose basic purpose is the formation of a single society dedicated to the common good. Indeed, Rawls even assumes a general understanding of common psychological principles so that the rational discourse among the participants in the original position will lead ultimately to the formulation of the two principles of justice.

Perhaps the clearest analogue of the original position in international life is the convening international conference. By this I mean a conference of great importance which establishes new principles for a coming era. The Congress of Vienna in 1815, the Versailles Conference, and that of San Francisco in 1945 are cases in point. The Congress of Vienna is the most central since it served to establish (or continue with modifications) the European balance-of-power system. Here, the "new beginnings" of 1815 are much like the basic structure of the original position. Sovereign rulers come together as participants to decide the rules of the new system to be established. A partial veil of ignorance is operative inasmuch as the Napoleonic Empire and the French ascendancy of the latter part of the eighteenth century would no longer exist and future trends could not be accurately anticipated. Rawls (1971, 378) himself suggests this interpretation when he states that one can "extend the interpretation of the original position and think of the parties as representatives of different nations who must choose together the fundamental principles to adjudicate conflicting claims among states."[6]

One sees in the Congress of Vienna an orientation to the future and an overriding European interest not to be found in most other international assemblies. Speaking of the Congress, Sir Harold Nicolson (1946, 57) noted that

> although the great protagonists of that age [Alexander and Talleyrand, Metternich and Castlereagh] were obliged to consider the rights and interests of their own countries, yet they were fully aware that more important than any such sectional desires was a general European interest, namely an assurance of peace, an acquired sense of security and a passionate need of civil repose.

The first and paramount outcome of the Congress of Vienna—recognition of the sovereignty of all member states—takes on a special significance in light of the Rawlsian analysis even if it is taken for granted in routine statements of international relations. The Napoleonic idea of empire was explicitly rejected in favor of Rawls' (1971, 302) first principle of "equal right to the most extensive total system of equal basic liberties compatible with a similar system of liberty for all." The cardinal principle of the new system was the preservation of the sovereignty of each of its members, something which the Napoleonic system had sought to limit. In this sense of simultaneously opposing the rise of any preponderant power and of any limitations on the liberty of the principals, the convening international conference (as at Vienna) and the Rawlsian scenario have identical consequences.

Rawls' second principle, the one pertaining to equal opportunity, also has a direct counterpart in the international system. This is the equal opportunity for any state to engage in alliances and have other diplomatic relations with any other state in the system. That is, each state is to have the same access as any other to opportunities the system may offer. In this sense of the near-total possibilities for access, the international balance-of-power process as identified in chapter 6 is more nearly fulfilling of this precept than is the domestic system, which is more restrictive as a result of private property and inheritance.[7] Alliances, as a primary good in the balance-of-power system, seldom are inherited.

A striking illustration of this principle in operation occurred during the Congress of Vienna barely one year after the first defeat of Napoleon and his exile to Elba. The conference had bogged down over the Polish–Saxon question, wherein Russia and Prussia were in dispute with Great Britain and Austria over the attempted annexations of Poland, by Russia, and Saxony, by Prussia.[8] The grand coalition of the former allies against France now broke down, and two of the former allies, Austria and Great Britain, signed the Triple Alliance of January 3, 1815, with France. It specified, among other obligations, mutual military support if any of the signatories was attacked. The targets of the alliance, of course, were Prussia and Russia. Thus, in the matter of a few months, the entire diplomatic landscape of Europe had changed. No longer did a grand coalition against France exist. Instead, France, under the adroit leadership of Talleyrand, fully reentered the diplomatic process of alliance and counteralliance in the European balance-of-power system.

At the very first opportunity, then, the absence of systematic exclusion became evident. An enemy, formerly possessing great power and posing an extraordinary threat, was now accepted as an ally to oppose the incipient hegemonic tendencies of Prussia and, especially, Russia. It is this absence of fixed barriers which highlights the similarity between the Rawlsian equal opportunity postulate and the European powers' equal access to the diplomatic process of the balance of power. Quoting again from Kaplan (1957, 23) as was done in a similar connection in chapter 6, "Permit defeated or constrained essential national actors to re-enter the system as acceptable role partners or act to bring some previously inessential actor within the essential actor classification. Treat all essential actors as acceptable role partners."

This randomness in the system's operation has been demonstrated empirically in the close fit of the Poisson to nineteenth century alliance formation (McGowan and Rood 1975), the absence of autocorrelated values in this process (Li and Thompson 1978), and the existence of equilibria in the formation and dissolution of alliances (Midlarsky 1981, 1983a). For each alliance which dissolved, on the average, another was formed to maintain the system's equilibrium. These findings indicate a randomness in the operation of the alliance system which signifies the equality of opportunity for access for any of the sovereign European states.

There also is a fixed aspect in Rawls' theory. Rawls recognizes that, despite equal opportunity for access, the natural differences among persons will lead to inequalities that require a compensatory mechanism. Hence, the difference principle, wherein gains to the most advantaged must also entail gains to the least advantaged. This principle must be met in all cases of territorial, demographic, and other inequalities in the nineteenth century balance-of-power system. No amount of alliance formation or dissolution could alter this structural aspect of power distributions. No formalized difference principle existed but, as we will see below, the positive-sum process suggested by the hierarchical equilibrium did operate to provide some compensatory advantage.

A version of the difference principle appeared in the process of resolving the conflict over the Polish–Saxon question referred to earlier. The Triple Alliance induced Russia and Prussia to negotiate. In the resulting agreement on February 11, 1815, Russia still received the lion's share in the form of tutelage over the Kingdom of Poland, and Prussia received approximately two-fifths of Saxony. But now Austria (which had originally opposed the annexations) had to be compensated. It received the Tyrol and Salzburg, in addition to promises of territories in Italy (which turned out to be Lombardy and Venetia), and the Illyrian provinces on the Adriatic. This, however, became possible because Italy was disunited and could not prevent the use of its territory in an overall settlement seeking an acceptable state of equilibrium. It may be said that the Rawlsian difference principle, here equivalent to the positive-sum feature of the hierarchical equilibrium, operated to benefit Austria. While Russia and Prussia, as the predominant (most advantaged) powers, received the major compensation, Austria, the least advantaged power, also received a share with promise of more to come.

The Polish Partitions

This entire process of territorial compensation at Vienna had been foreshadowed by the Polish partitions of the late eighteenth century. By 1763 (when Augustus III died), Poland had become extremely weak internally, and Catherine II of Russia had to send in armies to support her chosen ruler in Poland, Stanislaus Poniatowski. From 1767 to 1768, the Diet at Warsaw was surrounded by Russian troops, but then it rose against the Russians and formed the Confederation of the Bar. Savage battles were fought between the Confederates and the Russian soldiers. France and Austria began to support the Confederation, and then Turkey, upon desperate Polish appeal, also came to its support, thus precipitating the Russo-Turkish War of 1768–1774. The Eastern Question now became combined with the Polish Question. Catherine's successes against the Turks generated increased antagonism of the Austrians and the French, and according to Frederick the Great in his memoirs, the first Polish partition occurred precisely in order to avoid the outbreak of a general European war. Hötzsch concurs (1909, 668) in this evaluation, for as he suggests, "the amalgamation of the Polish and Eastern Questions gave rise to an international tension which nothing short of the first partition of Poland could bring to a close, unless it were to find vent in a great European War."

On February 17, 1772, the Russo-Prussian Treaty of Partition was signed at St. Petersburg, and on August 5, a seemingly reluctant but nevertheless participating Austria acceded to it. The second partition, in 1793, involved only Prussia and Russia, but the final act of dismemberment, in 1795, involved all three powers once again. Russia, in all three partitions, gained the lion's share of territory and population, with Prussia second and Austria a distant third.

The partitions of Poland illustrate two features of the Rawlsian scenario. First and most obviously, the difference principle is obeyed. Any gain to the most advantaged, Russia, is to be accompanied by some benefit to the least advantaged, Austria. To be sure, this is a perverse application in that there is a signal loser in these transactions—Poland. The elimination of Polish sovereignty in order to satisfy the needs of external powers cannot be justified on the basis of universal principles of justice or morality. But viewed from the perspective of the great powers (who assembled the major conferences—versions of the original position—that established the system mainly for their benefit), an element of justice did operate among the three beneficiaries.[9] Note also that all of this occurred before the rise of widespread nationalism. One might then argue that the needs of individual Poles could have been met just as well, if not better, by the more centralized and efficient monarchies of Austria and Prussia and, to a certain extent, even Russia. Although the participants tended to confuse the equity of the action with the equality of shares (Lewitter 1965, 335), the action must nevertheless be viewed within a prenationalist context in which the partitions of Sweden and Turkey were also openly discussed and in which entire nationalities such as the Dutch had been for centuries governed by foreign powers.

The partitions were excoriated among balance-of-power theorists,[10] but considering the difference principle and especially the need to avoid a general European war, the partitions had a logic of their own. It is in this latter area that the partitions conform to Rawlsian principles even more than is immediately apparent.

The Need for Abundance

We must turn back briefly to a fundamental proposition underlying the previous scenario. This is the assumption, never fully articulated by Rawls, that the system is expanding in material wealth. Recall that the difference principle requires that the least advantaged gain at least something as the more advantaged gain. In order for this to happen, the most advantaged obviously cannot take from the least advantaged for then the latter would lose, not gain. (A variant of this occurs in the Polish partitions where the least advantaged, the Poles, are dismissed as inessential actors.) Both societal sectors, therefore, gain from some external source, or as in the domestic case, they gain from the yields of an expanding economy.

Aside from the necessity for economic expansion inherent in the difference principle itself, the necessity for non-zero-sum activity can be seen in the indifference curves that Rawls (1971, 76) himself posits. These curves actually are straight lines which run parallel to the horizontal and vertical axes and intersect at right angles at the 45° line as shown in Figure 10.1. In this instance, any gain to x_1 does not have to come from x_2 and, of course, the converse holds true as well. Each of the actor's increases, as one moves

178

incrementally along the axes, is independent of the other's; x_1 and x_2 are entirely indifferent to each other. This is not the case for the utilitarian condition, which is indifferent to the method of maximizing net societal gain. In that case, curves of a very different sort can exist in which increments to x_1 are associated with losses to x_2, as shown in Figure 10.2. Thus, a condition of abundance, or at least the ability to draw upon resources not currently within the domain of either x_1 or x_2, is a fundamental property of the Rawlsian system. This is precisely the case in the Polish partitions, where x_1 and x_2 (Russia and Prussia, respectively) resolved their differences, avoided a general European war, and even extended territory to a third protagonist, Austria, by drawing upon resources outside of their possession at the time. The crucial difference between the domestic Rawlsian scenario and the international one centers on the ability, after the industrial revolution, to create new material abundance. For close to two centuries, the domestic systems of industrialized states—the prototypical societies for Rawls—were able to enjoy indifference curves very much like those shown in Figure 10.1 and to have the difference principle ameliorate the grosser sorts of inequities emerging out of capitalist systems. This is no longer the case. It should be noted that, in European societies, additional abundance materialized and the difference principle operated to the extent that it did, both domestically and internationally, in the eighteenth and nineteenth centuries as a consequence, in part, of the acquisition of colonies (see chapter 4). However, this source of abundance also came to an end and very likely hastened the coming of the great wars of this century.

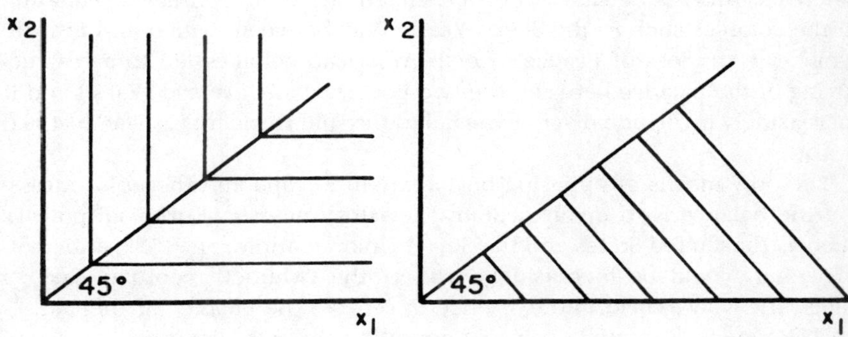

Figure 10.1	**Figure 10.2**
Independence condition	Utilitarian condition
(after Rawls 1971, 76).	(after Rawls 1971, 77).

Aside from the zero-sum-fixed (territorial-resource) aspect of the requirements of justice, the random, alliance-based process also tends toward some instability. This is the attempt to equilibrate by means of alliance formation in which the required precision of power calculation cannot be achieved. Although in possession of a new ally, as in an alliance between *A* and *B*, the statesmen in *A* (or *B*) cannot be certain that their ally's military forces are sufficiently professional and competent. Nor can they be sure that their ally, even if militarily effective, will actually honor the alliance commitment in the event of war. Prussia, for example, despite an excellent reputation for military expertise, was a notoriously unreliable ally, as the Poles discovered just prior to the second partition or as Napoleon found at the end of his long march out of Russia. Thus, power calculations, even when made with great numerical exactitude as done by Castlereagh at Vienna, were subject to serious uncertainties. Consequently, the system's territorial span expanded continually in order to avoid the zero-sum conflicts that would result from efforts to alter the balance by annexation of neighboring territory. Only in the case of extraordinarily weak and disunited powers such as Poland could such a process take place on the continent of Europe. Essentially, a positive-sum process, explicitly indicated by the hierarchical equilibrium, is put into effect in order to rescue the faltering balance-of-power process restricted to small confines.

Generally, it was outside of the continent that expansion efforts took place. European colonial expansion may be seen as a way of augmenting power via wealth and territory without having to rely on the vagaries of allies or bloody continental wars. In this sense, the Incas or the Aztecs of the New World were no different from the Poles of Europe in the vulnerabilities of their states to European expansion. Attempts at an extended balancing process outside of Europe sometimes led to conflicts originating in the colonies such as the Seven Years' War between Britain and France, which via the loss of France's North American colonies led to a restructuring of the balance between the two powers. Later, World Wars I and II increasingly involved powers external to the "old Occident" as Dehio (1962) put it.

The only means of opposing hegemony in Europe and thereby redressing the balance is to involve colonial territory or extra-European powers such as the United States and the Soviet Union. Canning, in 1826, anticipating what would be increasingly true of the twentieth century, said, "I called the New World into existence to redress the balance of the Old."[11] Such an ever-increasing radius of operation for the European powers in their task of establishing equilibrium may have helped bring about a bipolar system after World War II, which then relegated the old European powers to second- and third-rate status. Such are some of the ironies of international politics. Nevertheless, it is this property of seeking augmentations of the system that characterizes the equilibrium process, which, given the inexactness of its calculations and manipulations, requires an ever-widening area of operation. The hierarchical equilibrium, however,

180

can offer at least a partial solution to the problem by means of the existence of politically uncommitted small powers, as we shall see in the concluding section.

The Negative-Difference Principle

Finally, let us consider a feature of domestic life which does not seem to have any international counterpart and, in so doing, illustrate an inflexibility of the latter which may have led to considerable conflict. We know that Rawls' difference principle refers to domestic politics. If this principle, along with the principles of maximum liberty and equal opportunity, can be stabilizing to society, then the obverse condition of a decline, wherein any loss to the least advantaged is matched by some loss to the most advantaged, should also have some stability value. This may be termed the negative-difference principle to reflect the negative sum of both losses in contrast to the positive sum of the Rawlsian statement. Both sectors move in the same direction and a common fate or destiny is perceived throughout society. A strongly destabilizing condition develops, on the other hand, when the sectors do not move synchronously, when the most advantaged gain at the expense of the least advantaged or push forward without any gain at all to the least advantaged.

Viewing this negative principle as a condition for stability in declining circumstances, we can understand the outbreak of certain domestic revolutions. The recent Iranian case and that of Nicaragua reflect this property. In Iran, land redistribution, which actually led to financial losses for the peasantry, and increased unemployment in Tehran, due to a decline in the building boom, were not matched by proportionate or even discernible losses to the Shah or his family. The negative-difference principle certainly did not operate; if anything, the Shah and his family appeared to be gaining in wealth as both the countryside and the city declined in wealth. The case of Nicaragua is perhaps even more dramatic: the earthquake of 1972 disastrously impoverished the country, and the population perceived the Somoza family as actually profiting from Red Cross supplies and other aid. Here, too, the negative principle was not operating in a situation of widespread economic collapse. The perception of a common fate or destiny simply was not present.

The presence of a common identification between rulers and ruled is perhaps the critical factor here. A growing identification among the disadvantaged and their estrangement from the most powerful have been related to the onset of mass revolution.[12] This sense of identification may be used to understand the applicability of Davies' *J* curve to some instances of political violence but not to others.[13] It can be argued that if the sudden decline in relative well being after a period of increase (the *J* curve) affects all sectors of society equally (the negative-difference principle), a revolution might not occur—as none did during the Great Depression in the United States. (This point will be developed more fully later.) Most likely, it was in those instances where the decline affected the majority of the population strongly, but much less so the elites, that revolutions occurred. Whatever identification existed between rulers and ruled was lost as a consequence of the differential impact of the rapid decline.

This differential applicability may be the reason why the *J* curve did not quite explain the American disorders of the 1960s.[14] Whatever their previous circumstances, self-identification among blacks grew rapidly during this period, and it was often stated in explicit contrast with the white community. Under these circumstances, their declining or increasing economic circumstances alone might have been irrelevant to the onset of the disorders. The negative-difference principle, as an explicit assertion of a certain type of common identification between rulers and ruled but also as a derivative of Rawlsian theory, is now suggested to be a consequence of a theory of justice with strong implications for political stability. As such, it does not stand alone but can be understood as part of a much older and larger tradition.

The operation of the negative-difference principle can be used to explain the absence of serious attempts at revolution in a situation of blatant revolutionary potential. The Great Depression in the United States was obviously an economic catastrophe occurring after a period of economic increase, yet very little political violence emerged, not to speak of widespread revolutionary activity. Indeed, any violence that did occur was confined to eastern port cities which were subject to some European ideological influences, in contrast to the almost exclusively indigenous character of political action in the interior. The operation of the negative-difference principle seemed to have deterred major revolutionary activity in that wealth was lost not only by the poor but by the rich as well. The image of ruined investors leaping from high buildings was only the tip of the iceberg in which many of the affluent quietly lost large fortunes. Even if many of the rich did not suffer such a consequence, the imagery, not to say the symbolic value, of such losses and consequent suicides would put the negative-difference principle into operation.

Although, as we have seen, the positive form of the difference principle does, in its own fashion, operate in the international system, its negative form is far more difficult, if not impossible, to find. The positive form can be implemented by express agreement. Russia, Prussia, and Austria can enter into an agreement as a result of which they observe the positive form of the difference principle. But how can the international system spread the systematic accumulation of losses? Even in the midst of a depression or some other economic calamity, the international accoutrements of power and status are preserved. If one country experiences some loss in status, power, or economic well being, the economic disjointedness of the international system, or simply the differing circumstances of other countries, may lead them to experience the misfortune to a much lesser extent. For example, the effects of the depression were felt far more keenly in Germany than in Britain or France,[15] but the international advantages as set forth in the Treaty of Versailles were changed not at all. (This should have been another argument for the immediate relaxation of reparation requirements by the British and French in 1930–1931 to put into operation at least a modified negative-difference principle and thus avoid major conflict.) Nor were any adjustments made in the colonial powers' holdings outside of Europe as a result of these economic changes. To all appearances, the relative international positions of the principal European powers remained unchanged.

A modified version of a failed difference principle operated before World War I. The Entente powers, especially the British, continually benefited in wealth, status, and honors from their colonial holdings. But Germany, despite a rapid growth to power, could not do the same because of the rather modest size of its colonial empire and the virtual impossibility of obtaining new colonies at a time when colonial division of the non-Western world had already occurred.

It is this aspect of fixedness in territorial holdings, alliances, and even armaments which prevents the operation of the negative-difference principles in the realm of international *Realpolitik*. There is little commonality in the paraphernalia of wealth and status such that if one country were to experience a decline so would others, in contrast to the domestic situation of elites and mass (but, of course, not always) experiencing a simultaneous decrement. The absence of any formal mechanism for the institutionalization of common losses may be an important factor in the increased conflict potential of the international system. As the kaiser put it in a rather extreme statement of the negative-difference principle in the summer of 1914 when widespread hostilities became imminent, "if we are bled to death, England shall at least lose India."[16] Again, the argument in chapter 4 concerning the extreme inequalities in international resource development become relevant.

Conclusion

I have argued here that positive criteria do exist for the evaluation of justice as a property of the international system beyond extemporaneous condemnation or eulogistic moralizing so rejected by the theorists of *Realpolitik*. There are criteria generated for human societies which can be applied to international systems simply as additional forms of human association to be evaluated along with others. The historical balance-of-power system, as one such association stretching from the early nineteenth to the early twentieth centuries (at least that long and perhaps much longer), bears out certain elements of the Rawlsian scenario. But it also reveals a fixedness and lack of fluidity which do not allow for simultaneous adjustments when losses, economic or otherwise, are incurred by some in the system and the negative-difference principle as an elementary form of justice for all is required.

Both the Rawlsian (positive) difference principle and its international manifestation operate only when the system is expanding. This is necessary to satisfy the requirements of simultaneous gains to both the most and least advantaged and also to continually adjust by a positive-sum process the delicate balancing process. The success of the nineteenth century balance-of-power system, then, may have relied on this ever-expanding framework of colonial accession and new allies, much as the Euro-American democracies may have relied on an ever-expanding industrial largesse to maintain stable democracies. Both were extremely stable: the nineteenth century balance-of-power system lasted close to a century without major upheaval, and the Western democracies also experienced considerable longevity. But with the advent of increasing scarcities of territory and other resources, the balance-of-power system could no longer satisfy the difference principle (nor the equal opportunity principle), just as contemporary domestic economic systems may no longer be able to do so. Under these circumstances, domestic systems may show many of the strains and conflicts which ultimately destroyed the nineteenth century system of the balance of power.[17]

The relevance of the preceding arguments to the contemporary world scene derives not only from the demands for justice by Third World nations and, of course, the ever-present threat of systemic war but also from the possible reemergence of a new balance-of-power system. No longer do Europe, America, and Japan cleave together as one and Third World nations, especially the Islamic ones, now go their own way (not to mention the new role of China), but now it is a world without the possibility of substantial expansion. Certainly the rise of contemporary nationalisms, as in Vietnam and Afghanistan, has demonstrated the impracticality of territorial or quasi-imperial aggrandizement along nineteenth-century lines. It is a world of scarce resources with limited availability,[18] and these resources are greatly vulnerable, as in the Middle East. The positive-difference principle along Rawlsian lines would be extremely difficult to operate effectively under these circumstances. Thus, in addition to rapid technological change, only the random component of alternating allies (already happening) would be available for equilibrium purposes according to the classical balance-of-power argument. The hierarchical equilibrium's emphasis on the continued existence of a pool of politically uncommitted small powers helps alleviate this constraint, for it allows the simultaneous gain to two or more adversaries without engaging in partitions, colonialism, or any of the nastier efforts to institute positive-sum processes as ways of preventing major international conflict.

Notes

1 This emphasis on distributive justice can be found in works of scholars such as Hoffmann (1981), Shue (1980), and Beitz (1979). For specific applications of Rawls to problems of distributive justice, which sparked much of the current interest, see Amdur (1977) and Beitz (1975). Ethical imperatives for the redistribution of income are found in a systematic empirical analysis of such transfers in Russett (1978). Certain of the applications of Rawls to issues of distributive justice are not applicable to the nineteenth century European system treated here because of the nature of the mostly self-sufficient agrarian societies existing at the time and the consequent relative equality in average per capita income among the European states. The contemporary concern for the unequal distribution of natural resources also had much less relevance to a largely agrarian, state-centered world that was just beginning its industrialized dependence on such resources.

2 For comprehensive theoretical and historical treatments of the concept of the "just war," see Walzer (1977) and Ramsey (1983).

3 See, for example, Gulick (1955), Leckie (1817), Morgenthau (1973), Zinnes (1967), Organski (1968), O. R. Holsti (1976), and Fay (1930).

4 Metternich (1880–1884, 30), quoted in du Coudray (1936, 167).

5 See O. R. Holsti (1976, 364).

6 It is in this quotation from Rawls that we see the essentially state-centered universe that Rawls posits. As such, the needs of individual persons are not directly taken into account in this international universe of diplomatic representation. Interestingly, the state-centered assumption is much more tenable for the nineteenth century system treated here than for the twentieth century system with its far greater economic interdependence among nations. It is important to emphasize here that the agreements made at a convening international congress as a version of the original position apply only to the participants themselves and not to some party not represented at that congress. Thus, as we shall see, if only the major powers are represented at such a meeting, then "inessential actors" not represented can be fair game for any political action desired by the major powers.

7 Natural resources are inherited by nation-states, but in the largely self-sufficient agrarian states of the nineteenth century, they would have had much less importance than in the contemporary industrialized world of the major powers. Further, with a relatively unchanging weapons technology and the absence of citizen armies, the demographic and industrially linked natural resource inheritances would have been less critical than access to alliance partners for purposes of maintaining national security.

8 See Gulick (1955) and Nicolson (1946) for extensive descriptions of this dispute.

9 See note 6 for development of this idea.

10 See, for example, Metternich (1880, 9).

11 Quoted in Nicolson (1946, 273).

12 For a treatment of the consequences of fixedness or scarcity in domestic societies, see Midlarsky (1982).

13 See Davies (1962). For other theoretical treatments of the onset of political violence, see Gurr (1970), Tilly (1978), and Skocpol (1979). As in Davies' treatment, none of these works really emphasizes the importance of a common identification among societal sectors. One of the few writings that does strongly address this issue is Brickman and Campbell (1971). For a treatment of the diffusion of urban violence that presupposes a strong sense of identification among the disorder participants, see Midlarsky (1978).

14   This finding may be seen in Miller, Bolce, and Halligan (1977). This article sparked a lively debate in subsequent issues of this journal, in which Davies (1978) and later Crosby (1979) took issue with the overall approach taken by these authors. Of course, the authors of the original article provided rejoinders either following the critique or in a subsequent issue. Note that Davies' criticism is quite general and Crosby's is directed far more to the issue of implications for relative deprivation theory than to the findings by Miller *et al.* (1977) on the more specific issue of applicability of the *J* curve to the disorders.

15   This concept of a status inconsistency is derived here from the negative-difference principle but may be seen in a *sui generis* development in Galtung (1964). Tests of an international status inconsistency and its relationship to the onset of war are found in Wallace (1971) and in Midlarsky (1975, 94–144).

16   Quoted in Montegelas and Schücking (1924, 350).

17   Elections (or electioneering) in representative democracies, however, may often establish a sense of identification between rulers and ruled, at least by way of validating candidates for office. Additionally, if political leaders chosen in this manner also are not members of an economic elite (as is often the case among Labour leaders in Britain), then that identification may be sufficient to prevent serious instabilities even in severely declining circumstances. When there are clear barriers to such identification, as in post-World War II generational conflicts in Europe (with war seen as a major societal trauma), then even the mandating of candidates for office may not be sufficient to prevent political violence, as in the European violence of the late 1960s, especially in DeGaulle's France.

18   For an examination of the impact of scarcity on resource distributions, see Chapters 3 and 4, and Midlarsky (1982), which relied on earlier findings of the exponential distribution of land holdings found in Boxley (1971), Clark (1972), and Dovring (1973). These latter treatments, however, did not contain the justification in probability theory found here. The earlier works of Tanter and Midlarsky (1967) and Huntington (1968) are also relevant.

11

Conclusion: International Structure as an Information System

THE VARIOUS FORMAL aspects of the analysis are now complete. The hierarchical equilibrium theory has been formulated and tested and found to be associated with the absence of systemic war. Other elements of the model consequent upon the failure of such an equilibrium also have been examined empirically. In particular the inequality among great powers, as the result of some possessing colonies or other desiderata while others do not, is an especially egregious failure of that equilibrium. The principle of equality or equity in relations among the great powers is violated by the asymmetry of resource possession. Multipolarity has been tied analytically to this sort of inequality, with bipolarity as a much less likely candidate for that dubious distinction. Violations of the hierarchical equilibrium include the increase in number of disputes which remain unresolved, thus increasing the probability that some will overlap and, thereby, also increasing the probability of systemic war. A change (or impending change) in the delicately balanced force capabilities of the opposing coalitions may finally yield that consequence. Each later step in the sequence implies a greater probability of war after the preceding step has already occurred. A parallel consequence of increased coalition stability as the result of a hierarchical equilibrium also has been confirmed empirically. A normative justification for the expectation of peace upon the existence of such an equilibrium, especially its aspects of equality and positive-sum games, has been developed.

Having said all this, it also is appropriate to indicate the limitations of the previous analysis. Specifically, the systematic empirics of this treatment have been limited to the periods preceding World Wars I and II. Of course, this limitation was necessitated by the absence of systematic data for the earlier periods. Nevertheless, whatever the source of this deficiency, it should be clearly stated. In this sense the title of this book, *The Onset of World War*, surely is not a misnomer, for to the extent that World Wars I and II were the *only* truly global wars in extensity of participation and the systematic analysis of this book has been solely about their origin, then this title is especially apt.

At the same time, one should recognize the validity of corroborating historical evidence for the onset of other systemic wars. Because the systematic data are not available does not imply that the analysis should not be done. The topic of systemic war obviously is too important to be dealt with summarily in this fashion. Instead, a useful second line of attack and the only one generally available to the researcher of this subject is the use of historical materials. Fortunately, the wars analyzed here have been of sufficient importance to warrant extensive historical coverage which can then be used by the historical–political analyst. And this was the strategy adopted for this inquiry.

As a commentary on the material presented in this volume, it might seen as if ideological considerations or peoples' belief systems have been given short shrift. In one sense this is true and was necessitated by the particular focus of inquiry. Although it is manifestly the case that the Thirty Years' War, in its full scope and ferocity, is inconceivable without the occurrence of the Reformation one century earlier and that democracy in Athens versus oligarchy in Sparta became a major issue of the Peloponnesian War [as was republicanism (and regicide) in France versus the monarchism of the remaining great powers during the eighteenth century], the presence of these issues still begs the question. We want to know the conditions preceding a systemic war within some reasonably short time interval prior to its outbreak. This information can help distinguish between instances when such a war breaks out and those when it does not, even given the same degree of ideological conflict in both instances. For example, prior to World War I there were many instances when war could have broken out yet did not. The Moroccan crises, and the Bosnian crisis all were candidates for that dubious distinction, but war, in fact, erupted during the summer of 1914. One important function of the preceding analysis has been to detail the structural- and conflict-based reasons for that difference.

World War I offers another interesting facet of the issue for World War I, at its inception, was not an ideologically based conflict. Here, one observes the onset of a systemic war without major ideological input. Indeed, an alliance with at least some basis in ideological commonality—the *Dreikaiserbund*—was ruptured by tsarist Russia in favor of alliance with republican

France, ultimately in the Triple Entente. One cannot conceive of the onset of World War I without the presence of the Triple Entente, which existed as an alliance of ideologically dissimilar governments.

In the absence of systemic war after World War II, we have an instance of no systemic war in the presence of extreme ideological differences between the two contending blocs explained, in fact, by the hierarchical equilibrium analysis of chapter 2. Thus, in the presence of extreme ideological differences and animosity between the blocs after World War II, a systemic war was avoided while prior to World War I, without clear-cut ideological differences between the blocs, systemic war erupted. This is not to minimize the importance of ideology in establishing the bases for international controversy but that, under certain circumstances, it can be superseded by structural considerations. Ideology, of course, already has been singled out as important in distinguishing between systemic wars of the type just considered here and general wars of lesser conflict intensity, such as the War of the Austrian Succession and the Seven Years' War.

I shall not again address at length the various theoretical and policy implications which were developed in the preceding chapters. Several of the more compelling of these deserve at least a brief mention. Certainly the introduction of an effective SDI is a clear threat to the balance of power for the disadvantaged power and, therefore should be approached with extreme caution, as suggested in chapter 6. So, too, should any unilateral disarmament be viewed askance as also developed in that chapter. The placing of troops on the territory of small allies is a suggested consequence of chapter 9 with its emphasis on the determinants of coalition durability. Perhaps most important is the creation of disjoint sets of conflict relationships, such that great powers would not be subject to the threat of overlapping conflict universes with their implications for the onset of sytemic war. Allowing nonaligned nations to go their own way without undue interference is one way to avoid creating needless new disputes and, at the same time, generating the political independence from the superpowers required for these small powers to play a role in future positive-sum games. In a larger sense, this book may be seen as an effort to pursue the development of empirically valid theory (Mansbach and Vasquez 1981) that is not solely rooted in the traditional power politics paradigm (Vasquez 1983) and may be seen to have a certain kinship with neorealist theory (Keohane 1986).

Theoretically, in addition to the basics of the hierarchical equilibrium theory and the finding of the analytic instability of multipolar systems, there exists another, somewhat unexpected theoretical implication. The analysis of chapter 6 demonstrated that not only systemic wars were most probable to occur upon small changes in the balance of power but that this finding applied to all wars with memory. Instead of parity *or* preponderance as progenitors of peace, *both* are associated with the absence of war in polarized settings, with only small changes in the balance associated with this type of war. A new category of war has been generated with implications for future research directions.

At the same time, one must be careful to distinguish between the greater susceptibility to a small change in the balance of power for already formed and polarized coalitions in the systemic case, in contrast to the smaller susceptibility to such change in the dyadic instance. This difference arises from the greater number of sources of possible change in the systemic case. However, the path to the systemic war is lengthy and complex, as the Z process of Table 6.1 amply demonstrates, which accounts, in part, for the rarity of such wars despite the fragility of the balance between the opposing coalitions.

It is interesting to reflect on the relationship of these findings to another major theory of war, in addition to the theories of the balance of power, power transition, long cycle and power cycle considered throughout the volume. This is the expected utility theory of war developed by Bueno de Mesquita (1981b) as an extraordinarily successful systematic approach to the explanation of war, treated as a generic category. In this view, rational calculations of expected gain or loss to the interested powers govern the decision calculus of those who would initiate the conflict. Despite the persuasiveness of the theory, elegance of its formulation, and considerable evidence marshaled in its support, it is not especially relevant to the concerns of this volume. This is simply because, in the approach to the onset of a systemic war in contrast to other types of war (especially dyadic), the structural circumstances of hierarchical relations or their absence, polarities, neutralities, alliances, overlapping disputes, and changes in the balance of power become increasingly important constraints on the degrees of freedom of the decision makers. Whether they are involved in rational calculations of the sort invoked by Bueno de Mesquita and successfully applied to the mostly non-systemic cases of his war universe, becomes an increasingly less important question as the structural constraints develop over time.

Thus, it ultimately was not to Germany's advantage to have entered either World War I or World War II given the forces arrayed against her. (Consider in that light Bethmann Hollweg's response to the question about the origin of World War I: "Oh, if I only knew.") Nor would the Habsburgs have begun the Thirty Years' War at that time given the impending conflict with the Netherlands. (Bohemia's defeat and, ultimately, forced Catholicization of the largely Protestant population suggests that it was not to her advantage to ever have begun the revolt.) Indeed, the Habsburgs came out of the war as well as they did, which incidentally did involve a grave weakening of the empire, only because of the great military skill of a rogue general named Wallenstein and his private army, who were not even known to be available to the Habsburgs prior to the outbreak of the war (Pagès 1970). Subsequently, Louis XIV's wars nearly ended in disaster for

France. The French Revolutionary Wars began as a direct consequence of domestic matters in the French Revolution which initially bore no relation to war. And the Napoleonic Wars, as had those of Louis XIV, nearly brought France to ruin.

Similarly, the Peloponnesian War was not begun by either Athens or Sparta with any expectation of gain; there were serious reluctances and grave reservations on both sides, as the outcome, especially for Athens, amply indicates. Even Sparta suffered a weakening as the result of the war that increased the chances for a Theban victory during the subsequent period. Only in the Macedonian War begun by Philip II do we find calculation of gain amply justified by the subsequent conflict. And here we also find the greatest remoteness in time of the mobilization conflict from the initial structural war. It would appear as if a removal from the initial structural configuration which led to the earlier war may be required for the successful use of a rational calculus. In all other instances, the closeness in time of the mobilization war to the structural conflict likely led to the continued influence of the earlier structural conditions on the later war. One possible consequence of these persisting structural effects is the misperception of the likelihood of gain or loss such that perceptions of threat or hostility may govern the decision calculus instead of perceptions of capability (Zinnes *et. al.*, 1961) that would be expected under the rational calculus assumption.

Hitler was faced with the immediate consequences of World War I (particularly in the form of the Versailles Treaty), Napoleon with the apparent opportunities offered by the French victories at the end of the French Revolutionary Wars, and Louis XIV with the growing French ascendancy over Spain in the years immediately after the Thirty Years' War. Only Philip of Macedon was relatively free of the consequences of the preceding structural war, for so much had occurred after the Peloponnesian War to render the older Athenian–Spartan hostilities virtually irrelevant to the later conflict. Only the power vacuum remained to be exploited by Philip.

An interesting variant on this conception is found in the British hopes that Nazi Germany and Soviet Russia would turn against each other, possibly involving military action during the late 1930s. The resulting power vacuum presumably would be receptive to the restoration of British power on the continent. The failure of this effort was signaled by the greater likelihood of a systemic mobilization conflict initiated by one of the principal actors in the earlier structural war instead of the smaller dyadic war envisioned by the British.

Other implications of the analysis now can be explored. These include arms races as well as other conflictual and cooperative phenomena. Particularly important now will be the treatment of international structure as a type of information system, for even (and perhaps especially) armaments can serve a critical communications function. These implications of the model will be explored sequentially via the properties of (1) hierarchy, (2) the absence or, at least minimization of, memory, (3) minimization of entropy as a measure of uncertainty or disorder, as in information theory, (4) positive-sum games associated with the independent small powers, (5) effects on the balance of power, and (6) implications of any or all of these for the breakdown of superpower relations and the onset of systemic war.

Hierarchy

The hierarchical aspect of the hierarchical equilibrium has several interesting consequences for the arms race between two superpowers who lead two international coalitions. The conventional wisdom, of course, is that such arms races are destabilizing, with the possible consequence of a nuclear war. This is the often unstated premise of Richardson-type analyses of arms races as well as the more direct finding of studies of the relationship between arms races and war. However, studies of this type (Wallace 1982) seldom, if ever, disaggregate the incidents of war into systemic and nonsystemic components; the resulting number of cases of systemic war probably would be too small for inferential statistical analyses. Yet we require directed analyses of this type of war precisely because we know so little about its origins while, at the same time, it is so relevant for the future existence of humankind. Examination of the implications of the present theory of systemic war, one which has received at least some empirical validation, is one way to proceed. Although potentially unpleasant, these implications nevertheless should be explored, for the consequence of systemic instability is a concern shared by all powers, both great and small.

Arms Races

Consider now the two hierarchically organized blocs with the two super-powers engaged in a strategic (nuclear) arms race. One clear consequence of the arms race is the distance in strategic force capability between the leading power and its smaller allies. Even in NATO, where two former world powers—Britain and France—possess strategic weapons, the disparity in both quality and quantity of these armaments between the United States and its allies is immense. As such, the United States is still relatively free from concerns that these powers will "go it alone" again versus the Soviets, as was demonstrated in 1956 with fairly disastrous consequences for the two European powers. And even if these powers were to do so, the United States still is not reliant on their force capabilities for its own protection. Among the Warsaw Pact countries, the distance in force capability between the leading power and its smaller allies, of course, is even greater because of the absence of strategic weapons in the armies of the smaller powers. Thus, the nuclear arms race between the superpowers has the unintended but nevertheless important consequence of reinforcing the hierarchy.

At the same time, a minimization of memory also follows from the absence of important dependence of the leading power upon the smaller countries. The particular grievances of the smaller power would not be a basis for important decision making by the great powers. If we focus, then, specifically on systemic war as a dependent variable in contrast to all wars, the probability of such a war actually might be reduced by the strategic arms race as an unintended reinforcement of hierarchy within each of the two blocs.

What of the conventional arms race? Here, too, the superpowers are engaged in the development and manufacture of weapons. Once again, the conventional arms race actually can serve a positive function in supporting the international hierarchical structure.

A conventional arms race implies that each of the superpowers seeks to develop the most sophisticated weaponry in sufficient quantities to be tactically effective. As such, there really are only two countries with sufficient numbers of advanced weaponry to be decisive in a military confrontation with almost any nonsuperpower. Exceptions to this principle arise in the context of prolonged guerrilla wars, such as Vietnam or Afghanistan, or in the case of arms transfers of sophisticated weaponry to smaller allies. I will deal with these apparent exceptions momentarily.

Perhaps a classic instance of the successful operation of this principle is in the recent attack on Libya by the United States. Here, the use of sophisticated weapons such as the F-111 or F-16 essentially rendered the Libyan airspace defenseless against U.S. attack despite the existence of a fairly extensive Libyan missile defense. Even the one American aircraft that was downed apparently was not lost to the Libyan air defense but to a system malfunction on board the aircraft itself. Without the clear superiority of American conventional weapons, the outcome might have been different with a diminution of American prestige and a concomitant loosening of the NATO hierarchy. As it turned out, the Europeans, in their own fashion, followed the American lead in expelling large numbers of Libyan "diplomats" and others who likely were involved in terrorist activity in Europe. Thus, the decisive outcome of the military confrontation had a salutary effect on the integrity of the Western hierarchy.

An exception to this principle occurs in the instance of a protracted guerrilla war in which the sophistication and perhaps even the quantity of arms is not decisive. This points to the necessity of demonstrating the superiority of the superpower in a single engagement with portent for the future instead of in an ongoing guerrilla process which can only intensify a motivated population's will to resist.

Arms transfers from opposing superpowers also can undermine the technical superiority of a hierarchy leader, but, generally, superpowers do not transfer their latest technologies; they export armaments which are at least one or two generations removed from their latest efforts.

A counterargument to the position adopted here is that without the weapons often bought as newly obsolete from the superpowers (made obsolete, in fact, by the latest developments in the arms race), there would not even be the possibility of a challenge to the superpower from the smaller country. In this fashion the entire confrontation would be avoided if the conventional arms race was eliminated or, at least, substantially reduced in intensity. Yet, we know that technical achievements are not the sole province of the superpowers, especially in conventional weaponry, as weapons producers such as France, Brazil, Sweden, or Israel amply demonstrate. If the superpowers were to abandon the field to these smaller powers with their unique geopolitical concerns exclusive of the superpowers, then the arms production of the smaller powers likely would not be diminished; any confrontations with the superpowers would not be so distinctly to the advantage of the larger countries. Thus, on balance, both the conventional arms race and the strategic variant tend to reinforce the hierarchical structure with a consequent diminished probability of systemic war.

A destabilizing aspect of the nuclear arms race, however, is its potential impact on the balance of power, not so much in quantity of armaments but in technical breakthroughs. While increases in numbers of strategic weapons can be matched by the other side, major advances in the technical arena are likely to be destabilizing to the balance of power. As found in chapter 6, coalitions in a state of polarization (that is, fully formed in defensive alliances versus each other) were uniquely sensitive to changes in the balance of power. Such changes can come about as the result either of the expected imminent disintegration of a great power ally (World War I) or of a strategic breakthrough. In certain instances even a quantitative increase in very sophisticated strategic weaponry can be destabilizing, as in the Cuban missile crisis of 1962. In the early 1960s an approximate parity in nuclear armaments between the United States and USSR gave way to a strategic missile gap very much in favor of the United States. Indeed, so extreme was the disparity in favor of the United States that the decision to place missiles in Cuba, with all its dangers, was taken by the Soviet Presidium as a way of redressing the strategic imbalance (Allison 1971, 54–55).

In the approach to a missile preponderance by the United States in 1962, one may find a hint as to a possible outcome of a technical breakthrough such as the Strategic Defense Initiative. In the event of a successful SDI, likely known to the Soviets via its own information-gathering activities, a window of vulnerability might exist just before the system is completely operational. It is in this time period that a systemic war between the United States and USSR could erupt.

Thus, we find two possible consequences of the strategic arms race and one for the conventional arms race. Whereas the conventional arms race generally supports the hierarchical structure and, thus, minimizes the probability of systemic war, the strategic arms race has two contrasting outcomes. On the one hand, as we have seen, the existence of vast disparities in possession of strategic weapons reinforces the hierarchy and makes the potential rogue activities of an ally less likely to involve the hierarchy leader. On the other hand, technical and other strategic breakthroughs as a consequence of the arms race also can destabilize the balance between the superpowers. Thus, a delicate balance between these intrabloc and interbloc requirements is required for the avoidance of systemic war. A pell-mell crashing ahead to achieve new technical defenses, in all likelihood should be avoided, as should any unilateral disarmaments which would clearly weaken the hierarchy. What is also suggested by this analysis is not only that such a unilateral move would be destabilizing but that a bilateral nuclear disarmament could be equally destabilizing, for although in such an event the superpowers would have much less to fear from each other, their smaller allies also would have much less to fear from their hierarchy leaders. The likelihood of an adventurous stance by one or more of these smaller powers is substantially increased, with a concomitant increase in the probability of systemic war. Note that the current agreement between the United States and USSR on the elimination of intermediate range missiles is not likely to upset the hierarchical relations within blocs because of the continued possession of long-range strategic weapons which distinguishes the superpowers from their smaller allies.

Entropy

I shall now consider the impact of the hierarchy and the existence of the independent small powers (the second stipulation of the hierarchical equilibrium) on another dependent variable of concern, namely, the structural entropy. Here, the concern is not for an obvious, almost tactile variable, such as the arms race for which has been evinced so much concern, but for a measure of structure and, ultimately, of information which may have equally important consequences for the presence or absence of systemic war. As was seen in chapter 9, the entropy is a measure of disorder or uncertainty, for it is equal to zero when only one outcome is certain ($\log_b 1 = 0$) and it is at a maximum ($\log_b N$) when all of the outcomes are equally likely. This, of course is a condition of maximum uncertainty. Given the international system as one without central direction, there is a distinct advantage in minimizing the entropy or uncertainty of the prevailing international structure. Additionally, only the entropy has a particular structural uniqueness which is elaborated elsewhere (Ornstein 1973; Sinai 1976).

Maximizing the hierarchical structure clearly has the consequence of minimizing the entropy or uncertainty. The stronger the hierarchical structure, the more certain the great power at the head of the hierarchy would be as the source of decision making. Alternatively, the weaker the structure, the less certain the center of decision making; smaller powers could have greater influence on the hierarchy leader, such that the uncertainty of any decisional outcome is increased. Thus, a strong hierarchical structure minimizes the entropy of the international environment with regard to decision making within blocs and, consequently, the expectations of members of the opposing bloc. Knowing that the opposing bloc leader is the likely source of decisions, not some extraordinarily influential allied smaller power, clearly contributes to the clarity and therefore certainty of international discourse.

Structurally, in most configurations of this type, there is another aspect to the hierarchical equilibrium which is reflected by the existence of two opposing hierarchically organized blocs. Although the hierarchical equilibrium does not require that there be only two such blocs, in practice, this is usually the case, even within some multipolar system structures. Simple calculations reveal that the bipolar configuration minimizes the entropy versus any likely multipolar candidate (Midlarsky, 1984a). Given a bipolar structure with $H = 0.6931$ (using the logarithm to the base e) it would require a multipolar system (3, 4, or 5 powers) in which one power has at least 74% of the strategically relevant resources in order to match this entropy value for the bipolar structure. Since this capability distribution is an unlikely eventuality, the bipolar structure typically associated with the hierarchical equilibrium is the one with the least entropy and, therefore minimum uncertainty relative to other likely possibilities.

International Structure as an Information System

Thus far, we have analyzed the hierarchical equilibrium (with an emphasis on the hierarchy) in terms of its structure and the likely consequences of that structure for important aspects of international conflict. Now we will treat the hierarchical equilibrium in a somewhat different fashion, viewing it as an information system or, more exactly, as one which has certain likely informational consequences associated with it.

Claude Shannon (1948) was the first to use entropy not only as a measure of uncertainty or disorder but as a measure of information. The basic idea is that a certain amount of uncertainty is reduced when information is received; the greater that uncertainty reduction, the greater the information. Although information theory was somewhat derogated in the 1960s for not making startling breakthroughs in the meaning of information, it has more recently been appreciated for its abstract qualities. Precisely because it is abstract and, therefore, applicable to a variety of settings with vastly different informational meanings, it has enjoyed a widespread applicability of late. One of the more striking applications has occurred in genetics, in which the DNA code has been analyzed successfully using concepts of information theory (Gatlin 1972). Of course, the study of linguistics also has been greatly enhanced by the use of information theory (Campbell 1982).

The particular application here does not differ in certain essentials from those in linguistics or genetics. The basic problem is the same, namely, how to introduce a certain degree of redundancy into the informational structure, for in this fashion entropy or uncertainty is reduced. A high entropy letter sequence would be the essentially random one of

$$T\ Q\ B\ R\ Z\ P\ I\ L\ E\ A\ C\ U\ S\ .\ .\ .$$

A departure from uncertainty or randomness would consist of some repetitions of each of the letters, as in

$$T\ Q\ Q\ Q\ B\ B\ R\ R\ R\ R\ Z\ Z\ Z\ .\ .\ .$$

The entropy of this latter sequence is much less than that of the preceding one. Put another way, the uncertainty has been reduced by the redundancy of letters in the second sequence. Redundancy in both the learning of language and genetics has been found to be the principal way in which uncertainty is reduced and information transmitted. The redundancy also ensures that the message will be clearly received even in the presence of noise. Word or concept repetition is a principal means of avoiding the distortions due to noise, for even if one or more of these were to be lost in transmission, the redundant words or concepts still would be received.

Hierarchies and Context-Dependent Redundancy

There are essentially two ways in which redundancy can be introduced. The first is context free while the second is context dependent. In the former, as the name implies, the redundant letters or concepts simply appear without any warning or indication that they are to be expected. A string of alternate letters *I* in the sequence below would be an illustration of this type. The letters preceding *I* are essentially random.

$$Q\ I\ T\ C\ I\ L\ Q\ M\ T\ I\ B\ I\ B\ Z\ P\ I\ A\ I\ .\ .\ .$$

In the second type of redundancy, we are forewarned by the context in which the letter or concept occurs. A sequence of this type would be

$$A\,B\,+\,I\,Q\,L\,A\,B\,I\,R\,P\,A\,B\,I\,S\,\ldots$$

in which the letters A and B always precede the appearance of *I*, in addition to the remaining, essentially random letter sequences. Here we have a context-dependent redundancy. It is not only the repetition of the letter *I* which is the redundant element, but the ability to predict that *I* always follows A and B. In other words, context dependency is the key to the entropy or uncertainty reduction in this instance.

Learning processes generally have been facilitated by the context-dependent form of redundancy. It is, after all, the redundancy of language in meaningful ways which imparts information. Until the rules of language which make for creative combinations are thoroughly understood (even unconsciously) late in childhood or early adolescence, the chief method of teaching and learning is context-dependent redundancy. The context-free form also is important for daily communication and for the learning process. It is precisely these two forms of redundancy which are reflected by the hierarchical equilibrium structure—the context-dependent form in the hierarchy itself and the context-free type in relation to the independent small powers. These redundancies, in turn, give rise to entropy or uncertainty reductions in relations between the superpowers.

As a learning scenario, the context dependency occurs in the hierarchical structure. A particular set of nations, namely, the allied smaller powers, essentially cannot be dealt with in important matters by external powers independently of the leading power within the hierarchy. Of course, in matters which do not impinge on international security, such as cultural exchange or certain trade items, the allied smaller powers can be treated as fairly independent from the hierarchy leader. But in matters of international security, the context-dependency is strong if not unbreakable.

The post-World War II period witnessed just such a learning process driven by the geopolitics of a divided Europe. Each of the superpowers learned that any attacks on the smaller allied powers would be resisted by the superpowers even to the point of possibly initiating a nuclear war. Countries like Greece and Turkey would be defended by policy instruments such as the Truman Doctrine, and even small dependent cities such as Berlin would be defended forcibly. Within communist societies, any dissident movements, as in Hungary or Czechoslovakia, would be crushed with no serious interferences brooked by external powers.

The neutralization of Austria was, in effect, the first formal statement which established the perpetual neutrality of a formerly occupied territory and, in so doing, implied the obverse—that allied smaller countries are virtually in perpetuity tied to the hierarchy leader. One can say that it was this agreement which signaled a milestone in the learning process, for after this event there were few serious efforts to directly undermine the control of the opposing superpower over its European allies. From this perspective, one could have predicted after 1955 that the United States would not intervene in the Hungarian revolution or the Czechoslovakian imbroglio, nor would the Soviets make serious moves to engulf West Berlin, especially after the construction of the Berlin Wall as an affirmation of the obverse side of the Austrian neutrality agreement. Indeed, as found in chapter 2 in the analysis of disputes involving the superpowers between 1946 and 1964, only those specifically involving European powers were found to demonstrate systemic instability; when the dispute set was opened to include countries outside of Europe, systemic stability was demonstrated.

The smaller, non-European powers, principally in the Third World, essentially have become the venue of conflict discourse between the superpowers. This is likely because of the context-dependent learning process that occurred throughout the 1950s and early 1960s which implied the instability of any serious conflict activity on the European continent. The context-dependent learning process of the post-World War II period was facilitated by the redundancy of paired Soviet-allied small powers or U.S.-allied small power dyads. The United States and Italy or the United States and Turkey were, for security matters, essentially seen as one, as were the USSR and Bulgaria or the USSR and Hungary. In this fashion, the external entropy or uncertainty of that period was reduced. Momentarily, I shall turn to the normative implications of this scenario.

Independent Small Powers
and Context-Free Redundancy

A context-free redundancy has emerged alongside the older context-dependent one and, in fact, reinforces the older type. This second form of redundancy is found in relations between the superpowers and smaller non-European countries. When conflict between the superpowers is enacted essentially outside the European zone of sensitivity, each of these redundant conflicts conveys the basic message that the superpower ambitions remain outside of the European camp. Given the extreme instability that conflict in Europe threatens, the context-free redundancy of conflicts involving smaller powers outside of Europe constitutes a reinforcement of the earlier context-dependent learning process. As time passes, the superpowers increasingly institutionalize in their bureaucracies and other collective memories the importance of conflict avoidance in zones of extreme sensitivity.

To be sure, there are other areas of sensitivity, such as Central America for the United States or central Asia for the Soviets. As these conflicts appear and intensify, there seems to be a recognition, at least thus far, of the importance of treating these as context dependent with a minimal degree of interference by the opposing superpower in these ongoing conflicts. In

Vietnam in the 1960s or, more recently, Africa as essentially context-free zones of disputation between the United States and USSR, the likelihood of direct military confrontation by the opposing superpower was minimal, and so there could be more energetic involvement by the superpowers without serious fear of the onset of systemic war.

The communication process of context-free redundancy in the hierarchical equilibrium can be symbolized in the following way.

$$A_1\ A_2\ A_3\ A_4\ A_5\ .\ .\ .$$

Each of the subscripts refers to a different extra-European conflict with, to be sure, its own unique properties but having the property called A of a non-European location. The occurrence of each context-free A without serious threat of systemic war reinforces the absence of conflict in Europe which already has been learned to be context dependent and, therefore, extremely dangerous to system stability. It is the combination of the earlier learned context dependence and later reinforcement by context-free redundancy which reduces the entropy or uncertainty of the contemporary international system.

Contrast these two forms of entropy reduction with that of the traditional multipolar-balance-of-power system. Here, the insurance for system stability is the random formation and termination of alliances with any other major power. In this fashion, ongoing enmities are largely avoided with a consequent reduction in the likelihood and extent of systemic polarization. However, the entropy or uncertainty of such a system, virtually by definition, is very high and even approximates the entropy of the entirely random letter sequence given earlier in this chapter. Learning by either of the two forms of redundancy is absent here, for there are no contexts in the form of hierarchies nor independent small powers who effectively participate in the system. Only the number of major powers serves as an effective limit on the entropy of this system, for with a limited number of such powers some of the alliance sequences must be repeated. But only in this way is redundancy introduced. Any increase in the number of new major powers, as in fact occurred toward the end of the nineteenth century, would automatically increase the entropy and, therefore, the uncertainty of the international system.

The system of alliances, beginning in 1891 with the Franco-Russian Entente, was little better from this perspective. The only form of redundancy was context dependent in the ongoing alliance (but not hierarchical), and even here the entropy would be substantial because of the exclusive great power status of virtually all of the alliance members. There would not be the reduced entropy and, therefore, increased clarity of communication found in the hierarchically organized structure. The absence of a large number of neutral small powers in this configuration also implies the absence of the redundancy of communication found in the hierarchical equilibrium. This absence of context-free redundancy also applies to a bipolar system with hierarchically organized blocs, but without the independent small powers.

A hegemonic system, as in the existence of a single empire (for example, Rome), clearly allows for context-dependent redundancy but, at the same time, does not support the existence of context-free redundancy because of the inclination of such empires to include within their boundaries virtually all formerly independent small powers. Thus, of all the international systems which have existed historically, the hierarchical equilibrium is the only one which exhibits both forms of redundancy as reductions of entropy and as vehicles for learning.

There also exists an interesting comparison of this communication process with that of tit-for-tat (Axelrod 1984) in a prisoner's dilemma game. In tit-for-tat, as noted in chapter 2, the programmed player cooperates on the first move and reciprocates either cooperation or defection on all succeeding moves. The expectation is that after the first cooperative move, the other player will reciprocate, thus leading to an unending series of cooperations. This sequence can be written as

$$C\ C\ C\ C\ C\ C\ C\ C\ .\ .\ .$$

(I have intentionally omitted player and move subscripts for the sake of simplicity.) This clearly is a zero-entropy process with redundancy of communication having eliminated all uncertainty of communication. Unfortunately, if the first cooperative move is reciprocated by defection, then an unending series of defections could occur as follows.

$$C\ D\ D\ D\ D\ D\ D\ D\ .\ .\ .$$

This is almost a zero-entropy process, with only the first cooperative move raising the entropy from zero.

Here, the redundancy in both cases clearly is context dependent, for the entire series of moves is dependent on the initial move and the first response. There is no context-free redundancy as in the hierarchical equilibrium. Moreover, the context here is deterministic in contrast to the more probabilistic nature of the two forms of redundancy in the hierarchical equilibrium. In tit-for-tat, the outcome is an unending series of either cooperations or defections. Only a somewhat surprising cooperation after a preceding defection (possible, but not likely) could alter the defection sequence. In the hierarchical equilibrium, the contextual learning is reinforced by the rather unsurprising and unthreatening context-free redundancy, both of which together yield a stochastic process which does not have to veer either to complete cooperation or, as the likely alternative, to an unending feud which could spell mutual destruction. In some sense, the hierarchical equilibrium hedges our bets on the outcomes; it opts for a whole range of possibilities instead of the essentially binary tit-for-tat.

The redundancy of the smaller powers also has a game theoretic interpretation, namely, the possibility of positive-sum games or, what amounts to the same thing, an inducement to cooperate, as was seen in chapter 2 in connection with the small independent powers.

The Evolution of the International System

The context-dependent learning process of the hierarchy within the hierarchical equilibrium along with the reinforcement of the context-free process suggest certain evolutionary possibilities. One of these is the possibility of developing rules beyond those simply of context dependency. Arguments such as these have been strongly suggested to be the basis of evolutionary development in organisms (Gatlin 1972). Beyond a certain point in the context-dependent learning process, the organism begins to first understand and then later *generate* rules for its future ontogeny. The mere learning of new "vocabularies" is not enough; the organism begins to develop a sense of grammar or, what is the same thing, a set of rules for combining the letters and words in certain meaningful forms (Chomsky 1957). Rather than an ad hoc and fitful response to each new context-dependent move by the opponent, there can exist a set of rules which prescribe (and proscribe) certain conduct far into the foreseeable future.

Most desirable theoretically among all of these possible rule sets, of course, is world government which in perpetuity would generate and administer rules of interstate conduct. The recent failures of experimentation with this particular form suggest that perhaps the international system in 1919 and again in 1946 had not experienced sufficient context-dependent learning to embark on such an enterprise. SALT I and II are more limited and, therefore, perhaps more successful rule sets. Yet here we find something of a paradox, for SALT I and II as arms limitations agreements could have the consequence of limiting arms races to the point where the integrity of hierarchies could be affected with an increased probability of systemic war, as argued earlier in this chapter. Given the provisions of these treaties, however, this event is unlikely. Recent reinforcements of central elements of the hierarchies, which occurred when intermediate range nuclear missiles were placed in Europe, were within the permitted behavior of the SALT agreements. Nevertheless, the need to maintain hierarchy leadership by the superpowers may lead to the balking at future agreements which contain more comprehensive rule sets. It is this give-and-take between the generation of such rules and the fears that context-dependent learning may have been insufficient both within and between blocs that likely will limit the scope of future arms-control agreements.

The question remains, however, whether the two blocs indeed have reached a point where learning has been sufficient to allow for substantial rule generation. The signing of SALT II in 1979 and its likely ratification by the U.S. Senate suggested an affirmative response to this query, but the invasion of Afghanistan by the Soviets prevented that ratification. This, in turn, suggests that it is the uneven development of the system, in respect to both learning processes and perceived dangers, that is inimical to potential sophisticated rule making. The fear of fundamentalist Islam rising on the Soviet's central Asian border may have contributed much to the invasion of Afghanistan. If the Afghan population had somehow participated in processes designed to placate the Soviets (an unlikely and unpalatable event), then the risk of such an invasion probably would have diminished. The absence of such an invasion of Finland in the post-World War II era suggests the presence of precisely those context-dependent learning processes absent in Afghanistan in 1979. Whether rules, even at the level of sophistication of SALT II, can ever be generated again is, of course, an open question. Yet the fact that the current hierarchical equilibrium has allowed for such learning to take place via its two forms of redundancy suggests possibilities for the current system which likely were absent from the multipolar system of 1919 and the not-yet-risen bipolar one of 1946. As yet, we do not know whether that learning will be built upon successfully.

There exists a feedback mechanism between the informational output of the hierarchical equilibrium and its structural integrity. Strategic armaments of high technical quality may be necessary to maintain the hierarchy intact, but the communication of the intention to use them in certain ways may be as important as the armaments themselves. Probably more important than the range, payload, and other technical specifications of intermediate range missiles is the intention to place them on the territory of allied powers. Armaments treated this way as communication channels to both allies and potential opponents may be a more accurate understanding of their function in the contemporary hierarchical equilibrium than the destructive capabilities of the armaments themselves. The standing of Europe as still the most important zone of sensitivity in relations between the superpowers likely was reinforced by the placements of those missiles.

A somewhat surprising but nevertheless straightforward deduction from the analysis is the possible negative outcome of even a bilateral strategic disarmament by the superpowers. The resulting diminution in nuclear arms advantage by each of the hierarchy leaders vis-à-vis their own allies might, in the long run, have more serious consequences for systemic war than the improvement in political climate between the superpowers themselves. A nuclear monopoly, and a substantial one at that, may be required for the avoidance of systemic war in the foreseeable future. At the same time, any major technical breakthroughs such as a successful SDI might directly destabilize relations between the superpowers. Caution, therefore, is advised at both ends of the armaments spectrum. (Also see p. 195.)

The question of the evolution of the system is an intriguing one. It may well be that the time is ripe for some additional rule making; the learning achieved by both superpowers may have proceeded far enough to faciliate this process. The recent Chernobyl disaster with its implications for transnational concerns may have perversely and inadvertently increased the probability of such processes accelerating. On the other hand, the uneven development of the system may inhibit the rule-making process as we have seen immediately following the invasion of Afghanistan. A disturbing precedent exists in the resolution of certain basic conflicts (such as the Berlin–Baghdad railway) between the major powers in 1914 and the onset of systemic war immediately thereafter as the result of conflict processes begun in the Balkans outside of the great power arena itself. The war in Afghanistan alone likely does not have such destabilizing potential. If such a war were to spread in central Asia or Central America were to become an arena of superpower rivalry, on the other hand, then it is likely that more extensive and sophisticated rule making between the superpowers would be overcome by the consequent uncertainties and international crises.

Predictability and Timing

Although the theoretical framework developed here was not intended as a predictive device, nevertheless, given the enormous destructiveness of any future systemic war, it would be folly not to explore its implications for prediction. Indeed, there is one prediction that follows directly from the theory, namely, that any future systemic war is likely to arise from structural causes and not be a mobilization war. This is an immediate consequence of the theory because mobilization wars are suggested to follow upon the generally inconclusive consequences of structural wars. Although structural systemic wars have winners and losers, the outcome generally is not decisive in either case. Britain and France were the victors in World War I, yet they were considerably weakened by the war, as Germany, although a loser, was not so weakened that she could not rise again as a mobilized power in World War II. The French Revolutionary Wars, similarly, saw French power increased, but Austrian, Prussian, and British forces were hardly at all decreased preparatory to the Napoleonic Wars. The Thirty Years' War, which ended in 1648, was a virtual stalemate that encouraged Louis XIV to begin his mobilization efforts later in that century. The Peloponnesian War substantially weakened all of Hellas so that, ultimately, Philip of Macedon could rise as a successful mobilizing leader in a neighboring territory.

As we saw in chapter 7, this power interregnum between the two forms of systemic wars almost "invites" some aggressive response by a mobilizing polity. Clearly, such a condition does not exist at the present time nor in the foreseeable future simply because a structural systemic war has not occurred in the post-World War II era. This is not so say that the United States has maintained its hegemonic advantage enjoyed at the end of World War II (Keohane 1984; K. J. Holsti 1985). Rather, it suggests that, despite a substantial power decline in the post-World War II era vis-à-vis other countries (for example, the Soviet Union, Japan), the absence of any major upheaval during that period has enabled the United States and its power contenders to continually adjust or "fine tune" these relations. In this fashion, the extraordinary upheavals in those relations occasioned by a structural war are absent, with the diminished likelihood of the rise of a mobilizing polity to initiate a war of this type. Thus, if a systemic war was to come about, it would likely originate in the structural features of the system as initially outlined in the model of chapter 1. If such a war occurred, we could also predict a period of intense turmoil among the survivors until some kind of mobilization effort, pitiful as it might be, would put an end to the chaos, at least on a regional basis.

Clearly, the relationship between the structural and mobilization wars is not suggested to be deterministic. As in the specification of the overall model in chapter 1, relationships between all of the variables are probabilistic, hence the occurrence of a structural systemic war merely increases the probability of a later mobilization variant.

Based on the World War II experience and recent events, we can, interestingly, comment on mobilization efforts short of the systemic war and the conditions in which they arise. World War II began, in part, as the result of the mobilization efforts attendant upon what I have elsewhere called an authenticating revolution (Midlarsky 1982). These are revolutions which began not as redistributive efforts (as have so many recent revolutions, especially Marxist ones) but as efforts to return to what is perceived as the genuinely "authentic" in a national experience remote in historical time. The Nazi rise to power, with its emphasis on early pre-Christian myth, and the recent Iranian Revolution, with its return to fundamentalist Shiite norms, are cases in point.

Governments of this type tend to be warlike simply because they require some external validation for their existence. In contrast to the redistributive revolution that can validate itself simply by engaging in redistribution and increased social equality, which virtually all such revolutions have accomplished to some extent, the authenticating revolution has no such tangible material referent. Its reasons for being is found in some race-centered or God-centered concepts which cannot be immediately validated except by the granting of special favors, as in the conquest of other peoples and their subsequent extermination, subjugation, or conversion to the true faith. It is these outcomes, if successfully achieved, which can validate the essentially nonmaterial claims of the authenticating mobilizing elite. This partly explains the extraordinary international dynamism and aggressiveness of such revolutionary regimes.

Although it is unlikely that regimes of this type will come to power in the governments of the superpowers, including contemporary China, the likelihood is far greater for the rise of such regimes in smaller countries, such as Iran, with warlike potential. Wars, such as the Iran–Iraq War, consequent upon an authenticating revolution are unlikely in themselves to yield a systemic war. Yet the longer wars of this type persist, the greater the likelihood of some systemic involvement, although probably not at the level of widespread warfare. In order to avoid war at that level, a decision-making requirement for the superpower is to recognize the warlike potential of authenticating regimes and then to isolate these conflicts from those pitched solely at the superpower level. This is tantamount to the creation of disjoint dispute sets as suggested in the analysis of chapter 5.

Thus far, the timing of the onset of a systemic war has not been addressed. Clearly, it is dictated in part by the variable sequence given in chapter 1, p. 12. The absence of a hierarchical equilibrium, of course, begins the sequence and is followed by the development of inequalities and envies within a multipolar structure. Yet it is also clear that, at least at the outset of this process, some of the deterioration in interstate relations may be reversible. When does the slide toward the outbreak of war become more accelerated and irreversibility become more likely? The evidence certainly is not conclusive on this point, but the critical point for irreversibility appears to center on the occurrence of the overlap of conflict domains. When disputes involving exclusively major powers overlap with conflicts between great and small powers, the die appears to be cast for a systemic or general war.

When the conflicts between the Corintheans and Athenians over Corcyra and that between Athens and Potidae were brought to Sparta, the Peloponnesian War became much more likely to occur. When the Protestant revolt in Bohemia against the Habsburgs began to overlap in time with the expiration of the truce between Habsburg Spain and Protestant Holland, the Thirty Years' War began to assume a wider dimension. Similarly, the revolt in the Austrian Netherlands against Habsburg rule coinciding with the French Revolution and its international consequences for the Habsburgs vastly increased the probability of a systemic conflict. And in the approach to World War I, the overlap between exclusively great power conflicts and those involving smaller powers, especially in the Balkans, increased the probability of an extensive conflict. Our one instance of a structural general war exhibits this property in the overlap between the War of Jenkins' Ear, British concerns about the safety of Hanover, and the invasion of Silesia by Frederick the Great all vastly increasing the scope of heretofore small conflicts.

206

It is not merely the entry of a number of small countries into the conflict arena that signals the arrival of a wide-ranging conflict but more cogent considerations deriving from the theoretical framework itself. The beginnings of these disputes involving smaller powers suggests the decay of the hierarchical equilibrium. No longer is there a substantial power disparity between the major powers and smaller power allies or enemies. Additionally, the neutrality of many is now vitiated by the centrifugal aspects of the conflict itself. Perhaps most important as a signal of irreversibility is the fact that the decay of hierarchy is now manifest. It is there for all to see in the challenges to major powers by smaller ones (that is, Serbia, Bohemia, Spanish Netherlands, Potidae) and, therefore, requires some response by the threatened major powers, thus escalating the dispute to widespread warfare.

A distinction between the systemic and general war appears in the importance of deep internal conflicts within the initial conflict protagonists overlapping with external disputes in the case of the systemic war but much less so in the instance of the general war. It is the presence of the domestic *and* international overlap in the systemic case which probably makes this a point of greater irreversibility than in the general war where the domestic conflicts are much less deep and pervasive, if they exist at all beyond the level of the government itself.

A Historical Dynamic

It is possible to embed these findings within an even broader conception of history using the inequality analyses of chapters 3 and 4. As McNeill (1982, 148) observed in connection with the rise of great powers on the periphery of smaller or at least weaker powers, "The rise of such march states to dominance over older and smaller polities located near a center where important innovation first concentrated is one of the oldest and best-attested patterns of civilized history." Among the march states listed by McNeill are Akkad (ca. 2350 B.C.) in Mesopotamia, Ch'in (221 B.C.) in what is contemporary China, the Amerindian states (Aztec and Inca), and Macedon, familiar to us from our earlier analyses. We know from archeological and other historical sources that the earlier civilizations experienced serious warfare among the smaller constituent units (see, for example, Wesson 1967; Doyle 1986; or Mann 1986), prior to the eventual conquest by the march states. It was only after a fairly long period of such internecine warfare that the somewhat less developed but by now more vigorous peripheral states were able to conquer the older civilizations.

In the instance of the rise of Macedon and later of France subsequent to the Thirty Years' War, this pattern is respectively upheld and extended with modifications. Only after the exhaustion of the Peloponnesian War and its aftermath consequent upon the inequalities analyzed in chapter 3 was Philip II able to effectively exert his hegemony over Greece. Louis XIV attempted to achieve hegemony while on the periphery of the Central European scene of mass destruction among the small neighboring states during the earlier Thirty Years' War (also detailed in chapter 3) and a Spain now exhausted from her own efforts in that war as well as earlier struggles against the United Provinces. It was the size of the now less vigorous Central European core combined with a relatively new actor on the continent in this period (end of the seventeenth century), England, that defeated his purposes.

By the time of the French Revolutionary and Napoleonic Wars, the pattern had shifted. Population growth that McNeill (1982, 144–145) singles out as a principal driver of commercial and other forces of expansion had risen rapidly in France during the period after 1750. The rise of social class as a principal unit of importance in such circumstances of a scarcity-induced inequality (Midlarsky 1982; Midlarsky and Roberts 1985) led to the French Revolution as a major conflict event, not on the periphery of the would-be hegemon, but in its bowels. Effectively the rapid growth of population eliminated the distinction between civilization core and periphery on the European continent.

What is fascinating about Bismarckian diplomacy after 1871 is the apparent attempt to *create* a new area for legitimate conquest next to the European continent in which the European states *together* would constitute the hegemon. This was an effort to remove the locus of conflict away from Europe via colonial expansion, especially in Africa after 1885, as noted in chapter 3. The colonial powers of course made use of indigenous African conflicts wherever they could and even fomented many in order to achieve their colonial hegemony (Doyle 1986). This effort failed for reasons that were detailed in chapters 2 and 3, but what is noteworthy about the effort is its attempt to generate a form of European cooperation through a process similar to one that had much earlier antecedents and had become a fairly established pattern. In this, Bismarck was a brilliant observer of the contemporary and historical European condition. What Bismarck could not know was that the effort would be doomed to failure from the start because of the sequential acquisition processes developed in chapter 4.

Bismarckian diplomacy of this period can be seen as a response to the emerging inequality among European states on the continent (Table 3.1 and Figure 3.1) that on the one hand, would lead to the breakup of the *Dreikaiserbund* as a pillar of his eastern policy, and on the other a *revanchist* France in the west. Colonial acquisitions presumably would lead to an equalization of resource possession. However, attempts to create a new conquest area would only have the consequence of *deepening* an already existing inequality in colonial acquisition between Germany and its soon-to-be chief noncontinental rival, England, as was seen in chapter 4. Effectively a new distribution of even greater inequality (the Pareto log-exponential) was augmented as the result of German participation in a process that, for her, was brand new. Thus the process that was designed to provide some equalization in resource acquisition, with Germany as the initially too-favored unit on the continent, was to have the precise opposite consequence vis-à-vis another international actor, England, wherein Germany would emerge as the least-favored major power in colonial holdings (and even inferior to smaller states such as the Netherlands as in Table 4.2) as the result of earlier colonial acquisitions by England (and France) combined with newer additions after 1885. This failure to provide such resource equalization, especially for Germany, was to once again confine the principal conflict behavior to the European continent in 1914 and again in 1939.

It is ironic that a colonial process originally intended by Bismarck to dampen the conflict relations between Germany and France on the continent was to lead eventually, in the far less deft diplomatic hands of Wilhelm II and his military (especially Tirpitz), to an escalation of the naval arms race with England. A status quo power under Bismarck after 1871 was to be transformed into one seeking major changes in the international order as a result of its entry into a new category of "colonial power", but as a disadvantaged one. Here is one more instance of the inherent instability of a multipolar system.

In this sense, the analyses of Chapters 3 and 4 have revealed a dynamic for the historical regularity that McNeill has noted. Inequalities derivative of the processes detailed in chapters 3 and 4 lead to intense conflicts among the units comprising a civilization which in turn lead to its exhaustion and subsequent exposure to attempts at hegemonic conquest from outside the immediate region. Alternatively, under conditions of severe population growth and a consequent domestic inequality, social class can emerge as a relevant unit of international discourse. Some combination of the two processes also could be at work as was likely the case in the Peloponnesian War and its aftermath (Ste. Croix 1981) with serious efforts to utilize class conflict by the Greek city states against each other and by Philip II of Macedon against virtually all of them. It is also likely that social class was a relevant variable in the densely populated central European locus of the onset of the Thirty Years' War, as intimated by Wedgwood (1972, 28) and suggested in chapter 3. Certainly, the analysis of domestic political conditions within Austria-Hungary and Germany in chapter 5 suggests its importance in the onset of World War I as well. Further development of these ideas within a larger historical context will be found in a succeeding volume concerned with conflict and cooperation; their implications for the present analysis can now be explored further.

Issues of Domestic Inequality

In a deeper sense, issues of equality pervaded these conflicts directly from their onset, likely as the result of rapid population growth documented in all of our instances of structural systemic war. To this extent, the theoretical nexus with domestic conflict to be developed later in this chapter is a natural outgrowth of the overall analysis. In our four cases of structural systemic war, the more threatened and defensive power(s) tended to support hierarchical and explicitly inegalitarian domestic structures which were threatened by the more egalitarian policies associated with opposing states. Sparta and her frequently threatened domestic control over the Messenian helots clearly was wary of the more dynamic, democratic, and, ultimately, egalitarian Athens even in imperial guise (see chapter 5). In the Thirty Years' War, Calvinism was seen as an egalitarian version of Christianity, in comparison with the Roman Catholic variant expressed by the Holy Roman Empire under Habsburg tutelage. The Bohemian revolt as a political expression of this egalitarian form was intolerable to the Habsburgs for this and other reasons given in earlier chapters (see especially chapter 3). The French Revolutionary Wars witnessed the explicit threats to the monarchical states not only of French egalitarianism and regicide but also of the continued Austrian imperial control over the Austrian Netherlands. The First World War began with the strong threat emanating especially from Serbia to the traditional inequality of German-speaking dominance over the remaining peoples of the Austro-Hungarian Empire as detailed in chapter 5. In Germany itself, there were serious egalitarian movements, as documented by the rise of the Social Democrats, also detailed in chapter 5.

Thus, nested within the international inequality engendered by the multipolar environment preceding our four structural systemic wars, are issues of domestic inequality of a critical nature for the future of the concerned polities. World War I is an especially complex instance for, in addition to the Slavic threat to the continued Austro-Hungarian dominance within that state, the rise of German power not only posed the perceived international threat to Russia detailed in chapter 3 but likely, also by example, threatened the traditional domestic inequalities of tsarist Russia. The defeat inflicted by Japan in 1904–1905 and the subsequent revolution of 1905 revealed not only the archaic structure of Russian military organization but also the extreme unwillingness of the Russian peasantry to undergo hardships for the sake of the Russian Empire either at the front or at home. The inegalitarian social structure that failed in confrontation with the Japanese likely would be even more vulnerable when confronted by Imperial Germany.

Extensions to Regional Systemic Wars

Clearly, the concept of systemic war as it has been developed here is not confined to global war or even a continental variant as in the Thirty Years' War. Indeed, the Peloponnesian War was limited to Hellas, at least until the later mobilization variant arose out of neighboring Macedonia. Thus, one can treat a systemic war within a given region, such as the Middle East, much as we have done until now in this volume, and such a treatment can yield a similar structural–mobilization pairing for this region.

The 1967 Arab–Israeli War bears similarities to those of the structural systemic war.[1] It was the joining of Palestine Liberation Organization (PLO) activity to the north of Israel (ultimately with Syrian support) with Egyptian ambitions to the south which led to the systemic involvement of all Arab states bordering Israel. The PLO's goal of dismantling the Israeli state combined with Syrian desires for greater influence to her south coalesced with the ambitions of Nasser of Egypt for general leadership of the Arab world. The destruction of Israel would be an ideal vehicle for the attainment of that goal. It was not that Nasser or the Syrians initiated the early stages of that conflict. Instead, it was the increase in PLO activity, with Syrian support (or at least the absence of Syrian efforts to curtail that activity), that began the cycle of attack and counterattack on Israel's border which was to bring Syria, Egypt, and, ultimately, even Jordan into the war for essentially different reasons. Thus, as in the case of World War I, a prolonged crisis ensued. As such, the dispute activity was detectable as a rise in the number of conflict incidents and their spread throughout the region prior to the war. This can be seen clearly from plots of these conflict incidents (Midlarsky, Wilkins and Andrews 1972), much as the analysis of chapter 8 was able to demonstrate the diffusion of conflict behavior prior to World War I.

On the other hand, there was no such activity prior to the 1973 Arab–Israeli War, which clearly was a mobilization effort by Syria and Egypt. There was no structural joining of separate conflict axes and purposes as in 1967. Instead, the chief purpose was an effort to redress the balance of power by the reconquest of lost territory that clearly had shifted in Israel's favor after 1967 (Organski and Kugler 1980). It was clear that although Israel was perceived to be and, in many respects was, more powerful after 1967, she was not so powerful (given her small territory and population) that she could not be attacked and weakened if the mobilization effort were planned carefully. This was to be the case in 1973 with an attack on the holiest day of the Jewish year, Yom Kippur. Of course there was no increase or diffusion of confict incidents prior to 1973 as in 1967. From the perspective of the treatment of this book, the later conflict was predictable as a mobilization war consequent upon the earlier structural conflict.

In a fundamental sense, the antecedents of the structural conflict of 1967 were similar to those considered earlier in this volume. From the beginnings of the Jewish settlement in what is today Israel, a much different society developed during the preindependence period which culminated, in the 1960s, in a vastly increased GNP per capita (vis-à-vis the Arab states) and a semideveloped society and economy more akin to the European states. The envies and basic fears of this heretofore (but less so now) more successful society are reminiscent of Pericles' observations on the expected envy of Athens by the other Greek city-states (see chapter 3).

Yet caution is advised in this extrapolation from the findings of this study. The scale of the conflict in this regional systemic war clearly does not match that of the wars considered in this volume. The number killed, degree of destruction of cities, and civilian involvement all are vastly less than that of the systemic wars considered here. An obvious reason for this critical difference is the dependence of this regional system upon a global system with deeply interested superpowers. It is not that the Egyptians, Syrians, and Jordanians would have exercised self-restraint in destruction had they won the battles of 1967 and 1973, nor was the relative intactness of the Egyptian army in 1973 the result of Israeli mercy. Instead, it was the intervention of the superpowers in both wars, particularly in 1973, which prevented further destruction, especially of the Egyptian army perilously exposed now to Israeli onslaught. Thus, we have a system which cannot proceed solely on its own devices but is circumscribed by the limits imposed on it by far more powerful forces. This stands in bold contrast with the generally autonomous major power systems treated in this volume.[2]

In this extension of the theory and findings we now begin to approach the limits of their applicability, for as we have seen, what is required for the occurrence of the systemic war is a fair degree of system autonomy, and this is largely absent (at least for wars of this magnitude) in regional systems. The system must be large and powerful enough to proceed entirely on its own, even in the process of self-destruction. It is intriguing that such autonomy is often more likely to be found *within* nation-states, such as the United States in 1861, France in 1789, Russia in 1917, or China in 1946. Large states of this magnitude can exercise a more vigorous autonomy in deciding their own affairs, even by severe conflict, than smaller states in dependent regional systems.

Extensions to Domestic Conflict

The preceding discussion raises the possibility of extending the arguments of this analysis to domestic conflict. After all, the concept of system certainly is not confined to the international sphere but clearly has a domestic counterpart. Indeed, this sort of similarity was suggested by Quincy Wright's (1942, 381) observation that World War II was occasioned by "the revolts of Japan, Italy, and Germany from the public law of the world in 1931."

Similarities are to be found in at least four areas. First, there exists the presence of serious inequalities in both domestic and international conflict of a systemic order. We have seen this condition in international life preceding a systemic war, but one can also see this most clearly in a domestic conflict such as the American Civil War. Just as the more threatened protagonist in an international systemic war tends to be less egalitarian than its adversary, the American South, with its dependence on a one-crop economy and attendant slave labor (not to mention the poor whites in the rural areas surrounding the plantations), also was vastly less egalitarian than the North. The decade preceding the election of Lincoln in 1860 witnessed an intensification of this disparity in the emerging rapid industrialization of the North with its associated equalities of distribution, in comparison with the still agrarian and slave-dependent South.

Second, there exists the element of polarization in both domestic and international systemic conflicts. The Civil War divided the protagonists (here the American states) much in the same fashion as did our polarizing international systems. A southern state fought with the South and a northern one with the North, with only a few "border" states undecided until the last moment. It is in the paucity of undecided actors that the American Civil War is most like our polarizing systems and least like the balance of power as a process with its explicit demand for fluidity of association. The intensity with which the Civil War was fought also more closely approximates the intensity of the systemic war. The issues in the conflict are of paramount importance to the combatants.

A third similarity is to be found in the existence of overlapping conflicts in both revolutionary behavior and in the origins of systemic wars. In our structural systemic wars we have seen how overlapping conflicts were associated with the outbreak of the war. Especially important were the simultaneous occurrences of (1) conflicts among major powers only and (2) those between major powers which also involved midrange or central powers as detailed in chapter 5. In the case of mass or social revolution, Skocpol (1979, 154) found that it was the combination of (1) incapacitation of the central state machinery leading to conflict within the elite and (2) peasant revolts against landlords which were most characteristic of the social revolutions that she studied, namely, the French, Russian, and Chinese. The American Civil War also exhibits such simultaneity in the overlap between the vastly differing economic, demographic, and cultural circumstances as they were evolving in both North and South, on the one hand, and the moral issue of slavery as a cause celebre, on the other.

Fourth, a change in the balance of power prior to the conflict signals its onset in both the international and domestic instances. We have seen in chapter 6 how this process operated not only in our cases of systemic war but generally in the onset of war in polarized settings. Again, the American Civil War provides a good illustration in the election of Lincoln to the presidency in 1860. Now the federal government was to be actively committed to the antislavery cause which was an intolerable change in the balance of power for the South. Earlier, of course, there had been the explicit efforts to maintain the balance between slave and free states as in the Missouri Compromise of 1820, the entry into the Union of Maine (free) and Missouri (slave), the Kansas–Nebraska Act of 1854, and the Dred Scott decision of 1857.

Of course, a mobilization war did not follow upon the victory of the North in that structural conflict. The occupation of the South, tightening of the Union, and freeing of the slaves prevented that sort of response. Here, we find a basic difference between the international and domestic instances, for in the latter case the domination of the defeated opponent is virtually absolute and does not allow for a later mobilization effort as in the international instance. Yet within the limits imposed by the Northern victory, a kind of mobilization by the South did occur. A myriad of legal, economic, and personal methods were instituted to prevent true freedom for the former slaves and to largely perpetuate their former condition of servitude. Many other elements of the antebellum economy and social system also were retained in this fashion. The South's power within the federal government actually increased within a few years after the end of the Civil War due to the solid voting pattern for the Democratic Party and the seniority system in Congress which favored Southerners over others because of their ability to continue in office almost indefinitely. The ending of Reconstruction in 1878 (and even earlier) signaled this mobilization effort which was to prevent the realization of the goals of 1861 for nearly a century.

These similarities and differences suggest that it may be possible in the future to eliminate the designation "international" or "domestic" from cases of systemic conflict and, for many (but not all) analytic purposes, treat them all as a single category. Such a category itself could consist of a continuum of systemic conflict, beginning with revolutionary behavior in unitary states such as France at one end and ending with the international systemic war, with the civil war in federal systems and regional systemic wars somewhere between the two.

Normative Implications

There exists, finally, a disturbing normative implication of the analysis. This is the necessity for extra-European conflict in bipolar (or polarizing) systems in order to avoid the onset of a systemic war likely originating in Europe. Both the post-World War II bipolar system and the slowly polarizing multipolar system of the late nineteenth and early twentieth centuries gave evidence of this substitutability phenomenon in chapter 2. This is an unpleasant finding and, in some respects, exists as a historical parallel with the prevention of yet another general or systemic war in the eighteenth century by means of the Polish partitions as developed in chapter 10, or the delaying of World War I through the medium of colonial expansion. Is a Vietnam War engaged in by the United States or an intervention in Afghanistan by the Soviets required for the avoidance of systemic war in Europe? Fortunately, the COW data set upon which these findings are based includes not only high-intensity conflict incidents such as these but lower level

214

disputes which do not include overt violence and, sometimes, not even the serious threat of its onset. Thus, conflict between the superpowers does not have to be enacted upon the remains of smaller, weaker countries but can be kept at much lower levels of dispute behavior largely confined to diplomacy and short of the use of violence. Disputes entailing intense competition for the diplomatic support of small neutral powers can satisfy the substitutability requirement without necessarily vitiating their independence or imposing military constraints on their sovereignty.[3] If the superpowers can be persuaded to confine their activity to this level, then the price the world pays for system stability may not be too steep. Perhaps this is the lesson the Soviets have learned recently in Afghanistan as evidenced by their recent efforts to disengage from that conflict.

On the other hand, perhaps an overarching finding of this volume is that there exists a price to be paid for world peace. If we are aware of its cost in various guises, we may be able to minimize it for all parties concerned, including the sovereign non-European powers. The adage that there is "no such thing as a free lunch" may be transformed into "no free lunch but one that is affordable both in the ethics of the maintenance of the genuine sovereignty of all the world's countries and, at the same time, the preservation of world peace."

Notes

1 The Palestine War of 1948–1949 is not considered to be a regional systemic war because of the nature of the goals of the protagonists. (Note the naming of this war in contrast to the Arab–Israeli wars of 1967 and 1973.) It was the goal of the Jewish community to achieve an independent state—a purpose that was incompatible with the concept of the wholeness of the Arab nation which was then and, to some extent, still is a motivating force behind inter-Arab relations. (Witness the ultimately ill-fated attempts at Arab unification via the formation of the United Arab Republic joining Egypt and Syria in 1958.) To this extent, the threat of Israel was perhaps more symbolic than real, for a nation of little more than half a million population at that time, with future immigration likely to be limited by the confines of the original partition territory, could not pose a serious threat. This, then, raises the issue of minimal population size for states to participate in systemic wars much as the COW project chose a minimal population size for a country to be included in the system with a view to analyzing its participation in war. Of course, the 1956 Suez crisis involving Egyptian–Israeli conflict also would not qualify as a systemic conflict.
2 This raises the issue of extrasystemic involvement in the Peloponnesian War, especially that of Persia. Certainly the Persians were involved in the war, particularly in the aid given to Sparta toward the end of the conflict. However, we are concerned here with the *onset* of this war, not its later denouement, and here the Persians were largely absent as the result of the defeats of Salamis, Plataea, and Mycale by the Greeks prior to the Peloponnesian War.
3 One last normative concern should be addressed. By putting forward the hierarchical equilibrium structure and testing its stability, it might seem as if I am

stating a personal preference for inequality in the international system along the lines of structural relations within the two power blocs of the 1950s and 1960s. This is not true for at least three reasons. (1) The theoretical structure arose from the initial postulate of an average equality in number of disputes begun and ended within a given time interval and not on an a priori basis. (2) If a multipolar structure later were to evolve peacefully and an inequality were to arise in the history of that system (highly likely as suggested in chapter 3), then that inequality would be destabilizing. Thus, inequality in this instance is not desirable from the perspective of system stability. (3) If there is a hierarchical model that is personally persuasive to me (exogenous to the development of the hierarchical equilibrium here), it is the model of national political hierarchies that generally keep the peace domestically. The basic difference between domestic and international hierarchies, of course, is that in the former instance many, but certainly not all, obtain the consent of the governed in some sort of legitimating procedure such as a national election. This certainly is not true for the international hierarchy in which the threat of force is a far more common occurrence against the smaller entity than in domestic politics, and consent of the "governed" is all too infrequently obtained. My preference is for consent to be obtained in international circumstances as well. Alas, I see no ready way to institute such a procedure that would be politically effective.

In a similar vein, my preference is not for the existence of arms races, especially as they might increase the probability of dyadic war, but that we need to evaluate separately their consequences for the probability of systemic war, as was done in this chapter.

Mathematical Appendix A

THIS MATHEMATICAL APPENDIX contains derivations supplementary to
the expository material of chapter 2.

First, the Poisson distribution for the number of disputes in existence is to
be derived. Consider a small time element, t, within a larger time period, T.
Given the random distribution of disputes in this time period, let there be N
disputes distributed randomly throughout T. Given these circumstances,
then, the probability that a particular dispute will be found to exist in the
time interval t is clearly t/T and that it will not be found in t is $(T - t)/T$. Thus,
given these two independent probabilities in a random dispute configuration, the probability, $P_N(n)$, that some number n of the total of N disputes
will be found existing in t is given by the product of the two probabilities for
each of the n and $(N - n)$ disputes times the number of distinct ways or
combinations of choosing n disputes from the larger group of N, or the
binomial distribution:

$$P_N(n) = \frac{N!}{n! \, (N - n)!} \left(\frac{t}{T}\right)^n \left(\frac{T - t}{T}\right)^{N-n} \tag{1A}$$

Since the average value of n in a binomial distribution, is given by N_q, where
q, the probability of "success," is equal to t/T, we have

$$\langle n \rangle_{av} = N(t/T) \tag{2A}$$

which can, in turn, be set equal to m as the mean of this binomial
distribution.

Now, if we let N, the number of disputes in T, tend to infinity such that m remains constant, then the desired result will be obtained. To accomplish this we rewrite equation [1A] as

$$P_N(n) = \frac{1}{n!} N(N-1)(N-2)\ldots(N-n+1)\left(\frac{m}{N}\right)^n \left(1 - \frac{m}{n}\right)^{N-n}$$

$$= \frac{m^n}{n!} 1 \left(1 - \frac{1}{N}\right)\left(1 - \frac{2}{N}\right)\ldots\left(1 - \frac{n-1}{N}\right)\left(1 - \frac{m}{N}\right)^{N-n} \qquad [3A]$$

Letting $N \to \infty$ and keeping m and n fixed yields.

$$P(n) = \lim_{N \to \infty} P_N(n) = \frac{m^n}{n!} \lim_{N \to \infty} \left[\left(1 - \frac{1}{N}\right)\left(1 - \frac{2}{N}\right)\ldots\left(1 - \frac{n-1}{N}\right)\left(1 - \frac{m}{N}\right)^{N-}\right.$$

$$= \frac{m^n}{n!} \lim_{N \to \infty} \left(1 - \frac{m}{N}\right)^N \qquad [4A]$$

Recognizing that

$$\lim_{N \to \infty} \left(1 - \frac{m}{N}\right)^N = e^{-m} \qquad [5A]$$

gives us

$$P(n) = \frac{m^n e^{-m}}{n!} \qquad [6A]$$

which is the Poisson distribution for the number of disputes in existence with mean m.

One can now define a probability, p, that a single dispute existing during the interval t will be resolved. Now, the probability D of i disputes being resolved in t will be some function of p. Specifically, D_i is defined as the probability of some i disputes disappearing during t given an initial condition of n disputes existing in the interval t. The probability D_i, then, depends on the number n of disputes existing in t, as well as the probability p.

The expression for D_i is given by the probability p^i that some group of i disputes will disappear during t, the probability $(1 - p)^{n-i}$ that the remaining $(n - i)$ disputes do not, and the number of distinct ways of selecting i disputes from the starting group of n. The expression, then, is a binomial distribution in which

$$D_i = \frac{n!}{i!\,(n-i)!}\, p^i\,(1-p)^{n-i} \qquad\qquad [7A]$$

Carrying out the summation in equation [2.1] of chapter 2 and utilizing the expressions contained in equations [6A] and [7A] yield

$$C_i = \sum_{n=i}^{\infty} \frac{e^{-m}m^n}{n!} \times \frac{n!}{i!\,(n-i)!}\, p^i\,(1-p)^{n-i} = \frac{e^{-mp}(mp)^i}{i!} \qquad [8A]$$

which is a Poisson distribution for dispute initiation with mean mp.

If the transition probability from the state of having n disputes in time t to that of $n+j$ is $P(n, n+j)$, then this probability can be written as the product of the two independent probabilities D for disappearance and C for creation, or

$$P(n,\, n+j) = \sum_{i=0}^{n} D_i C_{i+j} \qquad\qquad [9A]$$

Similarly, for the transition probability $P(n,\, n-j)$ for the decrease of j disputes in t, we have

$$P(n,\, n-j) = \sum_{i=j}^{n} D_i C_{i-j} \qquad\qquad [10A]$$

From the expressions for C_i and D_i, given respectively by equations [8A] and [7A] and substituted in equations [9A] and [10A], we arrive at the equations

$$P(n,\, n+j) = e^{-mp} \sum_{i=0}^{n} \frac{n!}{i!\,(n-i)!}\, p^i(1-p)^{n-i} \times (mp)^{i+j}/(i+j)! \qquad [11A]$$

$$P(n,\, n-j) = e^{-mp} \sum_{i=j}^{n} \frac{n!}{i!\,(n-i)!}\, p^i(1-p)^{n-i} \times (mp)^{i-j}/(i-j)! \qquad [12A]$$

There exists a third variant of these equations which emerges upon setting $j = 0$ in equations [11A] and [12A], thus yielding

$$P(n,n) = e^{-mp} \sum_{i=0}^{n} \frac{n!}{i!\,(n-i)!} p^i(1-p)^{n-i} \frac{(mp)^i}{i!} \qquad [13A]$$

This equation gives the probability that the same number of disputes, n, will be observed on two successive occasions.

The Entropy

The entropy is defined as in equation [9.1]

$$H = -\sum_{i=1}^{n} p_i log_e p_i$$

where p_i is the probability of the ith event, there are n possible outcomes and the logarithm is taken to the base e. In most interpretations, the entropy is a measure of disorder or uncertainty, for if only one outcome is certain, then

$$p_i = 1$$
$$log_e p_i = 0$$

and

$$H = 0$$

since the logarithm of one always is equal to zero. Thus under conditions of certainty, the entropy is zero, but if all outcomes are equally likely, then $p_i = 1/n$, and

$$H = -\sum_{i=1}^{n} \frac{1}{n} log_e \frac{1}{n} = log_e n$$

The value of the entropy varies from a minimum of zero under conditions of certainty to a maximum of $log_e n$ when all outcomes are equally likely.

Mathematical Appendix B

THIS MATHEMATICAL APPENDIX contains a geometric derivation of the Pareto distribution supplementary to the material in chapter 4.

Sequential arrivals to scarce resources can be modeled geometrically in the following manner. This treatment is not intended to contribute anything new mathematically; it is intended to be virtually a pictorial account of the generation of a distribution of extreme inequality. The following is an expository geometric derivation in order to impart the particular flavor of the sequential sequestering of resources and also to emphasize the initial scarcity assumption which, to my knowledge, is never explicitly introduced in other derivations of the Pareto distribution. However, in one previous application (Badger 1980) the introduction of this assumption did make a substantial improvement in the fit of an entropy–utility model to the upper tail of an income distribution.

Consider a variation on the Koch curve which was used by Mandelbrot (1982, 34–45) as a basis for the generation of infinite sets and as a further basis for his theory of fractals. We consider, first, a straight line segment as in stage 1, Figure 1B. This is the geometric representation of scarcity; all operations must be performed within the confines of the line segment. No added quantities are allowed after stage 1. The middle one-third of the segment is then replaced by two pieces, each as long as the middle one-third, which are joined together as two sides in an equilateral triangle. This is shown as stage 2. Now, for the two remaining line segments on each side of the triangle, the middle one-third again is removed from each and two new equilateral triangles are formed on each side of the original but, of course, encompassing much smaller area as shown in stage 3. (In a non-modified Koch curve, the sides of the original triangle also would have their middle thirds removed and replaced by equilateral triangles but, for reasons that will become clear in a moment, only the remaining straight line segments will be treated here in this fashion.

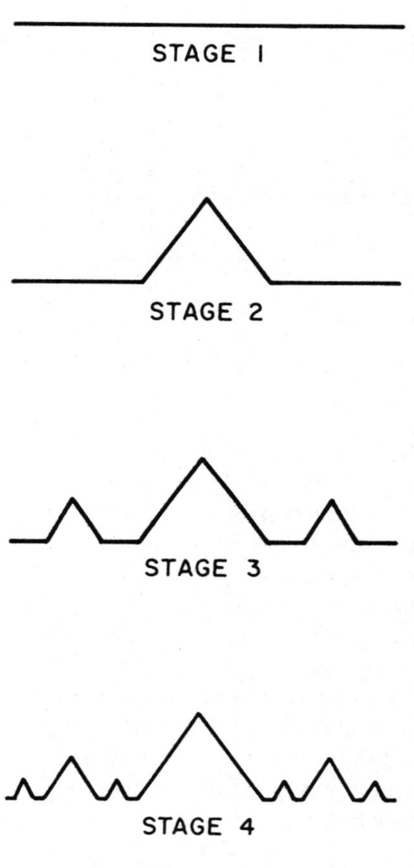

Figure 1B
Stages of sequential resource acquisition.

We continue this process of removing the middle one-thirds of remaining straight line segments and replacing them with equilateral triangles for as long as we please. Of course, this process can be infinitely long, for there is no limit to the number of straight line segments remaining at each stage of the procedure. Indeed, the generation of infinite Cantor sets often is the main purpose of such processes (Rucker 1982, 8; Sparrow 1982, 36); here the intention is quite different.

It is clear that the areas of each of the smaller triangles is some proportion of the larger ones. This is intuitively clear from the removal of the middle one-third of one segment for the formation of one triangle, thus leaving two proportionately much smaller segments on each side for the construction of two additional smaller triangles. It can be shown exactly that the area of each of the new triangles is one-ninth the area of its immediate predecessor. Given the original line segment (stage 1) as three unit lengths, with the middle third now of unit length, the area of the resulting triangle in stage 2 is equal to 0.4332 units squared. Each of the two smaller triangles constructed in stage 3 is equal to 0.0482, while those formed in stage 4 are equal to 5.348×10^{-3}. (All of these direct calculations of triangle areas are subject to rounding errors.)

It is also clear that the number of each of these triangles increases geometrically upon each new segmentation. The number of new triangles at each stage is equal to exactly twice the number constructed at the previous stage. Thus, one triangle is formed at stage 1 (leading to stage 2), two at stage 2, four at stage 3, eight at stage 4, sixteen at stage 5, etc. This is a geometric progression with parameter 2, or

$$(2), \ (2 \cdot 2), \ (2 \cdot 2 \cdot 2), \ (2 \cdot 2 \cdot 2 \cdot 2), \ (2 \cdot 2 \cdot 2 \cdot 2 \cdot 2), \ \ldots$$

Assuming that the probability of obtaining a triangle of a given area is directly proportional to its number, if we normalize the sequence so that the sum of the probabilities equals 1, we arrive at a probability distribution with parameter 1/2, or

$$(1/2), \ (1/2 \cdot 1/2), \ (1/2 \cdot 1/2 \cdot 1/2), \ (1/2 \cdot 1/2 \cdot 1/2 \cdot 1/2), \ \ldots$$

More generally, for any parameter, q, with r steps to the sequence, we have

$$q \, (1 - q)^{n-1} \qquad n = 1, 2, \ldots, r$$

which is a geometric distribution with parameter q.

The ordinary geometric distribution would be applicable if the areas of the triangles at each stage 1, 2, etc. differed from each other by some additive increment, ξ, that is, the highest probability (largest number of triangles) would be to attain one of the smallest triangles, the next highest for the smallest triangular area plus ξ, and so forth. The incremental gains for each successively "higher" stage (but achieved with lower probability) are additive. In Figure 1B, however, the differences in triangular area are not additive but multiplicative. Each area is exactly 1/9 of the preceding one. Thus if A is the area of the first triangle then $A/9$ is that of the second, $A/81$ is the area of the third, or the sequence

$$A, A(\tfrac{1}{3})^2, A(\tfrac{1}{3}\cdot\tfrac{1}{3})^2, A(\tfrac{1}{3}\cdot\tfrac{1}{3}\cdot\tfrac{1}{3})^2, A(\tfrac{1}{3}\cdot\tfrac{1}{3}\cdot\tfrac{1}{3}\cdot\tfrac{1}{3})^2, A(\tfrac{1}{3}\cdot\tfrac{1}{3}\cdot\tfrac{1}{3}\cdot\tfrac{1}{3}\cdot\tfrac{1}{3})^2,$$
$$\dots = A[1, (\tfrac{1}{3})^2, (\tfrac{1}{3})^3, (\tfrac{1}{3})^4, (\tfrac{1}{3})^5, (\tfrac{1}{3})^6, \dots]$$

To demonstrate that the logarithm of this sequence will yield an additive quantity, we simply take the logarithm to the base e of this sequence and

$$\log_e A + [2\log_e \tfrac{1}{3}, 3\log_e \tfrac{1}{3}, 4\log_e \tfrac{1}{3}, 5\log_e \tfrac{1}{3} \dots] = \log_e A + \log_e \tfrac{1}{3}$$
$$[2, 3, 4, 5, \dots]$$

or, more generally, setting $\log_e A$ and $\log_e \tfrac{1}{3}$ to constants we have

$$c + c_1 [2, 3, 4, 5 \dots]$$

Thus, each increment beyond the initial constant is additive and, by logging the variant, we retrieve the ordinary form of the geometric distribution, or

$$p(\log_e x_n) = q (1 - q)^{n-1} \qquad n = 1, 2, \dots, r \qquad [1B]$$

Passing to the exponential form as the continuous analogue of the geometric distribution (Feller 1968, 458), one which is more tractable in analysis and computation, we have

$$f(x) = A_1 e^{-k \log_e x} \qquad k>0, \; 1\leq x<\infty \qquad [2B]$$

where k is a constant and A_1 is a normalization constant designed to make the sum of the probabilities equal unity. In turn, the function $\log_e x$ transforms the ordinary exponential distribution into the Pareto distribution[1] (Gumbel 1958, 151; Johnson and Kotz 1970, 240),

$$f(x) = Bx^{-k-1} \qquad k>0 \; 1\leq x<\infty \qquad [3B]$$

Equations [2B] and [3B] are identical. The constant k here is the familiar Paretian exponent, α.

   This geometric derivation emphasizes the scarcity condition in that only the line segment in Figure 1B and the area above it are allowed to be acquired. It also shows explicitly the connection with the ordinary exponential as a distribution representing inequality derived from scarcity. Most important, the logarithmic function emphasizes extreme inequality derived from the sequential nature of resource acquisitions modeled directly in this geometric representation.

It is instructive to compare this geometric approach with that of Champernowne (1953), who also derived the Pareto distribution exactly but from analytic considerations based on a Markov chain defined on a logarithmic scale of income classes, u. Here, the Markovian assumption is

$$x_s\,(t+1) = \sum_{u=-\infty}^{s} x_{s-u}(t)\,p_{s-u,s}(t) \qquad [4B]$$

where $x_s(t)$ is the number of income earners in the logarithmic range s in year t and $p_{s-u,s}(t)$ are the transition probabilities for income earners going from one income range to the next in time t. If it is assumed that transitions are possible only in the range between $-n$ and $+1$ and the income distribution reaches an equilibrium, then equation [4B] reduces to

$$x_s = \sum_{u=-n}^{1} p_u\,x_{s-u} \qquad s>0 \qquad [5B]$$

Note that this is precisely the same assumption as in the preceding geometric derivation. In that instance each succeeding area is some constant proportion of the previous one, or

$$A_{t+1} = CA_t \qquad C>0 \qquad [6B]$$

where C is a constant equal, in fact, to 1/9 in the preceding numerical treatment. Each state of the system is linearly dependent only on the immediately preceding one which, of course, is a first-order Markov process. The Markovian assumption is never made explicit in the geometric representation; it emerges, nevertheless, as a consequence of the unfolding of the geometric process.

A nontrivial solution of the difference equation [5B] requires that the expectation of possible transitions is negative, or a shrinkage of incomes, or

$p_1 < p_{-1}$. This assumption leads directly to a geometric distribution of the form (Champernowne 1953, 326; Steindl 1965, 35)

$$x_s = N(1-b)b^s \qquad 0<b<1 \qquad\qquad [7B]$$

where N is the total number of incomes. Pareto's law now follows directly.[2]

Note that in Champernowne's formulation, the logarithmic scale had to be explicitly introduced; in the geometric derivation it emerged directly from the initial Koch curve construction. The mathematical expectation of shrinking income as time increases also had to be an explicit assumption by Champernowne (which to some was controversial, see Steindl 1965, 36 ff). Here, it emerged again as a direct consequence of the Koch curve and the initial scarcity assumption—never made explicit in the Champernowne formulation. The connection with the exponential distribution and its implication of inequality also is not a part of this derivation, although it does not have to be, for the passage from equation [1B] to equation [3B] is direct (see note 2). Mathematically, this is a more direct treatment than the passing from the geometric to the exponential as a limiting continuous form and the subsequent establishment of the connection between the log–exponential (equation [2B]) and the Pareto (equation [3B]) distributions as in the present treatment. Nevertheless, the avoidance of the exponential in its logarithmic form also avoids the substantive implications of severe inequality in a scarcity condition with all of its implications for the likelihood of potential conflict. This derivation also leads directly to the expectation that the Pareto distribution would be directly applicable only to the wealthy upper tail of the distribution because of the explicit sequestering of resources sequentially beginning at the most abundant stage in Figure 1B. Wage-related processes of economic growth, which rely on many different components, would likely be more relevant to the distribution form of the lower income levels.

The geometric derivation also has certain interesting parallels with other treatments. Consider, for example, Mandelbrot's (1960, 97) development of what he calls Pareto–Lévy stable distributions which include the Gaussian as well as the Pareto distributions. What distinguishes the Gaussian from the Pareto in this treatment is the approximate equality of contribution of various components to the Gaussian but inequality of contribution in the case of the Pareto. Thus, an overwhelming contribution to this distribution, say, by the sequestering of land or other scarce resources in a seriatum fashion, is consistent with this mathematical property of the Pareto–Lévy distribution.

There also exists a convergence with the work of Futia (1982), who demonstrated that a Markovian operator as in equations [5B] or [6B] converges at a geometric rate to yield an invariant distribution. This, of course, is also consistent with Mandelbrot's (1960) singling out of the weak

Pareto distribution as the only one (aside from the Gaussian) which is invariant upon the addition of several random variables of similar form. This finding further suggests that the distributions in equations [2B] or [3B] will emerge upon the simultaneous occurrence of several processes of the type outlined in Figure 1B. There can be N such simultaneously occurring processes in, say, different regions of a country, all of which together will yield the two distributions (equations [2B] and [3B]).

The Pareto distribution has been found to be applicable to the upper tails of income distributions among other random variables [see Chipman (1976) and Sahota (1978) for excellent reviews]. The applicability of this model to the tail of income distributions can be understood as follows. If there is some finite resource (it does not have to be scarce at the outset), such as the number of cities requiring railway connections between them in the nineteenth century, the first to exploit this societal need will take the lion's share, as in connections between the largest cities. After this has been done, say, by the Harrimans in the United States, distances between smaller cities, likely a less profitable venture, require railroad building and then the initial entrepreneurs in this activity will take the lion's share of that undertaking. We are left with still smaller and less profitable rail connections, and the process is once again repeated. In this fashion, a process quite similar to that detailed in Figure 1B takes place sequentially with each arrival getting a disproportionately smaller share of the total resources. Income will be proportional to the possession of these resources, hence the Pareto distribution will be applicable (Chipman 1976, 150). Note that the same persons or their descendants do not have to be in possession of the resources. All that is required is that there exist a hierarchical structure of resource possession along the lines of the preceding geometric argument occupied by some persons who will receive incomes proportional to their holdings.

This is the likely reason that the Pareto distribution has been found to apply only to the upper tail and not to the lower regions of the income distribution where the lognormal model is more applicable (Gumbel 1958, 151; Lydall 1976, 17; Brown 1976, 77). Indeed, Lydall (1968, 21) observes that "only the top 20 per cent or so of most income distributions can be said to approximate at all closely to the Pareto law." Additionally, the lognormal distribution instead of the Pareto has especially been found to apply to the incomes of communist countries of Eastern Europe (Lydall 1968, 130), a fact which confirms the importance of the sequestering process in the early stages of capitalist economies implied by the preceding geometric derivation. The dismantling of the pre-World War II capitalist economies in Eastern Europe also would have eliminated the possession of early sequestered resources, thus allowing the lognormal distribution to take hold. Here, the proportionality of growth to the existing level throughout the entire income range with many different components, as in an expanding economy with consistent wage increases over time, is the likely underlying dynamic. This, of course, is the principal basis of the derivation of the lognormal distribution (Aitchison and Brown 1957).

In its emphasis on the sequential sequestering of scarce resources, this geometric derivation of the Pareto distribution differs from all others of which I am aware. Typically, the dynamic interpretation of the origin of the Pareto distribution is in the tendency of elites to decline and selected members of the lower income levels to rise (Chipman 1976, 152–153). This is the meaning often attributed to Champernowne's (1953) assumption of the expected shrinkage of income. However, it was Sorel (1897), in a commentary that Pareto (1897) himself praised, who first interpreted the Paretian coefficient of inequality as a measure of the "difficulty of rising." Economically, this interpretation is consistent with the sequestering process outlined here.

Comparison of the Exponential and Log–Exponential Distributions

Intuitively, it appears obvious that the log–exponential (Pareto) distribution would represent a greater degree of inequality than the exponential itself. Perhaps an example will fix ideas more exactly. Table 1BP presents eight categories of resource holdings (land, financial, industrial, . . .). To represent the scarcity condition, the total number of resource units is approximately equal for both distributions (78,438 versus 80,000; it is difficult to achieve exact equality), but the two are sufficiently close for our illustrative purposes). The proportions of the population also are held constant; all that is allowed to vary is the exponential versus log–exponential distribution of these holdings. (I will now refer to this distribution as log–exponential to emphasize both its connection and contrast with the exponential distribution of scarce resources. Clearly it is also understood to be a Pareto distribution.) Even the overall means are approximately equal with $\bar{x} = 3.9362$ for the exponential and $\bar{x} = 4.0106$ for the log–exponential.

Table 1BP

Illustrations of exponential and log–exponential (Pareto) distributions.

Resource units (exponential)	Population	Proportion of population	Resource units (log-exponential)
2	10,000	0.5020	1
4	5,000	0.2509	2
6	2,500	0.1255	4
8	1,250	0.0627	8
10	625	0.0314	16
12	312.5	0.0157	32
14	156.25	0.0078	64
16	78.125	0.0039	128

Columns 1 and 3 together yield an exponential distribution, while columns 3 and 4 yield a log–exponential. Comparison of each of the categories indicates the extent of inequality. First, the richest 6% of the population holds 50% of the resources in the log–exponential with a mean of 34.13, while in the exponential distribution the top 6% holds 17% of the resources with a mean of 11.47, approximately one-third the mean value of the log–exponential. In the log–exponential, the poorer 75% of the population owns 25% of the resources with a mean of 1.33, while in the exponential they own 51% with twice the mean at 2.66. The rich are richer and poor are poorer in this distribution of extreme inequality. And this is in addition to the already blatant inequality in the exponential distribution itself.

Now consider another aspect of the increased inequality apparent here. In an earlier analysis (Midlarsky 1982), I traced the approach to greater equality upon the introduction of increased abundance. For each individual category (say, the first) this can be done and assumes the form

$$g(x) = e^{-1/x} \qquad 0 \leq x < \infty \qquad\qquad [8B]$$

where x is the mean resource availability (the "bar" over the x is dropped for convenience) and the unity in the numerator of the exponent signifies the first category. This function is shown as the solid line in Figure 2B. Now consider the mean of the log–exponential or $\log_e x$ in the denominator of the exponent in equation [9B]. This function now would represent the approach to infinite abundance of the log–exponential distribution as in

$$h(x) = e^{-1/\log_e x} \qquad 1 \leq x < \infty \qquad\qquad [9B]$$

This function is now shown in the dotted–dashed line of the figure. Two aspects of the curve are immediately apparent. First, it approaches the greater equality inherent in the infinite abundance condition far more slowly than the exponential. The maximum value for both the exponential and log–exponential function is unity, but the exponential function already has nearly reached this value at an abscissa of 90 while the log–exponential is still nowhere near this value. This is the second feature of the curve. It is likely that the log–exponential could *never* reach the equality implied by infinite abundance within realistic values of x. In order for the log–exponential to reach the same value as the exponential at $x = 90$, it would have to have a mean abundance of approximately $x = 1 \times 10^{40}$ (0.9890 exponential versus 0.9892 log–exponential). This clearly is not within the range of likely values to be achieved in any real-world circumstance. Thus, in contrast to the exponential distribution, which at least is amenable to an increased equality upon increased abundance, this tractable quality of the exponential is diminished considerably in the log–exponential.

A property of the Pareto distribution is that no matter how much you add to the available resource pool, the extent of inequality still will be severe.

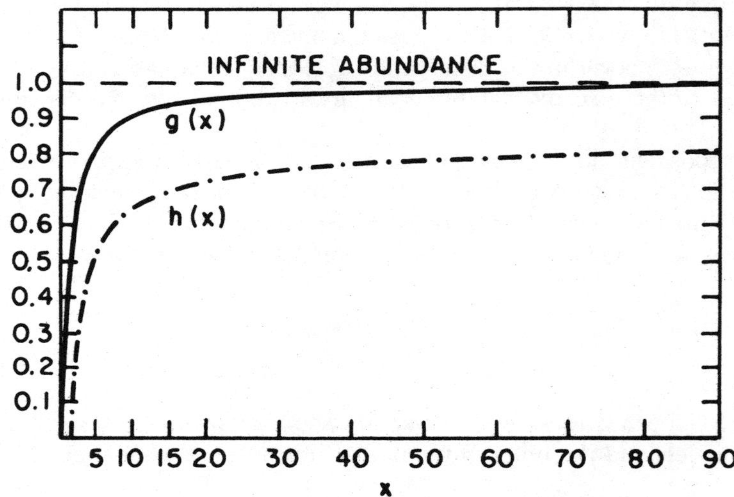

Figure 2B

Approach to infinite abundance and greater equality of the functions $g(x)$ and $h(x)$.

Notes

1 This is the most frequently encountered form of the Pareto distribution. For two other variations, see Johnson and Kotz (1970, 234).

2 Suppose that the proportionate income range is 10^h (the logarithmic assumption) and that the lowest income is Y_{min}; x_s is then the number of incomes in the range s whose lower bound is given by

$$Y_s = 10^{sh} \, Y_{min}$$

$$\log Y_s = sh + \log Y_{min}$$

The number of incomes exceeding Y_s is

$$F(Y_s) = Nb^s$$

$$\log F(Y_s) = \log N + s \log b$$

If we put $\alpha = (-1/h) \log b$, $q = \log N + \alpha \log Y_{min}$, we obtain Pareto's law in its logarithmic form

$$\log F(Y_s) = q - \alpha \log Y_s$$

Tabular Appendix A

THE FOLLOWING TABLES are supplementary to the analyses of chapter 2 and give more detailed evidence for the findings reported therein.

Applying equations [11A]–[13A] of Mathematical Appendix A to the 1816–1899 period for disputes involving two or more major powers yields the matrix of Table 1A. The value of p in the table was estimated by the ratio of the mean number of disputes initiated to the mean number in existence, as in Midlarsky (1981, 278). (The symbol p is used here to be consistent with earlier usages, and should not be confused with probability levels.) The observed entries in the table are the frequencies of transition from one state of the number of disputes in existence, n, to another state, k, in two successive years. The top line of each cell entry gives the observed value, while the bottom line is one predicted by the equation $z(n, k) = P(n, k)$, where $k = n+j$, $n-j$, or n, so that the values of $P(n,k)$ are given by equations [11A]–[13A] and $P(n)$ by values of the Poisson distribution for disputes in existence, as in Midlarsky (1981, 279).

Table 1A records 55 times when the system passed from 0 number of disputes in existence in one year to 0 in the succeeding year, with 53.09 predicted transitions of this type. Similarly, there were 8 instances where the system underwent a change from 0 disputes in one year to 1 in the next with 9.99 predicted transitions from 0 to 1. As can be seen, the chi-square goodness-of-fit statistic gives a probability value suggesting that the conflict system of the major powers exclusively was stable. A fit between observation and prediction will be rejected at $p < 0.10$ in order to adopt a fairly conservative policy on the acceptance of the equilibrium model. In practical terms, the higher the probability level for the chi-square value, the greater the confidence in the goodness of fit. Alternatively, the lower the probability level for chi square, the smaller the degree of confidence in the model.

An interesting property of equations [11A]–[13A] is the symmetry in transitions from *n* to *k* and from *k* to *n*. This, of course, is reflected in the predicted values in Table 1A (for example, 9.99 both for 0 to 1 and for 1 to 0) but also is found in several of the observed values in that table. Thus, there were eight cases of transition from 0 to 1 disputes in existence and eight from 1 to 0, and there were also two instances of transition from 0 to 2 disputes in existence and two from 2 to 0.

Table 1A

Observed and expected frequencies of occurrence of the pairs (*n,k*) of disputes between two or more major powers in the European system, 1816–1899 ($p = 0.6957$).[a,b,c]

n	*k* = 0	1	2
0	55[a]	8	2
	53.09	9.99	0.94
1	8	5	2
	9.99	6.25	1.00
2	2	2	0
	0.94	1.00	0.35

[a]The top line of each entry gives the observed value while the bottom line is one predicted by the equation $z(n, k) = P(n)P(n, k)$, where $k = n+j$, $n-j$, or n, so that the values of $P(n, k)$ are given by equations (11A)–(13A) and $P(n)$ by the values of the Poisson distribution for disputes in existence.

[b]For the chi-square test, predicted values less than 1.5 are combined with adjacent values until that figure is obtained as suggested in Gibbons (1971, 72).

[c]$\chi^2 = 4.576$, df $= 3$, $p < 0.30$.

When we analyze the somewhat wider range of conflict behavior extended to central powers (for example, Belgium, Denmark, Sweden, Netherlands, Serbia), the results suggest greater stability as in Table 2A, as

Table 2A

Observed and expected frequencies of occurrence of the pairs (*n,k*) of disputes between two or more major powers and those involving central powers in the European system, 1816–1899 ($p = 0.6852$).[a]

n	*k* = 0	1	2	3
0	32	12	2	1
	28.77	12.67	2.79	0.41
1	10	9	4	2
	12.67	11.06	3.64	0.71
2	3	3	1	1
	2.79	3.64	1.86	0.50
3	2	1	1	0
	0.41	0.71	0.50	0.19

[a]$\chi^2 = 8.217$, df $= 8$, $p < 0.50$.

indicated by the chi-square value. Here, as noted earlier, these countries tended to be formally neutral or, as in the case of Serbia, appeared as sovereign entities only toward the end of the century. Therefore this finding is to be expected because of the existence of hierarchy in the form of large disparities of power or the neutrality (or nonexistence) of many of the potential conflict protagonists.

Expanding the range of countries to include even the smallest powers (for example, Parma, Saxony, Tuscany, Kingdom of the Two Sicilies) yields the most stable pattern. Table 3A is based on the entire set of nineteenth century European disputes and no further conflicts could be added to the overall array. Thus, we have in this instance a highly equilibrated system.

Table 3A

Observed and expected frequencies of occurrence of the pairs (n,k) of disputes between two or more major powers and those involving any other countries in the European system, 1816–1899 $(p = 0.7231)$.[a]

n	$k = 0$	1	2	3	4
0	26	11	3	0	1
	22.49	12.44	3.44	0.63	0.09
1	11	12	3	3	0
	12.44	11.64	4.53	1.08	0.18
2	2	4	1	1	0
	3.44	4.53	2.49	0.78	0.16
3	2	1	1	0	0
	0.63	1.08	0.78	0.32	0.09
4	0	1	0	0	1
	0.09	0.18	0.16	0.09	0.03

[a] $\chi^2 = 7.097$, df $= 9$, $p < 0.70$.

For purposes of comparability with the later analysis of 1893–1914, the overall 1816–1907 period was divided into four intervals of 22 years each, and each interval was analyzed separately. All of the chi-square values were nonsignificant, at least at $p < 0.50$, with the highest attaining a value of 5.752 at $p < 0.50$ and the lowest reaching a value of 1.558 at $p < 0.95$. Thus, in this nineteenth century system all combinations of conflicts lead to a highly equilibrated system.

Note that several predictions of the theory have now been confirmed. First, that conflicts among great powers alone do not yield an unstable pattern; second, and most important, expansion of the range of conflict behavior to include the smallest and least consequential powers yields the greatest stability.

We now turn to an analysis of the 1893–1914 period and, as before, present the disputes solely involving two or more major powers. The pattern here is not substantially different from that shown in the earlier period and is acceptable, with a chi-square value of 3.439, df = 2, $p < 0.20$. (For the sake of parsimony, when a table repeats some earlier, already reported pattern, only the chi-square value is presented. All such tables are available from the author upon request.)

Extending the range of the conflict system to the central powers (because of the unifications of Italy and Germany, the only ones in existence now aside from the major powers) yields the first clearly unstable pattern. Table 4A shows the first statistically significant departure from the equilibrium condition of equation [2.1]. Substantively, we can say that the absence of equilibrium for this system was a consequence of the combined set of major power disputes alone and those involving central or midrange powers. By the early part of the twentieth century, many of the midrange conflict protagonists were independent (for example, Bulgaria, Serbia, Rumania) and were sufficiently large in size or power to challenge weaker great powers such as Austria-Hungary.

Table 4A

Observed and expected frequencies of occurrence of the pairs (n,k) of disputes between two or more major powers and those involving central powers in the European system, 1893–1914 $(p = 0.9474)$.[a]

n	$k = 0$	1	2	3
0	6	3	4	0
	4.40	3.45	1.35	0.35
1	3	0	0	0
	3.45	2.89	1.21	0.33
2	1	0	1	2
	1.35	1.21	0.54	0.16
3	2	0	0	0
	0.35	0.33	0.16	0.05

[a]$\chi^2 = 16.505$, df = 5, $p < 0.01$.

We have now distinguished between a multipolar system ending peacefully and a polarizing one ending in war. A major similarity is that, in both instances, the conflicts between great powers exclusively exhibited stable patterns, but when these systems were expanded to include other, smaller powers, the multipolar nineteenth century system evidenced increased stability whereas the polarizing system prior to World War I evidenced instability. More is said about this at a later point when the bipolar 1946–1964 period is examined.

Turning now to another polarizing period, 1919–1939, the overall pattern is similar to that evidenced in 1893–1914. An essential stability inherent in disputes involving major powers exclusively is demonstrated by a chi-square value of 3.780, df = 2, $p < 0.20$. Expansion of the system to include disputes involving other European powers once again yields patterns of instability similar to those discovered in the pre-World War I period, with a chi-square value of 14.706, df = 8, $p < 0.10$. (The global system including all sovereign states also is found to be unstable with a chi-square value of 17.429, df = 7, $p < 0.02$.) Although the European system is found to be formally unstable in 1919–1939, the less emphatic results here when compared to those of 1893–1914 suggest a different interpretation of the systemic instability of this time period, as is developed in chapters 7 and 8.)

Analyzing now the 1946–1964 period, the pattern changes substantially. First, the global system is the only relevant one because of the decline of Europe as the epicenter of global activity. Thus, all disputes considered are those taking place in a global context. As is seen shortly, though, Europe assumes a new significance within the context of a bipolar conflict.

Conflicts involving two or more major powers are analyzed and, as before, this set of disputes demonstrates no propensity toward instability as demonstrated by a chi-square value of 0.742, df = 1, $p < 0.50$. When this set is combined with those involving one or more European powers, a serious tendency toward instability emerges. Here, for example, we find the 1961 Berlin crisis involving the German Democratic Republic or the 1953 dispute at the death of Stalin involving Czechoslovakia and the USSR ranged against the United States and the United Kingdom. This pattern is shown in Table 5A.

Table 5A

Observed and expected frequencies of occurrence of the pairs (n,k) of disputes between two or more major powers and those involving any other countries in the European system, 1946–1964 ($p = 0.7000$).[a]

n	$k = 0$	1	2
0	4	6	0
	8.12	2.84	0.50
1	6	1	1
	2.84	2.21	0.60
2	0	1	0
	0.50	0.60	0.27

[a] $\chi^2 = 9.874$, df = 2, $p < 0.01$.

But, as suggested earlier, the global process is the central one in this time period, and when conflicts with at least one minor (non-European) power are included in this set, a pattern of stability develops as shown by a chi-square value of 10.619, df = 6, $p < 0.20$. Widening the conflict arena yields an element of stability. And when all of these conflicts are combined into one global set, including minor powers outside of the European continent, the result is a stable pattern which does not suggest systemic war, as indeed did not occur in this time period.

The findings of the analysis are summarized in Table 6A which includes all of the chi-square values for the various analyses.

Table 6A

Findings of the empirical tests.

| Time period | Disputes between | | | |
	Two or more major powers	Central (midrange)	Minor (smaller)	One major One minor[a]
1816–1899	Stability	Greater stability	Greatest stability	Stability
	(4.576, 3, 0.30)[b]	(8.217, 8, 0.50)	(7.097, 9, 0.70)	(0.292, 1, 0.70)
1893–1914	Stability	Instability	(No smaller powers in Europe)	Instability
	(3.439, 2, 0.20)	(16.505, 5, 0.01)		(6.513, 3, 0.10)
1919–1939	Stability	Instability	(No smaller powers in Europe)	Instability
	(3.780, 2, 0.20)	(14.706, 8, 0.10)		(11.952, 6, 0.10)
1946–1964	Stability	Instability (European)	Stability (global)	Stability
	(0.742, 1, 0.50)	(9.874, 2, 0.01)	(10.619, 6, 0.20)	(7.905, 6, 0.30)

[a]For 1893–1914, central powers only.

[b]The first number to the left of each entry gives the chi-square value, the second gives the degrees of freedom, and the third the probability value. Thus, for the stability of the major power system exclusively in 1816–1899, the chi-square value is $\chi^2 = 4.576$, df $= 3$, $p < 0.30$.

Tabular Appendix B

THE FOLLOWING TABLES, 1B and 2B, are the results of analyzing the disputes between two or more major powers and at least one central power, as in chapter 5, and are to be understood in conjunction with the tables in Tabular Appendix A. Table 3B also appears in connection with chapter 5, while Table 4B emerges from the analysis of wars with and without memory in Chapter 6.

Table 1B

Observed and expected frequencies of occurrence of the pairs (n,k) of disputes between two or more major powers involving at least one central power, 1816–1899 ($p = 0.7000$).[a]

n	$k = 0$	1	2	3
0	47	10	2	0
	46.10	11.39	1.41	0.12
1	10	9	1	1
	11.39	7.70	1.55	0.18
2	1	2	0	0
	1.41	1.55	0.60	0.10
3	1	0	0	0
	0.12	0.18	0.10	0.03

[a] $\chi^2 = 1.060$, df $= 5$, $p < 0.98$.

Table 2B

Observed and expected frequencies of occurrence of the pairs (n,k) of disputes between two or more major powers, involving at least one central power, 1893–1914 ($p = 0.5429$).[a]

n	$k = 0$	1	2	3
0	11	4	1	0
	11.25	2.65	0.31	0.02
1	3	1	0	1
	2.65	2.86	0.60	0.07
2	0	0	0	0
	0.31	0.60	0.36	0.07
3	1	0	0	0
	0.02	0.07	0.07	0.03

[a]$\chi^2 = 2.036$, df $= 2$, $p < 0.50$.

Table 3B

Observed and expected frequencies of occurrence of the pairs (n,k) of disputes between two or more major powers and those involving any other countries in the European system, 1893–1908 ($p = 0.9167$).[a]

n	$k = 0$	1	2	3
0	4	3	2	0
	4.14	2.68	0.87	0.19
1	3	0	0	0
	2.68	1.97	0.72	0.17
2	1	0	1	1
	0.87	0.72	0.29	0.08
3	1	0	0	0
	0.19	0.17	0.08	0.02

[a]$\chi^2 = 2.846$, df $= 3$, $p < 0.50$.

Table 4B

Wars with and without memory, 1850–1966.

War Name[a]	Years
Wars with memory[b]	
Crimean	1853–1856
Italian unification	1859–1859
Italo-Roman	1860–1860
Italo-Sicilian	1860–1861
Second Schleswig-Holstein	1864–1864
Spanish-Chilean	1865–1866
Seven Weeks'	1866–1866
Franco-Prussian	1870–1871
Russo-Turkish	1877–1878
Pacific	1879–1883
Greco-Turkish	1897–1897

Central American	1906–1906
Central American	1907–1907
First Balkan	1912–1913
Second Balkan	1913–1913
World War I	1914–1918
Greco-Turkish	1919–1922
Manchurian	1931–1933
Sino-Japanese	1937–1941
Russo-Japanese	1939–1939
World War II	1939–1945
Palestine	1948–1949
Korean	1950–1953
Sinai	1956–1956
Sino-Indian	1962–1962
Second Kashmir	1965–1965

Wars without memory[c]

La Plata	1851–1852
Anglo-Persian	1856–1857
Franco-Mexican	1862–1867
Ecuadorian-Colombian	1863–1863
Sino-French	1884–1885
Central American	1885–1885
Sino-Japanese	1894–1895
Spanish-American	1898–1898
Russo-Japanese	1904–1905
Spanish-Moroccan	1909–1910
Italo-Turkish	1911–1912
Hungarian-Allies	1919–1919
Chaco	1932–1935
Italo-Ethiopian	1935–1936
Russo-Finnish	1939–1940
Russo-Hungarian	1956–1956

[a]War names and years are taken initially from Ferris (1973, 141–142) and cross-checked for correct dates with Small and Singer (1982, 82–95).

[b]$\bar{x} = 3.580$, $\sigma^2 = 13.816$.

[c]$\bar{x} = 6.887$, $\sigma^2 = 44.262$.

Tabular Appendix C

THE FOLLOWING TABLES, 1C – 7C, are presented in conjunction with the comparison between the conflict processes preceding World Wars I and II as, respectively, structural and mobilization wars as developed in chapter 8.

Table 1C

Observed and Polya–predicted values of the distribution of conflict behaviors, 1893–1914[a]

Number of disputes (j)	Observed number of countries with j disputes	Predicted number of countries with j disputes ($b = 2, r = 6, s = 5$)
0	6	6.44
1	2	2.54
2	3	1.76
3	1	1.38[b]
4	0	1.14
5	1	1.00
6	0	0.88
7	1	0.80
8	0	0.70
9	1	0.66
10	1	0.58
11	1	0.54
12	1	0.48
13	0	0.42
14	1	0.38
15	0	0.28
16	1	0.02

[a]$\chi^2 = 4.045$, df $= 4$, $p < 0.50$; there exist three restrictions on the degrees of freedom for each of the parameters of the Polya distribution and one for the chi-square test itself.

[b]For the chi-square test, predicted values less than 1.5 are combined with adjacent values until that figure is obtained as suggested in Gibbons (1971, 72).

Table 2C
Observed and Polya–predicted values of the distribution of conflict behaviors, 1893–1907[a]

Number of disputes (j)	Observed number of countries with j disputes	Predicted number of countries with j disputes ($b = 2, r = 6, s = 5$)
0	9	7.48
1	2	2.94
2	0	2.02
3	2	1.56
4	1	1.30
5	1	1.10
6	1	0.96
7	1	0.82
8	1	0.72
9	1	0.62
10	0	0.50
11	1	0.20

[a]$\chi^2 = 3.299$, df $= 3$, $p < 0.50$.

Table 3C
Observed and Polya–predicted values of the distribution of conflict behaviors, 1908–1914[a]

Number of disputes (j)	Observed number of countries with j disputes	Predicted number of countries with j disputes ($b = 2, r = 4, s = 5$)
0	9	8.80
1	3	3.63
2	2	2.68
3	2	2.31
4	4	2.18
5	2	2.40

[a]$\chi^2 = 1.914$, df $= 2$, $p < 0.50$.

Table 4C
Observed and Polya–predicted values of the distribution of conflict behaviors, 1871–1892[a]

Number of disputes (j)	Observed number of countries with j disputes	Predicted number of countries with j disputes ($b = 2, r = 4, s = 5$)
0	9	5.98
1	0	2.47
2	1	1.79
3	1	1.50
4	2	1.33
5	1	1.26
6	2	1.26
7	1	1.43

[a]$\chi^2 = 4.611$, df $= 2$, $p < 0.10$.

Table 5C
Observed and Polya–predicted values of the distribution of conflict behaviors, 1919–1939[a]

Number of disputes (j)	Observed number of countries with j disputes	Predicted number of countries with j disputes ($b = 2, r = 10, s = 5$)
0	23	16.34
1	12	7.20
2	1	4.14
3	1	3.11
4	1	2.52
5	0	2.12
6	1	1.76
7	0	1.49
8	0	1.31
9	0	1.08
10	1	0.99
11	1	0.81
12	1	0.72
13	0	0.59
14	0	0.50
15	1	0.45
16	0	0.27
17	0	0.27
18	1	0.18
19	0	0.05
20	0	0.05
21	1	0.00

[a] $\chi^2 = 17.635$, df $= 7$, $p < 0.02$.

Table 6C
Observed and Polya–predicted values of the distribution of conflict behaviors, 1919–1932[a]

Number of disputes (j)	Observed number of countries with j disputes	Predicted number of countries with j disputes ($b = 2, r = 10, s = 5$)
0	26	18.09
1	5	6.84
2	5	4.45
3	2	3.29
4	1	2.57
5	2	2.12
6	0	1.71
7	0	1.40
8	1	1.17
9	1	0.95
10	0	0.77
11	0	0.59
12	0	0.45
13	1	0.32
14	0	0.23
15	1	0.09

[a] $\chi^2 = 8.547$, df $= 6$, $p < 0.25$.

Table 7C

Observed and Polya–predicted values of the distribution of conflict behaviors, 1933–1939[a]

Number of disputes (j)	Observed number of countries with j disputes	Predicted number of countries with j disputes ($b = 2, r = 10, s = 5$)
0	26	20.88
1	12	7.61
2	0	4.82
3	1	3.38
4	0	2.56
5	0	1.89
6	0	1.44
7	3	1.04
8	2	0.72
9	0	0.45
10	1	0.23

[a]$\chi^2 = 15.892$, df $= 3$, $p < 0.005$.

Bibliography

Aitchison, J., and Brown, J. A. C. 1957. *The Lognormal Distribution*. London: Cambridge Univ. Press.

Albertini, L. 1967. *The Origins of the War of 1914* (3 vols.) (I. Massey, translator and ed.). London: Oxford Univ. Press.

Allais, M. 1973. Inequality and civilizations. *Social Science Quarterly* 54: 508–524 (English translation of "Inegalité et Civilisations" In *Melanges en l'Honneur de Raymond Aron*. Paris: Editions Calmann-Lévy).

Allison, G. T. 1971. *Essence of Decision: Explaining the Cuban Missile Crisis*. Boston, MA: Little, Brown.

Amdur, R. 1977. Rawls' theory of justice: Domestic and international perspectives. *World Politics* 29: 438–461.

Aristotle, 1962. *Politics* (E. Barker, translator and ed.). New York: Oxford Univ. Press.

Aron, R. 1966. *Peace and War: A Theory of International Relations*. New York: Doubleday.

Aron, R. 1968. *Progress and Disillusion: The Dialectics of Modern Society*. New York: Praeger.

Ashby, W. R. 1963. *An Introduction to Cybernetics*. New York: Wiley.

Atkinson, C. T. 1934. The wars (1664–74). *The Cambridge Modern History, Vol. V* (A. W. Ward, G. W. Prothero, and S. Leathes, eds.). Cambridge: Cambridge Univ. Press.

Axelrod, R. 1984. *The Evolution of Cooperation*. New York: Basic Books.

Badger, W. W. 1980. An entropy–utility model for the size distribution of income. In *Mathematical Models as a Tool for the Social Sciences* (B. J. West, ed.). New York: Gordon and Breach.

Beaumont, W. 1907. Le suffrage universel en Autriche: La loi du 26 Janvier 1907. *Annales des Sciences Politiques* 22: 618–640.

Beer, F. A. 1981. *Peace Against War: The Ecology of International Violence*. San Francisco, CA: Freeman.

Beitz, C. R. 1975. Justice and international relations. *Philosophy and Public Affairs* 4: 360–389.

Beitz, C. R. 1979. *Political Theory and International Relations*. Princeton, NJ: Princeton Univ. Press.

Bharucha–Reid, A. T. 1960. *Elements of the Theory of Markov Processes and their Applications*. New York: McGraw-Hill.

Blum, J., Cameron, R., and Barnes, T. G. 1966. *A History of the European World*. Boston, MA: Little, Brown.

Boak, A. E. 1930. *A History of Rome to 565 A.D.* (Revised Ed.). New York: Macmillan.

Boxley, R. F. 1971. Farm size and the distribution of farm numbers. *Agricultural Economics Research* 23: 87–94.

Brams, S. J. 1985. *Superpower Games*. New Haven, CT: Yale Univ. Press.

Brecher, M. 1980. *Decisions in Crisis: Israel, 1967 and 1973*. Berkeley, CA: Univ. of California Press.

Brickman, P., and Campbell, D. T. 1971. Hedonic relativism and planning the good society. In *Adaptation–Level Theory* (M. H. Appley, ed.). New York: Academic Press.

Bridge, F. R., and Bullen, R. 1980. *The Great Powers and the European States System: 1815–1914*. London: Longmans.

Brody, R. A., and Benham, A. H. 1969. Nuclear weapons and alliance cohesion. In *Theory and Research on the Causes of War* (D. G. Pruitt and R. C. Snyder, eds.). Englewood Cliffs, NJ: Prentice-Hall.

Brown, J. A. C. 1976. The mathematical and statistical theory of income distribution. In *The Personal Distribution of Incomes* (A. B. Atkinson, ed.). London: Allen & Unwin.

Brunt, P. A. 1963. Introduction to Thucydides' *The Peloponnesian Wars* (B. Jowett, translator). New York: Twayne Publishers.

Bueno de Mesquita, B. 1978. Systemic polarization and the occurrence and duration of war. *Journal of Conflict Resolution* 22: 241–267.

Bueno de Mesquita, B. 1981a. Risk, power distributions, and the likelihood of war. *International Studies Quarterly* 25: 541–568.

Bueno de Mesquita, B. 1981b. *The War Trap*. New Haven, CT: Yale Univ. Press.

Bueno de Mesquita, B., and Singer, J. D. 1973. Alliances, capabilities, and war: A review and synthesis. In *Political Science Annual* (C. Cotter, ed.). New York: Bobbs-Merrill.

Campbell, J. 1982. *Grammatical Man: Information, Entropy, Language, and Life*. New York: Simon and Schuster.

Champernowne, D. G. 1953. A model of income distribution. *The Economic Journal* 63: 318–351.

Chatterjee, P. 1975. *Arms, Alliances and Stability*. Delhi: Macmillan Company of India.

Chatterji, S. D. 1963. Some elementary characterizations of the Poisson distribution. *American Mathematical Monthly* 70: 958–964.

Chenery, H. 1975. *Redistribution with Growth*. London: Oxford Univ. Press.

Chipman, J. S. 1976. The Paretian heritage. *Cahiers Vilfredo Pareto: Revue Européenne des Sciences Sociales* 14: 65–173.

Chomsky, N. 1957. *Syntactic Structures*. The Hague: Mouton.

Clark, C. 1972. The extent of hunger in India. *Economic and Political Weekly* 7: 2019–2027.

Clark, G. 1970. From the Nine Years War to the War of the Spanish Succession. In *The New Cambridge Modern History, Vol. 6* (J. S. Bromley, ed.). London: Cambridge University Press.

Claude, I. L., Jr. 1962. *Power and International Relations*. New York: Random House.

Craig, G. A., and George, A. L. 1983. *Force and Statecraft: Diplomatic Problems of Our Time*. New York: Oxford Univ. Press.

Crankshaw, E. 1963. *The Fall of the House of Habsburg*. New York: Penguin.

Crosby, F. 1979. Relative deprivation revisited: A response to Miller, Bolce, and Halligan. *American Political Science Review* 73: 103–112.

Davies, J. C. 1962. Toward a theory of revolution. *American Sociological Review* 27: 5–19.

Davies, J. C. 1978. Communication: The J-curve theory. *American Political Science Review* 72: 1357–1358.

Dehio, L. 1962. *The Precarious Balance: Four Centuries of the European Power Struggle* (C. Fullman, translator). New York: Knopf.

de Pradt, D. de Fourt. 1800. *La Prusse et sa Neutralité*. London: G. Cowie.

Derman, C., Gleser, L. J., and Olkin, I. 1973. *A Guide to Probability Theory and Application*. New York: Holt, Rinehart and Winston.

Deutsch, K. W., and Singer, J. D. 1964. Multipolar power systems and international stability. *World Politics* 16: 390–406.

Doran, C. F., and Parsons, W. 1980. War and the cycle of relative power. *American Political Science Review* 74: 947–965.

Dovring, F. 1973. Distribution of farm size and income: Analysis by exponential functions. *Land Economics* 49: 133–147.

Doyle, M. W. 1986. *Empires*. Ithaca, NY: Cornell Univ. Press.

du Coudray, H. 1936. *Metternich*. New Haven, CT: Yale Univ. Press.

Duncan, G. T., and Siverson, R. M. 1982. Flexibility of alliance partner choice in a multipolar system: Models and test. *International Studies Quarterly* 26: 511–538.

Fay, S. B. 1928. *The Origins of the World War* (2 vols.). New York: Macmillan.

Fay, S. B. 1930. Balance of power. In *Encyclopaedia of the Social Sciences, Vol. 2* (E. R. Seligman and A. Johnson, eds.). New York: Macmillan.

Feller, W. 1968. *An Introduction to Probability Theory and Its Applications, Vol. I* (3rd Ed.). New York: Wiley.

Feller, W. 1971. *An Introduction to Probability Theory and its Applications, Vol. II* (2nd Ed.). New York: Wiley.

Fénelon, F. 1920. *Ecrits et Lettres Politiques*. Paris: Editions Bossard.

Ferris, W. 1973. *The Power Capabilities of Nation-States*. Lexington, MA: D. C. Heath.

Finley, M. I. 1972. Introduction to Thucydides' *History of the Peloponnesian War* (R. Warner, translator). Baltimore: Penguin Books.

Fischer, F. 1967. *Germany's Aims in the First World War*. New York: W. W. Norton.

Futia, C. A. 1982. Invariant distributions and the limiting behavior of Markovian economic models. *Econometrica* 50: 377–408.

Galtung, J. 1964. A structural theory of aggression. *Journal of Peace Research* 1: 95–119.

Garnham, D. 1976a. Dyadic international war, 1816–1965: The role of power parity and geographical proximity. *Western Political Quarterly* 29: 231–242.

Garnham, D. 1976b. Power parity and lethal international violence. *Journal of Conflict Resolution* 20: 379–394.

Gatlin, L. L. 1972. *Information Theory and the Living System*. New York: Columbia Univ. Press.

Gaxotte, P. 1970. *The Age of Louis XIV* (M. Shaw, translator). New York: Macmillan.

Gentz, F. von. 1806. *Fragments on the Balance of Power*. London: Herries.

George, A. L., and Smoke, R. 1974. *Deterrence in American Foreign Policy: Theory and Practice*. New York: Columbia Univ. Press.

Gibbons, J. D. 1971. *Nonparametric Statistical Inference*. New York: McGraw-Hill.

Gilpin, R. 1981. *War and Change in World Politics*. New York: Cambridge Univ. Press.

Gochman, C. S., and Maoz, Z. 1984. Militarized interstate disputes, 1816–1976. *Journal of Conflict Resolution* 28: 585–616.

Goldstein, J. S. 1985. Kondratieff Wave as War Cycles. *International Studies Quarterly* 29: 411–444.

Good, I. J. 1963. Maximum entropy for hypothesis formulation, especially for multidimensional contingency scales. *Annals of Mathematical Statistics* 34: 911–934.

Grant, A. J. 1932. *A History of Europe from 1494 to 1610*. New York: Putnam.

Grey, E. 1925. *Twenty-Five Years: 1892–1916. Vol. 1*. New York: Frederick A. Stokes.

Gulick, E. V. 1955. *Europe's Classical Balance of Power*. New York: W. W. Norton.

Gumbel, E. J. 1958. *Statistics of Extremes*, New York: Columbia Univ. Press.

Gurr, T. R. 1970. *Why Men Rebel*. Princeton, NJ: Princeton Univ. Press.

Haas, E. B. 1953. The balance of power: Prescription, concept or propaganda? *World Politics* 5: 442–477.

Haas, M. 1970. International subsystems: Stability and polarity. *American Political Science Review* 64: 98–123.

Hardin, R., Mearsheimer, J. J., Dworkin, G., and Goodin, R. O. 1985. *Nuclear Deterrence: Ethics and Strategy*. Chicago: Univ. of Chicago Press.

Hart, P. E. 1962. The size and growth of firms. *Economica* 29: 29–39.

Hassall, A. 1907. The foreign policy of Louis XIV (1661–97). In *The Cambridge Modern History, Vol. 5* (A. W. Ward, G. W. Prothero, and S. Leathes, eds.). London: Cambridge Univ. Press.

Hatch, T., and Choute, S. P. 1929. Statistical description of the size properties of non-uniform particles. *Journal of the Franklin Institute* 207: 369–380.

Hayes, C. J. 1932. *A Political and Cultural History of Modern Europe, Vol. I*. New York: Macmillan.

Hayes, C. J., Baldwin, M. W., and Cole, C. W. 1967. *History of Western Civilization*. New York: Macmillan.

Henderson, N. 1940. *Failure of a Mission: Berlin, 1937–1939*. New York: Putnam.

Herdan, G. 1960. *Small Particle Statistics* (2nd Ed.). London: Butterworth.

Hermann, C. F. 1972. Threat, time, and surprise: A simulation of international crisis. In *International Crises: Insights from Behavioral Research* (C. F. Hermann, ed.). New York: Free Press.

Herz, J. H. 1959. *International Politics in the Atomic Age*. New York: Columbia Univ. Press.

Hoffmann, S. 1981. *Duties Beyond Borders: On the Limits and Possibilities of Ethical International Politics*. Syracuse, NY: Syracuse Univ. Press.

Hofstadter, D. 1985. *Metamagical Themas*. New York: Basic Books.

Holsti, K. J. 1985. *The Dividing Discipline: Hegemony and Diversity in International Theory*. London: Allen & Unwin.

Holsti, O. R. 1972a. *Crisis, Escalation, War*. Montreal: McGill-Queens Univ. Press.

Holsti, O. R. 1972b. Time, alternatives, and communications: The 1914 and Cuban missile crises. In *International Crises: Insights from Behavioral Research* (C. F. Hermann, ed.). New York: Free Press.

Holsti, O. R. 1976. Alliance and Coalition Diplomacy. In *World Politics: An Introduction* (J. N. Rosenau, K. W. Thompson, and G. Boyd, eds.). New York: Free Press.

Holsti, O. R., Brody, R. A., and North, R. C. 1964. Measuring affect and action in international reaction models. *Journal of Peace Research* 1: 170–190.

Holsti, O. R., North, R. C., and Brody, R. A. 1968. Perception and action in the 1914 crisis. In *Quantitative International Politics: Insights and Evidence* (J. D. Singer, ed.). New York: Free Press.

Holsti, O. R., Hopmann, P. T., and Sullivan, J. D. 1973. *Unity and Disintegration in International Alliances: Comparative Studies*. New York: Wiley.

Hötzsch, O. 1909. Catherine II. In *The Cambridge Modern History, Vol. 6* (A. W. Ward, G. W. Prothero, and S. Leathes, eds.). London: Cambridge Univ. Press.

Howard, M. 1983. *The Causes of Wars*. London: Allen & Unwin.

Huntington, S. P. 1968. *Political Order in Changing Societies*. New Haven, CT: Yale Univ. Press.

Ijiri, Y., and Simon, H. A. 1964. Business firm growth and size. *American Economic Review* 54: 77–89.

Ijiri, Y., and Simon, H. A. 1977. *Skew Distributions and the Sizes of Business Firms*. Amsterdam: North-Holland.

Jaynes, E. T. 1957. Information theory and statistical mechanics. *Physical Review* 106: 620–630.

Jervis, R. 1976. *Perception and Misperception in International Politics.* Princeton, NJ: Princeton Univ. Press.

Jervis, R. 1984. *The Illogic of American Nuclear Strategy.* Ithaca, NY: Cornell Univ. Press.

Job, B. 1976. Membership in inter-nation alliances, 1815–1965: An exploration utilizing mathematical probability models. In *Mathematical Models in International Relations* (D. A. Zinnes and J. B. Gillespie, eds.). New York: Praeger.

Johnson, N. L., and Kotz, S. 1970. *Continuous Univariate Distributions—1.* Boston, MA: Houghton.

Johnson, N. L., and Kotz, S. 1977. *Urn Models and Their Application: An Approach to Modern Discrete Probability Theory.* New York: Wiley.

Jutikkala, E. 1962. *A History of Finland* (P. Sjöblom, translator). New York: Praeger.

Kagan, D. 1969. *The Outbreak of the Peloponnesian War.* Ithaca, NY: Cornell Univ. Press.

Kagan, D. 1987. World War I, World War II, World War III. *Commentary* 83: 21–40.

Kahler, M. 1979. Rumors of war: The 1914 analogy. *Foreign Affairs* 58: 374–396.

Kalecki, M. 1945. On the Gibrat distribution. *Econometrica* 3: 161–170.

Kaplan, M. A. 1957. *System and Process in International Politics.* New York: Wiley.

Kecskemeti, P. 1961. *The Unexpected Revolution: Social Forces in the Hungarian Uprising.* Stanford, CA: Stanford Univ. Press.

Kennan, G. F. 1979. *The Decline of Bismarck's European Order: Franco-Russian Relations, 1875–1890.* Princeton, NJ: Princeton Univ. Press.

Kennan, G. F. 1984. *The Fateful Alliance: France, Russia, and the Coming of the First World War.* New York: Pantheon.

Kennedy, P. M. 1980. *The Rise of the Anglo-German Antagonism 1860–1914.* London: Allen & Unwin.

Keohane, R. O. 1984. *After Hegemony: Cooperation and Discord in the World Political Economy.* Princeton, NJ: Princeton Univ. Press.

Keohane, R. O. (ed.) 1986. *Neorealism and Its Critics.* New York: Columbia Univ. Press.

Khinchin, A. I. 1957. *Mathematical Foundations of Information Theory* (R. A. Silverman and M. D. Friedman, translators). New York: Dover.

Kissinger, H. A. 1957. *A World Restored: Metternich, Castlereagh and the Problems of Peace, 1812–1822.* Boston, MA: Houghton.

LaFeber, W. 1983. *Inevitable Revolutions: The United States in Central America.* New York: W. W. Norton.

Langer, W. L. 1966. *European Alliances and Alignments, 1871–1890* (2nd Ed.). New York: Knopf.

Lazear, E. D., and Michael, R. T. 1980. Family size and the distribution of real per capita income. *American Economic Review* 70: 91–107.

Lebow, R. N. 1981. *Between Peace and War: The Nature of International Crisis.* Baltimore, MD: Johns Hopkins Univ. Press.

Leckie, G. F. 1817. *An Historical Research into the Nature of the Balance of Power in Europe.* London: Taylor and Hessey.

Lefebvre, G. 1947. *The Coming of the French Revolution* (R. R. Palmer, translator). New York: Vintage.

Levy, J. S. 1983a. Misperception and the causes of war: Theoretical linkages and analytical problems. *World Politics* 36: 76–99.

Levy, J. S. 1983b. *War in the Modern Great Power System, 1495–1975.* Lexington, KY: Univ. Press of Kentucky.

Levy, J. S. 1985a. The Polarity of the system and international stability: An empirical analysis. In *Polarity and War: The Changing Structure of International Conflict* (A. N. Sabrosky, ed.). Boulder, CO: Westview Press.

Levy, J. S. 1985b. Theories of general war. *World Politics* 37: 344–374.

Lewitter, L. R. 1965. The partitions of Poland. In *The New Cambridge Modern History, Vol. 8* (A. Goodwin, ed.). London: Cambridge Univ. Press.

Li, R. P. Y., and Thompson, W. R. 1978. The stochastic process of alliance formation behavior. *American Political Science Review* 72: 1288–1303.

Liddell Hart, B. H. 1930. *The Real War: 1914–1918*. Boston: Little, Brown.

Liska, G. F. 1957. *International Equilibrium: A Theoretical Essay on the Politics and Organization of Security*. Cambridge, MA: Harvard Univ. Press.

Lydall, H. F. 1968. *The Structure of Earnings*. London: Oxford Univ. Press (Clarendon).

Lydall, H. F. 1976. Theories of the distribution of earnings. In *The Personal Distribution of Incomes*, (A. B. Atkinson, ed.). London: Allen & Unwin.

Mandelbrot, B. B. 1960. The Pareto–Lévy law and the distribution of income. *International Economic Review* 1: 79–106.

Mandelbrot, B. B. 1982. *The Fractal Geometry of Nature*. San Francisco, CA: Freeman.

Mann, M. 1986. *The Sources of Social Power, Vol. 1: A History of Power from the Beginning to A.D. 1760*. London: Cambridge Univ. Press.

Mansbach, R. W., and Vasquez, J. A. 1981. *In Search of Theory: A New Paradigm for Global Politics*. New York: Columbia Univ. Press.

Martens, G. F. von. 1795. *A Summary of the Law of Nations* (W. Cobbett, translator). Philadelphia, PA: Thomas Bradford.

Mayer, A. J. 1967. Domestic causes of the First World War. In *The Responsibility of Power* (L. Krieger and F. Stern, eds.). New York: Doubleday.

Mayer, A. J. 1969. Internal causes and purposes of war in Europe, 1870–1956. *Journal of Modern History* 41: 291–303.

McGowan, P. J. and Rood, R. M. 1975. Alliance behavior in balance of power systems: Applying a Poisson model to nineteenth-century Europe. *American Political Science Review* 69: 859–870.

McKay, D., and Scott, H. M. 1983. *The Rise of the Great Powers: 1648–1815*. London: Longmans.

McNeill, W. H. 1982. *The Pursuit of Power*. Chicago: University of Chicago Press.

Mearsheimer, J. J. 1983. *Conventional Deterrence*. Ithaca, NY: Cornell Univ. Press.

Metternich, Prince C. W. von. 1880. *Memoirs of Prince Metternich, Vol. 2* (A. Napier, translator). New York: Scribner's.

Metternich, Prince C. W. von. 1880–1884. "Memoires, documents et ecrits divers, Vol. 1." Quoted in H. du Coudray, 1936, *Metternich*. New Haven, CT: Yale Univ. Press.

Midlarsky, M. I. 1970. Mathematical models of instability and a theory of diffusion. *International Studies Quarterly* 14: 60–84.

Midlarsky, M. I. 1975. *On War: Political Violence in the International System*. New York: Free Press.

Midlarsky, M. I. 1978. Analyzing diffusion and contagion effects: The urban disorders of the 1960s. *American Political Science Review* 72: 996–1008.

Midlarsky, M. I. 1981. Equilibria in the nineteenth-century balance-of-power system. *American Journal of Political Science* 25: 270–296.

Midlarsky, M. I. 1982. Scarcity and inequality: Prologue to the onset of mass revolution. *Journal of Conflict Resolution* 26: 3–38.

Midlarsky, M. I. 1983a. Absence of memory in the nineteenth-century alliance system: Perspectives from queuing theory and bivariate probability distributions. *American Journal of Political Science* 27: 762–784.

Midlarsky, M. I. 1983b. Alliance behavior and the approach to World War I: The use of bivariate negative binomial distributions. In *Conflict Processes and the*

Breakdown of International Systems (D. A. Zinnes, ed.), Monograph Series in World Affairs, Vol. 20, Book 2. Graduate School of International Studies, University of Denver, Denver, CO.

Midlarsky, M. I. 1983c. The balance of power as a "just" historical system. *Polity* 16: 181–200.

Midlarsky, M. I. 1984a. Political stability of two-party and multiparty systems: Probabilistic bases for the comparison of party systems. *American Political Science Review* 78: 929–951.

Midlarsky, M. I. 1984b. Preventing systemic war: Crisis decision-making amidst a structure of conflict relationships. *Journal of Conflict Resolution* 28: 563–584.

Midlarsky, M. I. 1985. The coming of World War I: Conflict reinforcement in the period 1871–1914. In *Theories, Models, and Simulations in International Relations* (M. D. Ward, ed.). Boulder, CO: Westview Press.

Midlarsky, M. I. 1986a. *The Disintegration of Political Systems: War and Revolution in Comparative Perspective*. Columbia, SC: Univ. of South Carolina Press.

Midlarsky, M. I. 1986b. A hierarchical equilibrium theory of systemic war. *International Studies Quarterly* 30: 77–105.

Midlarsky, M. I. 1988a. A distribution of extreme inequality with applications to conflict behavior: A geometric derivation of the Pareto distribution. *Mathematical Modelling*, Special Issue, forthcoming.

Midlarsky, M. I. 1988b. Rulers and the ruled: Patterned inequality and the onset of mass political violence. *American Political Science Review*, forthcoming.

Midlarsky, M. I., and Roberts, K. 1985. Class, state, and revolution in Central America: Nicaragua and El Salvador compared. *Journal of Conflict Resolution* 29: 163–193.

Midlarsky, M. I., Wilkins, C., and Andrews, N. 1972. Periodic uncertainty and international crisis: The Arab–Israeli dispute in comparative perspective. Department of Political Science, University of Colorado, Boulder, CO.

Miller, A. H., Bolce, L. H., and Halligan, M. 1977. The J-curve theory and the black urban riots: An empirical test of progressive relative deprivation theory. *American Political Science Review* 71: 964–982.

Miller, S. E. (ed.) 1985. *Military Strategy and the Origins of the First World War*. Princeton, NJ: Princeton Univ. Press.

Modelski, G. 1978. The long cycle of global politics and the nation-state. *Comparative Studies in Society and History* 20: 214–235.

Modelski, G. 1983. Long cycles of world leadership. In *Contending Approaches to World System Analysis* (W. R. Thompson, ed.). Beverly Hills, CA: Sage.

Modelski, G., and Morgan, P. M. 1985. Understanding global war. *Journal of Conflict Resolution* 29: 391–419.

Montegelas, M., and Schücking, W. (eds.) 1924. *Outbreak of the War: German Documents Collected by Karl Kautsky*. New York: Carnegie Endowment for International Peace.

Morgan, P. M. 1977. *Deterrence*. Beverly Hills, CA: Sage.

Morgenthau, H. J. 1973. *Politics among Nations: The Struggle for Power and Peace* (5th Ed.). New York: Knopf.

Morgenthau, H. J., and Thompson, K. W. 1985. *Politics among Nations: The Struggle for Power and Peace* (6th Ed.). New York: Knopf.

Most, B. A. and Starr, H. 1983. Conceptualizing "war": Consequences for theory and research. *Journal of Conflict Resolution* 27: 137–159.

Most, B. A., and Starr, H. 1984. International relations theory, foreign policy substitutability and "nice" laws. *World Politics* 36: 383–406.

Most, B. A., and Starr, H. 1987. Polarity, preponderance and power parity in the generation of international conflict. *International Interactions* 13: 225–262.

Bibliography

Nicolson, H. 1946. *The Congress of Vienna, A Study in Allied Unity: 1812–1822*. New York: Harcourt, Brace.

Nomikos, E. V., and North, R. C. 1976. *International Crisis: The Outbreak of World War I*. Montreal: McGill-Queen's Univ. Press.

Ogg, F. A. 1913. *The Governments of Europe*. New York: Macmillan.

Oppenheim, L. F. 1947. *International Law: A Treatise, Vol. 1* (6th Ed., H. Lauterpacht, ed.). London: Longmans.

Ord, J. K., Patil, G. P., and Taillie, C. 1981. The choice of a distribution to describe personal incomes. In *Statistical Distributions in Scientific Work, Vol. 6* (C. Taillie, G. P. Patil, and B. A. Baldessari, eds.). Dordrecht, Holland: D. Reidel.

Organski, A. F. K. 1968. *World Politics* (2nd Ed.). New York: Knopf.

Organski, A. F. K., and Kugler, J. 1980. *The War Ledger*. Chicago: Univ. of Chicago Press.

Ornstein, D. S. 1973. *Ergodic Theory, Randomness and Dynamical Systems*. New Haven, CT: Yale Univ. Press.

Ostrom, C. W., Jr., and Hoole, F. W. 1978. Alliances and wars revisited. *International Studies Quarterly* 22: 215–236.

Pagels, H. 1982. *The Cosmic Code*. New York: Bantam Books.

Pagès, G. 1970. *The Thirty Years' War, 1618–1648* (D. Maland and J. Hooper, translators). New York: Harper.

Palmer, R. R. 1971. *The World of the French Revolution*. New York: Harper.

Pareto, V. 1897. La répartition des revenus. *Le Monde Économique* 7: 259–261.

Park, K. H. 1986. Income inequality and political violence. In *Inequality and Contemporary Revolutions* (M. I. Midlarsky, ed.). Monograph Series in World Affairs, Vol. 22, Book 2. Graduate School of International Studies, University of Denver, Denver, CO.

Pipes, R. 1957. *The Formation of the Soviet Union, Communism and Nationalism: 1917–1923*. Cambridge, MA: Harvard Univ. Press.

Pipes, R. 1974. *Russia under the Old Regime*. New York: Scribner.

Polanyi, K. 1944. *The Great Transformation*. Boston, MA: Beacon Press.

Polisensky, J. V. 1971. *The Thirty Years' War* (R. Evans, translator). Berkeley, CA: Univ. of California Press.

Polisensky, J. V. 1972. Social and economic change and the European-wide war. In *The Thirty Years' War* (T. K. Rabb, ed.). Lexington, MA: D. C. Heath.

Polisensky, J. V. 1978. *War and Society in Europe: 1618–1648*. London: Cambridge Univ. Press.

Pollard, A. F. 1923. The balance of power. *Journal of the British Institute of International Affairs* 2: 53–64.

Quester, G. 1977. *Offense and Defense in the International System*. New York: Wiley.

Ramsey, P. 1983. *The Just War: Force and Political Responsibility*. New York: University Press of America.

Rasler, K. A., and Thompson, W. R. 1983. Global wars, public debts, and the long cycle. *World Politics* 35: 489–516.

Rawls, J. 1971. *A Theory of Justice*. Cambridge, MA: Harvard Univ. Press.

Richardson, L. F. 1960. *Arms and Insecurity*. Chicago: Quadrangle Books.

Ritter, G. 1968. *Frederick the Great: A Historical Profile* (P. Paret, translator). Berkeley, CA: Univ. of California Press.

Rosecrance, R. N. 1966. Bipolarity, multipolarity, and the future. *Journal of Conflict Resolution* 10: 314–327.

Rostovtzeff, M. 1941. *Social and Economic History of the Hellenistic World*, 3 vols. London: Oxford Univ. Press (Clarendon).

Rucker, R. 1982. *Infinity and the Mind: The Science and Philosophy of the Infinite*. New York: Bantam Books.

Ruggie, J. G. 1986. Continuity and transformation in the world polity: Toward a neorealist synthesis. In *Neorealism and its Critics* (R. O. Keohane, ed.). New York, Columbia Univ. Press.

Russett, B. M. 1964. Inequality and instability: The relation of land tenure to politics. *World Politics* 16: 442–454.

Russett, B. M. 1968a. Components of an operational theory of international alliance formation. *Journal of Conflict Resolution* 12: 285–301.

Russett, B. M. 1968b. Is there a long-run trend toward concentration in the International system? *Comparative Political Studies* 1: 103–122.

Russett, B. M. 1978. The marginal utility of income transfers to the Third World. *International Organization* 32: 913–928.

Sabrosky, A. N. 1975. From Bosnia to Sarajevo: A comparative discussion of interstate crises. *Journal of Conflict Resolution* 19: 3–24.

Sahota, G. S. 1978. Theories of personal income distribution: A survey. *Journal of Economic Literature* 16: 1–55.

Schelling, T. 1960. *The Strategy of Conflict*. Cambridge, MA: Harvard Univ. Press.

Schmookler, A. B. 1984. *The Parable of the Tribes*. Boston, MA: Houghton.

Scramuzza, V. M., and MacKendrick, P. L. 1958. *The Ancient World*. New York: Holt.

Seton-Watson, H. 1957. Hungary 1945–1956. In *The Hungarian Revolution* (M. J. Lasky, ed.). New York: Praeger.

Shannon, C. E. 1948. A mathematical theory of information. *Bell Systems Technical Journal* 27: 379–423 and 623–656.

Shannon, C. E., and Weaver, W. 1949. *The Mathematical Theory of Communication*. Urbana, IL: Univ. of Illinois Press.

Shue, H. 1980. *Basic Rights: Subsistence, Affluence, and U.S. Foreign Policy*. Princeton, NJ: Princeton Univ. Press.

Simon, H. A. and Bonini, C. P. 1958. The size distribution of business firms. *American Economic Review* 48: 607–617.

Sinai, Y. G. 1976. *Introduction to Ergodic Theory* (V. Scheffer, translator). Princeton, NJ: Princeton Univ. Press.

Singer, J. D., and Small, M. 1966. Formal alliances, 1815–1939: A quantitative description. *Journal of Peace Research* 3: 1–32.

Singer, J. D., and Small, M. 1968. Alliance aggregation and the onset of war, 1815–1945. In *Quantitative International Politics* (J. D. Singer, ed.). New York: Free Press.

Singer, J. D. and Associates. 1979. *Explaining War: Selected Papers from the Correlates of War Project*. Beverly Hills, CA: Sage.

Singer, J. D., Bremer, S. and Stuckey, J. 1972. Capability distribution, uncertainty, and major power war, 1820–1965. In *Peace, War, and Numbers* (B. M. Russett, ed.). Beverly Hills, CA: Sage.

Siverson, R. M., and Duncan, G. T. 1976. Stochastic models of international alliance initiation, 1885–1965. *Mathematical Models in International Relations* (D. A. Zinnes and J. V. Gillespie, eds.). New York: Praeger.

Siverson, R. M., and Tennefoss, M. R. 1984. Power, alliance, and the escalation of international conflict, 1815–1965. *American Political Science Review* 78: 1057–1069.

Skocpol, T. 1979. *States and Social Revolutions: A Comparative Analysis of France, Russia, and China*. London: Cambridge Univ. Press.

Small, M. and Singer, J. D. 1982. *Resort to Arms: International and Civil Wars, 1816–1980*. Beverly Hills: Sage.

Smith, C. J., Jr. 1958. *Finland and the Russian Revolution: 1917–1922*. Athens, GA: Univ. of Georgia Press.

Snyder, G. H., and Diesing, P. 1977. *Conflict among Nations: Bargaining, Decision Making, and System Structure in International Crises*. Princeton, NJ: Princeton Univ. Press.

Snyder, J. 1984. *The Ideology of the Offensive: Military Decision Making and the Disasters of 1914*. Ithaca, NY: Cornell Univ. Press.

Sorel, G. 1897. La loi des révenus. *Le Devenir Social 3*: 577–607.

Sparrow, C. 1982. *The Lorenz Equations: Bifurcations, Chaos, and Strange Attractors*. New York: Springer-Verlag.

Statesman's Year-Book: Statistical and Historical Annual of the States of the World for the Year 1914. London: Macmillan (1914).

Ste. Croix, G. E. M. de. 1972. *The Origins of the Peloponnesian War*. Ithaca, NY: Cornell Univ. Press.

Ste. Croix, G. E. M. de. 1981. *The Class Struggle in the Ancient Greek World: From the Archaic Age to the Arab Conquest*. London: Duckworth.

Steindl, J. 1965. *Random Processes and the Growth of Firms: A Study of the Pareto Law*. New York: Hafner.

Stoessinger, J. G. 1964. *The Might of Nations: World Politics in Our Time*. New York: Random House.

Sullivan, M. P. 1975. *International Relations: Theory and Evidence*. Englewood Cliffs, NJ: Prentice-Hall.

Tanner, J. R. 1934. The Anglo-Dutch wars. In *The Cambridge Modern History, Vol. V* (A. W. Ward, G. W. Prothero, and S. Leathes, eds.). London: Cambridge Univ. Press.

Tanter, R., and Midlarsky, M. I. 1967. A theory of revolution. *Journal of Conflict Resolution 11*: 264–280.

Taylor, A. J. P. 1971. *The Struggle for Mastery in Europe: 1848–1918*. London: Oxford University Press.

Thompson, W. R. 1983. Cycles, capabilities, and war. In *Contending Approaches to World System Analysis* (W. R. Thompson, ed.). Beverly Hills, CA: Sage.

Thompson, W. R. 1986. Polarity, the long cycle, and global power warfare. *Journal of Conflict Resolution 30*: 587–615.

Thompson, W. R., and Zuk, L. G. 1982. War, inflation, and the Kondratieff long wave. *Journal of Conflict Resolution 26*: 621–644.

Thompson, W. R., Duval, R. D., and Dia, A. 1979. Wars, alliances, and military expenditures: Two pendulum hypotheses. *Journal of Conflict Resolution 23*: 629–654.

Thomson, D. 1966. *Europe since Napoleon* (2nd ed.). New York: Knopf.

Thucydides, 1954. *History of the Peloponnesian War* (R. Warner, translator). Baltimore, MD: Penguin Books.

Tilly, C. 1978. *From Mobilization to Revolution*. Reading, MA: Addison-Wesley.

Tintner, G., and Sengupta, J. K. 1972. *Stochastic Economics*. New York: Academic Press.

Tolkunov, B. F. 1975. Statistical methods for analyzing the impulse activity of neurons. In *Current Problems in Neurocybernetics* (A. B. Kogan, ed., N. Kaner, translator). New York: Wiley.

Toynbee, A. J. 1946. *A Study of History* (abridgement of Vols. I–VI). New York: Oxford Univ. Press.

Trevor-Roper, H. R. 1970. Spain and Europe 1598–1621. In *The New Cambridge Modern History, Vol. 4* (J. P. Cooper, ed.). London: Cambridge Univ. Press.

Vasquez, J. A. 1983. *The Power of Power Politics: A Critique*. New Brunswick, NJ: Rutgers Univ. Press.

Vattel, Emmerich de. 1870. *The Law of Nations, Vol. 3*. Philadelphia, PA: T. and J. W. Johnson.

Väyrynen, R. 1983. Economic cycles, power transitions, political management and wars between major powers. *International Studies Quarterly 27*: 389–418.

Veenendaal, A. J. 1970. The War of the Spanish Succession in Europe. *The New Cambridge Modern History, Vol. 6* (J. S. Bromley, ed.). London: Cambridge Univ. Press.

von Mises, R. 1957. *Probability, Statistics and Truth* (2nd Ed.). (H. Geiringer, translator). London: Allen & Unwin.

Walker, H. M. and Lev, J. 1953. *Statistical Inference*. New York: Holt, Rinehart and Winston.

Wallace, M. D. 1971. Power, status, and international war. *Journal of Peace Research* 8: 23–35.

Wallace, M. D. 1973. Alliance polarization, cross-cutting, and international war, 1815–1964. *Journal of Conflict Resolution* 17: 575–604.

Wallace, M. D. 1982. Armaments and escalation: Two competing hypotheses. *International Studies Quarterly* 26: 37–56.

Wallerstein, I. 1984. *The Politics of the World-Economy*. New York: Cambridge Univ. Press.

Waltz, K. N. 1979. *Theory of International Politics*. Reading, MA: Addison-Wesley.

Waltz, K. N. 1986. Reflections on *Theory of International Politics*: A response to my critics. In *Neorealism and its Critics* (R. O. Keohane, ed.). New York: Columbia Univ. Press.

Walzer, M. 1977. *Just and Unjust Wars: A Moral Argument with Historical Illustrations*. New York: Basic Books.

Ward, M. D. 1982. *Research Gaps in Alliance Dynamics*. Monograph Series in World Affairs, Vol. 19, Book 1. Graduate School of International Studies, University of Denver, Denver, CO.

Webster, C. K. 1921. *British Diplomacy, 1813–1815: Select Documents Dealing with the Reconstruction of Europe*. London: G. Bell and Sons.

Wedgwood, C. V. 1972. The futile and meaningless war. In *The Thirty Years' War* (T. K. Rabb, ed.). Lexington, MA: D. C. Heath.

Weede, E. 1976. Overwhelming preponderance as a pacifying condition among contiguous Asian dyads, 1950–1969. *Journal of Conflict Resolution* 20: 395–411.

Wesson, R. G. 1967. *The Imperial Order*. Berkeley, CA: Univ. of California Press.

Wilkie, J. W., and Haber, S. (eds.) 1983. *Statistical Abstract of Latin America, Vol. 22*. Los Angeles, CA: UCLA Latin America Center Publications.

Williams, N. 1969. *Chronology of the Expanding World, 1492 to 1762*. New York: David McKay.

Wright, Q. 1942. *A Study of War*. Chicago: Univ. of Chicago Press.

Young A. 1792. *Travels During the Years 1787, 1788, 1789*. London: Bury St. Edmund's.

Zagare, F. C. 1987. *The Dynamics of Deterrence*. Chicago: Univ. of Chicago Press.

Zinnes, D. A. 1967. An analytical study of the balance of power theories. *Journal of Peace Research* 4: 270–288.

Zinnes, D. A., North, R. C., and Koch, H. E., Jr. 1961. Capability, threat, and the outbreak of war. In *International Politics and Foreign Policy* (J. N. Rosenau, ed.). New York: Free Press.

About the Author

MANUS I. MIDLARSKY is Professor of Political Science and Director of the Center for International Relations at the University of Colorado, Boulder. He received his Ph.D. from Northwestern University in 1969 and specializes in the study of conflict behavior with particular emphasis on international war and national revolution. Dr. Midlarsky is the founding and immediate Past-President of the Conflict Processes Section of the American Political Science Association and the immediate Past-Vice President of the International Studies Association. He is the author of *On War: Political Violence in the International System* (1975), *The Disintegration of Political Systems: War and Revolution in Comparative Perspectives* (1986), and of the edited volumes *Inequality and Contemporary Revolutions* (1986) and *Handbook of War Studies* (1989).

Index

Absence of memory (*see* Memory)
Abundancy, 178-81
  infinite, 230
Admiral Horthy (Hungarian Regent), 129
Adriatic Sea, 177
Afghanistan, 184, 203-4, 215
Africa, 29, 62, 70, 72, 90, 107, 110, 200, 208
Aitchison, J., 118, 228, 244
Akkad, 207
Albania, 156
Albertini, Luigi, 62, 81, 244
Alexander I, tsar, 175
Alexander II, tsar, 60
Alexander III, tsar, 60-1
Alexander the Great, 135, 142
Algeciras, 98
Algeciras conference (*see* Conference)
Allais, Maurice, 78, 244
Alliance, 4-7, 13-14, 16, 18, 20-5, 28-32,
  35-40, 42-4, 46, 49
  Austro-German, 105
  Catholic League (1609), 67, 86, 98-9, 108,
  134
  Delian League, 31, 67, 99
  diadic, 163-4
  Dreikaiserbund, 188
  Dual, 7-8, 23, 26, 31, 33, 67, 79, 84, 90-1,
  95-7, 108, 129, 131, 152, 162
  durability of, 158-68
  equilibration, 180
  fluidity, 94-6, 100-2, 105-6, 109-10, 176,
  184
  Franco-Prussian, 132
  Franco-Russian, 11, 33, 59-62, 79, 91, 96,
  145, 152, 200
  Franco-Russian Entente, 200
  Franco-Spanish, 132
  memory, 92
  North Atlantic Treaty Organization
  (NATO), 163-4
  organizations, 163-4
  Peloponnesian (League), 31, 67
  polarization in, 106-12
  Protestant Union (1608), 55, 67, 86, 98,
  108, 134
  random alliance formation, 167
  randomness of, 94-6, 100-2, 105-6, 109-10,
  176, 200
  Reinsurance Treaty, 8, 105, 110, 125
  Rio Treaty, 163
  Triple Alliance, 96-8, 106-7, 125
  Triple Alliance (1815), 175-7
  Triple Entente, 7-8, 20, 23, 26, 31, 33, 44,
  46, 67, 79, 84, 90, 95-7, 107-8, 162,
  175-7, 183, 189
  Warsaw Pact, 163-5
Alliance Memory, 26-7
  in Triple Entente, 2
  in Dual Alliance, 23
Allies, 139-40
Allison, Graham, 194, 244
Alsace-Lorraine, 102, 115
Amdur, R., 185, 244
Amur River, 157
Andrews, Neil, 211
Antiochus III, 19
Aquinas, Saint Thomas, 170
Arab-Israeli wars (1967 and 1973, *see* War)
Arbenz, Jacobo, 85
Areas, of triangles, 222, 224
Aristotle, 48, 244
Arms races, 216
  conventional, 191-3
  naval, 153
  nuclear, 109, 191-3
Arms transfers, 194
Aron, Raymond, 68, 157, 244
Ashby, W. Ross, 127, 244
Asia, 67, 70
Athens, 13, 31, 53-4, 86, 89, 92, 131, 134,
  136, 140, 142, 147, 149, 191, 206, 210-11
Atkinson, C.T., 146, 244
Augsburg, Peace of, 55, 98
Augustine, Saint, 170
Augustus III (of Poland), 177
Austria, 22, 27-9, 32, 44, 54-5, 87, 100, 106,
  131-2, 134, 136, 138, 144-5, 149, 151,
  155, 157, 163, 169, 172, 175, 177-9, 182,
  204
  neutralization of, 198-9

Austria-Hungary, 6-8, 23, 26, 36, 41, 51, 58,
    60, 82-9, 91-2, 95-8, 108, 125, 127-9, 133,
    156, 204, 209-10, 234
Austrian Emperor, 102
Austrian Netherlands (*see* Belgium)
Austrian Succession, War of the (*see* War)
Austro-German Alliance (*see* Alliance)
Axelrod, Robert, 27-8, 40, 160, 201, 244
Axis powers, 129, 162
Aztecs, 180, 207

Baden, 28, 32, 42, 106
Badger, Wade W., 221, 244
Balance of power, 14, 20, 43, 92-130, 170-84,
    190, 192, 194, 200
    as condition, 94-130
    as process, 94-130
    change in, 101, 103-4, 112-30
    fluidity of, 106-12
    polarization in, 106-12
    theory, 5, 40
Baldwin, Marshall W., 86, 136, 247
Balkans, 22, 64, 91, 107-8, 152, 169, 206
Barnes, Thomas G., 68, 143, 245
Battenburg, Alexander von, 60
Battles:
    Leuctra, 135
    Mycale, 215
    Pavia, 134
    Plataea, 215
    Salamis, 215
    White Mountain, 86
Bavaria, 28, 32, 42, 106, 134
Beaumont, W., 87, 244
Beer, Francis A., 157, 244
Beitz, Charles R., 185, 244-5
Belgium, 32, 34-5, 42, 140, 142-3, 156, 232
Belgium (Austrian Netherlands), 86, 100,
    132, 206
Benham, A.H., 168, 245
Bentham, Jeremy, 171
Berlin, 134
Berlin-Baghdad railway, 96, 204
Berlin crisis (*see* Crisis)
Berlin wall, 199
Bethmann Hollweg, T. von (German
    Chancellor), 81, 144, 190
Bharucha-Reid, A.T., 122, 245
Binomial distribution (*see* Distribution)
Bipolar system, 201
Bipolarity, 30-1, 44-69, 105, 187, 196, 214
Bismarck, Otto von, 26, 59-62, 65, 68, 99,
    107, 128, 145, 153, 209
Bismarckian diplomacy, 208
Bismarckian period, 110, 127
Blank check, 82-4
Blum, Jerome, 68, 143, 245
Blum, Léon, 137

Boak, Arthur E., 19, 245
Bocskai, Stephen, 57
Bohemia, 54, 57-8, 86, 99, 111, 129, 131,
    134, 145, 190
Bohemian revolt (*see* Revolt)
Bolce, Louis H., 185, 250
Bolsheviks, 99
Bonini, C.P., 118-19, 252
Bosnia-Herzegovina, 83, 151
Bosnian crisis (*see* Crisis)
Bourbon monarchy, 136-8
Boxley, R.F., 186, 245
Brams, Steven J., 19, 245
Brandenburg-Prussia, 136
Brazil, 64, 194
Brecher, Michael, 84-5, 245
Bremer, Stuart, 93, 120, 252
Brickman, Philip, 68, 185, 245
Bridge, F.R., 26, 245
Britain (*see* Great Britain)
Brody, Richard A., 84-5, 168, 245
Brown, J.A.C., 118, 122, 227-8, 245
Brunt, P.A., 68, 245
Buchlau Agreement, 156
Bueno de Mesquita, Bruce, 9, 30, 43, 93,
    161, 168, 190, 245
Bulgaria, 22, 42, 59-62, 64, 66, 83, 156, 162,
    199, 234
Bullen, Roger, 26, 245

Cabinet durability, 87-8, 159
Caldicott, Helen, 1
Calvinism, 55-8, 63, 98-9, 134, 140, 210
Cameron, Rondo, 68, 143, 245
Campbell, J., 197, 245
Campbell, Donald T., 68, 185, 245
Canada, 113, 156, 166
Canning, George, 180
Cantor sets, 211
Caribbean, 90
Carlton, Sir Dudley, 56
Carthage, 19
Castlereagh, Viscount, 172-3, 175, 180
Castro, Fidel, 85
Catherine II (the Great), 177
Catholicism (Roman), 54-8, 98-9, 134, 140,
    190, 210
Central America, 28, 41, 85, 115, 199, 204
Central Asia, 199, 204
Central Limit Theorem, 118
Central powers (*see* Powers)
Ch'in, 207
Chamberlain, Neville, 133, 146
Champernowne, D.G., 225-6, 228, 245
Charles II (of Spain), 136
Charles V, Holy Roman Emperor, 134
Chatterjee, P., 41, 245
Chatterji, S.D., 68, 245

Chenery, Hollis, 52, 68, 245
Chernobyl, 204
Chi-square statistic, 33, 42, 119, 122, 130,
    150, 153, 157, 231-43
Chile, 29, 67
China, 67, 105, 130, 156-7, 184, 206-7,
    212-13
Chipman, J.S., 77, 227-8, 245
Chomsky, Noam, 202, 245
Choute, S.P., 118, 247
Christian I (of Saxony), 55-6
Christian (of Anhalt), 55
Christian Socialist Party (Austrian), 88
Christianity, 210
Civil War:
    American, 212-214
    Russian, 99
    Spanish, 141
Civilizations, disintegration of, 100-11
Clark, Colin, 186, 245
Clark, G., 146, 245
Claude, Inis L., 128, 245
Coalition (*see also* Alliance):
    Anglo-French, 139
    countervailing, 153
Coalition durability, 168, 189
Coalition formation, 134
Coalition stability, 159-61
Cole, Charles W., 86, 136, 247
Colonialism, 105
Colonial population distribution (*see*
    Distribution)
Colonies, 208-9
Concert of Europe, 41
Confederation of the Bar, 177
Conference:
    Algeciras, 96, 105, 128
    Congress of Vienna, 27-8, 122, 165, 170,
        172, 174-5
    Naval (London, 1908), 91, 153, 157
Conflict:
    Athenian-Spartan, 191
    continuum, 214
    diffusion, 21-3, 122-3
    domestic, 87-9, 139-40
    ideological, 139-40, 189
    no memory, 130
    overlapping, 79-91, 151, 213
    partitioning of, 104-9
    polarized, 92
    positive-sum, 29
    reinforcement, 21-3
    religious, 139-40
    zero-sum, 29
Conflict system, polarized, 92
Congress (American), 214
Congress of Berlin (1878), 59
Congress of Berlin (1884), 62

Congress of Vienna (*see* Conference)
Contagion, 150, 156
Cooperation, 27-9, 160-1, 191, 201-2
Corcyra, 13, 53, 82, 86, 92, 99, 131, 134,
    149, 206
Corinth, 13, 31, 53, 86, 131, 134-5, 149, 206
Correlates of War (COW), 3, 33, 42, 80, 162,
    165, 214
Counter-Reformation, 56-7
Craig, Gordon A., 19, 245
Crankshaw, Edward, 107, 110, 245
Crisis:
    1914 summer, 7, 26, 33-4, 42, 79, 81-5,
        105, 109, 112, 126, 148, 155, 188, 194
    Berlin, 34
    Bosnian, 23, 26, 42, 83, 90-1, 145, 152,
        157, 188
    Cuban missile, 7, 26, 33-4, 85, 105, 109,
        112, 126, 156, 194
    isomorphism to, 81-5
    Jülich Succession, 86
    Middle East (1967), 85
    Middle East (1973), 85
    Moroccan (crises), 58, 96, 105, 188
    Munich, 149
    Suez (*see also* War), 26-7
Crosby, Faye, 186, 245
Cuba, 8, 85, 90, 194
Cuban missile crisis (*see* Crisis)
Czechoslovakia, 22, 24, 99, 108, 133, 149,
    154, 156, 198-9, 235
Czech, Legion, 99

Davies, James C., 68, 181, 185-6, 246
DeGaulle, Charles, 186
Dehio, Ludwig, 41, 66, 180, 246
de Pradt, Abbé, 48, 172, 246
Delian League (*see* Alliance)
Democracies, Euro-American, 184
Democratic Party, 214
Denmark, 34, 54, 156, 232
Derivation:
    geometric, 71-2, 221-8
    of Pareto distribution, 71-2, 221-8
Derman, Cyrus, 120, 146
Deutsch, Karl W., 21, 45-6, 68, 246
Dia, A., 161, 253
Diesing, Paul, 19, 82, 252
Diet (at Warsaw), 177
Diet (German), 57
Difference principle, 14, 171-2, 177-84
    negative, 181-4
Diffusion, 24, 150-6
    nuclear weapons, 105
    of power, 122-3
    theory of, 122-3
Diffusion, process, 127
Diplomacy, Bismarckian, 105

Disarmament, unilateral, 189
Disjoint dispute sets, 89-90, 156, 189, 206
Disorders, urban, 182
Disputes, 217-19
  great power, 32-6, 80
  great power and others, 32-6, 80-1
Distribution:
  binomial, 68, 217-18
  colonial population, 69-78
  exponential, 51, 71-8, 120, 130, 226,
    228-30
  Gaussian, 226-7
  geometric, 221, 224-6
  income, 77, 225-6
  of inequality, 69-78
  land, 69-78
  log-exponential, 71-8, 224-30
  lognormal, 77, 117-23, 227-8
  Pareto, 69-78
  Pareto-Lévy, 226
  Pareto-log-exponential, 69-78, 208, 221-30
  Poisson, 68, 130, 161, 176, 217-19, 231-2
  Polya-Eggenberger, 151-6, 240-3
DNA, 197
Domestic conflict (*see* Conflict)
Doran, Charles F., 40, 123, 146-7, 246
Dovring, F., 186, 246
Doyle, Michael W., 207-8, 246
Dred Scott decision, 213
Dreikaiserbund, 11, 59-62, 208
du Coudray, H., 185, 246
Dual Alliance (*see* Alliance)
Dual Monarchy, 87
Dulles, John Foster, 30
Duncan, G.T., 95, 151, 161, 246
Durability of alliance (*see* Alliance)
Duval, R.D., 161
Dworkin, G., 19
Dyadic alliance (*see* Alliance)
Dynastic connections, 134

East Germany, 56, 235
Eastern Question, 177
Eastern Rumelia, 60, 62
Egypt, 41, 90, 105, 107, 211-12, 215
El Salvador, 73-4, 77
Elba, 175
Elector of Brandenburg, 56, 136
Elector of Saxony, 57
Elizabeth I (of Russia), 143
Empire (*see also* individual country entries):
  Austrian, 100, 111
  Austro-Hungarian, 110
  British, 32
  French, 32
  German, 43, 107, 153
  Napoleonic, 174-5
  Ottoman (Turkey), 22, 102, 106, 156

Emperor, Austrian, 86
Energy consumption, 164
England (*see* Great Britain)
Entropy, 159-66, 168
  as information, 168
  maximum, 15, 159-60, 162, 167, 195-201
  minimum, 7, 15, 159-60, 162-3, 192,
    195-201
  reduction of, 200
  zero, 201
Envy, 47-64, 92
Epaminondas, 135
Epidamnus, 53, 86
Equal opportunity, 175
Equality (*see also* Inequality), 25, 45-67, 137,
    160, 169-70, 185, 205
Equilibrium, 20-3, 31-2, 81, 84, 93, 171,
    173-6, 217, 231
  stable, 31-2
  unstable, 31-2
Ethiopia, 10, 22, 28, 29, 35, 41, 64
Europe, 34-7, 41, 50, 72, 80, 97, 127, 169,
    180, 183-4, 199
  post-Reformation, 48
  Central, 28, 44, 54, 58, 99, 106, 149
  Eastern, 77, 108, 144, 227
  Western, 115, 144, 167
Evolution, of the international system, 202-4
Exponential distribution (*see* Distribution)

Fair opportunity, 171
Fay, Sidney B., 20, 62, 81, 185, 246
Feller, William, 68, 151, 156, 224, 246
Fénelon, F., 20, 246
Ferris, Wayne H., 93, 112-14, 120-2,
    125-6, 246
Finland, 129, 156
Finley, Sir Moses, 54, 246
Fischer, Fritz, 7, 62, 143-5, 246
Fractals, 221
France, 7, 27, 35, 41, 55, 58-9, 70, 72, 78, 83,
    86-7, 96-100, 102, 115, 129, 132-3, 135,
    137, 142, 149, 154, 156, 167-8, 172, 174,
    177, 180, 183, 188-9, 191-2, 194, 204,
    207-9, 212-14
Francis Ferdinand Archduke, 97
Franco-Prussian alliance (*see* Alliance)
Franco-Prussian war (*see* War)
Franco-Russian alliance (*see* Alliance)
Franco-Spanish alliance (*see* Alliance)
Frederick I (of the Palatinate), 56
Frederick II (the Great), 13, 63, 86, 89,
    100, 132, 138, 141-3, 147, 177, 206
French revolution (*see* Revolution)
French Revolutionary Wars (*see* War)
Futia, Carl A., 226, 246

Galtung, Johan, 186, 246

Games (*see also* Conflict, Process):
  positive-sum, 29, 94
  zero-sum, 29, 46, 94
Garnham, David, 93, 246
Gatlin, L.L., 197, 202, 246
Gaussian distribution (*see* Distribution)
Gaxotte, P., 4, 246
General war, distinctions between systemic (*see also* War), 142-3, 207
Gentz, Friederich von, 48, 172, 246
Geometric distribution (*see* Distribution)
Geometric subdivision, 71
Geophysical dispersions, 22-3, 134
George, Alexander L., 19, 246
George II, 132
German Democratic Republic (*see* East Germany)
German General Staff, 146
German principalities, 55, 162
Germany (*see also* Prussia), 6-8, 23, 32, 34, 36, 42, 44, 58, 70, 72, 75, 78, 82-3, 85, 87-9, 91-2, 95-8, 106, 108, 110, 125, 127, 129-30, 133, 136, 139-40, 143-7, 149, 154, 157, 162-3, 167, 169, 183, 190, 204, 208-9, 212, 234
  Nazi, 130, 191
Gibbons, J.D., 42, 120, 232, 246
Gilpin, Robert, 4, 13, 19, 68, 246
Gleser, Leon J., 120, 246
Gochman, Charles S., 33, 102, 152, 246
Goldstein, Joshua, 146, 246
Good, I.J., 120-2, 246
Goodin, R.O., 19, 247
Gorbachev, Mikhail, 126
Grant, A.J., 134, 246
Great Britain, 7, 27, 35, 41, 44, 54, 58-9, 70, 72, 75, 78, 83, 86-7, 96-7, 99, 128, 132-4, 136-7, 154, 156, 167-9, 175, 180, 183, 191-2, 204, 206, 208-9, 235
Great Depression, 154, 182
Greece, 22, 41, 156, 198, 208, 211, 215
Greek City States (*see* Greece)
Grenada, 23
Grey, Sir Edward, 97, 128, 246
Gross National Product (GNP), 164
Guatemala, 85
Gulick, Edward V., 27, 46-7, 68, 173, 185, 247
Gumbel, E.J., 71, 224, 227, 247
Gurr, Ted R., 68, 185, 247
Gustavus Adolphus, 55

Haas, Ernest B., 94, 247
Haas, Michael, 45, 247
Haber, Saul, 74, 254
Habsburg monarchy, 13, 54-8, 86, 108, 129, 131, 134, 145, 149, 190, 206, 210
the Hague, 56

Halligan, Mark, 185, 250
Hanover, 28, 87, 136-7, 206
Hardin, Russell, 19, 247
Harriman family, 227
Hart, P.E., 122, 247
Hassall, A., 129, 247
Hatch, T., 118, 247
Hayes, Carlton H., 86, 136, 247
Hegemonic system, 201
Hellas (*see also* Greece), 53-4, 142, 204
Henderson, Nevile, 99, 247
Herdan, G., 118, 247
Hermann, Charles F., 84, 247
Herz, John H., 20, 247
Hesse-Darmstadt, 60
Hesse-Electoral, 28, 32
Hierarchical equilibrium, 5-11, 14-15, 17-18, 20-43, 45, 94, 102, 117, 155, 158, 169-71, 180-1, 184, 189, 196, 201-3, 206, 216
  as international learning, 198-204
  capsule description of, 24-5
  consequences of, 25-9
Hierarchy, 23-8, 40, 158-68, 192, 195-7, 216
  decay of, 207
  simultaneous, 36-8, 44
Historical dynamic, 15, 207-9
Historical referents, 52-65
Hitler, Adolph, 22-3, 30, 39, 133, 137, 139, 142, 144-6, 154-5, 191
Hoffmann, Stanley, 185, 247
Hofstadter, Douglas, 17, 247
Hohenzollerns, 132
Holland (*see* Netherlands)
Holsti, Kal J., 205, 247
Holsti, Ole R., 20, 84-5, 125, 145, 161, 185, 247
Holy Roman Empire, 58
Holy Roman Emperor, 54
Hoole, Francis W., 161, 251
Hopmann, P. Terrence, 161, 247
Hötzsch, Otto, 9, 68, 106, 112, 177, 247
Howard, Michael, 157, 247
Huntington, Samuel P., 186, 247
Hungary, 54-5, 57, 129-30, 162, 198-9

Iberia, 71
Ideology, 188
Ijiri, Y., 118, 247
Illyrian provinces, 177
Incas, 180, 207
Income distribution (*see* Distribution)
Independence, of conflict behavior, 21-3
India, 70, 183
Indifference curves, 178-81
Indonesia, 28
Inequality (*see also* Equality), 41, 47-78, 92, 152, 187, 208-10, 212-13, 216, 221-30
  domestic, 209-10

and multipolarity, 47-68
  programmed, 70-1, 221-8
Inequality distribution (*see* Distribution)
Information theory, 15, 192, 196-202
Instability (*see* Stability)
Intermediate range missiles, 203
International system, evolution of, 202-4
Iran, 181, 206
Irreversibility, 206-7
Islam, 203
Isomorphism, 16-17
  to crisis, 81-5
Israel, 90, 105, 107, 194, 211-12
Italy, 32, 35-6, 41-2, 44, 51, 54, 90-1; 96, 99,
  105-7, 110, 125, 133, 154, 156, 162, 177,
  194, 199, 211-12, 234

J Curve, 181-2, 185
Japan, 41, 51, 67, 154, 156, 162, 166, 184,
  205, 210, 212
Jaynes, E.T., 120-2, 248
Jervis, Robert, 19, 68, 248
Job, Brian, 95, 151, 161-2, 248
John Casimir (of the Palatinate), 55
John George (of Saxony), 57
Johnson, Normal L., 68, 71, 151-2, 224,
  230, 248
Jordan, 211-12
Journal of Conflict Resolution, 79
Jülich Succession crisis (*see* Crisis)
Justice, 14-15
  distributive, 185
  principles of (Rawlsian), 171
  Rawlsian, 170-85
Jutikkala, Eino, 129, 248

Kagan, Donald, 53, 144, 146, 157, 248
Kahler, M., 157, 248
Kaiser Wilhelm II, 59
Kalecki, M., 122, 248
Kansas-Nebraska Act, 213
Kaplan, Morton A., 48, 95, 128, 176, 248
Katkov, N.N., 60-2
Kecskemeti, Paul, 130, 248
Kennan, George F., 59-62, 65-8, 248
Kennedy, Paul M., 88, 248
Keohane, Robert O., 189, 205, 248
Khinchin, A.I., 160, 248
Khruschev, Nikita, 8, 33
Kingdom of the Two Sicilies, 233
Kissinger, Henry A., 28, 90, 96, 248
Koch, Howard E., Jr., 68, 254
Koch curve, 211, 226
Kolmogorov equations, 122
Kotz, Samuel, 68, 71, 151-2, 224, 230, 248
Kruger telegram, 59, 96
Kugler, Jacek, 5, 93, 128, 211, 251

Labour Party (British), 186
LaFeber, Walter, 77, 248
Land distribution (*see* Distribution)
Langer, W.L., 153, 248
Language rules, 198-9
Latin America, 37, 67, 70-1, 156
Lazear, E.D., 118, 248
League of Nations, 128
League of Torgau, 55
Learning (international), 198-202
Lebow, Richard N., 19, 248
Leckie, G.F., 20, 185, 248
LeFebvre, G., 63, 248
Legislative seats, 87-8
Lev, Joseph, 130, 254
Levy, Jack S., 4, 46, 68, 167, 248-9
Lewitter, L.R., 66, 178, 249
Li, R.P.Y., 95, 176, 249
Liberty, 171, 175
Libya, 22, 123, 128, 193
Liddell Hart, B.H., 110, 249
Limitations, analytic, 188, 212
Lincoln, Abraham, 213
Liska, George F., 20, 249
Log-exponential distribution (*see*
  Distribution)
Lognormal distribution (*see* Distribution)
Lombardy, 177
London Naval Conference (*see* Conference)
Long cycles, 43, 122-3, 190
Louis XIV, 14, 108, 129, 132-3, 135-6,
  141-4, 146, 204, 208
  wars of (*see* War)
Louis XV, 137
Low countries (*see also* Belgium,
  Luxembourg, Netherlands), 54, 86, 149
Lusitania, 140
Lutheranism, 55-8, 98-9, 129, 140
Luxemburg, 129
Lydall, H.F., 227, 249

Macedon, 207
Macedonian War (*see* War)
MacKendrick, Paul L., 19, 135, 252
Madrid, 54
Maine, 213
Major powers (*see* Powers)
Malta, 99
Manchuria, 22, 130
Mandelbrot, Benoit, 221, 226, 249
Mann, Michael, 137, 207, 249
Mansbach, Richard W., 189, 249
Maoz, Zeev, 33, 102, 152, 246
Maria Theresa, 89, 138, 143, 147
Marie Antoinette, 86, 102, 134
Markovian process (*see* Process)
Marne River, 140
Martens, G.F. von, 48, 249

Mathematical formalisms, 32
Mayer, A.J., 88, 249
McGowan, Patrick J., 43, 95, 161, 176, 249
McKay, Derek, 132-3, 249
McNeill, William H., 15, 207-9, 249
Mearshimer, John J., 19, 249
Mecklenburg-Schwerin, 32
Mediterranean, 99
Memory, 114-16
  absence of, 9-12, 94, 102-17, 170, 192
  alliance, 103-17, 146
  dyadic, 103-17
  minimization of, 193
  N-adic, 103-17, 146
  wars with, 114-17, 238-9
  wars without, 114-17, 239
Mesopotamia, 207
Messenian revolt (*see* Revolt)
Metternich, Prince C.W. von, 173, 175, 185, 249
Michael, R.T., 118, 248
Middle East, 27, 41, 90, 184, 211-12
Middle East crises (*see* Crisis)
Midlarsky, Manus I., 7, 26, 28, 36, 39, 41-3, 67-8, 71-2, 75, 79, 81, 88, 95, 98, 118-19, 127, 151, 153, 156, 159, 161-2, 169, 176, 185-6, 195-6, 205, 208, 211, 229, 231, 249-50
Military personnel, 164-8
Miller, Abraham H., 185, 250
Miller, S.E., 157, 250
Missile gap, 194
Missouri Compromise, 213
Mobilization wars (*see* War)
Mobilizing leader, 141-5
Models (*see also* Distribution), 16-17
  Lognormal, 117-22
  Markovian, 28, 102-4, 126-7
  Probabilistic, 16-17
Modelski, George, 40, 68, 123, 146, 250
Modena, 27, 32, 42, 106
Modernity, 138-40
Modes of inquiry, 15-18
Moltke, Helmut von, 144
Montegelas, M., 186, 250
Montenegro, 22
Moravia, 54
Morgan, Patrick, 19, 123, 250
Morgenthau, Hans J., 5, 12, 20, 40, 46, 92, 97, 126, 185, 250
Moroccan crises (*see* Crisis)
Moskovskie Vyedomosti, 60-61
Most, Benjamin A., 34, 43, 126, 250
Multiparty systems, 87-8
Multipolarity, 44-69, 92, 187, 189, 196, 200, 209, 216, 234
  and inequality, 47-68

Munich crisis (*see* crisis)
Mussolini, Benito, 137

Napoleon I, 132-3, 144, 146, 155, 172, 175, 180, 191
Napoleonic Wars (*see* War)
Nasser, Gamal Abdul, 27, 211
Naval Bill, English (1909), 91, 157
Naval conference (*see* Conference)
Negative difference principle (*see* Difference Principle)
Netherlands (*see also* United Provinces), 13, 32, 34-5, 42, 44, 54-5, 86, 108, 129, 131, 133, 136, 149, 156, 178, 190, 206, 209, 232
Nicaragua, 85, 181
Nicolas II, tsar, 140
Nicolson, Sir Harold, 175, 185, 251
No-memory wars (*see* War)
Nomikos, E.V., 81-2, 251
Normative concerns, 187
Normative implications, 41, 214-16
North, Robert C., 68, 81-2, 84-5, 247, 251, 254
North Africa, 27
North (the American), 213-14
North Atlantic Treaty Organization (NATO), 27, 166, 192-3
North Korea, 130
North Vietnam, 29, 64
Norway, 156
Nuclear armaments (*see also* Disarmament), 127
Nuclear proliferation, 168
Nuclear war (see War)

Occam's razor, 16
Ogg, Frederick A., 88, 251
Olkin, Ingram, 120, 246
Oppenheim, L.F., 20, 251
Ord, J.K., 77, 251
Organski, A.F.K., 5, 20, 40, 93, 126, 128, 185, 211, 251
Original position, 171
Ornstein, Donald S., 159, 195, 251
Ostrom, Charles W., 161, 251
Ottoman Empire (*see also* Empire, Turkey), 22, 102, 106
Overlapping conflicts (*see* Conflict)

Pacific Ocean, 62
Pagels, Heinz, 2, 251
Pagès, Georges, 13, 47, 55, 57, 68, 98, 190, 251
Palestine Liberation Organization (PLO), 90, 210
Palmer, R.R., 134, 251
Parable of the tribes, 65-6

Pareto, Vilfredo, 228, 251
Pareto distribution (*see* Distribution):
  invariance of, 77-8
Pareto-log-exponential distribution (*see*
  Distribution)
Park, Kang H., 68, 251
Parma, 27, 32, 35, 42, 233
Parsons, Wes, 40, 123, 146-7
Parthians, 19
Partitions:
  Dutch, 67
  Ottoman, 67
  Polish, 41, 66-7, 105-6, 112, 177-8, 215
  Swedish, 67
Patil, Ganapati P., 77, 251
Peace Corps, 161
Peace:
  of Amiens, 99
  Egyptian-Israeli, 107
Peloponnesian League (*see* Alliance)
Peloponnesian War (*see* War)
Pericles, 54, 147, 211
Persia, 19, 31, 135, 215
Philip II (of Macedon), 135-7, 141-2, 144,
  146, 191, 204, 209
Philip V (of Macedon), 19
Pipes, Richard, 99, 251
Poisson distribution (*see* Distribution)
Poland, 22, 28, 37, 55, 99, 106, 108, 132-3,
  149, 154, 156, 166, 172, 175, 178, 180
Polanyi, Karl, 128, 251
Polarity, 10-12, 44-68
Polarization, 9-11, 24, 92-130, 190, 194, 200,
  213
  systemic, 24-32
Polarizing systems (*see also* Polarization),
  30-2
Policy clarity, 160-1
Policy implications, 91, 126-8, 145-6, 166-7,
  189-95, 203-4
Polisensky, J.V., 13, 56-8, 98, 251
Polish Question, 177
Polish-Saxon Question (1814), 175
Political Science, 173
Pollard, A.F., 20, 251
Polya distribution (*see* Distribution)
Poniatowski, Stanislaus, 177
Population:
  growth of, 72, 208-9
  total, 164-8
Portugal, 54, 64, 136, 156
Positive-sum game (*see also* Conflict,
  Process), 8-12, 43, 192
Potidae, 13, 53, 82, 86, 99, 132, 134, 149,
  206
Power:
  cycle, 123, 190
  concentration of, 101, 117-23

deconcentration of, 40
disparities, 112-14
disparity ratio, 112-17
interregna, 135-7
memory, 130
parity, 92-4, 100-1, 123-6, 189-90
preponderance, 92-4, 100-1, 112-14, 123-6,
  189-90
transition, 128, 190
Power concentration, change in, 101
Powers:
  central, 30, 32-6, 42, 80-2, 99, 156, 232-8
  great, 32-6, 80-1, 163-4
  major, 32-6, 200, 232-8
  minor, 32-6, 232-8
  neutral, 34-5, 43
  small, 28-9, 32-6, 43, 162-4
Prague, 54
Predictability, 204-7
Presidium (Soviet), 194
Probabilistic models (*see* Models)
Process:
  constant-sum, 103-17
  learning, 198-204
  Markovian, 102-3, 118, 124-7, 225-6
  negative-sum, 109
  positive-sum, 104-17, 161, 180, 184, 189
  zero-sum, 103-17, 179
Protestant Union (*see* Alliance)
Protestantism, 54-8, 98-9, 134, 140, 190
Prussia (*see also* Germany), 28, 32, 38, 41,
  44, 63, 89, 100, 106, 132, 134, 137-8,
  142, 156, 167, 172, 175-80, 182, 204
Ptolemy IV (of Egypt), 19
Pyrenees, 99

Quester, George, 140, 251

Railroads, 227
Ramsey, Paul, 185, 251
Rapoport, Anatol, 27
Rasler, Karen, 43, 123, 251
Ratisbon, 57
Rawls, John, 14-15, 41, 48, 170-85, 251
Realpolitik, 170, 183
Reciprocity (*see also* Tit-for-tat), 160
Reconstruction (American), 214
Redistribution, 72
  income, 185
Redundancy, 201-2
  context-dependent, 197-202
  context-free, 197-202
Reformation, 56-7, 188
Reichsrath (Austrian), 88
Reichstag (German), 88
Reinforcement, 24
Reinsurance Treaty (*see* Alliance)
Revolt:

Bohemian, 89, 99, 108, 149, 206, 210
Messenian, 89
Revolution:
1905 (Russian), 210
Austrian Netherlands, 134, 149
authenticating, 205-6
Bolshevik, 63
Cuban, 63
French, 62-3, 89, 138-9, 142, 149, 206
Hungarian, 130, 198
Iranian, 63
Nazi, 63
redistributive, 205
Richardson, Lewis F., 146, 153, 192, 251
Ritter, Gerard, 13, 63, 86, 138, 251
Roberts, Kenneth, 72, 75, 208, 250
Rome, 19
Ronald Reagan, 94
Rood, Robert M., 95, 161, 176, 249
Rosecrance, Richard N., 45-7, 251
Rostovtzeff, Michael, 137, 251
Rucker, Rudy, 222, 251
Ruggie, Gerard, 2, 252
Rule sets, 202-4
Rumania, 33-5, 42, 156, 162, 234
Russett, Bruce M., 20, 118, 185, 252
Russia (*see also* Soviet Union), 7-8, 23, 27-8,
41, 59, 67, 82-3, 91, 96-8, 100, 106, 110,
125, 129, 138-9, 152, 156-7, 175-9, 180,
182, 188, 191, 210, 212-13

Sabrosky, Alan N., 83, 90, 252
Sahota, Gian S., 227, 252
Salzburg, 177
Sarajevo, 90
Sardinia (*see also* Italy), 32, 38, 156
Saxony, 28, 32, 132, 175, 233
Scarcity, 221-30
and inequality, 47
Schelling, Thomas, 19, 252
Schlieffen Plan, 140
Schmitt, Bernadotte, 62
Schmookler, Andrew B., 19, 65, 252
Schücking, W., 186, 250
Scott, H.M., 132-3, 249
Scramuzza, Vincent M., 19, 135, 252
Selassie, Haile, 9
Sengupta, Jati K., 118, 253
Sequential acquisition, 69-78
Serbia, 7, 22, 26, 33-5, 60, 64, 82-4, 87, 91,
97, 107, 110-11, 123, 127, 151, 155-6,
210, 232-4
Seton-Watson, Hugh, 129, 252
Seven Years' War (*see* War)
Shannon, Claude, 196, 252
Shah (of Iran), 181
Shue, Henry, 185, 252
Siberia, 67, 99

Sidgwick, Henry, 172
Silesia, 54, 63, 86, 132, 137-8, 142, 147, 206
Simon, Herbert A., 118-19, 252
Sinai, Y.G., 159, 195, 252
Singer, J. David, 21, 42, 45-6, 68, 80, 93-4,
100, 119-20, 129, 161, 169, 252
Siverson, Randolph M., 93, 95, 151, 161,
252
Skocpol, Theda, 130, 185, 213, 252
Small, Melvin, 42, 80, 161, 252
Small powers (*see* Powers)
Smith, C. Jay, Jr., 129, 252
Smoke, Richard, 19, 246
Snyder, Glenn, 19, 82, 252
Snyder, Jack, 19, 253
Social class, 208-9
Social Democratic Party (Austrian), 88
Social Democratic Party (German), 88
Somalia, 10, 28-9, 64
Somoza, Anastasio, 181
Sorel, Georges, 228, 253
South America, 64
South (the American), 213-14
South Vietnam, 29, 64
Soviet Central Asia, 203
Soviet Union (*see also* Russia), 26-8, 34-5, 38,
64, 85, 90, 99, 105, 130, 154, 156, 166-7,
192, 199-200, 205, 214, 235
Spain, 54-6, 64, 86, 129, 131, 133, 136-7,
154, 156, 206
Habsburg, 13
Spanish Succession, War of the (*see* War)
Sparrow, Colin, 222, 253
Sparta, 13, 31, 53, 86, 89, 131, 134-6, 140,
142, 149, 188, 191, 210
Stability (*see* System)
Stalin, Joseph, 22, 235
Starr, Harvey, 34, 43, 126, 250
Statesman's Year-Book, 75, 253
Status inconsistency, 186
Ste. Croix, G.E.M. de, 89, 134, 146, 209,
253
Steel production, 164-8
Steindl, Josef, 122, 226, 253
Stoessinger, John, 20, 253
Strategic Arms Limitation Talks I (SALT I),
127, 202
Strategic Arms Limitation Talks II (SALT II),
202-3
Strategic defense, 126-7
Strategic Defense Initiative (SDI), 19, 94,
105, 109, 189, 194, 204
Structural wars (*see* War)
Structure, international, 1-12
Stuckey, John, 93, 120, 252
Substitutability, 34-5
Substitutability phenomena', 214-15
Sudetenland, 149

Suez Canal, 27
Suez crisis (*see* Crisis)
Suez invasion, 168
Sullivan, John D., 161, 247
Sullivan, Michael P., 120-2, 126, 253
Surprise, in crisis, 84
Sweden, 34, 54, 129, 156, 166, 178, 194, 232
Switzerland, 34, 56, 99, 133, 156
Syria, 90, 211-12, 215
System:
    autonomy, 212
    balance-of-power, 153
    bipolar, 32-8, 44-68, 201, 203
    hegemonic, 201
    heterogeneity of, 36
    multipolar, 32-8, 44-68
    ontogeny, 202-4
    polarizing, 33-4, 234-5
    stability, 20-43, 167-8
Systemic war (*see also* War), 12-14, 236
    distinctions between general, 142-3, 207
    mobilization, 108
    structural, 108
    theory of, 25
    varieties of, 12-14

Taillie, Charles, 77, 251
Talleyrand, Charles-Maurice de, 172,
    175-6
Tanner, J.R., 146, 253
Tanter, Raymond, 186, 253
Taylor, A.J.P., 26-7, 58, 98, 107, 111, 128,
    253
Tehran, 181
Tennefoss, Michael R., 93, 252
Thailand, 35, 41
Thebes, 31, 135-6, 191
Theoretical deductions, 14-15
Third World, 184, 199
Thirty Years' War (*see* War)
Thompson, Kenneth W., 97, 126, 250
Thompson, William R., 40, 43, 46, 56,
    95, 123, 146, 161, 176, 251, 253
Thomson, David, 68, 253
Thucydides, 13, 31, 53-4, 68, 146, 253
Tilly, Charles, 185, 253
Timing, 141, 204-7
    of systemic war, 206-7
Tintner, Gerhard, 118, 253
Tirpitz, Alfred von, 209
Tit-for-tat (*see also* Reciprocity), 27-8, 160,
    201-2
Tolkunov, B.F., 130, 253
Toynbee, Arnold, 110-11, 253
Transition matrices, 232-5
Transitions, 231-2
Treaty (*see also* Alliance):
    Axis, 162

First Polish Partition, 177
Franco-Russian, 11
of Berlin (1885), 62, 72
(Peace) of Amiens, 133, 139, 141
Reinsurance (*see* Alliance)
Second Polish Partition, 177
Third Polish Partition, 177
Tordesillas (1494), 64
Versailles, 122, 174, 183, 191
Washington Treaty for the Limitation of
    Naval Armaments, 127
Westphalia, 54, 105, 107
Trevor-Roper, H.R., 145, 253
Truman Doctrine, 198
Turkey (*see also* Ottoman Empire), 20, 22,
    57-8, 83, 102, 106, 156, 177-8, 198-9
Tuscany, 32, 35, 106, 233
Two-party systems, 87-8
Tyrol, 54, 177

Uncertainty, 160-1, 167, 192, 195-7
Unifications:
    German, 119
    Italian, 119
Union of Soviet Socialist Republics (USSR
see Soviet Union)
United Arab Republic, 215
United Nations Security Council, 42
United Provinces (*see also* Netherlands), 5,
    54, 129, 208
United States of America, 8, 23, 26-8, 35, 41,
    51, 90, 113, 123, 128, 156, 166, 182, 184,
    193-4, 198-200, 203, 205, 212, 235
United States Senate, 203
Utiles, 49-52

Variance, infinite, 72
Vasquez, John, 189, 253
Vattel, Emmerich de, 48, 172, 253
Väyrynen, R., 146, 253
Veenendaal, A.J., 146, 254
Veil of ignorance, 171
Venetia, 177
Versailles (Court of), 100
Versailles (Treaty of, *see* Treaty)
Vienna, 88, 177, 180
Vietnam, 105, 184, 193, 200, 214
Vladivostok, 157
von Mises, Richard, 151, 254

Walker, Helen M., 130, 254
Wallace, Michael, 161, 186, 192, 254
Wallenstein, Albrecht von, 190
Wallerstein, Immanuel, 13, 254
Waltz, Kenneth N., 2, 17, 45-7, 91, 254
Walzer, Michael, 185, 254
War:
    Afghanistan, 215

Anglo-Persian, 239
Arab-Israeli (1967 and 1973), 211-12, 215
Austrian Succession, 5, 13-14, 63, 86-7,
  100, 111, 132-5, 137, 140-3, 147, 189
Austro-Prussian, 42
Balkan, 8, 23, 26, 42, 134
Central American (1885), 105, 107, 115,
  239
Central American (1906), 239
Central American (1907), 239
Chaco, 105, 107, 115, 239
Civil (American), 212-14
Cold, 33
Crimean, 18, 27, 59, 169, 238
Devolution (*see also* War: Louis XIV), 108,
  135
Dutch (*see also* War: Louis XIV), 108, 129,
  135-6
Dyadic, 103-4, 125, 190
Ecuadorian-Colombian, 239
First Balkan, 129, 239
First Peloponnesian, 89
First Punic, 19
Franco-Mexican, 239
Franco-Prussian, 3, 111, 164, 238
Franco-Spanish, 135, 142
French Revolutionary, 4, 13-14, 46, 63, 86,
  89, 100, 108, 133-5, 138-9, 142, 149, 156,
  191, 204, 208, 210
General, 13-14, 131-2, 137-8, 142-3, 207
General European, 179
Greco-Turkish, 7, 239
Hungarian-Allies, 239
Iran-Iraq, 205-6
Italian Unification, 119, 129, 238
Italo-Ethiopian, 141, 239
Italo-Roman, 238
Italo-Sicilian, 238
Italo-Turkish, 23, 96, 239
Jenkins' Ear, 86, 132, 137, 206
Jülich Succession, 134
"Just", 170, 185
Korean, 41, 130, 239
La Plata, 239
League of Augsburg (*see also* War: Louis
  XIV), 108, 136
Louis XIV (*see also* War: Devolution,
  Dutch, League of Augsburg, Spanish
  Succession), 108, 149, 191
Macedonian, 4, 14, 133, 135-7, 141-2, 149,
  191, 209
Manchurian, 239
Memory, 114-17, 238-9
Mobilization, 129, 131-47, 148-57, 191,
  204-7, 211
N-adic, 129
Napoleonic, 4, 13-14, 63, 99, 105, 108, 111,
  129, 132-3, 137-42, 149, 191, 204, 208

Nation months of, 100-1
no-memory, 114-17, 239
Nuclear, 1-2, 104-5, 109, 144
Pacific, 238
Palestine, 129, 215, 239
Peloponnesian, 4, 13-14, 31, 52-4, 58, 86,
  99, 129, 133-6, 138-42, 146-7, 149, 156,
  188, 191, 204, 206-10, 215
Protestant-Catholic, 107
Regional systemic, 210-12
Russo-Finnish, 129, 239
Russo-Hungarian, 129, 239
Russo-Japanese, 210, 239
Russo-Turkish (1768-1774), 177
Russo-Turkish (1877-1878), 59, 105, 108,
  111, 121, 238
Second Balkan, 111, 239
Second Kashmir, 239
Second Punic, 19
Second Schleswig-Holstein, 238
Seven Weeks', 238
Seven Years', 5, 13-14, 100, 106, 111, 132,
  137-43, 180, 189
Sinai, 239
Sino-French, 239
Sino-Indian, 239
Sino-Japanese, 141, 239
Spanish-American, 239
Spanish-Chilean, 238
Spanish-Moroccan, 239
Spanish Succession (*see also* War: Louis
  XIV), 4, 13-14, 99-100, 105, 108, 129,
  132-3, 136, 142-3, 149
Structural, 129, 131-47, 191, 204-7, 210
Suez (*see also* Crisis), 215
Vietnam, 193, 214
Systemic, 4, 12-14, 79-92, 103-4, 125,
  130-47, 188, 190, 193-4, 207, 236
Territorial, 105
Thirty Years', 4, 13-14, 52-8, 86, 89, 98-9,
  105, 110, 133-5, 138-42, 149, 156, 167,
  188, 190-1, 204, 206-10
World War I, 4-8, 12-15, 22-3, 40, 42, 45,
  52-3, 58-65, 69-70, 72, 75, 77, 79-91,
  94-130, 133-5, 138-46, 148-57, 167, 180,
  183, 188-91, 194, 204, 206, 208-10, 214,
  234-5, 239-40
World War II, 4-5, 12-15, 22-3, 25, 29,
  35-6, 38-9, 42, 44, 67, 99-100, 105, 108,
  111, 117, 119, 121-2, 125, 129, 132-3,
  139, 142, 145-7, 149-57, 167, 180, 186,
  191, 198-9, 204-5, 212, 214, 227, 239-40
World War III, 18, 105, 144, 155-6, 206-10
War aims, 143-5
Ward, Michael D., 161, 254
Washington Treaty for the Limitation of
  Naval Armaments (*see* Treaty)
Webster, C.K., 173, 254

Wedgwood, C.V., 57, 209, 254
Weede, Erich, 93, 124, 254
Wesson, Robert, 207, 254
West Berlin, 199
West Germany, 166
Westphalia, Peace of (*see* Treaty)
Wilhelm II (Kaiser), 75, 82, 144, 209
Wilkie, James W., 74, 254
Wilkins, C., 211, 250
William of Orange, 129, 136
Williams, N., 56-8, 68, 254
World War I (*see* War)
World War II (*see* War)

Wright, Quincy, 212, 254
Württemberg, 28

Yom Kippur, 211
Young, Arthur, 63, 254
Young Turks, 22, 91, 157

Z Process (*see* Process)
Zagare, Frank, 19, 254
Zero-sum game (*see* Conflict, Process)
Zinnes, Dina A., 20, 68, 84, 94, 98, 145,
    185, 191, 254
Zuk, L.G., 43, 253